Technology for Success
Computer Concepts

Second Edition

Jennifer T. Campbell

Mark Ciampa

Barbara Clemens

Steven M. Freund

Mark Frydenberg

Ralph E. Hooper

Lisa Ruffolo

Jill West

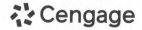 Cengage

THE SHELLY CASHMAN SERIES®

Australia • Brazil • Canada • Mexico • Singapore • United Kingdom • United States

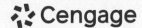

Technology for Success Computer Concepts,
Second Edition
Jennifer T. Campbell, Mark Ciampa,
Barbara Clemens, Steven M. Freund,
Mark Frydenberg, Ralph E. Hooper,
Lisa Ruffolo, Jill West

SVP, Product Management: Cheryl Costantini

VP, Product Management: Mark Santee

Portfolio Product Director: Rita Lombard

Senior Portfolio Product Manager: Amy Savino

Senior Product Assistant: Ciara Boynton

Learning Designer: Zenya Molnar

Senior Content Manager: Michelle Ruelos Cannistraci

Digital Project Manager: Jim Vaughey

Developmental Editor: MT Cozzola

Product Marketing Manager: Danae April

Content Acquisition Analyst: Callum Panno

Production Service: Lumina Datamatics Ltd.

Designer: Erin Griffin

Cover Image Source: Eugene Mymrin/Moment/ Getty Images

For product information and technology assistance, contact us at
**Cengage Customer & Sales Support, 1-800-354-9706
or support.cengage.com.**

For permission to use material from this text or product, submit all requests online at **www.copyright.com.**

Library of Congress Control Number: 2024906092

ISBN: 978-0-357-88323-5

Cengage
5191 Natorp Boulevard
Mason, OH 45040
USA

Cengage is a leading provider of customized learning solutions. Our employees reside in nearly 40 different countries and serve digital learners in 165 countries around the world. Find your local representative at **www.cengage.com.**

To learn more about Cengage platforms and services, register or access your online learning solution, or purchase materials for your course, visit **www.cengage.com.**

Notice to the Reader

Printed at CLDPC, USA, 08-24

Brief Contents

Contents

Module 10: Networking

Module 11: Digital Communication

Module 12: Digital Transformation

Module 13: Databases

Module 14: Digital Ethics and Lifestyle

Preface

About the Authors

Jennifer T. Campbell has written and co-authored several leading technology texts, including *Technology for Success*; *Discovering Computers: Digital Technology, Data, and Devices*; *Discovering the Internet*; *Web Design: Introductory*; *Microsoft Expression Web Introductory Concepts and Techniques*; *Computer Literacy Basics: Microsoft Office 2007 Companion*; and *Microsoft Office Quick Reference Pocket Guide*. For almost 30 years, she has served integral roles in computer educational publishing as an editor, author, and marketing manager. She holds a B.A. in English from The College of William and Mary.

Jill West authors Cengage courses for CompTIA Cloud+, CompTIA Network+, Data Communications, the Shelly Cashman Series, and the popular *Technology for Success*. She has taught kindergarten through college and currently teaches computer technology courses at Georgia Northwestern Technical College. With degrees in psychology, education, and IT, Jill innovates at the crossroads of IT and education, specializing in designing courses for popular IT certifications, presenting at conferences on IT education, and mentoring lifelong student learners in IT. Jill also teaches edutainment AWS courses with ACI Learning (formerly ITProTV) and is an AWS Academy Accredited Educator. Jill and her husband, Mike, live in northwest Georgia with their four children.

Dr. Mark Ciampa is Professor of Analytics and Information Systems and Program Director of the graduate Cybersecurity Data Analytics program in the Gordon Ford College of Business at Western Kentucky University in Bowling Green, Kentucky. Prior to this, he was an associate professor and served as the Director of Academic Computing at Volunteer State Community College in Gallatin, Tennessee, for 20 years. Dr. Ciampa has worked in the IT industry as a computer consultant for businesses, government agencies, and educational institutions. He has published over 25 articles in peer-reviewed journals and books. He is also the author of over 30 technology textbooks from Cengage, including *CompTIA Security+ Guide to Network Security Fundamentals, Eighth Edition*; *CompTIA CySA+ Guide to Cybersecurity Analyst, Third Edition*; *CWNA Guide to Wireless LANs, Third Edition*; *Guide to Wireless Communications*; *Security Awareness: Applying Practical Cybersecurity in Your World, Sixth Edition*; and *Networking BASICS*. Dr. Ciampa holds a PhD in technology management with a specialization in digital communication systems from Indiana State University and has certifications in security and healthcare.

Introduction

You probably use technology dozens of times a day on your phone, computer, and other digital devices to keep in touch with friends and family, research and complete school assignments, shop, and entertain yourself. Even though you use technology every day, understanding how that technology works and how it can work for you will give you the edge you want as you pursue your education and career. The concepts in this book help you become digitally literate and a strong digital citizen who not only understands technological concepts but recognizes the right ways to use technology.

Technology for Success: Computer Concepts 2e will explain the What, Why, and How of technology as it relates to your life so you can unlock the door to success in the workplace, at home, and at school. It also provides guidance on how to safely use digital devices. *Technology for Success: Computer Concepts* will help you master the computer concepts you need to impress at your dream job interview in this age of digital transformation. With new and expanded coverage of cutting-edge technologies like cloud computing, e-commerce, databases, digital ethics, and artificial intelligence, you'll be ready to put technology to work as you pursue your goals and live your life.

The book assumes no prior computer experience and uses clear, familiar language and brief lessons in order to provide a solid foundation of computer concepts. The real-life applications prepare you to continue building your skills, in future courses and beyond.

Changes to This Edition

- At least half of the End-of-Module questions have been updated. In addition, the number of questions by type has been standardized across all modules. Each module includes 12 Review Questions (with two True/False and 10 Multiple Choice), four Discussion Questions, four Critical Thinking Questions, and one Apply Your Skills exercise, a new feature that maps to the introductory case scenario and includes questions relating to each Learning Objective.
- Instructor supplements have been updated to reflect content changes. The PowerPoint presentations now include metacognitive opportunities and interactive activities.
- Throughout the text, key terms and figures have been updated and added to reflect important technological developments and our use of technology.

The following lists and describes all modules, including additional, changed, or expanded topics from the previous edition.

Module 1: Impact of Digital Technology (Technology use in society, both personal and professional)
- Key terms that students need for understanding later modules have been introduced, including cloud computing, Bluetooth, and network.

Module 2: The Web (The role of the web, accessing websites and webpages, e-commerce, and searching and conducting online research)
- New section on connecting to the Internet, which includes discussion of ISPs, Wi-Fi, and hotspots.
- New section on Net Neutrality (moved up from Module 10 in previous edition)

Module 3: Hardware and Processors (Types of hardware and processors, input and output devices, and hardware maintenance)
- Added figures that visually differentiate between how computers interact with data and information as well as differentiate between ROM and RAM.
- New section on use of QR codes as input methods.
- Rearranged content to group hardware devices with similar functions together.

Module 4: Operating Systems and File Management (Types and uses of operating systems, customizing an operating system, and managing files and folders)
- User interface coverage now includes NUIs (natural user interfaces).
- Expanded section on Selecting an Operating System.
- Presented content in a more device-diagnostic manner to ensure coverage goes beyond Windows and PCs and includes mobile devices.

Module 5: App Use (Types and purposes of apps, using productivity and graphics apps)
- Added content to clearly differentiate between "software" and "apps and programs."
- Added information to Presentation app section about presenting over the web.

Module 6: Cybersecurity and Safety (Cybersecurity risks, hazards of technology use, repelling cyber attacks, and protecting against hazards)
- New coverage of the importance of cybersecurity.
- Expanded information about authentication.
- Additional coverage on the risks of data collection.

Module 7: Digital Media (Uses of and creating digital media)
- New section on using digital media for business.
- New section on protecting your digital media creations with copyrights.
- Added coverage of emerging technologies, such as meme, NFT, and blockchain.

Module 8: App Development (Development roles, methods, phases, tools, and strategies, and how to sell apps)
- Focus changed from app use and development to just development.
- Added coverage on change management, including dealing with scope creep.
- New section on vendor proposals: types, evaluating, and making decisions.
- New section on project management techniques and tools.

Module 9: Web Development (Comparing HTML5, CSS, and JavaScript, strategies for creating and publishing websites, using data tools and analytics, and coding a website)
- New section on dashboards and website data analytics.
- Replaced and updated Case Study scenario.

Module 10: Networking (Connected network features, connecting to a network, and network security)
- Added comparison of 2.4 GHz Wi-Fi and 5 GHz Wi-Fi.
- Added content on networking with IoT devices.
- Updated information on wireless standards.

Module 11: Digital Communication (Comparing and using digital communication tools and evaluating their impact)
- Updated market statistics.
- Added coverage of new, popular social media sites.

Module 12: Digital Transformation (Cloud computing, doing business on the Internet, and AI and other new technologies)
- Added coverage of distributed computing.
- Added content on virtual reality and robotics.
- Expanded AI content to include generative AI tools and examples, plus coverage of prompt engineering.

Module 13: Databases (The importance of databases, using a database management system, and using data to make business decisions)

- Added coverage of ACID and BASE models.
- Added content on read replicas.
- Expanded coverage of cloud database services.
- Expanded coverage of how database types are selected for websites.

Module 14: Digital Ethics and Lifestyle (Responsibilities of a digital citizen, information accuracy, content accessibility, and promoting a healthy digital lifestyle)

- Expanded coverage of technology laws to include AI regulations and the Right to Be Forgotten.
- New coverage of deceptive technology practices: catfishing, deep fakes, AI misuse, and deceptive design.
- New coverage of ethical SEO practices and accessibility in web and app development.
- New coverage of content biases, including speech recognition and data pools.

Organization of the text

Technology for Success: Computer Concepts has the following components: a student text; activities and resources online in the MindTap platform; and a suite of instructor supplements. The textbook contains 14 modules, each with 3-5 learning objectives to which the text, activities, and assessments are aligned.

The book starts and ends with topics relating to being a digital citizen. Modules have been organized to be standalone topics, although the intent is to first introduce basic topics, such as apps and hardware, then delve into more specific ones such as digital media, databases, and cyber security. Module 1 includes an introduction and explanation of what it means to be a digital citizen, and the last module wraps up several concepts discussed in the book by framing them within an ethical standpoint.

Features of the text

Based on extensive research and feedback from students today, we've learned that students absorb information more easily if topics are broken down into smaller lessons that are authentic to everyday life. With this in mind, and to ensure a deeper understanding of technology in the real world, *Technology for Success: Computer Concepts* uses the following approach to helping you understand and apply its contents:

Module Objectives establish the goals of the module and what you should be able to achieve by the end.

In This Module

- Explain the evolution of society's reliance on technology
- Develop personal uses for technology to help with productivity, learning, and future career growth
- Explain the role of technology in the professional world

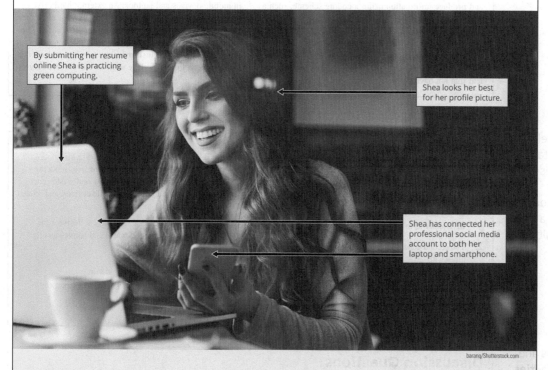

By submitting her resume online Shea is practicing green computing.

Shea looks her best for her profile picture.

Shea has connected her professional social media account to both her laptop and smartphone.

barang/Shutterstock.com

Shea Foley is finishing her degree in social media marketing. During her time at school, she has learned about how to use technology for productivity, and specifically how to use technology in social media marketing. Shea recently visited her school's career advisory center and received a list of tips to use technology to find an entry-level job in her field. She will use the technology with which she is familiar to search for openings, research the companies, schedule and keep track of interviews, and create a professional online presence.

Headings distill key takeaways to help you understand the big picture and serve as the building blocks of the module, designed to help you achieve mastery. Each module has 3-5 learning objectives. Each objective is a content heading in the module and is further broken down by subheadings that describe the technologies and how they are used.

Explain the Role of Technology in the Professional World

Nearly every job requires you to interact with technology to complete projects, exchange information with coworkers, and meet customers' needs. Technology careers span a range of specialities from software development to IT consulting to web marketing. And, no matter what business they're in, people interact with technology in almost every field, including business, education, and manufacturing. Whether you are looking for a job in a technology field or other area, you can use technology to prepare for and search for a job.

Explain Enterprise Computing

A large business with many employees is known as an enterprise. **Enterprise computing** refers to the use of technology by a company's employees to meet the needs of a large business. Each department of a company uses technology specific to its function. **Table 1-1** lists some of the uses of technology for different functional units.

Module Summary recaps the concepts covered in the module to help organize your learning experience.

Module 3 Summary

The hardware you use depends on what you are trying to accomplish, such as receive input, produce output, store data, play games, or connect to the Internet. Many hardware devices have more than one use. Input devices communicate instructions that the computer or device translates into data that the computer can read and use to produce information. Output devices convey information produced by a computer or device. Computers use the binary system to interpret data and produce information using a coding scheme, such as ASCII or Unicode.

Laptops, desktops, and all-in-ones are types of computers, as are mobile devices such as tablets and smartphones. Laptops are more common than desktops and all-in-ones because they are more portable. Smartphones are so prevalent that not having access to one is a factor in the digital divide. Peripheral devices extend the capability of a computer or device. Examples of peripheral devices include printers, keyboards, and speakers. You can connect a peripheral device wirelessly or using a port or USB hub.

Storage solutions include cloud storage and internal or external hard drives, as well as USB flash drives and optical media. All computers and devices come with an internal hard drive for storage. Solid state drives are common in mobile devices and laptops. An external hard drive can be used to extend the storage capacity of your computer. Cloud storage is popular because it allows for easier sharing and collaboration among multiple users in different physical locations. Flash memory devices and optical media are no longer widely used as more users rely on the cloud.

Review Questions help you test your understanding of each topic. These questions have been standardized to include 12 questions, which are a mix of True/False and Multiple Choice.

Review Questions

1. Data is _____.
    a. raw facts, such as text or numbers
    b. processed output
    c. the result of a calculation
    d. another term for software

2. The second generation of computers replaced vacuum tubes with _____.
    a. display devices
    b. glass crystals
    c. transformers
    d. transistors

6. (True or False) Green computing involves reducing electricity consumed and environmental waste generated when using computers, mobile devices, and related technologies.

7. A company's _____ department oversees the centralized computer equipment and administers the network.
    a. management
    b. technical support
    c. operations
    d. information security

Discussion Questions and **Critical Thinking Activities** help you relate your understanding of the module to the real world and reflect on your own experiences with technology.

Discussion Questions

1. How have embedded computers and the IoT impacted your daily life? What additional uses can you see yourself using? What security or other risks might you encounter with IoT?

2. How do the following technologies help you in your quest to become a digital citizen: kiosks, enterprise computing, and green computing?

3. What additional uses of technology can you see in the workplace? List ways technology impacts other careers not discussed in this module, such as finance, government, non-profits, and agriculture.

4. List guidelines for creating a professional online presence. View your own online presence and make a list of changes you should make in order to enhance how potential employers might view you. How should you go about making these changes? What additional advice would you give to others seeking jobs?

Critical Thinking Activities

1. You work in the educational software industry. Your boss asks you to give a brief lecture to other employees about the digital divide. Create a one-page document in which you define in your own words and give examples of the impact of the digital divide, and list ways your company can work to narrow the gap between students without reliable access to educational software, the Internet, and the hardware on which to run both. What is your role as a company and employee to address the digital divide? What aspects of the digital divide do you find most troubling or confusing?

2. You decide to reduce your environmental impact by recycling more, going paperless, and using environmentally safe cleaning products. List one or two reasons why you should add green computing to your efforts. Research five ways you can apply green computing to your daily life and rank them in order of importance. The next time you think about replacing a device, do you think this information will impact your decision? In what ways can you encourage others to do the same?

Apply Your Skills exercise ties in what you have learned in the module with the character introduced at the beginning of the module and supports you in applying what you've learned to an in-depth case scenario.

Apply Your Skills

Shea Foley is finishing her degree in social media marketing. During her time at school, she has learned about how to use technology for productivity, and specifically how to use technology in social media marketing. Shea recently visited her school's career advisory center and received a list of tips to use technology to find an entry-level job in her field.

Working in a small group or by yourself, complete the following:

1. How have past technological developments helped provide the basis for Shea's job and her ability to do her assigned tasks? If you could come up with an additional technological development that might occur in the future, what would it be, and what would Shea use it for? How might you apply the technologies you have learned about in this module to your current job or schoolwork, or to a job you have held in the past?

2. List three ways in which Shea will use technology to perform her daily tasks. Which technologies do you think will be most effective, and why?

3. What other departments might Shea interact with at work, and in what ways? List three. Which would be most important? Why? Which department interests you most? What skills might you need to be able to find a career in that department or field?

Course Solutions

Online Learning Platform: MindTap

Today's leading online learning platform, MindTap for Technology for Success, Second Edition, gives instructors complete control of a course to craft a personalized, engaging learning experience that challenges students, builds confidence and elevates performance.

MindTap introduces students to core concepts from the beginning of the course using a simplified learning path that progresses from understanding to application and delivers access to eTextbooks, study tools, interactive media, auto-graded assessments, and performance analytics.

Instructors can use MindTap for Technology for Success, Second Edition as is, or personalize it to meet specific course needs. Instructors can also easily integrate MindTap into a Learning Management System (LMS).

The online learning experience includes hands-on trainings and critical thinking challenges that encourage you to problem solve in a real-world scenario. *Technology for Success: Computer Concepts* is designed to help you build foundational knowledge and integrate it into your daily life with interactive experiences in the MindTap and SAM platforms.

- **Readings** cover focused, concrete content designed to reinforce learning objectives.
- **Skills Trainings** are comprised of brief, skills-based videos which are each followed by a multiple-choice question. SAM trainings are designed to give you concrete experience with specific technology skills.
- **Critical Thinking Challenges** place you in real-world scenarios to practice your problem-solving and decision-making skills.
- **Module Exams** assess your understanding of how the learning objectives connect and build on one another.
- **In The News activities** offer an opportunity to explore the latest technology news through various mediums to help you understand its impact on our daily lives, the economy, and society and to build lifelong learning habits.

To learn more, visit:

- MindTap – https://www.cengage.com/mindtap
- Introductory Computing – https://www.cengage.com/mindtap-collections/

Ancillary Package

Instructor Resources

Additional instructor resources for this product are available online. Instructor assets include an Instructor's Manual, Educator Guide, PowerPoint® slides, and a test bank powered by Cognero®. Sign up or sign in at www.cengage.com to search for and access this product and its online resources.

Test Banks: Questions written by the author are aligned with each module's learning objectives.

Instructor Manual: The module outline corresponds directly with the content in each module, and additional discussion questions and activities are aligned to headings in the book.

Educator Guide: The guide provides a detailed outline of the corresponding MindTap course.

PowerPoints: The icebreaker activity relates to the module topic, and the learning objectives and content slides align with the book. Activities and the self-assessment align with learning objectives and supplement the content in the book.

Solution and Answer Guide: The answers provided are written by the authors and correspond to the end of module activities.

Transition Guide: The guide is written by the authors and provides information on what has changed in this edition so that instructors know what to expect.

Acknowledgments

I would like to thank MT Cozzola for her expert editorial guidance, my co-authors Jill and Mark, for their collaboration, and Michelle, Zenya, Amy, Anne, and Ciara at Cengage for their contributions to the process. I couldn't do this without the inspiration from my two amazing children, Emma and Lucy, to whom I dedicate this book.

–Jennifer T. Campbell

Teaching is one of the greatest privileges of my life. I'm grateful to each and every one of my students that you allow me to accompany you on part of your educational and career journey. You inspire me to always do better. Thanks to all the Cengage folks who make these projects not only possible, but truly an evolution of academic progress. To our team members—MT, Zenya, Michelle, Anne, Ciara, and Amy—I have so enjoyed working with you again and getting to know you better. To my co-authors, Jennifer and Mark, it's been an honor to write alongside you. A special thank you to my husband for supporting me through the long months of intense deadlines. And thank you to my kiddos—Winn, Sarah, Daniel, and Zack—for your hugs, help, and encouragement.

–Jill West

It is a privilege to be a part of the team that worked so diligently on this project. Thanks to Amy, MT, Zenya, Michelle, and Anne, along with co-authors Jennifer and Jill.

–Mark Ciampa

Impact of Digital Technology

In This Module

- Explain the evolution of society's reliance on technology
- Develop personal uses for technology to help with productivity, learning, and future career growth
- Explain the role of technology in the professional world

By submitting her resume online Shea is practicing green computing.

Shea looks her best for her profile picture.

Shea has connected her professional social media account to both her laptop and smartphone.

baranq/Shutterstock.com

Shea Foley is finishing her degree in social media marketing. During her time at school, she has learned about how to use technology for productivity, and specifically how to use technology in social media marketing. Shea recently visited her school's career advisory center and received a list of tips to use technology to find an entry-level job in her field. She will use the technology with which she is familiar to search for openings, research the companies, schedule and keep track of interviews, and create a professional online presence.

In the course of a day, you might use technology to complete assignments, watch an online streaming video, flip through news headlines, search for map directions, make a dinner reservation, scroll through social media, or buy something online. At school, at home, and at work, technology plays a vital role in your activities.

In this module, you will learn how technology has developed over time, explore the ways technology impacts our daily home and work lives, and discover how to choose and prepare for a career in technology. As you reflect on what you learn in this module, ask yourself: How has your use of technology changed in your lifetime? How can you use technology to keep learning? What types of technology will be necessary for you to learn to help you in your career?

Explain the Evolution of Society's Reliance on Technology

Over the last quarter century, technology has revolutionized our lives. Because of advances in technology, you can access, search for, and share information more quickly and effectively than ever before. You can manage your finances, calendars, and tasks. You can play games and watch videos on your phone or computer for entertainment and relaxation. **Digital literacy** (also called **computer literacy**) involves having a current knowledge and understanding of computers, mobile devices, the web, and related technologies. Being digitally literate is essential for acquiring a job, using and contributing to global communications, and participating effectively in society and the international community.

A **computer** is an electronic device, operating under the control of instructions stored in its own memory, that can accept data, process the data to produce information, and store the information for future use. **Data** is raw facts, such as text or numbers. A computer includes hardware and software. **Hardware** is the device itself and its components, such as wires, cases, switches, and electronic circuits. **Software** consists of the programs and apps that instruct the computer to perform tasks. **Programs** and **apps** include a set of coded instructions written for a computer, such as an operating system program or an application program. The two terms are often used interchangeably, though "app" is a more accurate term for software applications while "program" may refer more broadly to instructions for operating systems as well. Software processes data into meaningful **information**.

Outline the History of Computers

People have relied on tools and machines to count and manipulate numbers for thousands of years. These tools and technologies have evolved from the abacus, a calculation tool that used a series of beads in ancient times, to the first computing machines in the nineteenth century, to today's powerful handheld devices such as smartphones and tablets and technologies that enable voice and motion interaction.

The first generation of computers used **vacuum tubes** (**Figure 1-1**), cylindrical glass tubes that controlled the flow of subatomic particles called electrons. The ENIAC and UNIVAC are examples of these expensive machines. Their use and availability were limited due to their large size, the amount of power they consumed, the heat they generated, and how quickly they wore out.

The second generation of computers replaced vacuum tubes with **transistors**, which were smaller, cheaper, and more reliable replacements for vacuum tubes. These computers contained many components still in use today, including tape and disk storage, memory, operating systems, and stored programs.

In the 1960s, computer engineers developed **integrated circuits**, which packed the equivalent of thousands of vacuum tubes or transistors into a silicon chip about the size of your thumb. In 1971, Ted Hoff and a team of engineers at the companies Intel and IBM introduced the microprocessor. A **microprocessor** is the "brains" of a computer, a chip that contains a central processing unit. Microprocessors were even faster, smaller, and less expensive than integrated circuits. Microprocessors often are called processors for short.

In the 1970s and 1980s, computers meant for personal use started to gain popularity. In 1978, Steve Jobs and Steve Wozniak of Apple Computer Corporation introduced the Apple II (**Figure 1-2**), a preassembled computer with color graphics and popular spreadsheet software called VisiCalc.

IBM followed Apple's lead in 1981, introducing its **personal computer (PC)**, which was designed for personal use, as opposed to commercial or industrial use. Other manufacturers also started making similar machines, and the market grew. Since 1981, the number of PCs in use has grown to the billions. However, many people today use tablets and smartphones in addition to or instead of PCs.

Computers have evolved into connected devices that can share data using the Internet or wireless networks. One of the many ways users communicate with each other is **email**, a system used to send and receive messages and files using the Internet. A **network** is a collection of two or more computers connected together to share resources. Wireless networks use **Wi-Fi** (short for wireless fidelity), a wireless data network technology that provides high-speed data connections that do not require a physical connection. You can save and share files over the cloud. **Cloud computing** is an Internet-based delivery of computing services, including data storage and apps. **Bluetooth** technology is wireless short-range radio connection that simplifies communications among Internet devices and between devices and the Internet.

Today's computers are smaller, faster, and have far greater capabilities than previous computers. In fact, your smartphone probably has more computing power than the computer that guided the U.S. Apollo mission to the moon in 1969! And while you might think of a PC when you think of a computer, a computer is any electronic device that includes instructions and processing power, including smartphones, tablets, and more.

Explain the Impact of the Internet of Things and Embedded Computers

The **Internet of Things (IoT)** is an environment where processors are embedded in every product imaginable (things), and these things communicate with one another via the Internet or wireless networks. Alarm clocks, coffeemakers, thermostats, streetlights, navigation systems, in-vehicle controls, and much more are enhanced by the growth of IoT. IoT-enabled

Figure 1-1: Electronic digital computer with vacuum tubes

Emkaplin/Shutterstock.com

Figure 1-2: Apple II computer

Trong Nguyen/Shutterstock.com

Figure 1-3: Smart devices use IoT to control home functions, such as a thermostat

devices often are referred to as **smart devices** (**Figure 1-3**) because of their ability to communicate, locate, and predict. Smart devices often have associated apps to control and interact with them directly or by using another device or control.

The basic premise of IoT is that objects can be tagged, tracked, and monitored through a local network or across the Internet. Communication technologies such as Bluetooth, RFID tags, near-field communications (NFC), and sensors have become readily available, more powerful, and less expensive. Sensors and tags can transmit data to a server on the Internet over a wireless network at frequent intervals for analysis and storage.

Recent technological developments have made it possible to efficiently access, store, and process the mountain of data reported by sensors. Mobile service providers offer connectivity to a variety of devices so that transmitting and receiving data can take place quickly.

An **embedded computer** is a computer that functions as one component in a larger product, and which has a specific purpose. Embedded computers usually are small and have limited hardware on their own but enhance the capabilities of everyday devices. Embedded computers perform a specific function based on the requirements of the product in which they reside. For example, an embedded computer in a printer monitors the ink levels, detects paper jams, and determines if the printer is out of paper.

Embedded computers are everywhere. This technology enables computers and devices to connect with one another over the Internet using IoT. You encounter examples of embedded computers multiple times a day, perhaps without being aware of it.

Today's vehicles have many embedded computers. These enable you to use a camera to guide you when backing up, warn you if a vehicle or object is in your blind spot, or alert you to unsafe road conditions. Some newer cars include screens that determine and guide your route, or that enable you to use touch or voice commands to control the temperature, car lights, and more. Recently, all new cars were required to include backup cameras and electronic stability control, which can assist with steering the car in case of skidding. All of this technology is intended to make driving safer (**Figure 1-4**).

Critics of in-vehicle technology claim that it can provide drivers with a false sense of security. If you rely on a sensor while backing up, parking, or changing lanes, you may miss other obstructions that can cause a crash. Reliance on electronic stability control may cause you to drive faster than conditions allow, or to pay less attention to the distance between your vehicle and others.

Figure 1-4: Some of the embedded computers designed to improve safety, security, and performance in today's vehicles

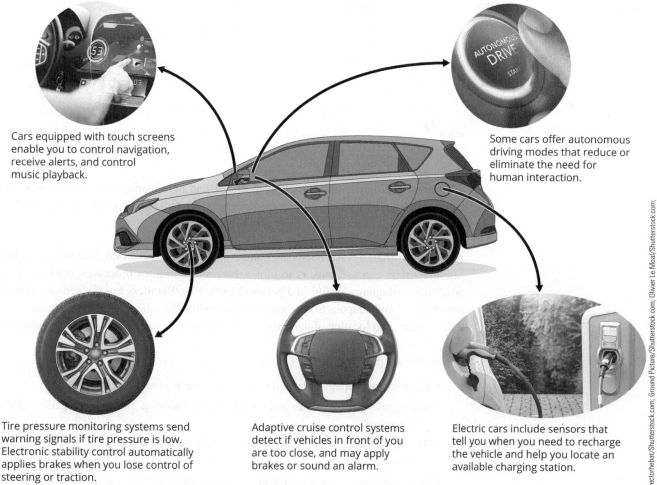

Cars equipped with touch screens enable you to control navigation, receive alerts, and control music playback.

Some cars offer autonomous driving modes that reduce or eliminate the need for human interaction.

Tire pressure monitoring systems send warning signals if tire pressure is low. Electronic stability control automatically applies brakes when you lose control of steering or traction.

Adaptive cruise control systems detect if vehicles in front of you are too close, and may apply brakes or sound an alarm.

Electric cars include sensors that tell you when you need to recharge the vehicle and help you locate an available charging station.

vectorhebat/Shutterstock.com; Ground Picture/Shutterstock.com; Olivier Le Moal/Shutterstock.com; Scharfsinn/Shutterstock.com; photobeps/Shutterstock.com; Evannovostro/Shutterstock.com

ATMs and Kiosks   Automated teller machines (ATMs) are one of the more familiar uses of IoT. You can use your ATM card to withdraw cash, deposit checks, and interact with your bank accounts. Recent innovations are improving card security, such as **chip-and-pin technology** that stores data on an embedded chip instead of a magnetic stripe.

ATMs are a type of kiosk. A **kiosk** is a freestanding booth usually placed in a public area that can contain a display device used to present information to the public or event attendees. Kiosks enable self-service transactions in hotels and airports, for example, to enable users to check in for a flight or room. Healthcare providers also use kiosks for patients to check in and enter information, such as their insurance card number.

IoT at Home   IoT enables you to manage devices remotely in your home, such as to start the washing machine at a certain time, view potential intruders via a webcam, or adjust the room temperature. Personal IoT uses include wearable fitness trackers that record and send data to your smartphone or computer about your exercise activity, the number of steps you take in a day, and your heart rate.

Figure 1-5: IoT-enabled devices can help you with daily tasks such as grocery shopping

Refrigerator detects milk is low. → Refrigerator sends a text to your phone that you need milk. → Refrigerator adds 'buy milk' to your scheduling app. → Phone determines the closest grocery store with the lowest milk price. → Phone sends store address to your vehicle's navigation system.

Figure 1-5 provides an example of how IoT can help manage your daily tasks. IoT continues to advance its capabilities, and can help you maintain a secure, energy-efficient, connected, voice-activated, remotely accessible home.

IoT in Business   All businesses and areas of business can take advantage of IoT. Manufacturers can use sensors to allow workers to monitor processes and ensure the efficiency and quality of finished goods (**Figure 1-6**). Retailers can use sensors to track inventory or send coupons to customers' phones while they shop. Shipping companies can track mileage and location of their trucks and monitor driving times to ensure the safety of their drivers.

A healthcare provider can use IoT to:

- Connect to a patient's wearable blood pressure or glucose monitor
- Send prescription updates and changes to a pharmacy, and alert the patient of the prescription
- Track and store data provided by wearable monitors to determine necessary follow-up care (**Figure 1-7**)
- Send the patient reminders about upcoming appointments or tests

The uses of IoT are expanding rapidly, and connected devices continue to impact and enhance business practices at all levels.

Figure 1-6: Manufacturing technology enables oversight of quality, safety, and procedures

Blue Planet Studio/Shutterstock.com

Figure 1-7: Wearable monitors enable users to monitor glucose levels and administer insulin

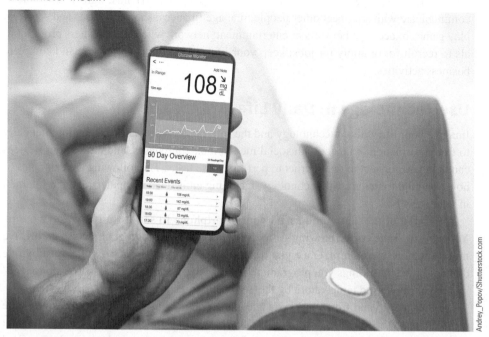

Andrey_Popov/Shutterstock.com

Recognize the Impact of the Digital Divide

All of this technology has many uses for both personal and business needs. However, it is not available to everyone. The **digital divide** is the gap between those who have access to technology and its resources and information, especially on the Internet, and those who do not. Socioeconomic (relative position in society), geographic (location), and demographic (population indicators, such as age or ethnicity) factors contribute to the digital divide, which can impact individuals, households, businesses, or geographic areas.

Imagine the educational opportunities when you have access to high-speed, unfiltered Internet content; your own laptop, tablet, or smart device; and software to create, track, and process data and information. Then compare these opportunities with the opportunities available to students who live in countries where the government restricts access to Internet content, and economics prevent them from owning their own devices and the software or apps used on them. Inequalities such as limited or no access to unfiltered information at a high speed can affect learning, knowledge, and opportunities and can have a lasting impact on the future of those affected.

Corporations, non-profits, educational institutions, and governments are working on solutions to narrow the digital divide so that all learners can become digitally literate.

Develop Personal Uses for Technology to Help with Productivity, Learning, and Future Career Growth

You can use technology to help with productivity, learning, and future career growth. In your daily life you interact with embedded computers in stores, public transportation, your car or truck, and more. Assistive technologies help people with disabilities to use technology. Green computing practices reduce the impact of electronic waste on the planet.

Just as any society has rules and regulations to guide its citizens, so does the digital world. As a **digital citizen**, you should be familiar with how to use technology to become an educated and productive member of the digital world.

Technology can enable you to more efficiently and effectively access and search for information; share personal ideas, photos, and videos with friends, family, and others; communicate with and meet other people; manage finances; shop for goods and services; play games or access other sorts of entertainment; network with other business professionals to recruit for or apply for jobs; keep your life and activities organized; and complete business activities.

Use Technology in Daily Life

Imagine your life without technology and the Internet. You probably use the Internet daily to find information, connect with social media, make purchases, and more. Your devices can help you connect to the Internet to perform these tasks. The following are examples of how you might interact with technology, including embedded computers and the Internet, in your daily life.

The sound of the alarm you asked your smartphone to set last night wakes you up. You can smell the coffee brewing from the coffee maker you programmed to go off five minutes before your alarm. Once you leave for work, your thermostat will adjust by five degrees based on settings you programmed into an app; later you can use the app to readjust to your preferred temperature by the time you arrive home.

On your way to and from work, you check the public transportation app on your phone to navigate to the subway station and check how much time you have before the next train arrives. Once there, you scan your phone to pay your fare and access the terminal (**Figure 1-8**). A screen in the station displays an alert when the train is incoming. As the subway speeds toward the next station, it relies on sensors to determine any oncoming traffic and report delays, changes in routes, and the next available stop.

After work, you need to pick up a new printer you previously researched using a technology review website, purchased using the store's app, and scheduled for a 5:30 PM pickup time. You go home and get in your car, which adjusts the seats and mirrors to your settings, and uses Bluetooth to start playing your favorite playlist (**Figure 1-9**). You program your vehicle's GPS to take you to the store. As you drive, your car senses the space between

Figure 1-8: Public transit apps enable you to pay electronically and monitor train arrivals

Figure 1-9: Bluetooth enables your car stereo to play music from your smartphone

Capix Denan/Shutterstock.com

you and the car ahead and slows your speed to keep a safe distance. Outside the store, you use your car's cameras to safely navigate into an open spot and use the store's app to let them know you have arrived.

At your next stop, you need to pick up a new top to wear to a friend's birthday party. Before heading into the store, you decide to check your balance on your debit card. Your banking app tells you how much money is in your checking account. You tap to transfer $40 to your smartphone's payment app, then you head to the store.

You walk into a bookstore, searching for a new book to read. You talk to a sales associate, who uses her tablet to look up your personal profile, including past purchases, based on your phone number. The sales associate tells you what genres you like to read, and what authors you have bought books by in the past few years. Together, you find a book by a new author that looks appealing to you. Before using the store's self-checkout, you check your store loyalty app on your smartphone to access available coupons.

Later, back at home, you log onto your school's network to access your assignments. You use video conferencing to discuss a group project with your classmates and complete a research paper using credible online sources and giving proper citations to the facts and quotes you find. You turn in your paper using the school's plagiarism checker and shut down your laptop for the night. You make sure your alarm is set for tomorrow and call it a night.

Use Technology to Assist Users with Disabilities

The ever-increasing presence of computers in everyone's lives has generated an awareness of the need to address computing requirements for individuals with certain disabilities, such as learning disabilities, mobility issues, and hearing and visual disabilities. **Accessibility** is the practice of removing barriers that may prevent individuals with disabilities from interacting with data or an app.

The **Americans with Disabilities Act (ADA)** requires any company with 15 or more employees to make reasonable attempts to accommodate the needs of workers with disabilities. The **Individuals with Disabilities Education Act (IDEA)** requires that public schools purchase or acquire funding for adaptive technologies. These laws were put in place to ensure that people with disabilities can access the same resources, information, and services as able-bodied individuals using the appropriate technology.

Figure 1-10: A Braille printer

Andy Shell/Shutterstock.com

Users with visual disabilities can change screen settings, such as increasing the size or changing the color of the text to make the words easier to read. Changing the color of text also can address the needs of users with certain types of color blindness. Instead of using a monitor, blind users can work with voice output. That is, the computer speaks out loud the information that appears on a screen. A Braille printer prints information on paper in Braille (**Figure 1-10**).

Screen reader technology uses audio output to describe the contents of the screen. Screen readers can read aloud webpages and documents or provide narration of the computer or device's actions. **Alternative text (alt text)** is descriptive text added to an object, such as a picture or drawing (**Figure 1-11**). A screen reader will read the alt text aloud so that the user understands the image and its purpose. Webpages and documents should include alt text for all images. Alt text can be as simple as the name of a famous individual shown in a photograph, or more complex, such as interpreting the results of a chart or graph. Productivity applications such as Microsoft Office and webpage creation apps prompt users to add alt text, and sometimes provide suggested alt text content.

Figure 1-11: Screen readers use alt text to describe an image

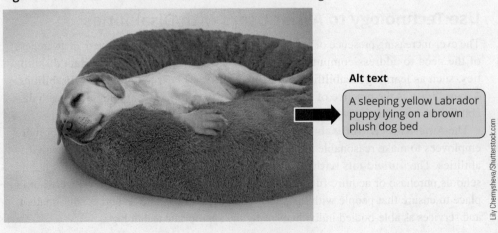

Alt text

A sleeping yellow Labrador puppy lying on a brown plush dog bed

Lily Chernysheva/Shutterstock.com

Figure 1-12: Specialized keyboard for users with mobility issues

Reshetnikov_art/Shutterstock.com

Deaf or Deaf-Blind individuals can instruct programs or apps to display words or other visual clues instead of sounds, such as for a notification from an app. Captioning software displays scrolling text for dialogue in a video. Cameras can interpret sign language gestures into text.

Mobility issues can impact a user's ability to interact with hardware, such as a keyboard or a mouse (**Figure 1-12**). Users with limited hand mobility can use an on-screen keyboard, a keyboard with larger keys, or a hand-mounted pointer to control the pointer or insertion point. Alternatives to mouse buttons include a hand pad, a foot pedal, a receptor that detects facial motions, or a pneumatic instrument controlled by puffs of air. Users with a physical disability that causes hands to move involuntarily can purchase input devices such as a keyboard or mouse that are less sensitive to accidental interaction due to trembling or spasms.

Users with learning disabilities might struggle with reading words on a screen, handwriting, or retaining information. Technologies that help these users learn or perform tasks include:

- **Audio books** to read information aloud to the user instead of reading on a printed page or on the screen
- **Speech recognition programs** so the user can input data or information verbally
- **Graphic organizers** to enable a user to create an outline or structure of information

Figure 1-13: Look for the Energy Star logo when purchasing appliances or devices

The basic premise of assisted technology is to improve accessibility for all users and provide the same opportunities to learn, work, and play as able-bodied users, no matter what disabilities a user has.

Apply Green Computing Concepts to Daily Life

People use, and often waste, resources such as electricity and paper while using technology. The practice of **green computing** involves reducing electricity consumed and environmental waste generated when using computers, mobile devices, and related technologies.

Personal computers, displays, printers, and other devices should comply with guidelines of the ENERGY STAR program (**Figure 1-13**). The United States Department of Energy (DOE) and the United States

US Environmental Protection Agency, ENERGY STAR program

Environmental Protection Agency (EPA) developed the ENERGY STAR program to help reduce the amount of electricity used by computers and related devices. This program encourages manufacturers to create energy-efficient devices. For example, many devices switch to sleep or power save mode after a specified amount of inactive time.

Electronic waste and trash have a negative effect on the environment where it is discarded. You can avoid electronic waste by not replacing devices every time a new version comes out, and recycling devices and products such as ink and toner when they no longer provide value.

Your personal green computing efforts should include:

- Purchasing and using products with an ENERGY STAR label
- Shutting down your computers and devices overnight or when not in use
- Donating computer equipment
- Using paperless communication
- Recycling paper, toner and ink cartridges, computers, mobile devices, and printers
- Telecommuting and using video conferencing for meetings

Organizations can implement a variety of measures to reduce electrical waste, such as:

- Consolidating servers
- Purchasing high-efficiency equipment
- Using sleep modes and other power management features for computers and devices
- Buying computers and devices with lower power consumption processors and power supplies
- Using outside air, when possible, to cool the data center or computer facility
- Allowing employees to telecommute to save gas and reduce emissions from vehicles

Green computing practices are usually easy to implement and can make a huge impact on the environment.

Explain the Role of Technology in the Professional World

Nearly every job requires you to interact with technology to complete projects, exchange information with coworkers, and meet customers' needs. Technology careers span a range of specialities from software development to IT consulting to web marketing. And, no matter what business they're in, people interact with technology in almost every field, including business, education, and manufacturing. Whether you are looking for a job in a technology field or other area, you can use technology to prepare for and search for a job.

Explain Enterprise Computing

A large business with many employees is known as an enterprise. **Enterprise computing** refers to the use of technology by a company's employees to meet the needs of a large business. Each department of a company uses technology specific to its function. **Table 1-1** lists some of the uses of technology for different functional units.

Table 1-1: Enterprise functional units

Functional unit	Technology uses
Human resources	Track employees' personal data, including pay rates, benefits, and vacation time
Accounting	Keep track of income and spending
Sales	Manage contacts, schedule meetings, log customer interactions, and process orders
Information technology	Maintain and secure hardware and software
Engineering and product development	Develop plans for and test new products
Manufacturing	Monitor assembly of products and manage inventory of parts and products
Marketing	Create and track success of marketing campaigns that target specific demographics
Distribution	Analyze and track inventory and manage shipping
Customer service	Manage customer interactions

Identify Uses of Technology in the Workplace

Technological advances, such as the PC, enabled workers to do their jobs more efficiently while at their desks. Today's workers can use smartphones, the Internet, the cloud, and more to work remotely, whether they are **telecommuting** (working from home), or traveling halfway around the world.

An **intelligent workplace** uses technology to enable workers to connect to the company's network, communicate with each other, use productivity software and apps, meet via web conferencing, and more. Some companies provide employees with computers and devices that come with the necessary software and apps, network connectivity, and security. Other workplaces have a **BYOD (bring your own device)** policy, enabling employees to use their personal devices to conduct business. Companies use online collaborative productivity software to allow employees to share documents such as reports or spreadsheets and to make edits or comments.

Outline Technology Careers

The technology field provides opportunities for people of all skill levels and interests, and demand for computer professionals continues to grow. The following sections describe general technology career areas.

Software and Apps   The software and apps field consists of companies that develop, manufacture, and support programs for computers, the web, and mobile devices. Some companies specialize in a certain area, such as productivity software or gaming. Other companies sell many types of software that work with both computers and mobile devices and may use the Internet to sync data and use collaborative features.

Technology Equipment   The technology equipment field consists of manufacturers and distributors of computers, mobile devices, and other hardware. In addition to the companies that make the finished products, this field includes companies that manufacture the internal components such as chips, cables, and power supplies.

Table 1-2: IT responsibilities

IT area	Responsibilities
Management	Directs the planning, research, development, evaluation, and integration of technology
Research and software development	Analyzes, designs, develops, and implements new information technology and maintains existing systems
Technical support	Evaluates and integrates new technologies, administers the organization's data resources, and supports the centralized computer operating system and servers
Operations	Oversees the centralized computer equipment and administers the network
Training and support	Teaches employees how to use the information system and answers user questions
Information security	Develops and enforces policies that are designed to safeguard an organization's data and information from unauthorized users

IT Departments   Most medium and large businesses and organizations have an **Information Technology (IT) department**. IT staff are responsible for ensuring that all the computer operations, mobile devices, and networks run smoothly. They also determine when and if the organization requires new hardware, mobile devices, or software. IT jobs typically are divided into the areas described in **Table 1-2**.

Technology Service and Repair   The technology service and repair field provides preventative maintenance, component installations, and repair services to customers. Some technicians receive training and certifications from manufacturers to become specialists in devices from that manufacturer. Many technology equipment manufacturers include diagnostic software with their computers and devices that assist technicians in identifying problems. Technicians can use the Internet to diagnose and repair software remotely, by accessing the user's computer or device from a different location.

Technology Sales   Technology salespeople must possess a general understanding of technology, as well as specific knowledge of the product they are selling. Strong people skills, including listening and communicating, are important. Some salespeople work directly for a technology equipment or software manufacturer, while others work for resellers of technology, including retail stores.

Technology Education, Training, and Support   Schools, colleges, universities, and companies all need qualified educators to provide technology-related education and training. Instructors at an educational institution typically have a background and degree related to the technology they are teaching. Corporate trainers teach employees how to use the technology specific to the business or industry. Help desk specialists provide support by answering questions from employees to help them troubleshoot problems.

IT Consulting   An IT consultant typically has gained experience in one or more areas, such as software development, social media, or network configuration. IT consultants provide technology services to clients based on their specific areas of expertise. Sometimes a company will hire a large group of IT consultants to work together on a specific task, such as building a new network infrastructure or database.

System Development   System developers analyze and create software, apps, databases, websites and web-based development platforms, cloud services, and networks. Developers identify the business requirements and desired outcomes for the system, specify the structure and security needed, and design and program the system.

Web Marketing and Social Media   Careers in web marketing require you to be familiar not only with marketing strategies, but also with web-based platforms and social media apps. Web marketers create social media plans, including the content and timing of marketing campaigns, posts, and emails. Search engine optimization (SEO) knowledge helps to create web content and layout that enhances the content's results when users search for content.

Data Storage, Retrieval, and Analysis   Employees in this field must be knowledgeable about collecting, analyzing, storing, and reporting data from databases or the web. Data scientists use analytics to compile statistics on data to create strategies or analyze business practices. Web analytics experts measure Internet data, such as website traffic patterns and ads (**Figure 1-14**). Digital forensics examiners use evidence found on computers, networks, and devices to help solve crimes.

Information and Systems Security   Careers in information and systems security require you to be informed about how to address and prevent potential threats to a device or network, including viruses and hacking. Security specialists need to know tools and techniques to prevent against and recover from digital attacks.

Figure 1-14: Web analytic data measures website traffic patterns

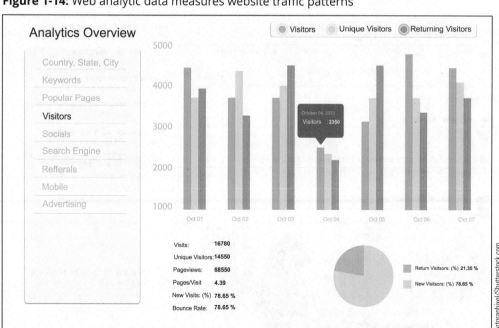

Explain How You Might Prepare for a Career in Technology

You can use both social media and job search websites to learn about technology careers and to promote yourself to potential employers. By creating a profile on a career networking site or creating a personal website or blog that showcases your talents, hiring managers can learn more about you beyond what you can convey in a traditional, one-page paper resume.

Professional Online Presence   Recommended strategies for creating a professional online presence include:

- Do not use humorous or informal names for your account profiles, blog, or domain name.
- Include a photo that represents you in a confident, professional manner.
- Upload an electronic copy of your resume.
- Include links to videos, publications, or digital content you have created.
- Proofread your resume, blog, website, or profile carefully to avoid spelling and grammar mistakes.
- Enable privacy settings on your personal social media accounts, and never post anything online that you would not want a potential employer to access.

Online social networks for professionals can help you keep up with past coworkers, instructors, potential employers, and others with whom you have a professional connection. You can use these networks to search for jobs, learn about a company before interviewing, join groups of people with similar interests or experiences, share information about your career, and communicate with contacts. LinkedIn (**Figure 1-15**) and other professional networking websites also offer online training courses to keep your skills up-to-date.

Certifications   Some technology careers require you to have certain certifications. A certification demonstrates your knowledge in a specific area to employers and potential employers. Online materials and print books exist to help you prepare for a certification

Figure 1-15: LinkedIn is a career-based social networking site

LinkedIn Corporation

exam. Most certifications do not require coursework assignments, but instead require you to pass an exam that demonstrates your proficiency in the area. Tests typically are taken at an authorized testing center. Some tests are multiple choice, while others are skills-based. You likely will have to pay a fee to take the exam. Some areas that offer certifications include:

- Application software
- Data analytics, database, and web design
- Hardware
- Networking
- Operating systems
- Programming
- Cybersecurity

Obtaining a certification requires you to spend time and money. Certifications demonstrate your commitment to your chosen area and can help you land a job.

Technology in K-12 Education   Schools use social networking tools to promote school events, work cooperatively on group projects, and teach concepts such as anti-bullying. Online productivity software enables students to work collaboratively on projects and send the finished assignment to the teacher using email, reducing the need for paper printouts. These factors and more create an **intelligent classroom**, in which technology is used to facilitate learning and communication.

Technology in Higher Education   A college or university might use a **learning management system (LMS)** to set up web-based training sites where students can check their progress in a course, take practice tests, and exchange messages with the instructor or other students. Students also can view instructor lectures online and take classes or earn a degree online. Ebooks let students read and access content from their tablet or device, and access digital assets like videos associated with the content.

Technology in Healthcare   Physicians use computers to monitor patients' vital signs and research symptoms and diagnoses. The **mobile health (mHealth)** trend refers to healthcare professionals using smartphones or tablets to access health records stored in the cloud, and to patients using digital devices to monitor their conditions and treatments, reducing the need for visits to the doctor's office. For example, mHealth apps can track prescription information and text reminders to take medication, or even contact the pharmacy to refill the prescription. Medical monitoring devices, such as electronic bracelets, collect vital signs and send the data to a specialist. Patients can ingest smart pills that contain sensors to monitor medication or tiny cameras to enable a physician to view the patient's internal organs without invasive procedures. Healthcare also uses 3-D printers to manufacture skin for burn patients, and prosthetic devices and casts.

Figure 1-16: Codes on packages can be scanned to determine their location

Technology in the Transportation Industry   Transportation workers use handheld computers to scan codes on packages or containers of products before loading them on a vehicle, train, ship, or plane (**Figure 1-16**). You then can track the progress of your package as it makes its way to you. Computers find an efficient route for

Figure 1-17: Robots often are used in computer manufacturing

Gorodenkoff/Shutterstock.com

the packages and track their progress. Drivers use GPS to navigate quickly and safely, avoiding traffic and hazardous conditions. Soon, self-driving trucks will use robotics for mechanical control. Automated vehicles increase independent transportation options for people with disabilities.

Technology in Manufacturing   Manufacturers use **computer-aided manufacturing (CAM)** to streamline production and ship products more quickly. With CAM, robots perform work that is too dangerous, detailed, or monotonous for people (**Figure 1-17**). In particular, they play a major role in automotive, metal and plastics, and electrical and electronics manufacturing. In the automotive industry, for example, robots typically paint the bodies of cars because painting is complex, difficult, and hazardous. Pairing robotic systems with human workers also improves quality, cost efficiency, and competitiveness. Computers and mobile devices make it possible to order parts and materials from the warehouse to assemble custom products. A company's computers monitor assembly lines and equipment using **machine-to-machine (M2M)** communications.

Module 1 Summary

Computers have evolved from large, inefficient, and expensive devices that used technology such as vacuum tubes to smaller, more powerful connected devices such as PCs, smartphones, and more.

Computers impact your daily life in many ways, including the use of embedded computers in vehicles, ATMs, and stores, and the Internet of Things (IoT) that allows smart home appliances and other devices to communicate over the Internet or a wireless network. IoT has many applications

within both the personal realm (such as wearable fitness trackers and managing appliances) and the business world (such as manufacturing sensors or retail inventory tracking). Differences in access to technology, especially the Internet, have led to a digital divide that limits opportunities for many.

Users with disabilities can use many different devices and software that enable them to access and use technology. These are crucial in providing everyone with the same opportunities to learn, work, and play. Many technologies exist to help provide accessibility to all users, and laws such as the Americans with Disabilities Act (ADA) require workplaces to provide accessible products.

There are many ways you can employ green computing practices to help reduce your impact on the environment, including donating old computer equipment, telecommuting, and purchasing ENERGY STAR products.

Technology has had a large impact on the professional world. Enterprise computing refers to the needs of large companies to provide technology for their different functional units, such as customer service and accounting. Intelligent workplaces enable employees to communicate and perform tasks efficiently. Education, transportation, healthcare, and manufacturing all use technology to reduce costs and increase safety and efficiency.

There are many careers available to you in the technology field, including software development, technology equipment, IT, service and repair, education and training, consulting, system development, marketing and social media, data storage and analysis, and security. To prepare for a career in technology, you should create a professional online presence and take advantage of certification options.

Review Questions

1. Data is _____.
   a. raw facts, such as text or numbers
   b. processed output
   c. the result of a calculation
   d. another term for software

2. The second generation of computers replaced vacuum tubes with _____.
   a. display devices
   b. glass crystals
   c. transformers
   d. transistors

3. The premise that objects can be tagged, tracked, and monitored through a local network or across the Internet refers to _____.
   a. intelligent workspaces
   b. the digital divide
   c. the Internet of Things
   d. networking

4. The gap between those who have access to technology and its resources and information, especially on the Internet, and those who do not, is known as the _____.
   a. Internet of Things
   b. digital divide
   c. information abyss
   d. accessibility factor

5. Descriptive text added to an object is called _____ text.
   a. associative
   b. alternative
   c. accessible
   d. assistive

6. (True or False) Green computing involves reducing electricity consumed and environmental waste generated when using computers, mobile devices, and related technologies.

7. A company's _____ department oversees the centralized computer equipment and administers the network.
   a. management
   b. technical support
   c. operations
   d. information security

8. The use of technology by a company's employees to meet the needs of a large business is called _____ computing.
   a. enterprise
   b. macro
   c. ultra
   d. resourceful

9. A company's BYOD policy refers to allowing employees to bring their own _____.
   a. dogs
   b. data
   c. documents
   d. devices

10. Colleges set up web-based training sites where students can check their progress in a course, take practice tests, and exchange messages with the instructor or other students using a _____ management system (LMS).
    a. learning
    b. linked
    c. locational
    d. live

11. A company's computers monitor assembly lines and equipment using _____ communications.

    a. CAM
    b. AI
    c. IT
    d. M2M

12. (True or False) When looking for a job, you should use humorous or informal names for your account profiles, blog, or domain name to make yourself stand out.

Discussion Questions

1. How have embedded computers and the IoT impacted your daily life? What additional uses can you see yourself using? What security or other risks might you encounter with IoT?

2. How do the following technologies help you in your quest to become a digital citizen: kiosks, enterprise computing, and green computing?

3. What additional uses of technology can you see in the workplace? List ways technology impacts other careers not discussed in this module, such as finance, government, non-profits, and agriculture.

4. List guidelines for creating a professional online presence. View your own online presence and make a list of changes you should make in order to enhance how potential employers might view you. How should you go about making these changes? What additional advice would you give to others seeking jobs?

Critical Thinking Activities

1. You work in the educational software industry. Your boss asks you to give a brief lecture to other employees about the digital divide. Create a one-page document in which you define in your own words and give examples of the impact of the digital divide, and list ways your company can work to narrow the gap between students without reliable access to educational software, the Internet, and the hardware on which to run both. What is your role as a company and employee to address the digital divide? What aspects of the digital divide do you find most troubling or confusing?

2. You decide to reduce your environmental impact by recycling more, going paperless, and using environmentally safe cleaning products. List one or two reasons why you should add green computing to your efforts. Research five ways you can apply green computing to your daily life and rank them in order of importance. The next time you think about replacing a device, do you think this information will impact your decision? In what ways can you encourage others to do the same?

3. Research the history of the IDEA and the ADA. List achievements and developments of both, and compare how they impact both students and employees. What examples of the impact of both have you seen in your school or workplace?

4. In addition to the developments outlined in this module, list and describe other technological advances of which you are aware that occurred before you were born and after. Which advancement has had the most impact on you, personally? Why?

Apply Your Skills

Shea Foley is finishing her degree in social media marketing. During her time at school, she has learned about how to use technology for productivity, and specifically how to use technology in social media marketing. Shea recently visited her school's career advisory center and received a list of tips to use technology to find an entry-level job in her field.

    Working in a small group or by yourself, complete the following:

1.   How have past technological developments helped provide the basis for Shea's job and her ability to do her assigned tasks? If you could come up with an additional technological development that might occur in the future, what would it be, and what would Shea use it for? How might you apply the technologies you have learned about in this module to your current job or schoolwork, or to a job you have held in the past?

2.   List three ways in which Shea will use technology to perform her daily tasks. Which technologies do you think will be most effective, and why?

3.   What other departments might Shea interact with at work, and in what ways? List three. Which would be most important? Why? Which department interests you most? What skills might you need to be able to find a career in that department or field?

The Web

In This Module

- Explain the role of the web in daily life
- Describe websites and webpages
- Use e-commerce
- Explain how information literacy applies to web searches and research
- Conduct online research

Unathi connects to the Internet while on his commute using his ISP's wireless network.

Unathi uses the web throughout the day to collaborate with his classmates, post updates to his blog, conduct research at educational websites, read sports and news articles, and check his social networks such as Instagram and Facebook.

VAKS-Stock Agency/Shutterstock.com

Unathi Mwange uses the web in every aspect of his life, even as he commutes to school. Connecting to the cloud with his mobile phone, he stores, retrieves, and shares files. He uses his browser to log onto his school's LMS to check his grades, participate in web-based lectures, and gather content for class projects from reliable online resources. He completes assignments using web apps, compares deals on headphones at e-commerce websites, and uses an online auction website to buy and sell sports memorabilia.

You probably use the web dozens or hundreds of times a day to do things such as locate and reserve a place for lunch, keep track of your budget, shop for new clothes, post a comment on a blog or message board, or search for photos or facts you need to complete a project at school or work. As a vast library of content, the web is where you go for entertainment, bargains, news, and information of all kinds. To find what you need on the web, you should understand the types of resources the web provides.

In this module, you will examine the role of the web in daily life. You will explore the components of websites, webpages, and e-commerce, determine how to connect to the Internet, gain an understanding of information literacy, and learn about tools for trustworthy web searches and online research. As you reflect on what you learn in this module, ask yourself: How would your life be different if you didn't have access to the web? What types of websites are most useful to you? How can you ensure you are participating in e-commerce safely? What impact does net neutrality have on how you access the Internet? How do you ensure that the information you find online is accurate?

Explain the Role of the Web in Daily Life

While sometimes used interchangeably, the Internet and the web are two different things. The **Internet** is a global collection of millions of *computers* linked together to share information worldwide. The **web**, originally known as the **World Wide Web**, is a collection of *webpages* located on computers around the world, connected through the Internet. The web has changed the way people access information, conduct business transactions, and communicate (**Figure 2-1**). Almost everyone can use the web because it is part of the Internet. Today, billions of people use the Internet and the web. The more you know about the web and how to access its contents, the more you can benefit from using it.

Figure 2-1: The web can be used to communicate, shop, share information, travel, and more

Viewvie/Shutterstock.com

Define Web Browsing Terms

When you use a mobile phone or other device to access the web, you are accessing a collection of webpages located on computers around the world, connected through the Internet. A **webpage** (**Figure 2-2**) is an electronic document that can contain text, graphics, sound, video, and links to other webpages. The main page in a website is called the **home page**. Webpages can be either static or dynamic, depending on how the content is presented. A webpage that is **static** is one where the content does not change very often. A webpage that

Figure 2-2: Webpage

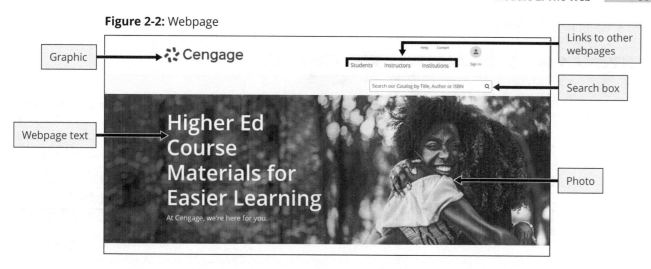

is **dynamic** is one with content that changes as you interact with it, such as a news site that updates based on breaking news, or for a weather website that displays content based on the visitor's location or preferences.

Successful websites are designed to be visually appealing, and to present the content in a logical format. Most web designers use the concept of **responsive web design**, which is a way to provide content so that it adapts appropriately to the size of the display on any device, such as on a laptop or a smartphone (**Figure 2-3**).

A collection of webpages (often shortened to "pages") makes up a **website** (often shortened to "site"). A company, organization, institution, group, or person creates and maintains a website. In general, websites focus on a specific topic, business, or service.

Figure 2-3: Responsive web design adapts content to fit different devices

Figure 2-4: Comparing websites

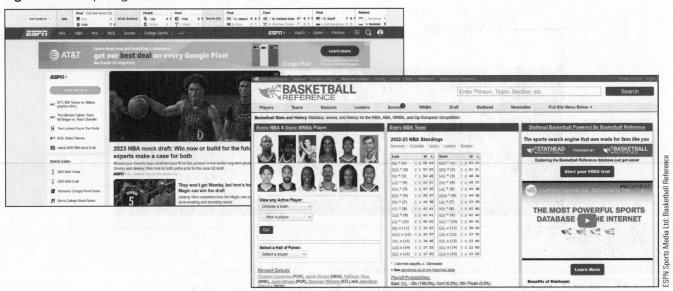

When you visit a website for the first time, figure out its purpose so you know what type of content to expect and which actions are appropriate. For example, the purpose of the ESPN website is to provide sports news and entertainment for free, while the Basketball Reference website provides statistics only, and has additional information for subscribers. Both websites are dedicated to sports, but each has a different purpose (**Figure 2-4**).

Browsers   To access the web, you open a **browser**, which is an app designed to display webpages. Google Chrome, Apple Safari, Mozilla Firefox, and Microsoft Edge are examples of popular browsers. You use the tools in a browser to **navigate** the web, or move from one webpage to another.

The webpage that appears when you open a browser is called the **home page** or **start page**. To display a different webpage, you use a link, short for **hyperlink**, which is a specially formatted word, phrase, or graphic that, when clicked or tapped, lets you display a webpage on the Internet, another file, an email, or another location within the same file, or perform another action, such as sending an email message. Links enable you to pursue information in a nonlinear fashion, clicking relevant links if and when their content appeals to you.

Webpage Identification   To keep track of billions of webpages, the Internet assigns each one a **uniform resource locator (URL)**, a web address used by a browser to locate a website on the Internet. A URL can consist of the parts described in **Figure 2-5**.

Figure 2-5: Parts of a URL

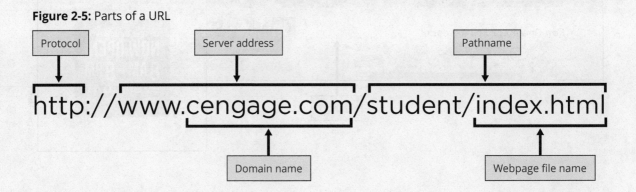

Table 2-1: URL parts

URL part	Definition
Protocol	A standardized procedure computers use to exchange information
Server address	The address of the server storing the webpage
Pathname	The address to the folder containing the webpage
File name	The name of the webpage file

If you can interpret a URL, you can learn about the sponsor, origin, and location of the webpage and catch a glimpse of how the web works. **Table 2-1** defines each part of a URL.

When the URL for a webpage starts with http://, the browser uses the **Hypertext Transfer Protocol (HTTP)**, the most common way to transfer information around the web, to retrieve the page. Often when giving a URL, the http:// prefix is omitted, but the browser knows to fill it in.

A server is a powerful networked computer that provides resources to other computers. A **web server** stores webpages and delivers them to computers requesting the pages through a browser. In the server address www.cengage.com, the www indicates that the server is a web server, cengage is the name the Cengage company chose for this website, and .com means that a commercial entity runs the web server.

The server address in a URL corresponds to an Internet Protocol (IP) address, which identifies every computer on the Internet. An **Internet Protocol (IP) address** is a unique number that consists of four to six sets of numbers from 0 to 255 separated by periods, or dots, as in 69.32.132.255. Although computers can use IP addresses easily, they are difficult for people to remember, so domain names were created. A **domain name** identifies one or more IP addresses, such as cengage.com. URLs use the domain name in the server address part of the URL to identify a particular website.

In addition, each file stored on a web server has a unique pathname. The pathname in a URL includes the names of the folders containing the file, the file name, and its extension. A common file name extension for webpages is .html, sometimes shortened to .htm. For example, the pathname might be student/index.html, which specifies a file named index, saved in the .html format, and stored in a folder named student.

Not all URLs include a pathname. If you don't specify a pathname or file name in a URL, most web browsers open a file named index.html or index.htm, which is the default name for a website's main page.

Web Navigation   The **address bar** is the part of a browser window that displays the location of the current webpage (**Figure 2-6**). You can also use the address bar to type the URL of the webpage you want to display, or enter terms for which you want to search.

Figure 2-6: Navigating the web with a browser

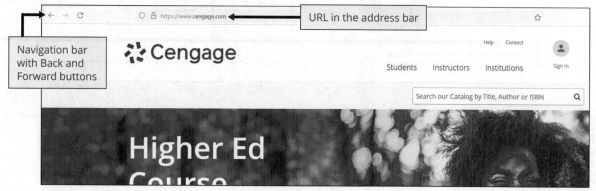

As you navigate websites, your browser keeps a copy of each page you view in a **cache**, so that the next time you go to a webpage, it loads more quickly. The browser also keeps track of pages you have viewed in sequence by tracking **breadcrumbs**—the path you followed to display a webpage. The **navigation bar** in a browser includes buttons such as Back and Forward that you can use to revisit webpages along the breadcrumb path.

Connect to the Internet

In order to access the Internet, you first must create a connection between the Internet and your device. You can connect your computers or devices to the Internet using wired or wireless technology. With a wired connection, a computer or device physically attaches via a cable or wire to a communications device that transmits data and other items over transmission media to the Internet. A **modem**, a device that sends and receives data over telephone or cable lines and is connected to your computer, is an example of a communications device. Wireless communications can use technologies including cellular radio, satellite, or Wi-Fi to connect to the Internet. **Wi-Fi** is a wireless data network technology that provides high-speed data connections that do not require a physical connection. It is used for mobile devices.

Before you can connect to the Internet, you need to select an Internet Service Provider. An **Internet Service Provider (ISP)** is a company that sells Internet access. Methods to connect to the Internet include cellular networks, Wi-Fi hot spots, and mobile hot spots. A **hot spot** is a wireless network device that provides Internet connections to mobile computers and devices. A **mobile hot spot** enables you to connect a phone, computer, or other device to the Internet through the cellular network. Various types of cellular networks, including 4G and 5G ("G" stands for "generation") can provide Internet services in most locations where cellular service is offered (**Figure 2-7**). 5G networks provide higher-speed data transmission.

Figure 2-7: How a cellular network might work

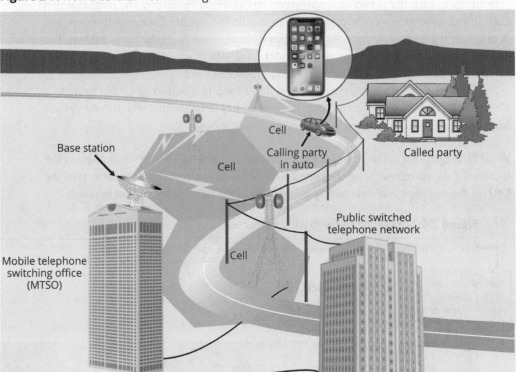

Table 2-2: Popular TLDs in the United States

TLD	Generally used for
.biz	Unrestricted use, but usually identifies businesses
.com	Most commercial sites that sell products and services
.edu	Academic and research sites such as schools and universities
.gov	U.S. government organizations
.int	International treaty organizations
.mil	Military organizations
.mobi	Sites optimized for mobile devices
.net	Network providers, ISPs, and other Internet administrative organizations
.org	Organizations such as political or not for profit (any website can have the .org TLD but, traditionally, only professional and nonprofit organizations such as churches and humanitarian groups use it)
.pro	Licensed professionals

Explain the Purpose of a Top-Level Domain

In a web address, the three-letter extension after the period in a domain name indicates a **top-level domain (TLD)**, such as the "com" in "cengage.com". The TLD identifies the type of organization associated with the domain. As you visit websites, you might notice some that have TLDs other than .com, such as .edu for educational institutions and .gov for U.S. government agencies. The TLD provides a clue about the content of the website.

An organization called Public Technical Identifiers (PTI) approves and controls TLDs, such as those in **Table 2-2**, which lists popular TLDs in the United States. For websites outside the United States, the suffix of the domain name often includes a two-letter country code TLD, such as .au for Australia and .uk for the United Kingdom.

Describe Internet Standards

Have you ever wondered who is in charge of the web? Who maintains the webpages? Who makes sure all the parts of the complex system work together? One organization is the **Internet Engineering Task Force (IETF)**. This group sets standards that allow devices, services, and applications to work together across the Internet. For example, the IETF sets standards for IP addresses, as well as rules for routing data, securing websites, and developing guidelines for responsible Internet use.

Another leading organization is the **World Wide Web Consortium (W3C)**, which consists of hundreds of organizations and experts that work together to write web standards. The W3C publishes standards on topics including building webpages, technologies for enabling web access from any device, and browser and search engine design.

Describe Websites and Webpages

People around the world visit websites and webpages to accomplish the types of online tasks (**Figure 2-8**). In addition, you can use websites to play games; access news, weather, and sports information; download or read books; participate in online training; attend classes; and more.

Identify Types of Websites

Chances are, a certain type of website provides whatever service or content you're looking for. Most websites fall into one or more of the following categories:

banking and finance	entertainment	portals
blogs	government or organization	retail and auctions
bookmarking	health and fitness	science
business	information and research	search sites
careers and employment	mapping	travel and tourism
content aggregation	media sharing	website creation and management
e-commerce	news, weather, sports, and other mass media	web apps and software as a service (SaaS)
educational	online social networks	wikis and collaboration

Besides displaying information and other content, some websites provide ways to interact with them. You can contribute ideas, comments, images, and videos to an online conversation through interactive community pages, social media sites, and **blogs**, which are informal websites with time-stamped articles, or posts, in a diary or journal format.

A **content aggregator** site gathers, organizes, and then distributes web content. As a subscriber, you choose the type of content you want and receive updates when new content is available.

Figure 2-8: Tasks you can accomplish using websites

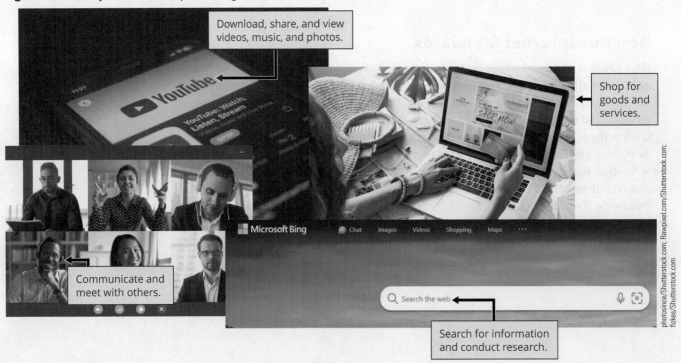

Download, share, and view videos, music, and photos.

Shop for goods and services.

Communicate and meet with others.

Search for information and conduct research.

Figure 2-9: Educational website

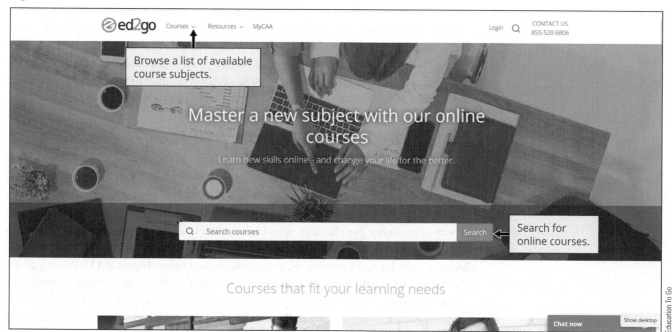

An educational website such as ed2go (**Figure 2-9**) offers formal and informal teaching and learning. The web contains thousands of tutorials where you can learn how to build a website or cook a meal. For a more structured learning experience, companies provide online training to employees, and colleges offer online classes and degrees.

On entertainment websites, you can view or discuss activities ranging from sports to videos. For example, you can cast a vote on a topic for a television show.

With a **media sharing site**, such as YouTube or TikTok, you can display and view various types of media, such as photos, videos, and music, share it with other site members, and manage it. Use a media sharing site to post, organize, store, and download media.

An **online social network**, also called a **social network** or **social media** site, is an online community where users can share their interests, ideas, stories, photos, music, and videos online with other registered users. In many online social networks, you can communicate through text, voice, and video chat, and play games with other members. Facebook, X (formerly known as Twitter), WhatsApp, Instagram, Pinterest, and Tumblr are some websites classified as online social networks. You interact with an online social network through a website or mobile app on your computer or mobile device (**Figure 2-10**).

A **web portal**, or **portal**, is a website that combines pages from many sources and provides access to those pages. Most web portals are customized to meet your needs and interests. For example, your bank might create a web portal that includes snapshots of your accounts and access to financial information.

Using a search site such as Google, you can find websites, webpages, images, videos, news, maps, and other information related to a specific topic. A **search engine** is software used by search sites to locate relevant webpages by creating a simple query based on your search criteria and storing the collected data in a search database. You also can use a search engine to solve mathematical equations, define words, find flights, and more.

Figure 2-10: Online social networking websites

General-purpose search sites such as Google, Yahoo!, and Bing help you locate web information when you don't know an exact web address or are not seeking a specific website.

As the web becomes more interactive, an increasing amount of content is supplied by users. You can contribute comments and opinions to informational sites such as news sites, blogs, and wikis. A **wiki** is a collaborative website where you and your colleagues can modify and publish content on a webpage. One use of wikis is for companies to keep track of procedures and policies, and to enable employees to contribute notes and additional information.

Explain the Pros and Cons of Web Apps

In addition to using a browser to visit websites and display webpages, you can use it to access a **web app**, which is an app stored on an Internet server that you can run entirely in a browser. A web app resides on a server on the Internet, rather than on your computer or mobile device. For example, Microsoft Office provides Excel, PowerPoint, and Word as web apps. Other popular web apps include Slack for group collaboration, Trello for project management, and Google Docs, which, like Microsoft Office, offers a suite of productivity apps for word processing, presentations, and more (**Figure 2-11**). When you use a web app, you usually store your data on the web app's server using cloud computing.

You can run many apps as traditional installed apps or as web apps. Examples include Box, for storing and exchanging files in the cloud, and Skype, which lets you communicate with others using video and voice. **Table 2-3** summarizes the pros and cons of using web apps.

Figure 2-11: Web apps running in a browser

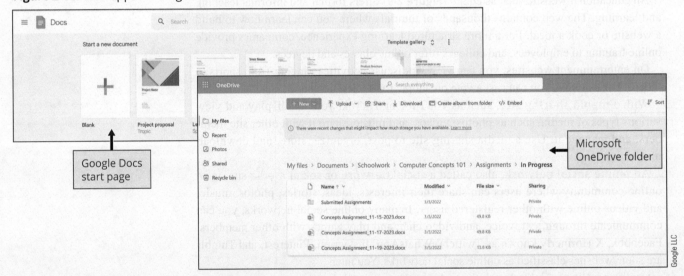

Google Docs start page

Microsoft OneDrive folder

Google LLC

Table 2-3: Pros and cons of web apps

Pros	Cons
Access web apps from any device with a browser and Internet connection.	You must be online to use web apps.
Collaborate with others no matter their location.	Your files are more vulnerable to security and privacy violations.
Store your work on the app's website so you can access it anytime and anywhere.	If the web app provider has technical problems, you might not be able to access your work.
Save storage space on your device.	If the web app provider goes out of business, you can lose your files.
Access the latest version of the app without installing updates.	Web apps often offer fewer features and may run more slowly than installed apps.

Identify the Major Components of a Webpage

Although web design is constantly evolving, webpages typically include five major areas: header or banner, navigation bar or menu, body, social media links, and footer (**Figure 2-12**). Each area can include text, graphics, links, and media such as audio and video.

- **Header**: Located at the top of a webpage, the header or banner usually includes a logo to identify the organization sponsoring the webpage and a title to indicate the topic or purpose of the webpage. Headers and navigation bars can also provide a Search tool for searching the website.

- **Navigation bar**: A bar or menu lists links to other major parts of the website.

- **Body**: The body is the main content area of the webpage, and can provide text, images, audio, and video.

- **Social media links**: An area that includes links to social networking accounts and platforms. These often appear in a sidebar on the webpage, near the navigation bar, or in the footer.

- **Footer**: Located at the bottom of a webpage, the footer contains links to other parts of the website and lists information about the webpage, such as who owns the content.

Figure 2-12: Parts of a webpage

Figure 2-13: Secure website

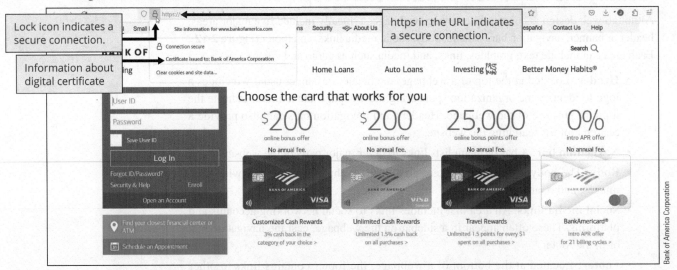

Bank of America Corporation

Identify Secure and Insecure Websites

Before you make a payment on a website or provide sensitive information such as a credit card number, make sure the website is secure. Otherwise, an unauthorized web user could intercept the payment or information and steal your funds or identity. **Figure 2-13** demonstrates how you can identify a secure website.

A secure website uses encryption to safeguard transmitted information. **Encryption** is a security method that scrambles or codes data so it is not readable while being transmitted until it is decrypted.

A secure website connection displays https instead of http in the URL. The "s" in https stands for "secure," so https means **Hypertext Transfer Protocol Secure**. Most websites, especially banks and online retail stores, use the https protocol to make a secure connection to your computer. Secure websites often use a **digital certificate**, which is technology that contains the website's special key used for encryption that has been "signed" by a trusted third party.

An insecure website URL starts with "http," indicating an unprotected protocol for transmitting information. The address bar in the Chrome browser identifies such websites as "Not secure."

Use E-commerce

E-commerce, short for electronic commerce, refers to business transactions on an electronic network such as the Internet. If you have bought or sold products such as clothing, electronics, music, tickets, hotel reservations, or gift certificates, you have engaged in e-commerce. **Table 2-4** describes three types of e-commerce websites.

Table 2-4: Three types of e-commerce websites

Type of E-commerce	Description	Example
Business-to-consumer (B2C)	Involves the sale of goods and services to the general public	Shopping websites
Consumer-to-consumer (C2C)	Occurs when one consumer sells directly to another	Online auctions
Business-to-business (B2B)	Consists of businesses providing goods and services to other businesses	Market research websites

Table 2-5: E-commerce pros and cons for consumers

Pros	Explanation
Variety	You can choose goods from any vendor in the world. Websites have more models, sizes, and colors, for example, than a physical store.
Convenience	You can shop no matter your location, time of day, or conditions, such as bad weather. You save time by visiting websites instead of stores.
Communication	Chat features, contact forms, frequently asked question pages, and other tools enable you to ask or find additional information relevant to your purchase.
Budget	By searching effectively and comparing prices online, you can find products that meet your budget.
Cons	**Explanation**
Security	At insecure e-commerce sites, you risk unauthorized users intercepting your credit card information and other personal data.
Fraud	Some shopping websites are fraudulent, designed to look legitimate while accessing your account information.
Indirect experience	You cannot experience a product directly to verify its color, quality, or texture. You lose the social interaction that is a natural part of shopping at a physical retailer.

Explain the Role of E-commerce in Daily Life

Consumers use e-commerce to access products and services without stepping foot in a store. Businesses use e-commerce to generate revenue and communicate with customers. You should understand the advantages and risks of using e-commerce to make your online transactions satisfying and safe. **Table 2-5** outlines the pros and cons of e-commerce for consumers.

Use E-commerce in Business Transactions

B2B e-commerce involves transferring goods, services, or information between businesses. In fact, most e-commerce is actually between businesses. B2B services include advertising, technical support, and training. B2B products include raw materials, tools and machinery, and electronics. The Shiply website is a B2B site that helps businesses ship goods (**Figure 2-14**).

Figure 2-14: B2B website

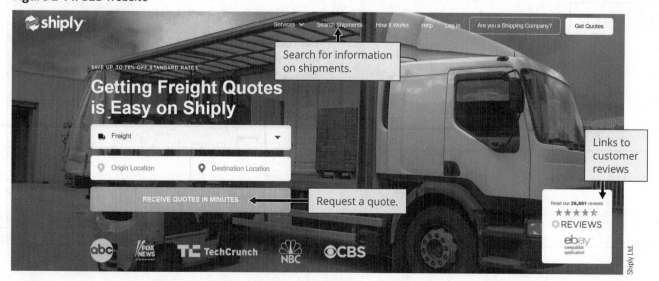

The more you know about B2B websites, the more valuable you can be to your employer. B2B websites are different from B2C websites. For example, consumer-focused shopping websites offer fixed, consistent pricing; for B2B purchases, pricing can vary based on the level of service provided, negotiated terms, and other factors.

At B2C websites, the consumer is the decision maker. In a B2B transaction, a team of people often need to review and make a purchasing decision. They usually have to follow company procedures, which can lengthen or complicate the transaction.

Use E-commerce in Personal Transactions

You can purchase just about any product or service at a B2C e-commerce website. Doing so is sometimes called e-retail or e-tail (short for electronic retail). To make a purchase online, you visit an **electronic storefront**, an e-commerce website that sells products or services. This type of storefront usually contains product descriptions, images, and a shopping cart to collect items you want to purchase. When you're ready to complete the sale, you enter personal data and the method of payment, which should be through a secure Internet connection.

A B2C website tracks your selected items using **cookies**, small text files created by the website that store information on your computer. These cookies act like a storage bin for the items you place in your shopping cart. Cookies store shopping cart item numbers, saved website preferences, and other information.

B2C websites are usually designed to be easy to use so you can find what you want fast (**Figure 2-15**). They include reviews from other customers to help you make purchasing decisions, special offers for web customers only, and wish lists to encourage you to return to the site. Many B2C websites let you research online and then pick up the purchased item in a physical store.

Figure 2-15: B2C website

Online classified ads and online auctions are examples of C2C e-commerce websites. An online auction works much like a real-life auction or yard sale. You bid on an item being sold by someone else. The highest bidder at the end of the bidding period purchases the item. eBay is one of the more popular online auction websites.

C2C sites have many sellers promoting the goods, rather than a single merchant hosting a B2C site. Many C2C sites use email forwarding, which hides real email identities, to connect buyer with seller and still protect everyone's privacy. You pay a small fee to the site if you sell an item.

E-commerce Security   To make e-commerce payments in a B2C transaction, you can provide a credit card number. **3D Secure** is a standard protocol for securing credit card transactions over the Internet, and is used by online merchants. Using both encryption and digital certificates, 3D Secure provides an extra layer of security on a website.

Besides the https protocol, e-commerce sites also use **Transport Layer Security (TLS)** to encrypt data and provide other services. This technology helps protect consumers and businesses from fraud and identity theft when conducting commerce on the Internet.

To provide an alternative to entering credit card information online, some shopping and auction websites let you use an online payment service, such as PayPal, Venmo, and Zelle. To use an online payment service, you create an account that is linked to your credit card or funds at a financial institution. When you make a purchase, you use your online payment service account, which manages the payment transaction without revealing your financial information.

You can also use smartwatches and smartphones to make e-commerce payments. ApplePay and Google Wallet are two of several mobile payment and digital wallet services available on smartphones and smartwatches. Scan the watch or phone over a reader, often available in stores, to make the electronic payment.

Another payment method is to use a one-time or virtual account number, which lets you make a single online payment without revealing your actual account number. These numbers are good only at the time of the transaction; if they are stolen, they are worthless to thieves.

Explain How to Find E-commerce Deals

You can find online deals in at least two ways: visiting comparison shopping sites and using digital deals.

Websites such as BizRate and PriceGrabber are comparison shopping websites that save you time and money by letting you compare prices from multiple vendors, as well as read industry and user reviews to find product.

Digital deals can be gift certificates, gift cards, or coupons. Groupon and NewEgg are examples of deal-of-the-day websites, which help you save money on restaurant meals, retail products, travel, and personal services. Digital coupons consist of promotional codes that you enter when you check out and pay for online purchases. Sites and apps such as RetailMeNot and browser extensions such as PayPal Honey provide coupon codes and offer alerts for e-commerce discounts (**Figure 2-16**).

Figure 2-16: Some websites and shopping apps offer deals and coupons

Redemption rates are high with mobile phones because customers carry them with them.

Andrey_Popov/Shutterstock.com

Explain How Information Literacy Applies to Web Searches and Research

You can search for and find virtually any information you want on the Internet. Search engines let you enter search criteria and then compile a list of webpages that match your criteria. Of the billions of webpages you can access using Google or another search site, some are valuable and some are not.

Define Information Literacy

Information literacy is the ability to find, evaluate, use, and communicate online information. Being able to distinguish legitimate websites and information sources is part of being a digital citizen. If you have information literacy, you can do the following:

- Navigate many sources of information, including the Internet, online libraries, and popular media sites.
- Select the right tool for finding the information you need.
- Recognize that not all information is created equal.
- Evaluate whether information is misleading, biased, or out of date.
- Manage information to become a knowledgeable decision maker.

Information literacy is gained by understanding and selecting the tools, techniques, and strategies for locating and evaluating information (**Figure 2-17**).

Explain How Search Engines Work

Suppose you're working on a presentation about mobile phone technology and need to know about current innovations.

To find information quickly, you could start a **general search engine** such as Google, Bing, or Yahoo!, which is designed to find general results, and enter a search term or phrase such as *net neutrality*. Within seconds, the first page of search results lists a dozen webpages that might contain the information you need.

Figure 2-17: Viewing and evaluating search results

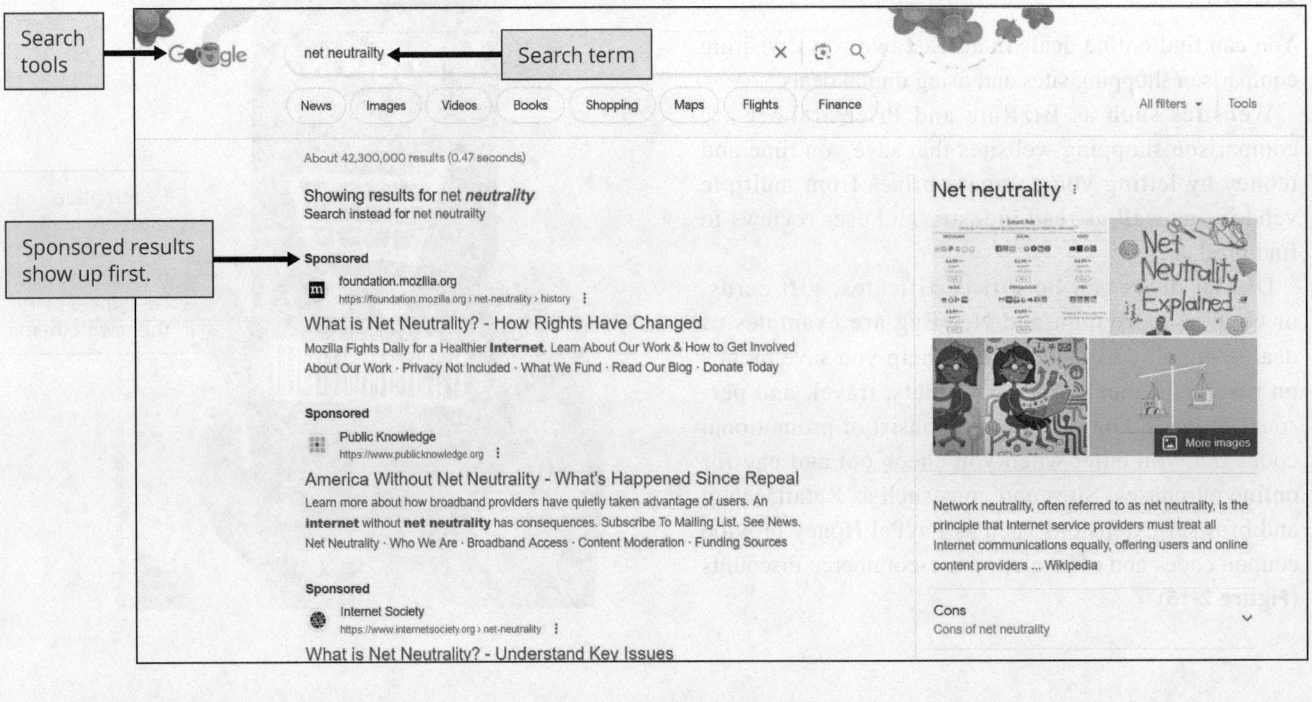

When you perform a search, a general search engine does not search the entire Internet. Instead, it accesses a database of information about webpages. It uses programs called **spiders** or **crawlers**, software that combs the web to find webpages and add new data about them to the database. These programs build an **index** of terms and their locations.

When you enter a search term, or **query**, a general search engine refers to its database index and then lists results that match your search term, ranked by how closely they answer your query.

Each search engine uses a different method to retrieve webpage information from an index and create a ranked list of results. The ranking depends on how often and where a search term appears on the webpage, how long the webpage has been published, and the number of other webpages that link to it. Website creators and content writers use **search engine optimization (SEO)**, which includes tools to allow search engines to better find or index your website. SEO strategies include arranging content order, including keywords, and ensuring other content is linked to yours.

Use Search Tools and Strategies

A **search tool** finds online information based on criteria you specify or selections you make. Search tools include search engines and search boxes on webpages. The more effectively you use search tools, the more quickly you can find information and the more relevant that information will be.

Another type of search tool is a **web directory**, or **subject directory**, an online guide to subjects or websites, usually arranged in alphabetic order.

Search engines and web directories take different approaches to searching for information. Instead of using an index created by digital spiders, a human editor creates the index for a web directory, selecting categories that make sense for the information the web directory provides. The editor usually reviews sites that are submitted to the directory and can exclude those that do not seem credible or reliable. For this reason, a web directory is often a better choice than a search engine if you are conducting research online.

A **specialized search tool** concentrates on specific resources, such as scholarly journals or the United States Congress. Examples include the Directory of Open Access Journals, Congress.gov Legislative Search (**Figure 2-18**), and Google Books. If you need to research the latest academic studies or look up the status of a bill, using a specialized search tool is more efficient than using a general search engine such as Google.

Figure 2-18: Specialized search tool

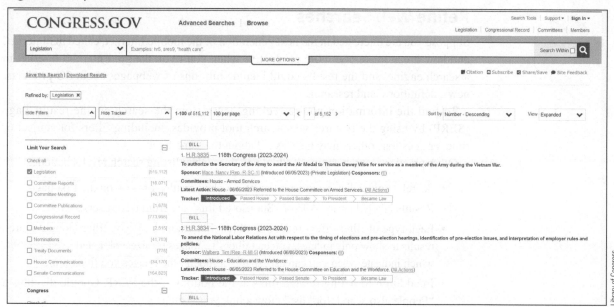

Library of Congress

Figure 2-19: Search strategy

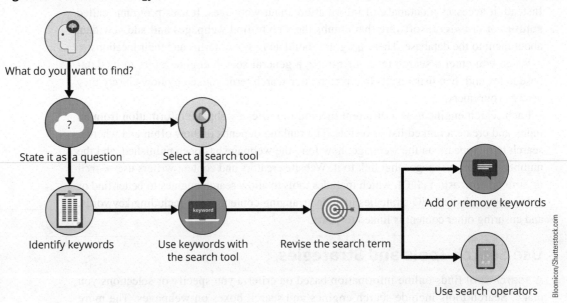

What do you want to find?

State it as a question

Select a search tool

Identify keywords

Use keywords with the search tool

Revise the search term

Add or remove keywords

Use search operators

Bloomicon/Shutterstock.com

To get the most out of a web search, develop a search strategy, which involves performing the following tasks before you start searching:

- State what kind of information you are seeking, as specifically as possible.
- Phrase the search term as a question, as in "How do businesses use augmented reality?"
- Identify the keywords or phrases that could answer the question.
- Select an appropriate search tool.

Next, perform the search. For example, if you want to know about how website designers use SEO, you could search using *search engine optimization strategies* as the **keywords**, the descriptive words you enter to obtain a list of results that include the words or phrase. If you find the results you need, you can stop searching.

If the term you use is too general, you are likely to find millions of webpages that mention the term. If the term you use is too specific, you might miss useful webpages related to your term. In either case, you need to refine the web search to narrow or broaden the results. **Figure 2-19** summarizes an online search strategy.

Refine Web Searches

Suppose you are interested in the next generation of the mobile Internet, called 5G Internet, and how it can make you more productive when you're on the go. Enter *5G internet* in a search engine, and the results could include millions of webpages about 5G products, news, definitions, and research.

To find the information you're seeking, learn from the search engine results page (SERP) by using the features your search tool provides, including filters for subject or time, or questions others may have asked about the same topic.

Other practices search engines follow practices when listing search results include:

- Search engines list the most relevant matched results, or **hits**, on the first page.
- Results labeled as an "Ad" or "Sponsored link" are from advertisers.
- Each type of filter offers related features. For example, if you filter Google search results to show only images, you can filter the images by size, color, and **usage rights**, which indicate when you can use, share, or modify the images you find online.
- In addition to listing related links at the bottom of the SERP, Google displays a "People also search for" list below a link you visited.

Table 2-6: Common search operators

Operator	Means	Example
" " (quotation marks)	Find webpages with the exact words in the same order	"augmented reality" in business
| (vertical bar)	OR	augmented | virtual
- (hyphen)	NOT	augmented reality -virtual
*	**Wildcard** (placeholder for any number of characters)	augment* reality
#..#	Find webpages within a range of numbers	augmented reality 2017..2022

Table 2-7: Examples of web searches

Keywords	Possible results	Suggested change
Looking for a used smartphone	A list of all used phones; returns too many hits	Add the word "Android."
Looking for a used Android smartphone	Still too many hits	Remove common words such as "the" and "an"; remove verb.
Used Android smartphone	Results still include other smartphones	Search for an exact phrase by entering it in quotation marks.
Used "Android smartphone"	List of used Android smartphones	Results are targeted; no changes are needed.

You can also refine a web search by using one or more **search operators**, also called **Boolean operators**, which are characters, words, or symbols that focus the search. **Table 2-6** lists common search operators.

Now you're ready to try a new search. **Table 2-7** lists examples of keywords you might use to find information on buying used Android smartphones.

Many search sites have advanced search operators, which are special terms followed by a colon (:). For example, *site:* means to search only the specified site, as in *site: www .cengage.com sam*, which finds information about SAM on the cengage.com website. You can find the advanced search operators by referring to the site's help pages.

To broaden a search, you can use a **word stem**, which is the base of a word. For example, instead of using *businesses* as a keyword, use *business*. You can also combine the word stem with an asterisk (*), as in *tech** to find technology, technician, and technique.

Evaluate the Pros and Cons of Net Neutrality

The concept of **net neutrality** is that one website has the same value or priority as other websites, resulting in equal, unrestricted access to each site. When net neutrality is enforced, ISPs must provide the same level of service to all websites, regardless of their content or purpose. Net neutrality supports the concept that the Internet should be neutral and all traffic should be treated equally.

Networks transmit data over a communication channel, which can be a wire or over the air (wireless). Each type of communication channel can support a certain amount of data being transferred at a given time. **Bandwidth** is a term commonly used to describe the capacity of a communication channel. When a communication medium or connection supports transferring a large amount of data at one time, it is said to be a high-bandwidth connection. High-bandwidth connections (also called broadband connections) support capacity for transferring content such as videos, music, and other large files, and can support online gaming. Low-bandwidth connections (also called narrowband connections) support only slower transfer speeds as they have less capacity. These connections are suitable for performing functions such as sending and receiving email, transferring small files, and viewing basic websites.

Supporters of net neutrality like the fact that access to websites and other Internet services cannot be restricted based on factors such as content or bandwidth requirements. Those who oppose net neutrality argue that the ability for users to access certain types of high-bandwidth content such as music and movies might result in slower Internet speeds for others who are also connecting to the Internet using the same ISPs. Without net neutrality, Internet Service Providers could charge more money for those wanting access to content requiring more resources (such as streaming music and movies) and charge less money to those who require access to less resource-intensive services.

Although the Internet is a global resource, the U.S. Federal Communication Commission (FCC) is responsible for releasing rules surrounding Internet access for U.S. users. Other countries or areas have different governing bodies and rules. Some individuals feel the government should not control Internet access and its content, but one primary goal of the FCC is to guarantee accessibility to all Internet users.

Conduct Online Research

When you need to conduct online research for an assignment or project, using search engines designed for research yields more reliable results, saving you time and effort and ensuring the validity of the content you find.

Use Specialty Search Engines

Where do you go to find academic information for your research? Try using a **specialty search engine**, which lets you search databases, news providers, podcasts, and other online information sources that general search engines do not always access.

Much of the information on the web is stored in databases. To access this database information, you need to use a special search form and may need to enter a user name and password. For example, Google Scholar searches scholarly literature from many disciplines and includes articles, books, theses, and abstracts.

Other specialty search tools let you find information published on certain types of sites. For example, use Google News or Alltop to find news stories and Listen Notes to search podcasts.

Figure 2-20: CARS checklist

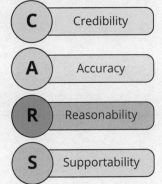

Evaluate Online Information

On the Internet, anyone can publish anything to a website, a blog, or a social media site, regardless of whether the information is true. How can you tell if a website is worth your time? In general, look for sites from trusted, expert institutions or authors. Avoid sites that show bias or contain outdated information.

When you use the Internet for research, be skeptical about the information you find online. Evaluate a webpage before you use it as an information source. One way to evaluate a webpage is to use the CARS checklist (**Figure 2-20**) to determine whether the online information is credible, accurate, reasonable, and supportable.

Credibility: When someone is providing you information face to face, you pay attention to clues such as body language and voice tone to determine whether that information is credible, or believable. Obviously, you can't use that same technique to evaluate the credibility of a webpage.

To determine the credibility of a website:

- Identify the author of the webpage and check their credentials. This information is often listed on the Contact Us page or the About page.
- If you find biographical information, read it to learn whether the author has a degree in a field related to the topic.
- Use a search engine such as Google or the professional networking site LinkedIn to search for the author's name and see whether the author is an expert on the subject.

Accuracy: You're attending a classmate's presentation on the history of the personal computer, and he mentions that Bill Gates invented the first PC for home use in 1980, citing an online resource. You know it was actually Steve Wozniak and Steve Jobs in 1976. That inaccuracy makes you doubt the accuracy of the rest of the presentation.

To check the accuracy of a website:

- Verify its facts and claims. Consult an expert or use fact-checking sites such as snopes.com and factcheck.org to find professionally researched information.
- Evaluate the information source. Be wary of web addresses that contain slight modifications of legitimate sites, use unusual domain names, or have long URLs.
- Find out more about an organization that has no history, physical location, or staff.
- Check to see if the source has a bias and evaluate the information with the bias in mind.
- Check the webpage footer for the date the information was published or updated. For many topics, especially technology, you need current information.

Reasonableness: Along with credibility and accuracy, consider how reasonable an online information source is. Reasonable means fair and sensible, not extreme or excessive.

To check how reasonable a website is:

- Identify the purpose of the webpage. Is the page designed to provide facts and other information, sell a product or service, or express opinions?
- Evaluate whether the webpage offers more than one point of view.
- Emotional, persuasive, or biased language is often a sign that the author is not being fair or moderate. Even opinions should be expressed in a moderate tone.
- Look for a conflict of interest. For example, if the page reviews a certain brand of smartphone and the author sells those types of phones, he or she has a conflict of interest.

Support: Suppose a webpage refers to a study concluding that most people consider computer professionals to be highly ethical. But the page doesn't link to the study itself or mention other sources that support this claim. The page is failing the final criterion in the CARS checklist: support.

To evaluate a webpage's support:

- Look for links or citations to reputable sources or authorities. Test the links to make sure they work.
- Check other webpages and print material on the topic to see if they cite the same sources.
- Look for quotations from experts.
- For photos or other reproduced content, a credit line should appear somewhere on the page that states the source and any necessary copyright information.

Gather Content from Online Sources

As you conduct research online, you gather content from webpages, including text, photos, and links to resources. Follow ethical guidelines and be aware of ownership rights to avoid legal, academic, and professional sanctions and be a responsible member of the online community.

Intellectual property is unique and original works, such as ideas, inventions, art, writings, processes, company and product names, and logos. If you copy a photo from the Internet and use it in a report, you might be violating the photographer's **intellectual property rights**, which are legal rights protecting those who create works such as photos, art, writing, inventions, and music.

A **copyright** gives authors and artists the legal right to sell, publish, or distribute an original work. A copyright goes into effect as soon as the work exists in physical or digital form.

If you want to use a photo in your report, you need to get permission from the photo's owner. Contact the photographer by email, and explain what you want to use and how you plan to use it. If a copyright holder gives you permission, keep a copy of the message or document for your records. The holder may also tell you how a credit line should appear. Acquiring permission protects you from potential concerns over your usage and protects the copyright holder's intellectual property rights.

Some online resources, such as e-books, newspapers, magazines, and journals, are protected by **digital rights management (DRM)**, which refers to a collection of technologies used by software publishers and trade groups to fight software piracy and prevent unauthorized copying of digital content. It is a violation of copyright law to circumvent these protections to obtain and then use the materials. To avoid legal trouble, only use materials to which you have legal access, and then follow accepted usage laws for any information you obtain.

Some work is in the **public domain**, which means that the item, such as a photo, is available and accessible to the public without requiring permission to use, and therefore not subject to copyright. This applies to material for which the copyright has expired and to work that has been explicitly released to the public domain by its owner. Many websites provide public domain files free for you to download. Much information on U.S. government sites is in the public domain (**Figure 2-21**), although you must attribute the information and be aware that the sites might contain other copyrighted information.

For any online source, if you don't see a copyright symbol, look for a statement that specifically defines the work as being in the public domain. For quotations and other cited material, the United States **fair use doctrine** allows you to use a sentence or paragraph of text without permission if you include a citation to the original source.

Figure 2-21: Copyright information from the U.S. Department of Agriculture site

Digital Rights and Copyright

Most information presented on the USDA Web site is considered public domain information. Public domain information may be freely distributed or copied, but use of appropriate byline/photo/image credits is requested. Attribution may be cited as follows: "U.S. Department of Agriculture."

Some materials on the USDA Web site are protected by copyright, trademark, or patent, and/or are provided for personal use only. Such materials are used by USDA with permission, and USDA has made every attempt to identify and clearly label them. You may need to obtain permission from the copyright, trademark, or patent holder to acquire, use, reproduce, or distribute these materials.

U.S. Department of Agriculture

Figure 2-22: Creative Commons site

If the discussion about rights and legal trouble makes you nervous, you're not alone. Clearly, it can be hard to know what is acceptable to use and what's not. Most people are not legal experts, so how can you know what you can use and how you can use it? If you make your writing, photographs, or artwork available online, how do you specify to others how they can use that content?

Creative Commons   Creative Commons (CC) is a U.S. nonprofit organization that makes it easy for content creators to license and share their work by supplying easy-to-understand copyright licenses; the creator chooses the conditions under which the work can be used. As a creator, set these conditions by you selecting a CC license that explains how others can use your work. For example, you can choose whether to allow commercial use of your poem, or allow derivative works, such as translations or adaptations. People who use content that carries a Creative Commons license must follow CC license rules on giving credit for works they use and displaying copyright notices.

CC licenses are based on copyright law and are legal around the world. The CC organization is helping to build a large and ever-growing digital commons (**Figure 2-22**), a collection of content that users can legally copy, distribute, and expand.

Apply Information Literacy Standards

Part of information literacy involves the ethical use of the information you find on the web. When you use the Internet for research, you face ethical decisions. Ethics refers to the moral principles that govern people's behavior. Many schools and other organizations post codes of conduct for computer use, which can help you make ethical decisions while using a computer.

Ethically and legally, you can use other people's ideas in your research papers and presentations as long as you cite the source for any information that is not common knowledge. A citation is a reference to a source, such as a published work.

Thorough research on technology and other topics usually involves books, journals, magazines, and websites. Each type of information source uses a different citation style, or sequence of elements, such publication name and author name, and the punctuation between them. Instructors often direct you to use a particular citation style, such as MLA, APA, or Chicago. You can find detailed style guides for each style online. Some software, such as Microsoft Word, helps you create and manage citations and then produce a bibliography, which is an alphabetical collection of citations.

If you use the content from a Wikipedia article or any other source, but change some of the words, you have to cite the source for that material. Otherwise, you are guilty of **plagiarism**, which is copying or using someone else's work and claiming them as your own.

To avoid plagiarism, cite your sources for statements that are not common knowledge. Even if you **paraphrase**, which means to restate an idea using words different from those used in the original text, you are still trying to claim someone else's idea as your own. Cite sources when you borrow ideas or words to avoid plagiarism.

Module 2 Summary

The Internet is a global collection of millions of computers linked together to share information worldwide, and the web is one part of the Internet. A webpage is an electronic document that can contain text, graphics, sound, video, and links to other webpages, while a website is a collection of webpages. You use a browser to display webpages and enter web addresses, or URLs, which identify the location of webpages on the Internet. Webpages can be static or dynamic. Web designers use responsive web design to optimize how webpages appear on different devices.

You connect to the Internet using wired or wireless technology, and connect through an ISP using devices such as a modem or hotspot.

Nonprofit organizations set the rules for the Internet, such as the names of top-level domains. The IETF sets standards for IP addresses. The W3C publishes standards for websites and webpages.

Websites can be classified into one or more categories, such as blogs, content aggregators, or entertainment sites. A web portal combines pages from many sources and provides access to those pages. Search sites use search engines, software designed to find webpages based on your search criteria.

In addition to using a browser to visit websites and display webpages, you can use it to access web apps, which are apps you run in a browser. A web app offers the advantages of convenience and portability, but involves risks to security and privacy. Webpages typically include the following areas: header or banner, navigation bar or menu, body, social media links, and footer.

A secure website uses encryption to safeguard transmitted information. Signs of a secure website are a lock icon and the https protocol in the address bar. In an insecure website, the URL starts with "http," indicating an unprotected protocol for transmitting information.

E-commerce refers to business transactions on an electronic network such as the Internet. The three types of e-commerce are business-to-business (B2B), business-to-consumer (B2C), and consumer-to-consumer (C2C). For consumers, e-commerce websites provide the benefits of variety, convenience, and cost, but have the drawbacks of reduced security, fraud, and indirect experience.

B2B e-commerce involves transferring goods, services, or information between businesses. Most e-commerce is actually between businesses. To make a purchase at a B2C website, you visit an electronic storefront, collect items in a shopping cart, and then enter personal data and the method of payment to complete the purchase.

To make secure online payments, use e-commerce websites with the 3D Secure or TLS protocol. You can also use an online payment service to scan your mobile phone or smartwatch, or a virtual account number.

To find deals for goods and services online, visit comparison shopping sites and use digital deals. Comparison websites let you compare prices from multiple vendors. Digital deals come in the form of gift certificates, gift cards, and coupons.

How you find, evaluate, use, and communicate online information depends on your information literacy. You become information literate by understanding and selecting the tools, techniques, and strategies for locating and evaluating information.

When you perform an online search, a general search engine compiles a database of information about webpages. The search engine refers to its database index when you enter a search term and then lists pages that match the term, ranked by how closely they answer your query.

A search tool finds online information based on criteria you specify or selections you make. Search tools include search engines, search boxes on webpages, and web directories, which are online guides to subjects or websites, usually arranged in alphabetic order. Net neutrality refers to the concept of equal, unrestricted access to all websites for all users.

To find academic information for research, you can use a specialty search engine, which lets you search databases, news providers, podcasts, and other online information sources that general search engines do not always access.

When evaluating online information, look for sites from trusted, expert institutions or authors. Avoid sites that show bias or contain outdated information. Evaluate a website using the CARS (credibility, accuracy, reliability, supportability) checklist.

As you gather content from webpages, follow ethical guidelines and be aware of ownership rights to avoid legal, academic, and professional sanctions. Observe intellectual property rights and copyrights to be a responsible member of the online community.

When you use the Internet for research, you face ethical decisions. Ethically and legally, you can use other people's ideas in your research papers and presentations as long as you cite the source for any information that is not common knowledge.

Review Questions

1. (True or False) The web is a global collection of millions of computers linked together to share information worldwide.

2. Most web designers provide content so that it adapts appropriately to the size of the display on any device using _____ web design.

   a. adaptive
   b. responsive
   c. alternative
   d. reactive

3. Each webpage is assigned an address that identifies the location of the page on the Internet, called a(n) _____.

   a. Internet Protocol (IP)
   b. uniform resource locator (URL)
   c. top-level domain (TLD)
   d. Hypertext Transfer Protocol (HTTP)

4. An ISP is a company that _____.

   a. manages and assigns top-level domains
   b. promotes net neutrality
   c. manages C2C e-commerce
   d. sells Internet access

5. A(n) _____ website gathers, organizes, and then distributes web content.

   a. content aggregator
   b. media sharing
   c. entertainment
   d. search engine

6. Which of the following indicates an encrypted website connection?

   a. https in the URL
   b. http in the URL
   c. The message "secure website" in the address bar
   d. A shield icon in the address bar

7. Which of the following best describes business-to-business (B2B) e-commerce purchases?

   a. The consumer is the decision maker.
   b. Pricing can vary based on level of service.
   c. Customers bid on items being sold by other customers.
   d. Customers can pick up the purchased item in a physical store.

8. A business-to-consumer (B2C) website tracks the items you place in a shopping cart using _____.

   a. a digital wallet
   b. the Transport Layer Security (TLS) protocol
   c. crawlers
   d. cookies

9. Who or what creates the index for a web directory?

   a. A digital spider
   b. A human editor
   c. A wiki
   d. A search operator

10. Bandwidth refers to the _____.

    a. capacity of a communication channel

    b. speed of an Internet search

    c. size of a search directory

    d. security of a website

11. In the CARS checklist, the A stands for _____.

    a. accessibility

    b. adaptability

    c. accuracy

    d. authority

12. (True or False) Creative Commons licenses are legal only in the United States.

Discussion Questions

1. What is the difference between the Internet and the web? How does each affect your daily life?

2. Media sharing websites let you post photos and videos to share with other people. Social media websites enable you to share thoughts, follow others, and post content. What are the benefits and drawbacks of using these websites?

3. Explain the concept of net neutrality. Why is it important? What drawbacks might there be to enforcing it? Has it impacted you? If so, how?

4. On the Internet, anyone can publish anything to a website, a blog, or a social media site, regardless of whether the information is true. Recent years have seen a spike in misleading or false "news" and hoaxes that are shared as fact on social media. How can you tell fake news stories from real ones?

Critical Thinking Activities

1. You are a part time student going back to school to finish your degree. Knowing you will often research topics using your mobile phone and laptop, you want a fast, secure browser that is also easy to use. Evaluate and compare reviews of three browsers, at least one of them a mobile browser. Consider Google Chrome, Microsoft Edge, Apple Safari, Mozilla Firefox, Opera, and others you might find in your research. Recommend two browsers: one for when you use your laptop, and one for when you use your mobile phone. What factors did you use to make your recommendation? Which is more important to you: speed or security? Why?

2. You are starting a new job in the Sales and Marketing Department of a financial services company and are part of a team redesigning the company's website. You want to become better acquainted with current website design principles, including SEO and responsive web design. Search for tips on how to incorporate both strategies into your website. List three that you find most important. Why did you select these strategies? What might be the downside of not following either principle? What other current trends in website design did you find?

3. You want to purchase a new bicycle that you can use to get from school to home and your job. You know you can use the web to find reviews of bikes, help you find the type of bike you need, purchase accessories, and connect with people selling bikes on social media or a local online marketplace. Outline your strategy for researching, selecting, and purchasing a bike. What websites will you use? How can you ensure your purchase is secure?

4. You have been putting off writing a research paper, and now it's due in two days. You have gathered a few notes, but forgot to write down your sources, and aren't sure if your notes are paraphrased or in your own words. You decide it's best to start your research over. What strategies should you use to verify your sources and cite them properly? Why is this important? What consequences might there be if you fail to follow good practices?

Apply Your Skills

Unathi Mwange uses the web in every aspect of his life, even as he commutes to school. Connecting to the cloud with his mobile phone, he stores, retrieves, and shares files. He uses his browser to log onto his school's learning management system to check his grades, participate in web-based lectures, and gather content for class projects from reliable online resources. He completes assignments using web apps, compares deals on headphones at e-commerce websites, and uses an online auction website to buy and sells sports memorabilia.

Working in a small group or by yourself, complete the following:

1. Describe how Unathi can connect to the Internet. List the parts of a URL. What additional ways can you think of that Unathi can benefit from using the web? Imagine your life without the Internet. What would be the biggest change?

2. Identify the main parts of a webpage. How can this knowledge help you navigate a webpage or website? What types of webpages do you visit most frequently?

3. Explain how Unathi can keep safe while shopping online. What tools can he use to find online deals or coupons? Do you use digital coupons or deals? How does this impact you?

4. Come up with an example of something Unathi might have to research for his job or school. What search tools and terms should he use? How can he evaluate the content for accuracy and relevance? What strategies for refining searches and verifying results did you learn from this module? How will you use those going forward?

5. Imagine an example of how Unathi might use the Creative Commons. Describe the responsibility of Unathi to properly cite his sources. If you were an artist or writer and found your content being used without attribution, what impact would that have on you?

Hardware and Processors

In This Module

- Categorize the various types of hardware and processors
- Demonstrate familiarity with input and output devices
- Maintain hardware components

Celeste's laptop allows her to easily transport work between locations.

Celeste needs a large screen monitor to work on graphic design projects.

Celeste uses a headset to listen to podcasts while she works without disturbing others.

Celeste uses a mouse and keyboard for input, and connects them wirelessly to her computer.

Pressmaster/Shutterstock.com

Celeste Rosa is an office manager at a small graphic design firm with ten employees in Denver, Colorado. In addition to supporting the designers who create professional graphics for large corporations worldwide, Celeste is responsible for maintaining the staff's computers and mobile devices. Each employee is issued a laptop they can bring home to use in telecommuting and a tablet they can use in presenting work to potential and current customers, and all share a variety of printers and projectors.

When you perform activities on a smartphone, tablet, or computer, you are using hardware, the physical components that allow your device to operate properly. Hardware can include externally connected devices, and also can include internal components that you can't see, such as the processor. Hardware is used to accept data and transmit information. Like any equipment, hardware and its components must be maintained.

In this module you will learn about the many different types of hardware, how to choose hardware that will best meet your needs, and methods for maintaining and troubleshooting hardware problems. As you reflect on what you learn in this module, ask yourself: How can you use different types of hardware effectively? What methods of input and output are most relevant to your school or work? How can you address hardware maintenance needs and prevent or minimize problems?

Categorize the Various Types of Hardware and Processors

The type of hardware you use depends on what you are trying to accomplish. Most hardware devices have more than one purpose. For example, a laptop can receive input, display output, store data, and connect to the Internet to facilitate communication. The components residing within your computer are also considered hardware. These components help translate data into information, provide storage, and control the device's memory.

Differentiate between Input and Output Devices

An **input device** communicates instructions and commands to a computer, which then translates the input into data that the computer can interpret. On a computer, the most common input device might be a keyboard, which can communicate text and instructions. On a mobile phone, the most common input device is its touchscreen. A **touchscreen** is a display that lets you touch areas of the screen to interact with software. Additional types of input devices include, but are not limited to, a mouse, stylus, scanner, webcam, microphone, and game controller (**Figure 3-1**).

Figure 3-1: Input devices send data to a computer or device

Figure 3-2: Output devices produce or display information from a computer or device

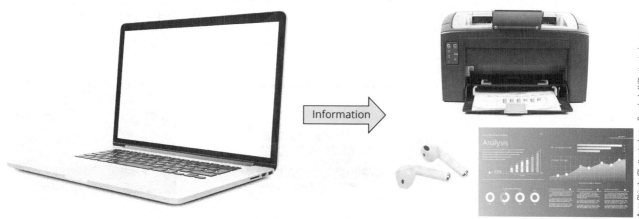

An **output device** conveys information from the computer to the user, based on the data and instructions that are input by the user. On a computer or mobile device, the most common output device might be its display device. Other types of output devices include speakers, headphones, projectors, and printers (**Figure 3-2**).

Explain How Computers Represent Data

Most computers are digital and use a binary system to operate. The **binary system** is a number system that has two digits, 0 and 1. The digit 0 indicates the absence of an electronic charge, and a 1 indicates the presence of an electronic charge. These electronic charges (or absence thereof), when grouped together, represent data. Each 0 or 1 is called a bit. A **bit** (short for binary digit) is the smallest unit of data a computer can process. When 8 bits are grouped together, they form a **byte**. A byte can represent a single character in the computer or mobile device (**Figure 3-3**).

When you enter numbers, letters, and special characters using an input device such as a keyboard, microphone, or stylus, the computer translates them into the corresponding bits and bytes that it can understand. This translation spares you from having to manually enter or translate the bits for each number, letter, or special character. When you display text on an output device such as a screen, the computer translates the various bits back to numbers, letters, and special characters that you can understand (**Figure 3-4**).

When a computer translates a character into bits and bytes, it uses a text coding scheme. Two popular text coding schemes are ASCII and Unicode. **ASCII** is an 8-bit coding scheme, which means that 8 bits are used to represent uppercase and lowercase letters,

Figure 3-3: Eight bits grouped together as a unit are called a byte

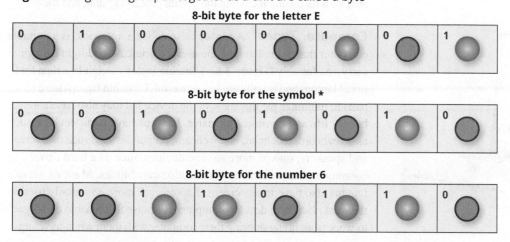

8-bit byte for the letter E

| 0 | 1 | 0 | 0 | 0 | 1 | 0 | 1 |

8-bit byte for the symbol *

| 0 | 0 | 1 | 0 | 1 | 0 | 1 | 0 |

8-bit byte for the number 6

| 0 | 0 | 1 | 1 | 0 | 1 | 1 | 0 |

Figure 3-4: Converting a letter to binary form and back

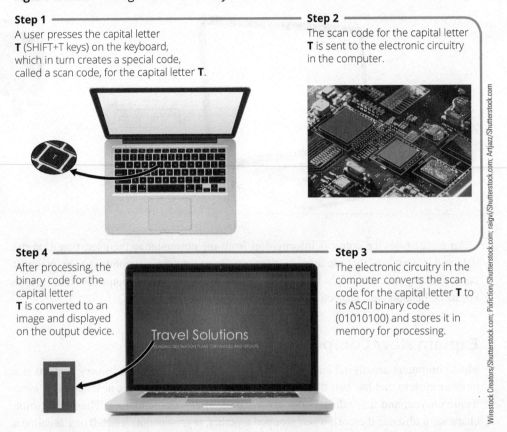

Step 1

A user presses the capital letter **T** (SHIFT+T keys) on the keyboard, which in turn creates a special code, called a scan code, for the capital letter **T**.

Step 2

The scan code for the capital letter **T** is sent to the electronic circuitry in the computer.

Step 4

After processing, the binary code for the capital letter **T** is converted to an image and displayed on the output device.

Travel Solutions

Step 3

The electronic circuitry in the computer converts the scan code for the capital letter **T** to its ASCII binary code (01010100) and stores it in memory for processing.

Wirestock Creators/Shutterstock.com; Pixfiction/Shutterstock.com; raigvi/Shutterstock.com; Artjazz/Shutterstock.com

mathematical operators, and logical operations. **Unicode** is a 16-bit coding scheme that is an extension of ASCII and can support more than 65,000 symbols and characters, including Chinese, Japanese, Arabic, and other pictorial characters.

Identify Types of Computers and Processing Components

Various types of computers exist, including laptop computers, desktop computers, and all-in-one computers. Mobile devices, such as tablets and smartphones, also are computers. A **mobile device** is a portable or handheld computing device, such as a smartphone or a tablet, with a screen size of 10.1 inches or smaller. Peripheral and storage devices are other types of hardware for input and output. Processing components are also associated with hardware, including the central processing unit, and memory.

Figure 3-5: Typical laptop

ifong/Shutterstock.com

Computer Types   A **laptop**, also called a notebook, is a portable computer that is smaller than the average briefcase and light enough to carry comfortably (**Figure 3-5**). Ultrathin laptops weigh less than traditional laptops and usually are less powerful. Ultrathin laptops have fewer parts to minimize the thickness of the device but may also have a longer battery life and be more expensive. Laptops have input devices, such as a keyboard, touchpad, and webcam; output devices, such as a screen and speakers; one or more storage devices, such as a hard drive; and communication and Internet connection capabilities. Many of today's laptops also have touchscreens. Laptops are more commonly used in the workplace than desktop computers because they enable employees to work from home or bring their computer with them when traveling.

Figure 3-6: Typical desktop computer

Den Rozhnovsky/Shutterstock.com

Figure 3-7: Typical all-in-one computer

Krisda/Shutterstock.com

A **desktop computer** typically consists of the system unit, monitor, keyboard, and mouse (**Figure 3-6**). Because desktop computers consist of multiple separate components, they are not very portable. However, these computers often can be more powerful and contain more storage than mobile equivalents such as laptops and tablets. Hardware components such as hard drive and memory can be more easily upgraded in desktop computers than in other types of computers. You might use a desktop computer in a location where you do not need the ability to frequently move the device from place to place.

An **all-in-one computer** is similar to a desktop computer, but the monitor and system unit are housed together (**Figure 3-7**). All-in-one computers take up less space than desktop computers and are easier to transport but typically are more difficult to service or upgrade because the components are housed in a very limited space. All-in-one computers sometimes are more expensive than a desktop computer with equivalent hardware specifications. Because of their expense and limited portability, they are not as common as laptops. Unlike a desktop computer, with an all-in-one you cannot choose a monitor that meets your needs, such as one with a large screen or touchscreen capabilities.

A **tablet** is a small, flat computer with a touch-sensitive screen that accepts input from your fingertip, your voice, a digital pen, or a stylus (**Figure 3-8**). Tablets often are less powerful than other types of computers, but provide an easy, convenient way to browse the web, read

Figure 3-8: Typical tablet

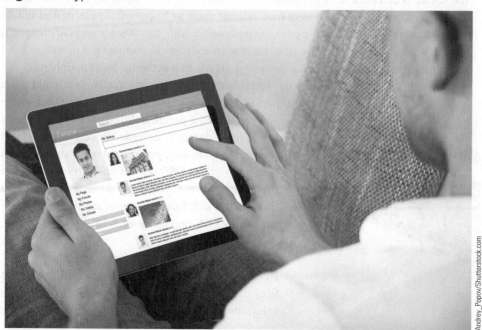

Andrey_Popov/Shutterstock.com

Figure 3-9: Typical smartphone

Kaspars Grinvalds/Shutterstock.com

and respond to emails, and create simple documents. Tablets are also easy to transport, making them ideal to take to classes and meetings for accessing information and taking notes. Tablets are used in a variety of professions, such as the medical profession, to easily collect data from patients for storage in their permanent medical records. While the primary method of input on a tablet is by using a fingertip, digital pen, microphone, or stylus, you also may be able to connect a wireless Bluetooth keyboard to make it easier to type. It often is not possible to upgrade a tablet; if your tablet's performance begins to deteriorate or cannot keep up with the latest operating systems and apps, it may be necessary to replace the device.

Two popular types of tablets are slate and convertible. A slate tablet resembles a letter-sized pad and does not contain a physical keyboard. A convertible tablet is a tablet that has a screen in its lid and a keyboard in its base, with the lid and base connected by a swivel-type hinge. You can use a convertible tablet like a traditional laptop, or you can rotate the display and fold it down over the keyboard so that it looks like a slate tablet.

A **smartphone** is an Internet-capable phone that usually also includes a calendar, an address book, and games, in addition to apps (**Figure 3-9**). Because many companies and organizations assume everyone has a smartphone these days, providing things like boarding passes and transit cards through apps instead of in physical form, those who do not have use of a smartphone find themselves on the wrong side of the digital divide. If you have a smartphone you likely use it to communicate, look up information, and use apps and games.

Peripheral Devices   An add-on device, also referred to as a **peripheral device**, is a device such as a keyboard, mouse, printer, or speakers that can connect to and extend the capability of a computer or mobile device. For example, if you need to share hard copies of documents you create, you can send the document to a printer. If you plan to work in a quiet location while listening to a podcast or music, you should consider using a headset or earbuds. If you will need to regularly bring files from one computer to another, and do not want to rely on the cloud, you could purchase an external storage device that you can connect to various computers. Peripheral devices can be used for input, output, or a combination of both.

When purchasing a peripheral device for your computer, you should make sure that the device is compatible. A peripheral device may only be compatible with a device- or platform-specific operating system such as those made by Microsoft, Apple, or Android. In addition to making sure that the device is compatible with the software on your computer, you also should make sure you have the necessary ports to connect the device or have the capability to attach the shared device wirelessly to a network. Most peripherals have the capability to connect wirelessly. To connect to a device physically, you might use a port or hub. A **port** is a slot on the computer where you can attach a peripheral device. For example, if a peripheral device is designed to connect to a USB port on the computer, you should make sure that you have an available USB port. If all USB ports on your computer are in use, you might consider purchasing a USB hub. A **USB hub** is an external device that contains many USB ports (**Figure 3-10**).

Figure 3-10: USB hub

Willem Marnix Boer/Shutterstock.com

Storage Solutions   One of the benefits of using a computer or mobile device is the ability to store files that you download or create. Various storage solutions exist, each with its own set of strengths

Figure 3-11: Internal magnetic hard drives have a disk and other moving parts

hadescom/Shutterstock.com

Figure 3-12: Solid state drives have no moving parts

Peter Gudella/Shutterstock.com

and weaknesses. For example, if you want to completely back up the contents of your computer, you might store those contents on an external hard drive or in cloud storage. However, your internal hard drive might store your operating system and apps you currently are using. If you want to move several files from one computer to another, consider using a USB flash drive. Finally, you might use a DVD or other type of optical disc to store a movie.

All computers, including smartphones and tablets, come with internal storage, such as one or more internal hard drives (**Figure 3-11**). A **hard drive** is the most computer common storage medium, and can be magnetic or solid state. Internal hard drives are installed in the computer or device you are using. For example, if you are creating a file on your work computer and store it on an internal hard drive, you will not be able to access the file from a different computer unless you send it electronically, or copy the file to a location on the cloud, an external hard drive, or a USB flash drive. Magnetic hard disk drives (HDDs) typically have greater storage capacity and are less expensive than their solid state equivalents, but have several moving parts, making it inadvisable to move the computer while they are running. A **solid state drive (SSD)** is a hard drive without moving parts, and is faster and more durable than a magnetic drive (**Figure 3-12**). Solid state drives often are used on mobile devices such as laptops and tablets and come in various physical sizes.

In addition to storing data and information on an internal hard drive, you also can store it on an external hard drive. **External hard drives** are housed in a separate case, and typically connect to your computer using a USB cable (**Figure 3-13**), instantly adding storage capacity to your computer. Similar to internal hard drives, external hard drives can use either magnetic or solid state technology. External hard drives also can be transported from one computer to another, so if you are working on a file and save it to the external hard drive, you can connect the drive to a different computer to continue working on that same file. An external hard drive can enable you to store large files and can be a good solution if you are unsure of access to the cloud, but only enable you to access the stored files if you can transport and connect the external hard drive to a computer or mobile device.

Figure 3-13: External hard drive

Anton Starikov/Shutterstock.com

Cloud storage involves storing electronic files on the Internet, not on a local computer, a practice called storing data "in the cloud." Cloud storage enables you to store your files remotely on servers that could be in a different city, state, or part of the world. Storing files

Figure 3-14: Cloud storage

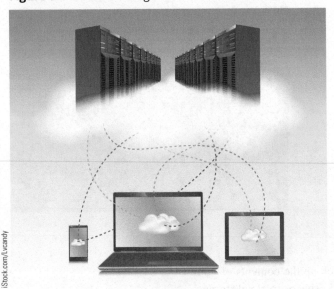

iStock.com/Lvcandy

Figure 3-15: USB flash drive

IB Photography/Shutterstock.com

to and retrieving files from cloud storage typically requires only a computer or mobile device with an Internet connection (**Figure 3-14**). With cloud storage, you might not require as much storage on your computer because you can store your files remotely. Examples of cloud storage include Google Drive, Microsoft OneDrive, and Box. Disadvantages to cloud storage include that you must be connected to the Internet, may be limited to the amount of free storage available, and could have concerns about security. However, the ease of access to files stored on the cloud, and the ability to share and collaborate with others, makes cloud storage a popular storage method.

Flash memory is a type of nonvolatile memory that can be erased electronically and rewritten. This type of memory typically is less expensive than most types of RAM, and can retain its contents in the absence of power. SSDs are a type of flash memory. Two other widely used types of flash memory storage include memory cards and USB flash drives. A **memory card** is a removable flash memory storage device, usually no bigger than 1.5 inches in height or width, that you insert and remove from a slot in a computer, digital camera, mobile device, or card reader/writer. Memory cards enable mobile uses to easily transport files to and from devices. A **USB flash drive**, also known as a flash drive, pen drive, jump drive, or thumb drive, is a removable storage device that you plug into a USB port on your computer, making it easy to transport files and folders to other computers or devices (**Figure 3-15**). Storage capacities of USB flash drives and memory cards vary. They are easily portable, but also easy to lose because of their small size. Like most physical storage, their uses are being phased out because of the reliance on cloud storage.

Optical media include CDs, DVDs, and Blu-ray discs (BDs) and use laser technology for storage and playback. Optical media were once widely used to distribute installation files for programs and apps, but saving files to optical media required special software or capabilities within the operating system. While optical media is easy to transport, if the discs get damaged, you might not be able to access your stored files. Because of the rise in availability of streaming services for music or video, and the cloud for storage, optical media's use as storage is declining.

The CPU   The **central processing unit (CPU)** is a complex integrated circuit consisting of millions of electronic parts and is primarily responsible for converting input (data) into meaningful output (information). Data travels in and out of the CPU on embedded wires collectively called a **bus**. The location of the CPUs in varies, depending on the type of computer or mobile device (**Figure 3-16**).

When you purchase a device, you might notice that processors can be advertised as having one or more cores. A processor core is a unit on the processor with the circuitry necessary to execute instructions. Processors with more cores typically perform better and are more expensive than processors with fewer cores. A processor with multiple cores is referred to as a **multi-core processor**. Computers and devices rely more on multi-core processors today than in the past, as the performance requirements for the devices have increased.

If a processor uses specific data frequently it can store that data in a processor cache. A **processor cache** stores frequently used data next to the processor so that it can easily and quickly be retrieved.

Figure 3-16: Central processing units

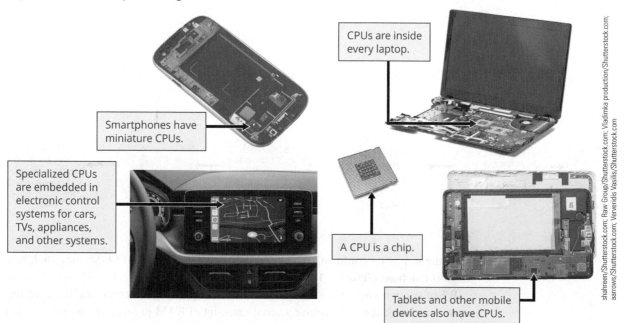

Smartphones have miniature CPUs.

CPUs are inside every laptop.

Specialized CPUs are embedded in electronic control systems for cars, TVs, appliances, and other systems.

A CPU is a chip.

Tablets and other mobile devices also have CPUs.

When a CPU executes instructions as it converts input into output, it does so with the control unit and the arithmetic logic unit (ALU). The **arithmetic logic unit (ALU)** is responsible for performing arithmetic operations in the CPU. The **control unit** manages the flow of instructions within the processor. Instructions executed by the CPU go through a series of four steps, often referred to as a machine cycle or an instruction cycle. This cycle includes the steps the CPU completes to run programmed instructions, make calculations, and make decisions. The four steps in the machine cycle include fetching, decoding, executing, and storing. The fetching and decoding instructions are performed by the control unit, while the executing and storing instructions are performed by the ALU (**Figure 3-17**).

Figure 3-17: Machine cycle

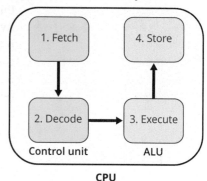

1. Fetch   4. Store

2. Decode   3. Execute

Control unit   ALU

CPU

Memory   Memory is responsible for holding data and programs as they are being processed by the CPU. Different types of memory exist, including random access memory (RAM), read-only memory (ROM), and virtual memory.

Random access memory (RAM) is the storage location that is part of every computer and that temporarily stores open apps and document data while a computer is on. On a computer, RAM is stored on one or more chips connected to the main circuit board, also referred to as the motherboard. The **motherboard** contains the microprocessor, the computer memory, and other internal devices. RAM temporarily stores data needed by the operating system and apps you use. When you start an app, the app's instructions are transferred from the hard drive to RAM. Although accessing an app's instructions from RAM results in increased performance, the contents of RAM are lost when power is removed. Memory that loses its contents when power is removed is said to be **volatile memory**. **Nonvolatile memory** does not lose its contents when power is removed.

Read-only memory (ROM) is permanently installed on your computer and is attached to the motherboard. The ROM chip contains the BIOS (basic input/output system), which tells your computer or device how to start. At startup, the BIOS also performs a **power-on self test (POST)**, which tests all components for proper operation. The ROM also provides the means of communication between the operating system and hardware devices. Manufacturers often update the instructions on the ROM chip, which are referred to as **firmware**. These updated instructions, or firmware version, can enable your computer to perform additional tasks or fine-tune how your computer communicates with other devices.

Figure 3-18: Differences between ROM and RAM

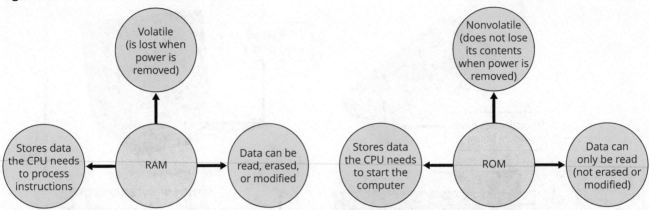

While it may be confusing to differentiate between RAM and ROM, they each have distinct functions (**Figure 3-18**).

When you run your operating system and other apps on your computer, the operating system and each app will require a certain amount of RAM to function properly. As you run more apps simultaneously, more RAM will be required. If your computer runs low on RAM, it may need to swap the contents of RAM to and from the hard drive. When this takes place, your operating system uses its **virtual memory** capability, temporarily storing data on a storage medium until it can be swapped into RAM. A **swap file** or **paging file** is a file that contains the area of the hard that cannot fit in RAM, and which is stored in the hard disk's virtual memory. Depending on the type of hard drive installed on your computer, using virtual memory may decrease your computer's performance (**Figure 3-19**).

Various types of random access memory exist, and the different types vary in cost, performance, and whether or not they are volatile. **Table 3-1** lists common types of RAM.

Figure 3-19: How a computer might use virtual memory

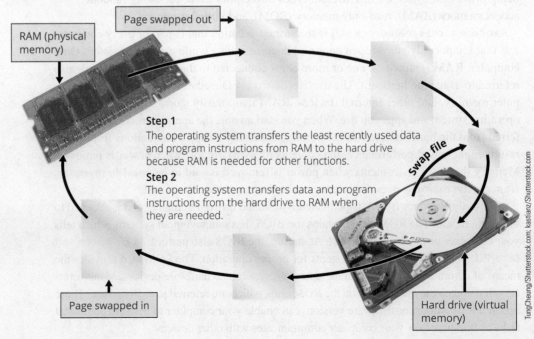

Page swapped out

RAM (physical memory)

Step 1
The operating system transfers the least recently used data and program instructions from RAM to the hard drive because RAM is needed for other functions.

Step 2
The operating system transfers data and program instructions from the hard drive to RAM when they are needed.

swap file

Page swapped in

Hard drive (virtual memory)

TungCheung/Shutterstock.com; kastianz/Shutterstock.com

Table 3-1: Types of RAM

Type of RAM	Description	Volatile or nonvolatile
Dynamic RAM (DRAM)	Memory needs to be constantly recharged or contents will be erased	Volatile
Static RAM (SRAM)	Memory can be recharged less frequently than DRAM, but can be more expensive than DRAM	Volatile
Magnetoresistive RAM (MRAM)	Memory uses magnetic charges to store contents, and can retain its contents in the absence of power	Nonvolatile
Flash memory	Fast, inexpensive memory that can retain its contents in the absence of power	Nonvolatile

While RAM is used to temporarily store instructions used by apps, storage devices are designed to store data and information for extended periods of time. The type and amount of data you want to store will help you determine the most appropriate storage device to use.

Explain Considerations When Purchasing a Computer

With the powerful capabilities of tablets and smartphones, you may not need to purchase a laptop or desktop of your own. However, many feel that the larger screen, built-in keyboard, and pointing device make a personal laptop or desktop computer still necessary. Your employer may also place restrictions on personal uses of company-issued computers. When purchasing a computer, understanding your needs will help you to select the most appropriate device.

If your primary needs are to do activities such as check your email, use social media, do online banking, and browse the web, your hardware and software needs will be different than if you will be creating and editing video content or other multimedia and graphics, which require more processing power and a larger monitor. When choosing a computer, you should select one with the platform, hardware, form factor, and add-on devices that best meet your needs. **Table 3-2** identifies factors to consider when buying a computer, as well as questions that will help you in making the most appropriate choices.

Platform refers to the software, or operating system, a computer or device uses. It typically is easier to transfer files between computers and devices that use the same platform. If you are purchasing a computer to do schoolwork, for example, consider purchasing one that uses the same operating system as the computers at your school. If you have a job

Table 3-2: Factors to consider in buying a computer

Consideration	Questions
Platform	• Do I need to use software that requires a specific platform? • Does the computer need to be compatible with other devices I own that use a particular platform?
Hardware	• Do I require specific hardware to perform intended tasks? • How much data and information do I plan to store on the computer?
Hardware specifications	• Will the tasks I perform or software I want to run require certain hardware specifications?
Form factor	• Will I be using this computer in one location, or will I need it to be mobile?
Add-on devices	• What additional devices will I need to perform my intended tasks?

and want the ability to do some work both on your office and home computer, consider purchasing a computer that uses the same operating system as your work computer. The operating systems used elsewhere in your home, both on computers and mobile devices, also might play a role in the selection. For example, if you own an iPhone or iPad, you might choose to purchase an Apple computer for maximum compatibility between the devices. A Chromebook is a type of laptop that runs the ChromeOS operating system. While these are budget friendly, they often do not have as many advanced features or support as many apps as computers running Windows or macOS, which are the leading desktop operating systems.

When you buy a computer, you should review the computer's hardware specifications so that you purchase one that meets your needs. Computers are available in a variety of brands. Each brand might include models that have varying types of processors, amounts of memory, storage devices, and form factors. You can find specifications about a computer on the computer's packaging, on signage next to the computer's display in a store, or on the manufacturer's or retailer's website (**Figure 3-20**).

Your budget will play a big role in the computer you purchase, and there may be many computers available in the same price range. For example, one computer available for $1,000 might have a great processor and a mediocre hard drive, but another computer at the same price might have a mediocre processor and a great hard drive. It is important to evaluate what each computer has to offer so that you can select the device that best meets your needs.

A common way to determine the required hardware specifications for your computer is to evaluate the minimum hardware requirements, also called system requirements, for the software you plan to use. Each program or app you plan to use has its own system requirements. The system requirements for one program or app might conflict with the system requirements of the other(s), so you will need to select the computer with the hardware specifications that can accommodate a variety of programs or apps. **Table 3-3** describes how to evaluate conflicting system requirements.

Figure 3-20: Detailed hardware specifications

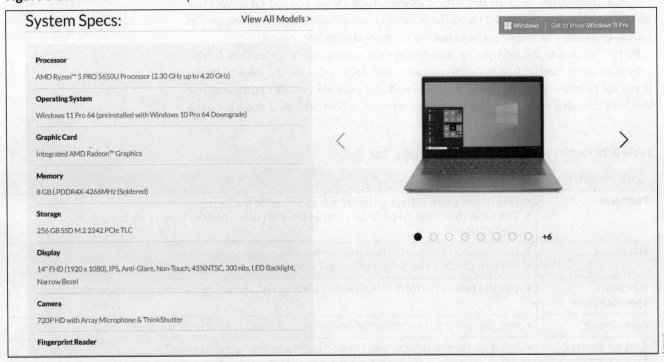

System Specs: View All Models >

Processor
AMD Ryzen™ 5 PRO 5650U Processor (2.30 GHz up to 4.20 GHz)

Operating System
Windows 11 Pro 64 (preinstalled with Windows 10 Pro 64 Downgrade)

Graphic Card
Integrated AMD Radeon™ Graphics

Memory
8 GB LPDDR4X-4266MHz (Soldered)

Storage
256 GB SSD M.2 2242 PCIe TLC

Display
14" FHD (1920 x 1080), IPS, Anti-Glare, Non-Touch, 45%NTSC, 300 nits, LED Backlight, Narrow Bezel

Camera
720P HD with Array Microphone & ThinkShutter

Fingerprint Reader

Windows | Get to know Windows 11 Pro

Lenovo

Table 3-3: Evaluating system requirements

Specification	Recommended solution
Different processor requirements	Identify the program or app with the greatest processor requirement and select a computer with a processor that meets or exceeds the requirement.
Different memory requirements	Identify the program or app with the greatest memory requirement and select a computer with a memory type and capacity that meets or exceeds this requirement. Computers with as little as 4 GB of RAM are adequate for basic web browsing and very basic productivity tasks, while virtual reality applications, high-end gaming, and other intensive tasks often require as much as 32 GB.
Different storage requirements	Add the storage requirements for each program or app you want to use, and select a computer with the storage capacity that exceeds the sum of all storage requirements.
Other differing hardware requirements	In most cases, identify the program or app with the greatest requirement and select a computer that at least meets or exceeds this requirement.

Although following these guidelines will help you select an appropriate computer, keep in mind that you likely want the computer to meet your needs for the next three to five years. If you select a computer that exactly meets the system requirements for the present software you intend to use, you might not be able to install or use additional programs or apps in the future. In addition, you should purchase a computer that has enough storage capacity not only for the programs and apps you want to use, but also for the files you intend to store on the computer (homework, photos, videos, important documents, etc.). Cloud storage can extend the capabilities of your computer, so consider your access and storage limits to cloud storage drives when evaluating storage needs. While purchasing the most expensive computer you can afford might meet your needs, you might not ever use all available resources. For example, if the system requirements for the programs and apps you want to use call for 12 gigabytes (GB) of memory, it might be reasonable to select a computer with 16 GB of memory, but it could be a waste of money to purchase a computer with 32 GB of memory. If you intend to use a computer to play games, you might consider a computer built specifically for gaming applications. These computers typically have a large amount of RAM, as well as other supporting hardware to support an immersive gaming experience. Evaluate your options carefully and seek advice from professionals if you are unsure of your exact needs.

After you have determined the platform and hardware requirements for the computer you want to purchase, you will select a form factor. The **form factor** refers to the shape and size of the computer. Not all form factors may support the hardware you need. For example, a tablet might not contain adequate hardware specifications for editing videos. Choosing between a desktop and laptop usually comes down to whether you need to be able to easily transport your computer. You also should consider the need for peripheral devices such as a keyboard, mouse, webcam, speakers, and printer. Depending on your needs, it may also be necessary to use two monitors that can display different documents or apps (**Figure 3-21**).

Figure 3-21: Two monitor setup

Demonstrate Familiarity with Input and Output Devices

Input and output devices are necessary to provide information to and receive information from a computer. Manual input devices include keyboards. Touchscreens are another common method of input used by mobile devices, and increasingly on computer monitors. Audio, visual, and gaming are other types of input. Output can be display, audio, or print.

Investigate Input Devices

Various types of input devices are available, such as keyboards, pointing devices, touchscreens, microphones, webcams, digital cameras, scanners, and game controllers. Some input devices are peripheral devices, such as printers, which are shared by multiple devices or users on a network. Others are built into the computer or device. For example, most laptop computers today come with a keyboard, pointing device, touchscreen, microphone, and webcam, and smartphones also include a microphone, digital camera, and webcam.

Manual Input A **keyboard** is an input device that contains keys for entering letters, numbers, punctuation, and symbols, and issuing commands (**Figure 3-22**). Desktop computers have keyboards connected either wired or wirelessly, and laptop computers have a keyboard built-in. Mobile devices such as tablets and smartphones typically have an on-screen keyboard; that is, an image of a keyboard displays on the screen, and you touch the appropriate keys to enter letters, numbers, and symbols.

A **pointing device** is used to point to and select specific objects on the computer screen. Pointing devices can be used to select objects, move objects, and position or draw items on the screen. Examples of pointing devices include a mouse, touchpad, and trackball (**Figure 3-23**).

Figure 3-22: Typical computer keyboard

Volodymyr Krasyuk/Shutterstock.com

- A **mouse** is the most common type of pointing device used with computers. A mouse fits under your hand and can connect to your computer either with a wire or wirelessly. Moving the mouse on a flat surface, such as a desk, moves a pointer on the screen. When the pointer is positioned over an object you want to select, you can press a button on the mouse to select the object. This action is referred to as clicking the mouse.

Figure 3-23: Typical pointing devices

Mouse

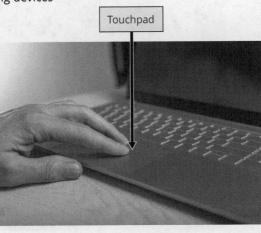

Touchpad

Trackball

New Africa/Shutterstock.com; valiantsin suprunovich/Shutterstock.com; Mikhail Gorshenin/Shutterstock.com

- A touchpad is a pointing device that is commonly used on laptops. A **touchpad** is a flat surface that is touch-sensitive, and you move your finger around the touchpad to move the pointer on the screen. When the pointer is over an item on the screen you wish to select, you can tap the touchpad with your finger to select the object.
- A **trackball** is a stationary pointing device with a ball anchored inside a casing, as well as two or more buttons. Moving the ball moves the pointer on the screen, and pressing the buttons issues the commands to the computer.

Touchscreen Input   In addition to responding to the touch of your fingers, touch-screens also may be able to respond to a stylus or digital pen to enter commands. **Multitouch screens** can respond to multiple fingers touching the screen simultaneously. This is useful when you are performing a gesture such as pinching or stretching an object to resize it. Other touchscreen input methods include tapping (to select an object or command), and swiping (to move the screen).

Pen input is used to make selections or draw on a touchscreen with more precision than a finger. Common pen input devices include a stylus and a digital pen. A **stylus** is a pen-shaped digital tool that you can use to make selections or enter information on a touchscreen, as well as draw, tap icons, or tap keys on an on-screen keyboard. A **digital pen** is similar to a stylus, but is more capable because it has programmable buttons. Some digital pens can also capture your handwriting as you write on paper or on the screen (**Figure 3-24**).

Figure 3-24: Digital pen

Mak3t/Shutterstock.com

Audio and Visual Input   An option for issuing instructions to your computer without using your hands is using your voice. A **microphone** is used to enter voice or sound data into a computer. Examples of activities that might require a microphone include video conferencing, voice recognition, and recording live music. Many laptops and tablets have built-in microphones, but you can connect a microphone to other types of computers either using a wire or wirelessly. Using a microphone, you can record audio, issue commands to the computer, or speak while the computer translates your words to text in a document. Microphones are also essential if you are using the computer to have an audio or video conversation with one or more other people.

A **digital camera** creates a digital image of an object, person, or scene, and allows you to download or send pictures or videos to a computer. Most computers come with a built-in camera called a **webcam**, a type of digital video camera that captures video and still images as well as audio input, primarily for use in videoconferencing, chatting, or online gaming (**Figure 3-25**). If the computer does not have a built-in webcam, or you would like to connect a different type of camera to your computer, you can do so either via a wired or wireless connection.

A **scanner** is an input device that converts an existing paper image into an electronic file that you can open and work with on your computer. For example, if you want to convert a printed logo to digital form so that you can edit and duplicate it, you could use a scanner to convert the printed logo to a format a computer can understand. In addition to scanning printed materials such as logos and documents, 3D scanners can scan three-dimensional objects, which then can be manipulated and possibly printed. You can also use a scanner to scan a printed document so that you can edit it using an app on your computer.

Figure 3-25: Webcam

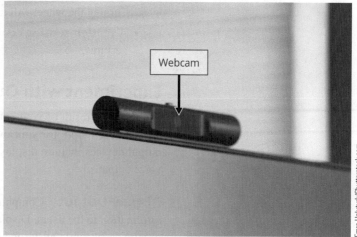

Webcam

Emre Unluturk/Shutterstock.com

Figure 3-26: QR code

Figure 3-27: Gaming wheel

Tinxi/Shutterstock.com

Another common type of visual input is QR codes. A **QR code** is a square-shaped graphic that corresponds to a web address or other information (**Figure 3-26**). QR is short for quick response. QR codes often appear on flyers, menus, or other printed materials, including books and signs. The advantage of a QR code is that they are easy and free to generate, and can enable users to use their smartphone's camera to easily navigate to a specific website.

Gaming Input   A **game controller** is an input device you use when playing a video game. Various types of game controllers exist such as joysticks, gamepads, dance pads, wheels, and motion-sensing controllers.

- A **joystick** includes a handheld vertical lever, mounted on a base, that you move in different directions to control the actions of the simulated vehicle or player.
- A **gamepad** is held in both hands and controls the movement and actions of players or objects. On gamepads, users press buttons with their thumbs or move sticks in various directions to trigger events.
- A **dance pad** is a flat, electronic device divided into panels that users press with their feet in response to instructions from the video game.
- A **wheel** mirrors the functionality of a steering wheel in a vehicle (**Figure 3-27**). Turning the wheel will turn the vehicle you are driving in the game.
- A **motion-sensing controller** allows users to guide on-screen elements with air gestures.

Experiment with Output Devices

Output is the result of your actions, creations, or commands, and can be print or digital. You can use output for your own purposes or share output with others. Commonly used output devices include display devices, speakers, headphones, printers, projectors, and voice output.

Display Output   Computers use display devices as output devices to communicate information to the users. Display devices are connected to desktop computers via a cable or wirelessly, while all-in-one computers, laptops, tablets, and smartphones have built-in display devices. Display devices come in a variety of sizes. If you are simply using a computer to browse the web and check your email, you might consider a smaller display device. However, if you are working with graphics or large spreadsheets, you might use a larger display device, and/or multiple display devices, which allow you to display one app or document window on one screen and another app or document on another.

To present onscreen information to a group, you might consider using a projector. **Projectors** can display output from a computer on a large surface such as a wall or screen (**Figure 3-28**). Projectors are often used in classroom or conference room environments where individuals give presentations. Projectors are connected to computers or device using a cable or wirelessly and can either duplicate what is on your monitor or screen or act as an extension of the monitor (your monitor might display one thing while the projector displays another). Some projectors are small and easy to transport, while others are larger and may be permanently mounted in a room. Many conference rooms and classrooms now have screens that connect directly to a computer or device, eliminating the need for a projector.

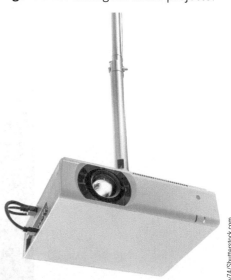

Figure 3-28: Ceiling mounted projector

v74/Shutterstock.com

Audio Output
Speakers are used to convey audio output, such as music, voice, sound effects, or other sounds. While speakers often are built into computers, tablets, and smartphones, you can also connect speakers via a wired or wireless connection. For example, if you want to play music in a small office setting and would like others to hear it, you might connect a separate speaker to your computer so that it can play more loudly. If you prefer to listen to audio in a public space without disturbing others, consider using headphones. **Headphones** consist of a pair of small listening devices that fit into a band placed over your ears. As an alternative to headphones, **earbuds** are speakers that are small enough to place in your ears (**Figure 3-29**). If you prefer a device that provides audio output while being able to accept voice input, consider a headset. **Headsets** include one or more headphones for output, and a microphone for input.

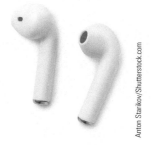

Figure 3-29: Earbuds

Anton Starikov/Shutterstock.com

In addition to output being displayed or printed, computers can also provide voice output. A **voice synthesizer** converts text to speech. Some apps and operating systems have a built-in voice synthesizer. In addition to this form of output being convenient for some, it is also helpful for those with visual impairments.

Print Output
A **printer** creates hard copy output on paper, film, and other media. A printer can be connected to a computer via a cable, a network, or wirelessly. **Table 3-4** describes the various types of printers.

Table 3-4: Types of printers

Type of printer	Description
Ink-jet printer	Prints by spraying small dots of colored ink onto paper
Laser printer	Uses a laser beam and toner to print on paper
Multifunction device (MFD)	Also called an all-in-one printer; can serve as an input device by copying and scanning, as well as an output device by faxing and printing
Mobile printer	Small, lightweight printer that is built into or attached to a mobile device for mobile printing
Plotter	Large-format printer that uses charged wires to produce high-quality drawings for professional applications such as architectural blueprints; plotters draw continuous lines on large rolls of paper
3D printer	Creates objects based on computer models using special plastics and other materials

Figure 3-30: 3D printer

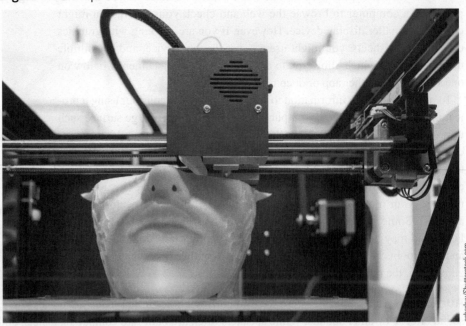

A **3D printer** uses a process called additive manufacturing to create an object by adding material one horizontal layer at a time to print solid objects, such as clothing, prosthetics, eyewear, implants, toys, parts, prototypes, and more (**Figure 3-30**). 3D printers and the materials required to use them are expensive, limiting their use. While some personal users have 3D printers, they often are associated with manufacturing, scientific and medical, and other industrial uses. For example, in manufacturing, 3D printers can produce parts quickly and efficiently. Medical professionals can create organ models that can be used in training or preparation for complex surgeries.

Explain How to Install Computer Hardware

When you purchase a desktop or laptop computer, you should determine an ideal location to use the computer. Select an area that is free from clutter, is not subject to extreme temperatures or water, and is comfortable for you to work. Before you turn on your computer or device for the first time, you should make sure that all necessary components are included and that the device is charged or connected to a power source. You should also inspect the computer or device to make sure it is free from damage.

If you are installing a desktop or all-in-one computer, carefully unpack all components from the box and place them in their desired locations. Connect all components and accessories, such as your keyboard and mouse, and then connect the power. Finally, you can turn on the computer and follow all remaining steps on the screen. Most computer manufacturers include installation instructions with their computers, so be sure to follow any additional steps included in those instructions.

If you are installing a laptop, carefully unpack the laptop and place it in a location next to a power source. It is a good idea to fully charge the laptop's battery before using the device for the first time.

In addition to installing a computer, you might buy peripheral devices, such as a printer or scanner, to connect to the computer. These peripheral devices communicate with the computer through a port. Some devices, called **plug-and-play** devices, will begin functioning properly as soon as you connect them to your computer. Other devices might require that you manually install special software, called a device driver, to work properly. A **device driver** is a program that controls a device attached to your computer, such as a printer, monitor, or video card. If you have to install a program or app for your device to work, make sure you are signed in to the computer with a user account that has the necessary permission to install programs and apps. Some components must be installed inside your computer. If you are uncomfortable or inexperienced in opening a computer and installing or replacing components, contact a professional.

Devices can also connect to a computer wirelessly. To connect a wireless device to your computer, follow the installation instructions that come with the device.

Maintain Hardware Components

After purchasing a computer or device, you will want to make sure it runs optimally and is well maintained to guarantee proper performance. Some methods for ensuring performance include measuring the performance of computer hardware, troubleshooting problems with hardware and peripherals, and maintaining hardware and software.

Measure Hardware Performance

When searching for a computer or device to purchase, you should be able to evaluate the hardware specifications so that you can select one that best meets your needs. The following methods evaluate the processor and other factors that impact efficiency.

- A processor's **clock speed** measures the speed at which it can execute instructions. Clock speed can be measured in either megahertz (MHz) or gigahertz (GHz). Megahertz specifies millions of cycles per second, while gigahertz specifies billions of cycles per second.
- A **cycle** is the smallest unit of time a process can measure. The efficiency of a CPU is measured by instructions per cycle (IPC).
- The **bus width** determines the speed at which data in a computer travels, and is also referred to as **word size**. The wider the bus, the more data that can travel on it. A 64-bit bus, for example, transfers data faster than a 32-bit bus. If you have a fast CPU but the bus speed is slow, that can cause a condition called bottlenecking.

While manufacturers advertise performance factors such as clock speed and bus speed, there are other factors that can affect processor performance. For this reason, you should research benchmark test results for the processor(s) you are considering. A **benchmark** is a test run by a laboratory or other organization to determine processor speed and other performance factors. Benchmarking tests compare similar systems performing identical tasks. You typically can find benchmarking information online.

Troubleshoot Hardware Problems

At some point you probably will experience a technology problem with your computer or device that requires troubleshooting. Technology problems that remain unresolved may impact your ability to use your device. Often issues with powering on or holding a battery charge stem from a faulty device used to plug in the device, such as the adapter. Laptops often come with **adapters**, which are external batteries that provide power to the laptop and help its battery recharge.

Table 3-5 outlines some common problems you might experience with a computer or device, as well as some recommended solutions. Before troubleshooting, you should properly turn off the computer or device and remove it from its power source, and make sure your files are backed up to the cloud or external storage. Failure to do so might result in damaging the computer's physical components.

Table 3-5: Troubleshooting hardware problems

Problem	Recommended solution(s)
Computer or device does not turn on	It might be in sleep or hibernate mode; to wake it up, try pressing a key on the keyboard, pressing the power button, or tapping the touchscreen.
	Make sure power or charging cables are plugged securely into both the external or wall outlet and the device itself.
	Make sure the battery is charged if not connected to an external power source. If the battery is charged, connect the adapter or charging cord and attempt to turn on the computer or device. If it still does not turn on, the problem may be with the computer or device.
Computer or device gets wet	Turn off the computer or device, remove the battery, and dry off visible water with a cloth. Fill a plastic bag or box with uncooked rice, submerge the computer or device and battery into the rice so that it is surrounded completely, and then do not turn on the computer or device for at least 24 hours. If the computer or device does not work after it is dry, contact a professional for your options.
Battery does not hold a charge or drains very quickly	Verify that the adapter, cable, and/or charging cord used to charge the battery are all working properly. If the computer or device can run from the adapter or charging cord without a battery installed, you may need to replace the battery.
The device issues a series of beeps	Refer to your user manual to determine what the beeps indicate, as different sequences of beeps may indicate different hardware problems specific to your model of computer.
Device turns on, but operating system does not run	Disconnect all nonessential peripheral devices, remove all storage media, and then restart the computer or device.
	If the problem persists, the operating system might need to be restored or the device reset. If these measures do not work, the hard drive might be failing.
Display device does not display anything	On a desktop, verify that the monitor is turned on and set to the right input, and that the video cable is connected securely to the computer and monitor and plugged in to an outlet.
	Restart the computer or device.
	There might be a problem with the video card, requiring it to be replaced. The **video card** is a circuit board that processes image signals.
	If you have access to a spare monitor, see if that monitor will work. If so, your original monitor might be faulty. If not, the problem may be with the hardware or software configuration.
Peripheral device does not work	Verify that the peripheral device is connected properly.
	If it is wireless, make sure it is turned on and is charged or has working batteries, and then attempt to pair it again with the computer or wireless receiver.
	If you have access to a spare device, see if it will work. If so, your original peripheral device might be faulty. If not, the problem may be with the hardware or software configuration.
Sound does not work	Verify that speakers, headphones, or earbuds are connected, charged, and turned on.
	Make sure the volume is not muted and is turned up on the computer or mobile device.
Hard drive makes noise	If the computer is not positioned on a flat surface, move it to a flat surface.
	If something has impacted the hard drive, it might have caused the hard drive to fail.
	If the problem persists, contact a professional.

Problem	Recommended solution(s)
Program or app does not run	Restart the computer or device and try running the program or app again.
	If feasible, uninstall the program or app, reinstall it, and then try running it again. If the problem persists, the problem may be with the operating system's configuration.
Computer or device displays symptoms of a virus or other malware	Make sure your antivirus software is up to date, and then disconnect the computer or device from the network and run antivirus software to attempt to remove the malware. Continue running scans until no threats are detected and then reconnect the computer to the network.
	If you do not have antivirus software installed, obtain and install a reputable antivirus program or app and then scan your computer in an attempt to remove the malware. You should have only one antivirus program or app installed on your computer or mobile device at one time.
	If you are unable to remove the malware, take your computer to a professional who may be able to remove the malicious program or app.
Screen is damaged physically	Contact a professional to replace the screen; if the computer or device is covered under a warranty, the repair may be free.
	Replacing a broken screen on a computer or device might be more costly than replacing the computer or device.
Touchscreen does not respond	Clean the touchscreen. Restart the computer or device.
Computer or device does not connect to a wireless network	Verify that you are within range of a wireless access point.
	Make sure the information to connect to the wireless network is configured properly on the computer or device.
	Make sure the wireless capability on the computer or device is turned on.
	Make sure your router or modem is turned on properly.
Computer or device cannot synchronize with Bluetooth accessories	Verify that the Bluetooth device is turned on.
	Verify that the Bluetooth functionality on your computer or device is enabled.
	Verify that the computer or device has been paired properly with the accessory.
	Make sure the Bluetooth device is charged.
Device continuously has poor mobile phone reception	Restart the device.
	If you have a protective case, remove the case to see if reception improves.
	If you are using the device inside a building, try moving closer to a window or open doorway.
	Contact your wireless carrier for additional suggestions.
Printer does not print	Verify that the printer is plugged in and turned on.
	Verify that the printer is properly connected to the computer either via a wired or wireless connection.
	Verify that there is paper in the paper tray.
	Verify that there is sufficient ink or toner.

If you are uncomfortable performing any of the recommended solutions or the solutions are not solving the problem(s), you should consult a professional (independent computer repair company, technical support department, or computer or mobile device manufacturer) for further assessment and resolution. If the problem you are experiencing is not listed, you can perform a search on the Internet to identify potential solutions.

Before attempting to resolve computer or mobile device problems on your own, be sure to follow all necessary safety precautions. Contact a professional if you require additional information.

Maintain Computer Hardware

You should perform tasks periodically to keep your hardware in good condition and the software functioning properly. Failure to properly maintain hardware can result in decreasing its lifespan and/or its performance.

Table 3-6: Maintaining hardware

Recommendation	Proactive steps
Keep it clean	Keep your computer and device away from dusty or cluttered areas.
	Use a damp cloth to clean the screen or monitor gently. Do not use any special cleaners to clean the display.
	Periodically use a can of compressed air to free your keyboard from any dirt and debris. Always hold the can of compressed air upright to avoid damaging the keyboard.
	If the computer has an air vent where a fan removes heat, make sure the vent is free of dust and debris. If the air vent is dirty, contact a trained professional to have it cleaned properly. Do not attempt to clean the air vent yourself, as it is possible that dirt and debris can enter the computer.
Avoid water and moisture	Avoid exposure to water and moist air by keeping liquids away and keeping the computer or device in a climate-controlled space when possible.
Monitor available storage to ensure the computer or device runs efficiently	Make sure you have enough free space on your hard drive. When computers or devices run low on available hard drive space, performance can quickly deteriorate. If you are unable to free enough space on your hard drive to run properly, consider archiving or moving files to the cloud, deleting files, or purchasing additional internal or external storage hardware.
Don't allow overheating	Extreme temperatures or humidity can damage the electronics. Many devices will alert you when the temperature is too high or will automatically shut down. For a laptop, consider purchasing a cooling pad that protects it from overheating.

Hardware maintenance involves performing tasks to keep the computer's physical components in good working order. **Table 3-6** lists maintenance recommendations that will help keep your computer functioning properly.

Following these maintenance recommendations will enable you to prevent many common problems from occurring in the first place. Another proactive step you can take to protect desktop and laptop computers is to avoid power fluctuations such as power spikes or power surges. To do so, consider purchasing and connecting an uninterruptable power supply (UPS) or a surge suppressor. An **uninterruptable power supply (UPS)** maintains power to computer equipment in case of an interruption in the primary electrical source, usually in the form of a short-term battery backup that comes on automatically in case of power loss (**Figure 3-31**). A **surge suppressor** is a device that prevents power fluctuations from damaging electronic components.

Figure 3-31: Uninterruptible power supply

Nor Gal/Shutterstock.com

Restore a Device

If you are experiencing a problem with your computer or device, you might need to take corrective actions such as restoring the operating system, correcting display problems, or updating device drivers.

If you are experiencing a problem with your operating system, often characterized by programs and apps not properly starting, persistent error messages, or slow performance, you should consider restoring the operating system. Before you attempt to restore the operating system, you should copy all personal files to a separate storage device such as a USB flash drive or external hard drive. When you **restore** an operating system, you are reverting all settings back to their default, or migrating back to the operating system's previous version. To restore your operating system, review the help documentation and follow the specified steps (**Figure 3-32**). You should always regularly back up your files to the cloud or to an external hard drive as a preventative measure.

Figure 3-32: Windows includes a feature to restore your operating system

Module 3 Summary

The hardware you use depends on what you are trying to accomplish, such as receive input, produce output, store data, play games, or connect to the Internet. Many hardware devices have more than one use. Input devices communicate instructions that the computer or device translates into data that the computer can read and use to produce information. Output devices convey information produced by a computer or device. Computers use the binary system to interpret data and produce information using a coding scheme, such as ASCII or Unicode.

Laptops, desktops, and all-in-ones are types of computers, as are mobile devices such as tablets and smartphones. Laptops are more common than desktops and all-in-ones because they are more portable. Smartphones are so prevalent that not having access to one is a factor in the digital

divide. Peripheral devices extend the capability of a computer or device. Examples of peripheral devices include printers, keyboards, and speakers. You can connect a peripheral device wirelessly or using a port or USB hub.

Storage solutions include cloud storage and internal or external hard drives, as well as USB flash drives and optical media. All computers and devices come with an internal hard drive for storage. Solid state drives are common in mobile devices and laptops. An external hard drive can be used to extend the storage capacity of your computer. Cloud storage is popular because it allows for easier sharing and collaboration among multiple users in different physical locations. Flash memory devices and optical media are no longer widely used as more users rely on the cloud.

Processing components include the CPU and memory. The CPU converts input into output using the control unit and the ALU. More computers and devices rely on multi-core processors because of their enhanced performance. Two types of memory are RAM, which is volatile, and ROM, which is nonvolatile.

When purchasing a computer or device, you should consider the platform (operating system), hardware type and specifications needed to complete tasks, form factor (shape and size), and any add-on devices you may need. You also will need to consider your budget and evaluate the system requirements, such as processor speed, memory, and storage.

Input devices are used to input data. Input devices can be peripheral and shared with others or be built into the computer or device. The type of device you use depends on what type of input you are entering: manual (keyboard or pointing device), touchscreen (fingertip, stylus, or digital pen), audio or visual (microphone, digital camera, webcam, scanner, or QR codes), and gaming (game controllers such as joysticks). Output devices display print or digital information. The type of device you use depends on what type of output

you want to present or distribute: display (monitor, screen, or projector), audio (speakers, headsets, or earbuds), or print (printers that produce paper or 3D output).

When installing hardware, you should inspect all components and ensure that everything is present and undamaged. When installing peripheral devices, plug-and-play devices begin functioning automatically, while other devices may require you to install a device driver. When measuring hardware performance, consider the clock speed, cycle, and bus width and research benchmark tests.

You should know how to troubleshoot common problems and determine if you might fix them or if you require professional help. Hardware maintenance involves making sure the computer's physical components work properly. Maintenance can address issues, such as using a cooling pad for a laptop if you must use the device in uncomfortably warm conditions, and prevent issues, such as using a surge protector to avoid damage caused by power spikes. If troubleshooting and maintenance are not resolving an issue, you may need to restore the operating system to revert all settings back to their default.

Review Questions

1. A keyboard is an example of a(n) _____ device.
   a. output
   b. input
   c. pointing
   d. processing

2. The binary system is a number system that has two digits, _____.
   a. a and b
   b. 0 and 1
   c. positive and negative
   d. small and large

3. A slot on the computer where you can attach a peripheral device is called a(n) _____.
   a. port
   b. bus
   c. outlet
   d. node

4. The form factor refers to the _____ of a computer.
   a. operating system
   b. bandwidth
   c. purpose
   d. shape and size

5. A QR code is a square-shaped graphic that corresponds to a _____.
   a. web address
   b. byte
   c. peripheral device
   d. binary code

6. A 3D printer uses a process called _____ manufacturing to create an object.
   a. predictive
   b. incremental
   c. additive
   d. virtual

7. (True or False) A plug-and-play device will begin functioning properly as soon as you connect it to your computer.

8. The smallest unit of time a process can measure is a _____.
   a. cycle
   b. clock speed
   c. bit
   d. byte

9. (True or False) The clock speed determines the speed at which data travels.

10. A circuit board that processes image signals is called a(n) _____.

    a. ALU

    b. video card

    c. scanner

    d. USB flash drive

11. To prevent power fluctuations from damaging electronic components, you should use a(n) _____.

    a. surge suppressor

    b. UPS

    c. ALU

    d. adapter

12. When you _____ an operating system, you are reverting all settings back to their default.

    a. rewind

    b. reverse

    c. restore

    d. reconnect

Discussion Questions

1. When you are purchasing a computer or device, you might be tempted to get the most expensive one you can afford. Why might this not be a good idea? What questions should you ask that can help you determine what type of computer or device to purchase? Does your current computer or device meet your needs? If not, what would you consider if you were able to replace it?

2. What is the difference between input and output devices? What types of input and output devices are necessary for a college student? Why? What types of input and output devices are necessary for an employee in the field in which you work or plan to work? What types of input and output devices do you rely on? Why are they important?

3. Despite how well you might take care of your computer or device, problems can always arise. When troubleshooting problems you encounter, at what point should you engage a professional for assistance? Why? At what point might you consider purchasing a new computer or device? Have you ever had a situation in which you were able to troubleshoot a problem?

4. List and describe three types of storage solutions available for use. What should you do if you run out of space on your device? What type of storage is available with your device? Which do you prefer? Why?

Critical Thinking Activities

1. You are pursuing a degree in graphic design. What hardware specifications should you look for if you were to purchase a new computer to help with your studies? Why did you choose the central processing unit? Why did you choose the amount of RAM? Why did you choose the storage solution? How does the computer you chose compare with your current device?

2. You are a financial advisor who works in an open office with coworkers nearby. You advise clients in person, over the phone, and using video calls. What types of input and output devices might you require to do your job? If you were working in this role, are there other input or output devices you feel might make your work easier or more enjoyable?

3. You are working part time providing computer support for a veterinarian's office. When you arrive to work one morning, the receptionist informs you that the computer monitor is not displaying anything. List at least three steps you will perform to troubleshoot the problem, and list three possible causes.

4. Explain how a computer represents data. What is the role of an input device? What is the role of an output device? Do you think it is important for the average user to understand how computers represent data? Why or why not?

Apply Your Skills

Celeste Rosa is an office manager at a small graphic design firm with ten employees in Denver, Colorado. In addition to supporting the designers who create professional graphics for large corporations worldwide, Celeste is responsible for maintaining the staff's computers and mobile devices. Each employee is issued a laptop they can bring home to use in telecommuting and a tablet they can use in presenting work to potential and current customers, and all share a variety of printers and projectors.

Working in a small group or by yourself, complete the following:

1. List three types of storage solutions that Celeste should ensure her employees can access. What are the benefits and drawbacks of each? Have you ever run out of storage? How did/could you solve the problem?

2. In addition to a laptop and tablet, and shared printers and projectors, name one input and one output device Celeste should consider for employees to have access. What would be the purpose of these additional devices? How might it benefit employees to have access to them? Which of the ones that you chose would you consider the most important? Why?

3. Celeste wants to help her employees know how to troubleshoot various common issues, but also know how to do so safely and when they should instead call on someone in the technical support department. Describe a common problem and how the employee might solve it on their own. Have you ever had to rely on a professional technical support person to help you with a problem? Did you learn anything useful about your device during the experience?

Operating Systems and File Management

In This Module

- Examine the types of operating systems
- Explain how an operating system works
- Personalize an operating system to increase productivity
- Manage files and folders

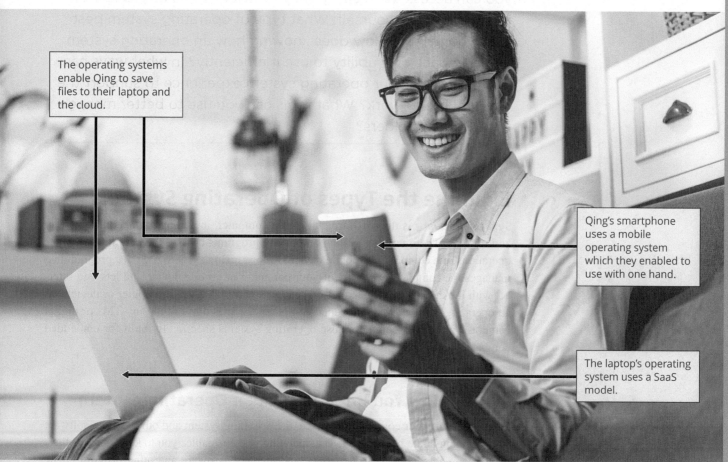

The operating systems enable Qing to save files to their laptop and the cloud.

Qing's smartphone uses a mobile operating system which they enabled to use with one hand.

The laptop's operating system uses a SaaS model.

Art_Photo/Shutterstock.com

Qing Chan has an internship with an accounting firm, which has provided them with a laptop and a smartphone. The laptop runs Microsoft Windows as its operating system and the phone uses the Apple iOS operating system. Qing uses the apps and utilities provided with their devices to share and collaborate on files, send communications, and participate in web conferences. Qing recently made modifications to the operating systems' settings to personalize them so that they can work more efficiently.

The system software on your computer or device, including the operating system, determines how your device runs and how you interact with it. Most computers and devices come preloaded with system software. Some factors that affect an operating system's capabilities include the time in which it responds to your instructions, its reliability, the tools available to enable you to work productively and efficiently, and how and where you store your files.

In this module, you will learn about different types of operating systems and compare options of each type. You will begin to understand how an operating system works to help your computer or device function. You will explore methods to personalize your operating system and program settings to increase your productivity. Lastly, you will learn how to manage the files and folders you store on your computer or device so that you can access them easily. As you reflect on what you learn in this module, ask yourself: What type of operating system best suits your needs? How does knowing how an operating system works impact your ability to use it efficiently? In what ways can you customize your operating system experience to support the way you like to work? What tools can you use to better manage your files and folders?

Examine the Types of Operating Systems

System software is the software that runs a computer, including the operating system and utilities. The operating system and utility programs control the behind-the-scenes operations of a computer or mobile device. An **operating system (OS)** is a program that manages the complete operation of your computer or mobile device and lets you interact with it. An operating system also is called a platform. Every computer or device has an operating system, even embedded computers such as those found in ATMs or digital cameras. Embedded computers use operating systems specifically built for embedded computers.

Explain How You Interact with an Operating System

When you start your computer or device, the operating system and other system software starts running in the background. The operating system enables you to keep track of files, print documents, connect to networks, and manage hardware and other programs. The operating system is critical to using your computer or device; without the operating system, the computer or device cannot function. Most programs and apps you run on your computer come in versions specific to your operating system and are optimized to take advantage of the operating system's features.

Suppose you are writing a report and want to save the document to your hard drive. **Figure 4-1** lists the steps the operating system takes to enable you to perform this task.

Figure 4-1: Interacting with the operating system

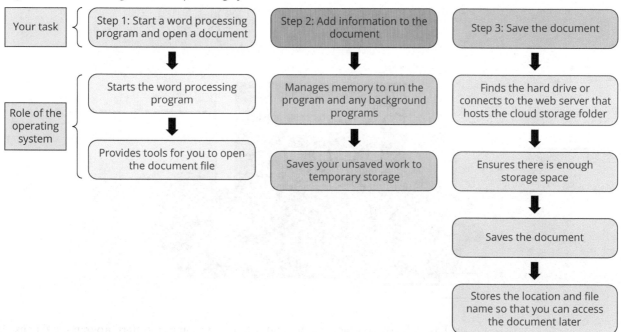

Operating System Features   One of the main roles of an operating system is to provide a way for you to interact with your computer. An operating system provides a **graphical user interface (GUI)**, which is a collective term for all the ways you interact with the device; a GUI controls how you interact with menus, programs and apps, and visual images such as icons by touching, pointing, tapping, or clicking buttons and other objects to issue commands.

A **natural user interface (NUI)** is a GUI interface that enables you to train it to respond to your gestures and voice commands. As you continue to work with a NUI, it learns more about you and enables you to improve efficiency and perform more complex tasks. NUIs are especially helpful to those who require assistive technologies that do not require either a pointing device and/or a keyboard.

The main workspace of an operating system is called the **desktop** or, for mobile devices, **home screen** (**Figure 4-2**). This area contains icons for programs and files, as

Figure 4-2: The main workspace of an operating system

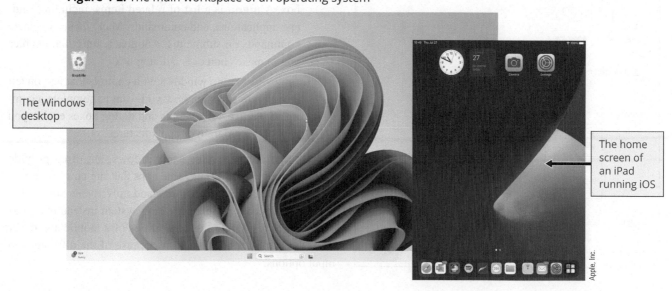

The Windows desktop

The home screen of an iPad running iOS

Apple, Inc.

Figure 4-3: GUI objects

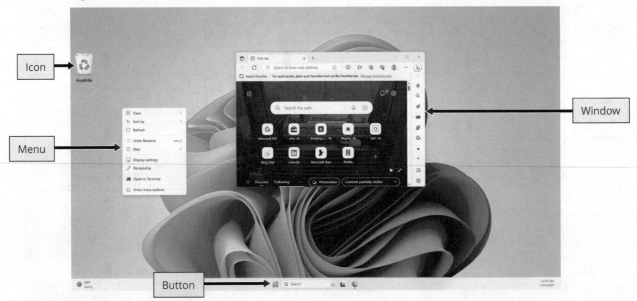

Icon

Menu

Window

Button

well as toolbars, taskbars, menus, and buttons you can use to start programs and apps. A notification area displays the date and time, as well as shortcuts to utilities such as audio controls and network connections.

GUIs use visual objects that you can select by tapping, clicking, or double-clicking to perform tasks or issue commands (**Figure 4-3**). These objects include:

- **Icons**, which are small pictures that represents an app, file, or peripheral device.
- **Buttons**, which are icons you tap or click to execute commands you need to work with an app.
- **Windows**, which are rectangular-shaped work areas that display an app or a collection of files, folders, and tools. Every time you open a new program or file, a new window opens. You can switch between windows to access different information or resources.
- To perform tasks, make selections, or execute commands on a desktop you might use a menu or a dialog box. A **menu** is a list of related items, including folders, applications, and commands. Many menus organize commands on submenus. Another feature that enables you to make choices is a dialog box.
- **Dialog boxes** are windows with controls that let you tell the operating system how you want to complete a command (**Figure 4-4**). Menus and dialog boxes enable you to access a program or app's features.

Figure 4-4: A dialog box

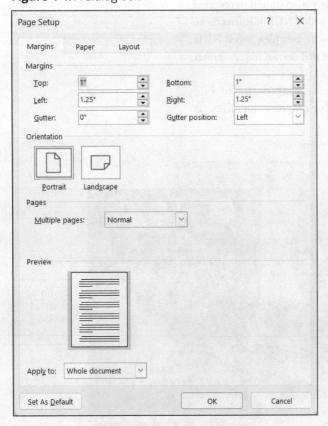

Mobile operating systems use windows, but often provide scaled down versions of the same apps that run on a desktop or laptop computer. Simple gestures and movements are used to perform tasks on a mobile operating system instead of menus or dialog boxes. Often the capabilities of a mobile app differ from those of a desktop version because of the difference in input options.

Classify Operating System Types

Operating systems differ based on the purpose, manufacturer, development method, and form factor of the computer or device. The type of operating system you select or have access to will depend on several factors, including whether it is one you select or if it comes with a computer or device issued by your job or school.

Operating System Models   Operating system names identify the manufacturer and program name, and sometimes specify the purpose, year, or release number. For example, Microsoft Windows is a popular operating system. Microsoft Windows 11 indicates the number assigned to the release of the program, whereas Microsoft Windows Server indicates that the purpose of the version is to provide system software for a server.

Some software manufacturers are doing away with version numbers, and instead offering Software as a Service. **Software as a Service (SaaS)** is software that is distributed online for a monthly subscription or an annual fee (**Figure 4-5**). Instead of releasing a new complete version of the program to purchase, the company will provide updates to its subscribers that include fixes for issues or additional functionality. Your tablet or smartphone's operating system likely will update automatically with any changes or fixes, or to the latest version of the operating system compatible with your device.

Closed vs. Open Source   Another classification when choosing an operating system is open vs. closed source. **Closed source** programs keep all or some of the code hidden, enabling developers to control and profit from the program they create. Closed

Figure 4-5: SaaS subscription information

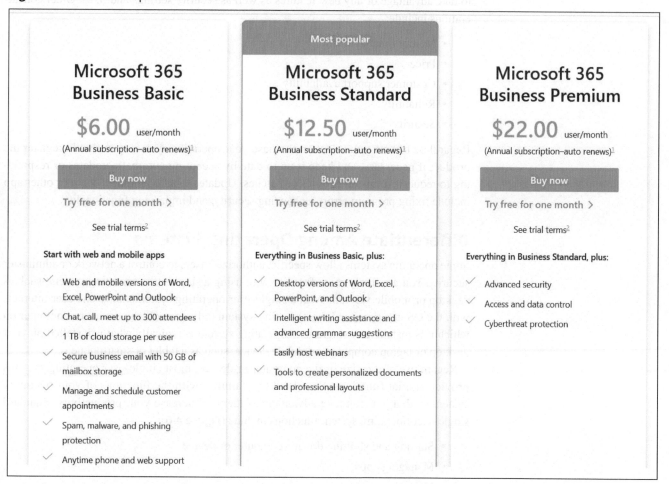

source programs have standard features and can only be customized using the operating system's tools. Microsoft Windows and macOS are examples of closed source operating systems.

Open source programs and apps (including operating systems) have no restrictions from the copyright holder regarding modification and redistribution. Users can add functionality and sell or give away their versions to others. Proponents of open source programs state that because the code is public, coders can examine, correct, and enhance programs. Some have concerns about unscrupulous programmers adding malicious code that can damage a user's system or be used to gather data without the user's knowledge. Unix is an example of an open source operating system.

Select an Operating System

Whether you are choosing an open or closed source operating system, program, or app, be sure to research carefully and read reviews to ensure you are getting the highest quality program.

If you receive a laptop or have access to a computer through your school or workplace, you likely will not have a choice in operating system. If you purchase a computer or device for yourself, you may not have a choice as certain computers and devices only run operating systems designed specifically for the computer or device. You also might want to choose a computer or device because of its operating system.

If you do have a choice when selecting an operating system, compare factors such as available programs and apps, hardware and software support, and security. Determine your needs and priorities to choose the operating system that will help you be productive. Always choose the most updated version of an operating system, or choose a SaaS model, to take advantage of any new features as well as security settings and fixes. Other considerations include:

- Memory management
- Price
- Customer support availability
- Reliability
- Security

Regardless of how you select or purchase your operating system, you should register the product if necessary, and keep it up to date by accepting automatic updates or responding to requests to install updates or patches. Updates to an operating system or other app include fixing program errors, enhancing security, and improving functionality.

Differentiate Among Operating Systems

Some operating systems allow specific, authorized users to control a network or administer security. You are likely more familiar with using a single-user operating system, such as desktop or mobile version. With a single-user operating systems, only one user interacts with the OS at a time, and the operating system only controls the device or computer on which it is installed. A single-user operating system is typically what is installed on your desktop or laptop computer, or mobile device, such as a tablet or smartphone.

Regardless of the size of the computer or device, most single-user operating systems provide similar functions. You should be familiar with the functions of your operating system so that you can take advantage of them to increase your productivity. Standard single-user operating system functions include (**Figure 4-6**):

- Starting and shutting down a computer or device
- Managing apps
- Managing memory

Figure 4-6: Common operating system functions

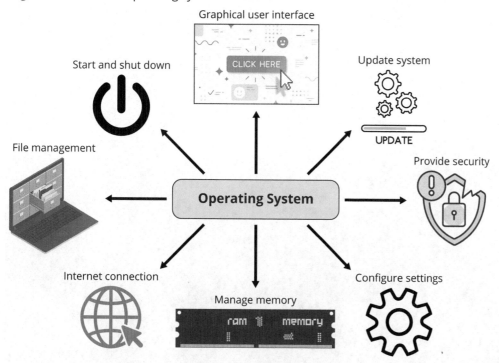

- Coordinating tasks
- Configuring peripheral devices
- Establishing an Internet connection
- Monitoring performance
- Providing file management
- Updating operating system software
- Monitoring security
- Controlling network access

Operating systems also provide **utilities**, apps or programs that enable you to perform maintenance-type tasks related to managing the computer or device (**Figure 4-7**). The tools you use to manage files, search for content or programs, view images, install and uninstall programs and apps, compress and back up files, secure your device, and maintain the computer or device are all utilities.

Desktop Operating Systems An operating system installed on a single laptop or desktop computer is called a **desktop operating system** or a **PC (personal computer) operating system**. Most are single-user operating systems. Examples include Microsoft Windows and Apple's macOS (**Figure 4-8**). Other operating systems include:

- UNIX, a multitasking operating system with many versions, as the code is licensed to different developers.

Figure 4-7: Utilities can help manage storage and other functions

System › Storage › **Storage Sense**

Cleanup of temporary files

☑ Keep Windows running smoothly by automatically cleaning up temporary system and app files

Automatic User content cleanup

◯ On

Storage Sense runs when disk space is low. We clean up enough space to help your system run its best. We cleaned up 0 bytes of space in the past month.

Configure cleanup schedules

Run Storage Sense

During low free disk space (default)   ⌄

Delete files in my recycle bin if they have been there for over:

30 days (default)   ⌄

Delete files in my Downloads folder if they haven't been opened for more than:

Never (default)   ⌄

Locally available cloud content

Storage Sense can free up space by removing unused cloud-backed content from your device.

Content flagged as "Always keep on this device" will not be affected.

Click here for more information

Figure 4-8: macOS desktop operating system

Apple, Inc.

Figure 4-9: Android mobile operating system

Google LLC

- Linux, which is distributed under the terms of a General Public License (GPL), which allows you to copy the OS for your own use, to give to others, or to sell.
- ChromeOS, which is based on Linux, uses the Google Chrome browser as its user interface, and primarily runs web apps.

Mobile Operating Systems   Smartphones, tablets, and other mobile devices use a mobile operating system (**Figure 4-9**). A **mobile operating system** has features similar to those of a desktop operating system but is focused on the needs of a mobile user and the capabilities of the device. A mobile operating system, often referred to as a mobile OS, works especially well with mobile device features such as touchscreens, voice recognition, and Wi-Fi networks. They also are designed to run using the limited memory of most mobile devices, and to optimize the display for smaller screen sizes. They are programmed to manage tools common to mobile devices, including video and photo cameras, media players, speech recognition, GPS, wireless capabilities, rotating screen displays that adjust when you switch orientation of your device's screen, and text messaging. **Table 4-1** describes popular mobile operating systems.

Server Operating Systems   A **server operating system** is a multiuser operating system because it controls a single, centralized server computer that supports many users on networked computers. A server operating system manages the network. It also controls access to network resources, such as network printers. Web servers are Internet computers that store webpages and deliver them to your computer or device.

Table 4-1: Mobile operating systems

OS	Notable features
Android	Developed by Google based on Linux, and designed to be run on many types of smartphones and tablets.
iOS	Runs only on Apple devices, including the iPhone and iPad; derived from macOS. Apple watches run ApplewatchOS.

Table 4-2: Server operating systems

OS	Notable features
Windows Server	The server version of Windows. It includes advanced security tools and a set of programs called Internet Information Services that manage web apps and services.
macOS Server	Supports all sizes of networks and servers. One unique feature is that it lets authorized users access servers using their iPhones or other Apple devices.
UNIX	A multipurpose operating system that can run on a desktop PC or a server. Many web servers use UNIX because it is a powerful, flexible operating system

Although desktop operating systems include network capability, server operating systems are designed specifically to support all sizes of networks. Many also enable virtualization. **Virtualization** is the practice of sharing computing resources, such as servers or storage devices, among computers and devices on a network. Virtualization supports green computing initiatives because it limits the number of machines required, thereby reducing e-waste, emissions, and the environmental impacts of producing multiple machines.

Although you may not realize it, you take advantage of a server operating system whenever you download mail or files, access networked resources such as a printer or database, or access information on the web. When you instruct your computer or device to do those tasks, the computer or device interacts with a server and its operating system to complete the request. Unless you are a network administrator, you likely will not directly interact with a server operating system, but you should be familiar with its capabilities. **Table 4-2** lists popular server operating systems.

Explain How an Operating System Works

An operating system takes care of the technical tasks of running the computer or device so that you can work on school or professional projects, watch videos, connect with friends, or play games. Operating systems process data, manage memory, control hardware, and provide a user interface. You interact with the operating system to start programs, manage files and folders, get help, and customize the user interface. The operating system is critical to the start process of the computer or device.

Explain the Role of an Operating System

When you enter instructions and data, your computer or device coordinates the resources and activities to process them and then provides information from the system back to you. The operating system also manages interactions between hardware and software. For example, if you want to print a flyer you created in your word processing program, the operating system establishes a connection to the printer, sends the flyer document to the printer, and lets other software know the printer is busy until it finishes printing the flyer. During this process, the operating system directs internal components such as the processor, RAM, and storage space to manage and complete its task.

Files and Folders   A **file** is a collection of information stored on your computer, such as a text document, spreadsheet, photo, or song. You use an operating system to manage files. Files can be divided into two categories: data and executable. A **data file** contains words, numbers, and pictures that you can manipulate. For example, a spreadsheet, a database, a presentation, and a word processing document all are data files. Graphic and media files also are data files. An **executable file** contains the instructions your computer or device needs to run programs and apps. Unlike a data file, you cannot open and read an executable file. You run it to perform a task, such as opening a program or app.

Files are stored in folders. A **folder** is a named location on a storage medium that usually contains related documents. You name the folder so that you know what it contains, and in the folder you store related files. An operating system comes with tools to manage files and folders. These tools allow you to create new, named folders; choose the location of folders; move files between folders; and create a folder hierarchy that includes subfolders (**Figure 4-10**). The term subfolder refers to a folder that is inside another folder. Every file you save will have a destination folder—by choosing the correct folder, or adding new folders, you can help keep your files accessible and organized.

A **library** is a special folder that catalogs specific files and folders in a central location, regardless of where the items are actually stored on your device. Library files might include pictures, music, documents, and videos. Your operating system most likely comes with a few libraries. You can customize your libraries to add additional folders, and include

Figure 4-10: Creating a folder hierarchy helps keep files organized

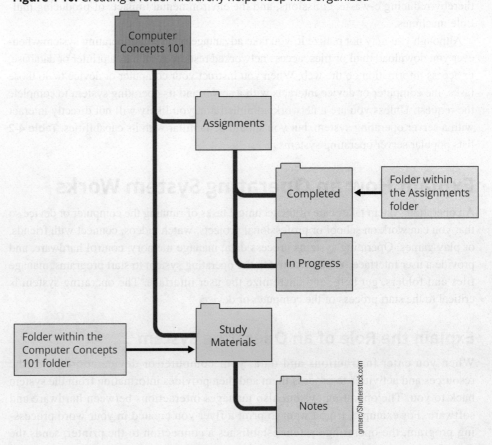

grmarc/Shutterstock.com

Table 4-3: Common file extensions

File type	Extensions
Microsoft Office	.docx (Word), .xlsx (Excel), .pptx (PowerPoint)
Text file	.txt, .rtf
Webpage	.htm or .html, .xml, .asp or .aspx, .css
Graphics	.jpg, .png, .tif

files from the Internet or a network. Libraries are helpful to find all files of a certain type, no matter where they are located on your computer or device. Windows computers use libraries, but mobile devices typically do not.

File format refers to the organization and layout of data in a file. The file format determines the type or types of programs and apps that you can use to open and display or work with a file. Some files only can be opened in the program with which they were created. Others, such as graphics files, can be opened in multiple programs or apps. A file extension is three- or four-letter sequence, preceded by a period, at the end of a file name that identifies the file as a particular type of document, such as .docx (Microsoft Word document), or .jpg (a type of graphic file). When you save a file, the program or app assigns the file extension. **Table 4-3** shows some common file extensions by file type.

Describe How an Operating System Manages Memory

The purpose of memory management is to optimize the use of a computer or device's internal memory to allow the computer or device to run more efficiently. Memory consists of electronic components that store instructions waiting to be executed by the processor, data needed by those instructions, and the results of processing the data into information.

The operating system uses RAM to temporarily store open apps and document data while they are being processed. It carefully monitors the contents of memory, and releases items when the processor no longer requires them. Frequently used instructions and data are stored in the temporary storage area designed to help speed up processing time, called a cache.

Every program or app, including the operating system, requires RAM. The more RAM a device has, the more efficiently it runs. If several programs or apps are running simultaneously, your computer or device might use up its available RAM. When this happens, the computer or device may run slowly.

The operating system can allocate a portion of a storage medium, such as a hard disk, to become virtual memory to function as additional RAM. Virtual memory temporarily stores data in an area of the hard drive called the swap file until it can be swapped into RAM. Because a page is the amount of data and program instructions the operating system can swap at a given time, the technique of swapping items between memory and storage is called paging. Paging is time consuming. When an operating system spends more of its time paging instead of executing apps, the whole system slows down and it is said to be thrashing. You may be able to adjust the settings on your operating system to free up virtual memory in order to enable your computer or device to run more quickly.

List Steps in the Boot Process

To start an operating system, you simply turn on the computer or device. Before you can interact with the operating system, the computer or device goes through the **boot process**, which triggers a series of steps and checks as the computer loads the operating system. The boot process includes the following steps:

1. The computer or device receives power from the power supply or battery and sends it to the circuitry.

2. The processor begins to run the bootstrap program, which is a special built-in startup program.

3. The **bootstrap program** executes a series of tests to check the components, including the RAM, input devices, and storage, and identifies connected devices and networks and checks their settings.

4. Once the tests are completed successfully, the computer or device loads the operating system files into RAM, including the kernel. The **kernel** is the core of an operating system, which manages memory, runs programs, and assigns resources.

5. The computer or device loads the system configuration information, prompts you for user verification if necessary, establishes connections with networks and peripheral devices, and loads all startup programs, such as antivirus programs or apps.

The boot process starts automatically when you turn on your computer or device. You cannot use the computer or device until the boot process is complete. Depending on your operating system, you may be able to customize your settings to instruct that certain programs or apps you frequently use be started at the same time as your operating system.

If a computer or device is slow in accepting or providing input or output, the operating system uses buffers. A **buffer** is an area of memory that stores data and information waiting to be sent to an input or output device. Placing data into a buffer is called **spooling**. An example of spooling is when a document is sent to the buffer while it waits for the printer to be available. By sending data to a buffer, the operating system frees up resources to perform other tasks while the data waits to be processed. While the buffer and cache may both serve the purpose of freeing up RAM, a buffer typically is used for input and output processes, while a cache is used when reading and writing from the disk.

Personalize an Operating System to Increase Productivity

When you start using a computer or device, the operating system and related software and hardware have default settings. **Default settings** are standard settings that control how the screen is set up and how a document looks when you first start typing. As you continue to work with your computer or device, you may decide to customize the settings to be more productive.

Customize an Operating System

Every operating system has its own tools for customization. Operating systems allow you to make adjustments such as:

- Changing the brightness of the screen
- Adding a desktop theme, which is a predefined set of elements such as background images and colors
- Adjusting the screen resolution, which controls how much content you can see on a screen without scrolling
- Adding a sound scheme, which associates sounds such as a bell chime with an event, such as closing a window or receiving a message

Figure 4-11: Windows Settings dialog box

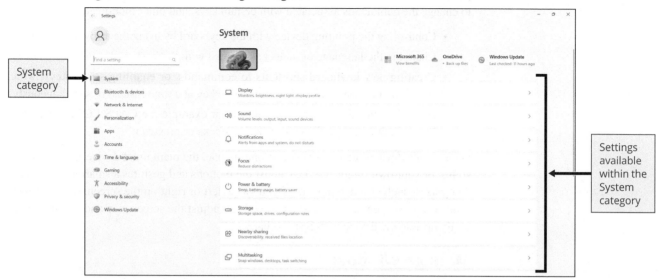

- Adjusting or silencing the volume of media playback and/or notifications
- Pinning frequently used apps to the taskbar or home screen for easy access
- Selecting items to appear in the Notification area

You also can use these tools to link your devices and computers to each other and to networks and peripheral devices, uninstall apps, add accounts, manage your network connections, and adjust privacy settings.

On a Windows computer, you use the Settings dialog box. To open the Settings dialog box, click the Start button on the Windows taskbar, and then click the Settings icon. In the Windows Settings dialog box (**Figure 4-11**), click an option to access further options. For example, if you click System, you can adjust settings such as the display, sounds, power, battery, storage, and more.

You also can customize the desktop on a computer by moving the taskbar or other items, creating and organizing icons and folders for apps and files, and more. In addition, you can create links to files and apps called **shortcuts**. Shortcuts do not place the actual file, folder, or app on the desktop—the object remains in the location where it is saved on your computer or device. A short-cut merely allows you to access the object from the desktop without going through a file manager or a program menu such as the Start menu.

Access to settings on a mobile device differs depending on the device. For instance, on an Android smartphone, you swipe down from the top of the screen, then tap the Settings button to open the Settings screen (**Figure 4-12**).

Customize Hardware Using System Software

Pointing devices let you interact with your computer by controlling the movement of the pointer on your screen; examples include a mouse, trackball, touchpad, or for touch-enabled devices, a stylus or your finger. You can change the settings of your pointing device. For example, you can switch the mouse buttons if you are left-handed, or adjust the sensitivity of your touchpad.

On a desktop computer or laptop, the keyboard is the main input device. The keyboard contains not only characters such as letters, numbers, and

Figure 4-12: Settings window on an Android smartphone

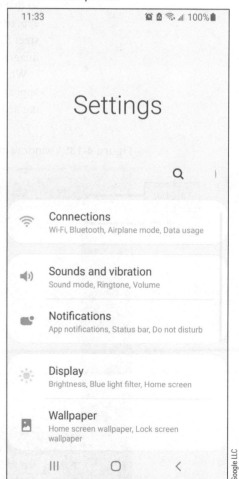

punctuation, but also keys that can issue commands. You can adjust the keyboard settings to change the commands associated with certain keys, and other modifications, including:

- Controlling the pointing device with the keyboard by using the arrow and other keys
- Changing the language or dialect associated with the keyboard
- Creating new keyboard shortcuts to commands, or enabling sticky keys, which allow you to press keyboard shortcuts one key at a time instead of simultaneously
- Adjusting the settings for toggle keys, for example the CAPS LOCK key, which turn a feature on or off each time a user clicks or presses it

On a mobile device, such as a tablet or smartphone, the main input device is a digital pen, stylus, or your own finger. You can adjust the motions and gestures a smartphone or tablet recognizes, such as what happens if you swipe left or right on the screen, using a fingerprint sensor to open or close apps, and you can adjust the screen size and layout to more easily operate the device with just one hand.

Manage Windows

When you open an app, file, or folder, it appears in a window. Most windows share common elements: the center area of the window displays its contents, and a title bar at the top displays the name of the app, file, or folder (**Figure 4-13**). When there is more information than fits on the screen, vertical and horizontal scroll bars appear that you drag to display contents currently out of view.

On a desktop or laptop computer, a **Maximize button** and **Minimize button** on the title bar enables you to expand a window so that it fills the entire screen or reduce a window so that it only appears as an icon on the taskbar. A **Close button** closes the open window, app, or document. The **Restore Down button** reduces a window to its last non-maximized size. Some windows include a ribbon, toolbar, or menu bar that contains text, icons, or images you select to perform actions and make selections.

When you have multiple windows, files, and apps open at a time, the windows can appear side-by-side or stacked. Most mobile devices only display stacked windows, with the active window in the foreground and maximized to fit the screen. The **active window**

Figure 4-13: A window in macOS

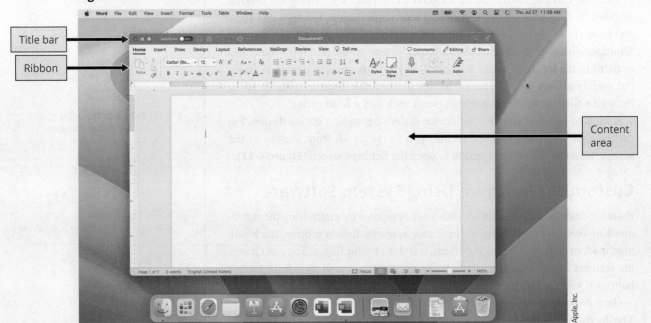

Title bar

Ribbon

Content area

Apple, Inc.

Figure 4-14: Apple Dock

Apple, Inc.

is the window you are currently using, which appears in front of any other open windows. The steps to switch between windows depends on the type of device or operating system you are running.

- On a mobile device, you might have a button near the Home button that displays all open windows in a stack. When you select it, it displays the stack of open windows and apps. You can select a window to make it the active window, close individual windows, or close all open windows.

- On a computer, you can click an icon on the Windows taskbar or the Dock on the macOS desktop (**Figure 4-14**). You also can use keyboard shortcuts to cycle through thumbnails of open windows. If multiple windows are open and visible on the screen, you can click in each desired window as needed to switch or toggle between one and another.

There are two types of windows: a **program window** displays a running program; a **folder window** displays the contents of a folder, drive, or device. To start a Windows program, you click the Start button on the taskbar, and then click the program name. To start a Mac program, click the Launchpad (rocket) icon on the dock, then click the app icon. Or, for either Mac or Windows, you can click a shortcut to the app on the desktop. To open a folder window, open your system's folder management tool, such as File Explorer or Finder, and then navigate to the folder you want. To close any type of window, tap or click its Close button. To open a window on a mobile device, you click its icon on the screen. You can arrange your apps on a mobile device into folders by category so that you can easily find your games, travel apps, and other app types.

You can rearrange windows on a computer's desktop to work effectively and to access other items on the desktop. To move a window, point to its title bar, and then drag the window to its new location. To resize a window to display more or less of its content, point to a border or corner of the window, then drag the resizing pointer to make it smaller or larger. Windows and other desktop operating systems allow you to drag a window to the left or right side of the screen, where it "snaps" to fill that half of the screen and displays remaining open windows as thumbnails you can click to fill the other half of the screen. Mobile device windows tend to take up the full screen.

Use Administrative Tools

An operating system controls the **resources** of a device, which are the components required to perform work, such as the processor, RAM, storage space, and connections to other devices and networks. The operating system tracks the names and locations of files, as well as empty storage areas where you can save new files. It alerts you if it detects a resource problem, such as too many programs or apps are open for the memory to handle, or the printer is not turned on, or if your hard drive is out of space. To manage RAM resources, an operating system keeps track of the apps, processes, and other tasks the system performs. Microsoft Windows, for example, displays this information

Figure 4-15: Windows Task Manager dialog box

				8%	64%	3%	0%
Task Manager		Type a name, publisher, or PID to search					
Processes			Run new task / End task / Efficiency mode ⋯				
Name		Status		CPU	Memory	Disk	Network
Apps (6)							
> Microsoft Edge (11)				6.1%	311.9 MB	0.1 MB/s	0.1 Mbps
> Microsoft Outlook (8)				0.9%	257.9 MB	0.1 MB/s	0 Mbps
> Microsoft Word (4)				0%	205.2 MB	0 MB/s	0 Mbps
> Settings				0%	38.5 MB	0 MB/s	0 Mbps
> Task Manager				0.2%	80.9 MB	0 MB/s	0 Mbps
> Windows Explorer				0%	145.8 MB	0 MB/s	0 Mbps
Background processes (133)							
Acrobat Collaboration Synchr...				0%	2.0 MB	0 MB/s	0 Mbps
Acrobat Collaboration Synchr...				0%	0.8 MB	0 MB/s	0 Mbps
> Acrobat Update Service (32 bit)				0%	0.3 MB	0 MB/s	0 Mbps
Adobe Content Synchronizer (...				0%	15.2 MB	0.1 MB/s	0 Mbps
> Adobe Genuine Software Mon...				0%	0.5 MB	0 MB/s	0 Mbps
Application Frame Host				0%	7.8 MB	0 MB/s	0 Mbps
> Background Task Host (2)				0%	6.3 MB	0 MB/s	0 Mbps

Side menu: ☰, Processes, Performance, App history, Startup apps, Users, Details, Services, Settings

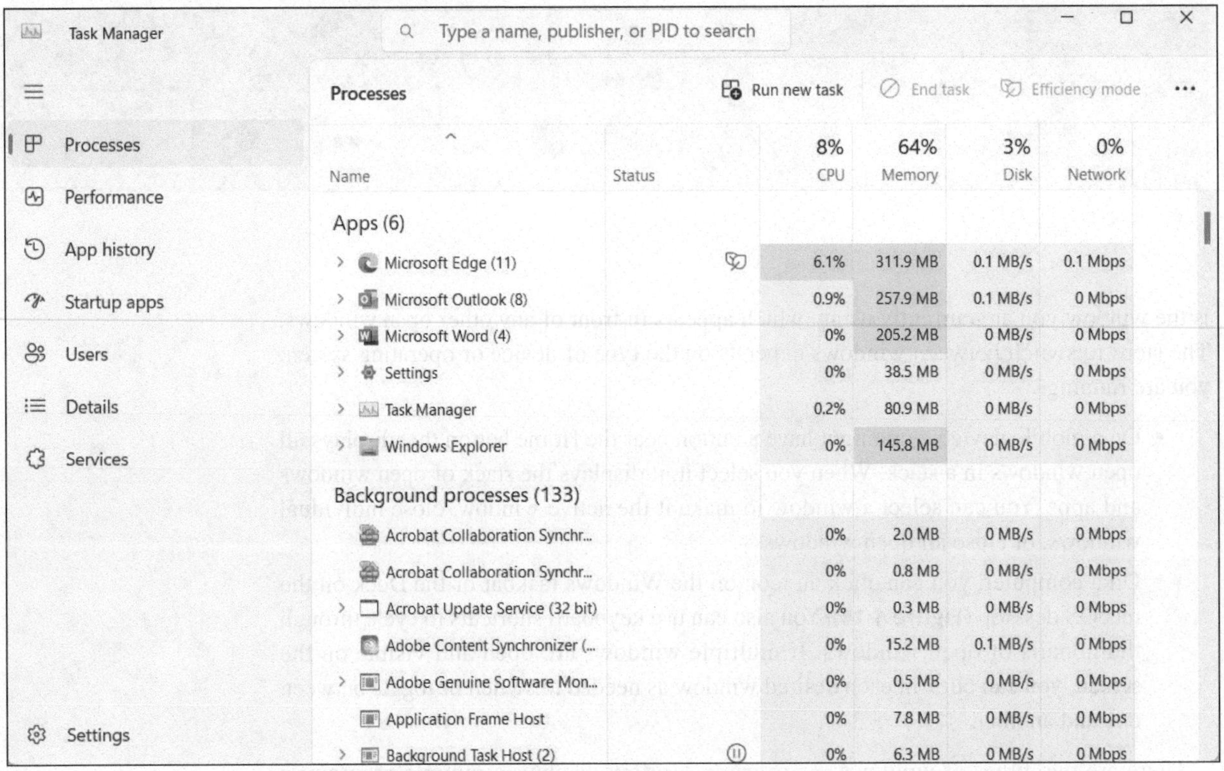

in the Windows Task Manager dialog box (**Figure 4-15**). You can open your computer or device's version of the task manager to view running programs and see the percentage of RAM being used. You can shut down programs and apps in the task manager to free up RAM.

Utilities Regardless of the operating system you're using, if your computer starts to slow down or act erratically, you can use a utility to diagnose and repair the problem. A common solution is to use a cleanup utility that archives files by backing up infrequently used or older files to the cloud, and then deletes them from the computer or device. Some cleanup utilities will remove files that the system determines are no longer needed, such as old website cookies or files related to the operation of an uninstalled program.

The Recycle Bin, or Trash folder, is another type of disk utility. This folder stores files you designate to be deleted. When you move a file to the Recycle Bin or Trash, it still takes up storage space, but no longer appears in the folder or location where it was created. The file only is permanently deleted when you empty the folder or run a cleanup utility. To avoid wasting time searching for files you have saved, or to manage file locations and sizes, you can use file utilities. A file management tool gives you an overview of stored files and lets you open, rename, delete, move, and copy files and folders. A search tool finds files that meet criteria you specify, such as characters in a file name, or the saved date.

Adjust Power Settings

You may keep your computer or device running constantly, or you may choose to shut it down, either to save power or prevent it from being shut down suddenly and unexpectedly, such as by a thunderstorm (if connected to a power source that uses an electrical outlet) or battery issue. Operating systems provide shut-down options so that you can close programs and processes properly. You can instruct the device to completely shut down, which turns off the power, and may close any open files or apps. Some operating systems have a Sleep option to use low power instead of shutting down. Sleep stores the current state of open programs and files, saving you time when you resume using your device.

Since you tend to keep your desktop computer or laptop plugged in while in use, battery life is a bigger concern with mobile devices. You can switch to a low power mode, which limits data usage, dims the screen brightness, and makes other adjustments to slow down battery usage. You also can purchase a portable charger you can plug in with a USB cord to charge your device, use a wireless charging station, or use a replacement battery to switch when your battery power gets low.

Run More than One Operating System

A **virtual machine (VM)** enables a computer or device to run another operating system in addition to the one installed. You might want to enable a virtual machine if you have an app that is incompatible with your current operating system, or to run multiple operating systems on one computer. To run a virtual machine, you need a program or app that is specifically designed to set up and manage virtual machines (**Figure 4-16**). You also will need access to installation files for the operating system you want to run on the virtual machine.

The virtual machine runs separately in a section of the hard disk that functions like a separate disk, called a **partition** or a **volume**. You can only access one partition of a hard disk at a time. To use the virtual machine, you need to perform the following steps:

1. Run the virtual machine software.
2. Select the virtual machine you want to run.
3. Click the button to run the virtual machine.
4. When you are finished using the virtual machine, shut down the operating system similarly to how you would shut down your computer.
5. Exit the virtual machine software.

With many companies allowing or requiring employees to work remotely, virtualization, such as use of VMs, has increased dramatically. Companies may enable temporary or contract employees to set up a VM on their own device, which incorporates greater security than the user's device might normally use. In addition, if VMs are set up for a specific

Figure 4-16: Windows VM running on macOS

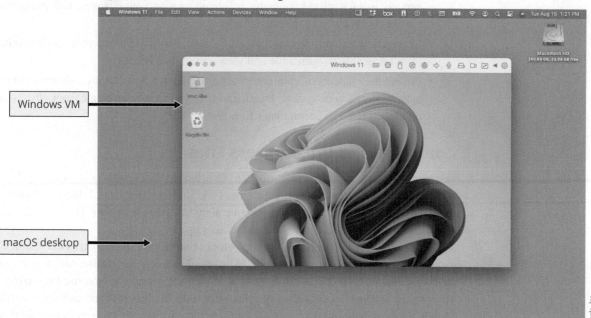

Windows VM

macOS desktop

Apple, Inc.

purpose, such as a project, and then abandoned, the VM should be removed so as not to crowd the servers with unnecessary resources. VM management software can track access, permissions, and activity on a VM.

Manage User Accounts

User accounts identify the resources, such as apps and storage locations, a user can access when working with the computer. User accounts protect your computer against unauthorized access. A user account includes information such as the user name or ID, and a password. You can set preferences for each user account on your computer or device, as well as set permissions to certain folders or files. A standard user account is designed for the everyday user, who will be using the computer or device for work or recreation. An administrator account provides full access to the computer. Additional responsibilities associated with an administrator account include installing programs and apps, adjusting security settings, and managing network access. On a computer you use at your home, you likely will not have a separate administrator account—the main user account will have administrator capabilities. On a networked computer, such as at your school or workplace, you will not have access to the administrator account.

Manage Files and Folders

There are many ways to manage files and folders on your computer or device. You can change or view the properties of a file, compress a file to save storage space, move or rename a file or folder, and more.

Protect Files

Whether you are working on a presentation for a school assignment, keeping a journal, or tracking your budget in a spreadsheet, you do not want to lose the information in your files. Guidelines for protecting your files and folders include:

- Saving them to a cloud folder and regularly backing up. A cloud folder likely has regular backup and encryption, and, unlike your hard drive, is not as susceptible to loss due to physical damage.
- When you are planning to make major changes to a file, consider saving it as a new version, using a related file name, before attempting your changes. This preserves a version to which you can revisit if necessary.
- Encrypt or password-protect files and folders. This will prevent unauthorized others from being able to open a file and view or edit its contents.
- Protect the contents of your computer or device from malicious code by installing apps that scan your system, email, and files you receive or create from viruses and other apps that can corrupt your files and system.

Compress and Uncompress Files

File size is usually measured in kilobytes (KB) (thousands of bytes of data), megabytes (MB) (millions of bytes of data), gigabytes (GB) (billions of bytes of data), or terabytes (trillions of bytes of data; a terabyte is equivalent to 1,000 gigabytes). The more data, the larger the file and the more storage space it takes up.

You often need to compress files and folders before you share or transfer them. For example, by attaching a compressed file to an email message the smaller file travels faster to its destination. Before you can open and edit a compressed file, you need to extract or uncompress it. Desktop operating systems offer tools to compress and uncompress files. Mobile operating systems do not always include these by default, but you can install them.

To compress a file or folder, select it in your operating system's file management tool, and then instruct the tool to zip or compress the file. To uncompress, double-click the file in the file management tool, and either drag selected files to another folder, or instruct the tool to extract all files into a new folder.

Save Files and Folders to File Systems

The first time you save a file, you need to name it. On a computer running a locally installed version of an app, instructing the computer to save a new file opens a Save As dialog box or screen, depending on the program or app. Save As includes controls that let you specify where to store the file, and what file name to use. Navigate to the correct folder on your computer or device, or to another location such as a flash drive or cloud folder. Type the file name, select the file extension if necessary, and then click Save. You then should frequently use the save command to save any changes, or enable the AutoSave feature. If using a web app, such as Microsoft Office 365 or Google Docs, your file is automatically saved once you start it, but you still will need to name it. Any changes you make as you work on a file using a web app automatically are saved.

Besides saving files to your hard drive or on a flash drive, you can save them in the cloud. The cloud is a storage area located on a server that you access through the Internet or a network. You can upload files to cloud storage to share them with others or to back up your files to a secure, offsite location. You can access files stored on the cloud from any device connected to the Internet. To access a cloud storage location, you may need to download an app, or create an account. Popular cloud storage apps include Dropbox, Microsoft OneDrive, Google Drive, and iCloud. You can save a file to OneDrive from within any Microsoft Office program if you have the required permissions.

Determine File Properties

Every file has properties such as its name, type, location, and size (**Figure 4-17**). File properties also include the dates when the file was created, modified, and last accessed. The modified date is useful if you have several versions of a file and want to identify

Figure 4-17: File properties

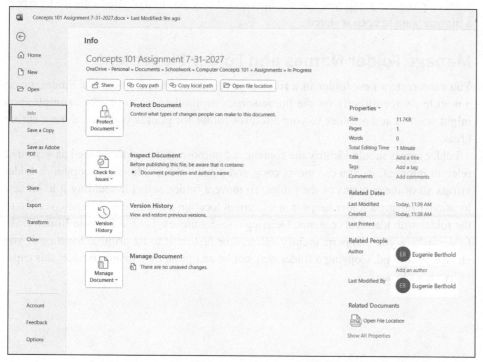

the most recent version. The operating system assigns some properties to files, such as type or format, and updates other properties, such as date, size, and location. Some file types have unique properties. For example, an image might contain information about the dimensions (size) of the image, while a song or media file might include the artist(s) names.

You can view a file's properties to determine information not shown in the file manager, such as the original creation date, the program used to create the file, and more.

Manage File Names and File Placement

Every file has a name. Most file names contain an extension that tells something about its contents, such as the type of platform or app on which the file can be used. File name extensions are added automatically when you save a file, but you can change the extension in some cases.

While you can have many files on your computer or device that have the same name, each folder can only include one file with the same name of the same type. To differentiate a version of a file without overwriting the original, you could add additional characters such as numbers, the date, or the initials of the person who modified the file.

You should be specific when naming files to clearly identify the contents of each, to make them easier to find and organize. A file name should identify the content and purpose of the file, as well as any other information, such as whether the file is a draft or final. For instance, a specific file name such as Q1_Budget_For_Review_Draft-1 is more specific than Budget.

If you want to copy or move files from one location to another, you must first select the files. You can select them from a file management tool, the desktop, or another location. You can select multiple files at once, or just a single file. You also can drag files and folders between or within file management tool windows.

You open a saved file using the same techniques as when saving the file, except you use a different dialog box or window. To open a file, you must first find its location. You can locate a file in Windows using File Explorer, or the Finder in macOS. On a mobile device, you can use the search tool if you are unsure of in which folder the file is stored. From within a program or app, you can use the Open dialog box to navigate to the folder where a file you want to open is stored.

Manage Folder Names and Folder Placement

You can create a new folder in a file manager such as File Explorer or Finder, or on a mobile device directly on the home screen or another location. For example, you might want to add a folder to your Pictures folder for photos you took during spring break.

Folder names should identify the content and purpose of the folder, as well as any other relevant information. You can move, copy, and delete folders. Moving or copying a folder affects all of the contents of the folder. To move a folder, select it and drag it to its new location. Copying a folder keeps it in its current location and also creates a new version of the folder with identical contents. Deleting a folder moves it to the Recycle Bin or Trash folder, where you can permanently delete it or restore it to its original location if you change your mind. Copying a folder may not be an option on a mobile device; this capability varies by app.

Module 4 Summary

The system software on your computer or device, which includes the operating system, determines how your device runs and how you interact with it. Every computer has an operating system, also called a platform, that manages its operations and allows you to interact with it. Your operating system will have a GUI (or possibly a NUI) that includes visual objects, such as buttons or icons, that you click or tap to select options, or issue commands.

Operating systems often are offered using SaaS subscription models that automatically provide access to updates and fixes. An operating system's code may be closed or open, depending on whether the manufacturer enables others to access, modify, and distribute versions of the system. Windows and macOS are examples of closed source operating systems. Desktop and mobile operating systems are single-user systems that enable the computer or device's user to start and shut down the computer or device, manage apps and memory, coordinate tasks, configure peripheral devices, establish an Internet connection, monitor performance, manage files, update system software, monitor security, and control network access. A server operating system is a multiuser system that controls a single computer that supports others on a network. Some server operating systems enable virtualization, which is the practice of sharing computing resources.

The operating system coordinates interactions between hardware and software. Files include data files such as text documents and photos, as well as executable files. The operating system can manage your files and help you store them in folders or libraries to keep them organized so that you can find them. Every program or app, including the operating system, requires RAM. The operating system manages memory and uses RAM to temporarily store open apps and data while they are being processed. It also uses processes such as buffering, spooling, and swapping to efficiently use

memory. When you start your computer or device, it goes through a boot process that loads the operating system using the bootstrap program to load the kernel and other operating system files.

You can customize your operating system to meet your needs by changing how the screen is set up, adjusting the screen brightness or resolution, adding a theme or sound scheme, and pinning or creating shortcuts to items to the taskbar or home screen. You also can configure input devices to change commands for keys on a keyboard, or to use a mobile device with one hand.

Administrative tools help you manage resources. Adjusting your power settings can help you manage the power and battery charge efficiently. Utilities help you with a variety of maintenance-type tasks, such as diagnosing and repairing problems, cleaning up your disk, and restoring deleted files or folders. Using a virtual machine enables you to run more than one operating system on a computer or device. You also can use the operating system to set up and manage user accounts for multiple users on a device.

You can manage files and folders using your operating system. Protecting files by storing them safely and using password protection can help prevent loss or unauthorized access. Compressing the file size reduces the storage space that it takes up, making it easier to store, share, or transfer. You can save your files to folders and file systems in order to keep them organized. Determining the file properties helps you identify the name, type, location, and size, as well as when the file was created, modified, or accessed. A file name contains an extension that tells the platform or app on which the file can be used. File and folder names should be specific to the contents and purpose of the item. Folders and files can be copied or moved or placed in the Recycle Bin or Trash folder.

Review Questions

1. A GUI controls the _____ of an operating system.

   a. memory

   b. interface

   c. boot process

   d. type

2. The practice of sharing computing resources among multiple computers or devices is called _____.

   a. virtualization

   b. spooling

   c. utilizing

   d. buffering

3. (True or False) A data file contains the instructions your computer or device needs to run programs and apps.

4. The core of an operating system is its _____ .

   a. source code

   b. kernel

   c. nugget

   d. executable file

5. Standard settings that control how the screen is set up are called _____ settings.

   a. typical
   b. average
   c. normal
   d. default

6. An operating system controls the components required to perform work, called the _____.

   a. resources
   b. functions
   c. settings
   d. devices

7. (True or False) When you move a file to the Recycle Bin or Trash, it still takes up storage space, but no longer appears in the folder or location where it was created.

8. The separate hard disk space on which a virtual machine functions is called a(n) _____.

   a. buffer
   b. partition
   c. external hard disk
   d. cloud folder

9. The user account that provides full access to the computer is called a(n) _____ account.

   a. standard user
   b. administrator
   c. controller
   d. default

10. Which of the following units measure billions of bytes of data?

    a. Kilobytes
    b. Megabytes
    c. Gigabytes
    d. Terabytes

11. Microsoft Office 365 and Google Docs are examples of _____.

    a. file management tools
    b. multiuser operating systems
    c. web apps
    d. desktop operating systems

12. You can locate a file in the macOS using the _____.

    a. File Explorer
    b. search engine
    c. source code
    d. Finder

Discussion Questions

1. What characteristics are common among operating systems? List types of operating systems, and examples of each. How does the device affect the functionality of an operating system? Explain the benefits of a SaaS model. What operating system is installed on your computer or device? If you had the choice, would you change it? Why or why not?

2. Discuss how an operating system manages the computer's memory. What is virtual memory, and why is it important? Have you ever had issues with the memory on your computer or device? What steps can you take to make sure you have ample memory?

3. List three administrative tools and utilities and explain how they are used. What utilities have you used, and for what purpose?

4. Explain what you can determine about a file by looking at its properties. List two types of information a file name should include. Have you ever been unable to find a file that you created? How can you be sure to avoid this problem?

Critical Thinking Activities

1. You are a coder who is working with a team to create a new mobile operating system. At your last meeting, the team discussed whether to make the code open source or closed source. What are benefits to each for the developer and for the user? What concerns might a developer have to ensure the quality of an open source program? Would you use an open source operating system? Why or why not?

2. You are a teaching assistant for an introductory computer concepts course at your local community college. The instructor asks you to prepare a lecture explaining the boot process and the role of the operating system. List four important steps in the boot process. How could learning about the boot process help you if you had any issues with starting your computer or device?

3. You have purchased a new laptop and want to customize the operating system to meet your needs. List three ways you might customize your operating system, and explain why and what tools or types of tools you might need. Have you ever customized your operating system? How did/might you do this to improve your user experience?

4. You work with a lot of different documents in your internship with a software development company. What kinds of actions can you take to keep your files and folders organized? Discuss the importance of file naming, folder names, and folder structure in keeping yourself organized.

Apply Your Skills

Qing Chan has an internship with an accounting firm, which has provided them with a laptop and a smartphone. The laptop runs Microsoft Windows as its operating system, and the phone uses the Apple iOS operating system. Qing uses the apps and utilities provided with their devices to share and collaborate on files, send communications, and participate in web conferences. Qing recently made modifications to the operating systems' settings to personalize them so that they can work more efficiently.

Working in a small group or by yourself, complete the following:

1. List common operating system functions. What differences are there between single-user and multiuser operating systems? What differences are there between desktop and mobile operating systems? List three factors Qing might use when selecting an operating system. Have you ever interacted directly with a server operating system? How might you have indirectly interacted with a server operating system without realizing it?

2. Differentiate between a data file and an executable file. In what circumstances might Qing use each? Differentiate between a folder and a library. Have you ever used a library? How did/ might you benefit from using one?

3. For a project Qing is working on, they need to run two operating systems on their laptop. Explain how they can accomplish this. Have you ever used a virtual machine? Why might you use a virtual machine over using two computers running different operating systems?

4. Explain why Qing may want to compress and uncompress files and folders, and how they might accomplish this. Have you ever compressed a file or folder or received one?

App Use

In This Module

- Explain apps and their purposes
- Use common features of productivity apps
- Recognize graphics apps

Sara uses spreadsheet software to graph her income and expenses.

Sara designed her company's logo using a graphics app.

Because her files are stored in the cloud, Sara can use mobile apps to access the same information on her smartphone or tablet.

Foxy burrow/Shutterstock.com

Sara Jackson is starting her own interior design consulting firm. While she is based in the United Kingdom, her customers will be from all over the world. She will need to use a variety of apps to create presentations and drawings for customers and graphics for her firm's website. She will write work proposals and contracts using a word processing app, manage her firm's income and expenses in a spreadsheet, and track her customers in a database. Sara uses graphic software to adapt customers' photos and videos of their space to demonstrate how it would look with different furnishings.

Everything you do with your smartphone, computer, or tablet requires an app. Whether you are sending messages, watching videos, browsing the web, or checking the news, apps help you accomplish these tasks. Businesses and home users use apps to manage documents, spreadsheets, presentations, and databases. With graphics apps, you can edit and enhance digital images and videos.

In this module, you will learn about different types of apps and how they are used in your personal and work life. You will learn about different kinds of productivity apps. You will explore how digital artists use drawing, paint, video, and photo editing apps. As you reflect on what you learn in this module, ask yourself: What are the benefits and drawbacks to using mobile apps? How can you use productivity software to do your job? What can a graphic artist accomplish using graphics apps?

Explain Apps and Their Purposes

The terms software, program, and apps often are used interchangeably. Software is any set of instructions that tell the computer or device how to operate. Apps (also called programs or application software) are programs that help you perform specific tasks when using your computer or smartphone. All apps are software, but not all software is an app; the main difference is that if end-user interaction is required, the software is an app. With apps, you can create documents, edit photos, record videos, read the news, get travel directions, go shopping, make online calls, manage your device, and more (**Figure 5-1**).

Figure 5-1: People use a variety of apps

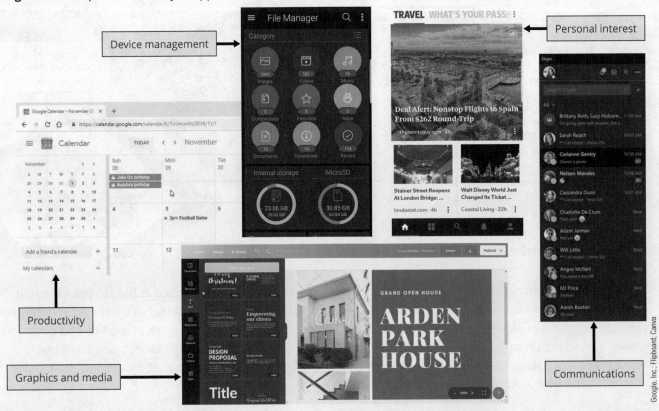

Describe Types of Apps

While all apps allow you to accomplish a task, the device on which you access them and the way you obtain the app can determine its capabilities. Desktop- or laptop-installed native versions of the apps generally provide the most complete and advanced capabilities. Web, mobile, and portable versions are often simpler, or lightweight, and contain the most basic and most popular basic features.

- A **native app**, also called a local app, is an app written for a specific operating system and installed on a computer or mobile device. Native apps can take advantage of specific features of the devices on which they are installed, such as a smartphone's camera, microphone, or contacts list. You may install native mobile apps by downloading them from an app store. Many native apps require an Internet connection to provide full functionality. Some apps can run offline and will store information on your device until they can synchronize with the cloud.

- **Mobile apps** are native apps that you access on a smartphone or tablet. Usually you download and install these from your device's app store. Because screens on mobile devices tend to be small, mobile apps might focus on a single task, such as checking email, searching the web, or sending a text message. **Figure 5-2** compares mobile and web apps.

- Web apps are stored on an Internet server that can be run entirely in a web browser. Because these programs run over the Internet, web apps often offer collaboration features, and store the files or documents you create in the cloud.

- **Mobile web apps** are stored on an Internet server and can be run entirely in a web browser using a smartphone or tablet. Like all web apps, they do not require device storage space or updates, as they run from a browser.

- **Portable apps** run from a removable storage device such as an external hard drive or flash drive, or from the cloud. When using an external hard drive or flash drive, you connect the storage device to your computer and then run the application. When installed in the cloud, you can access portable apps from a folder in your cloud storage. Portable apps are useful when you have limited storage space on your computer, or if you are using a very specific type of app that you need to be able to use on multiple devices.

Figure 5-2: Mobile and web apps

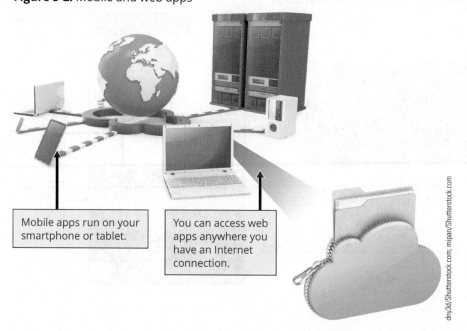

Mobile apps run on your smartphone or tablet.

You can access web apps anywhere you have an Internet connection.

dny3d/Shutterstock.com; mipan/Shutterstock.com

Figure 5-3: Mobile and web apps can synchronize data

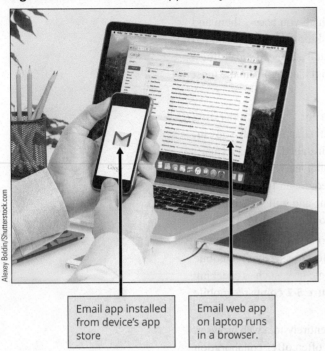

Alexey Boldin/Shutterstock.com

Email app installed from device's app store

Email web app on laptop runs in a browser.

Identify Common Features of Apps

Apps have many common features, regardless of whether they run on a computer or mobile device. They:

- Usually are represented on your computer's desktop or smartphone's home screen by an icon
- Can be run by double-clicking or tapping the icon
- Open in a window that has buttons, icons, menus, and a workspace
- Have menus that give you options to access different features of the program or app
- Have buttons to click or tap to give commands or perform actions

Some apps are available as both a web app and a native app. In this case, you typically can **synchronize** the data, settings, preferences, and apps so they are set up the same way on all your devices. For example, you might look at your Gmail account on your smartphone or tablet, and access Gmail on your computer via its website (**Figure 5-3**). In both cases, the email messages displayed in your inbox are the same. If you delete an email message using the email app on your mobile device, it will not appear when you check email using the email application on your laptop later.

Use Mobile Apps

To interact with a mobile app, you touch or tap the screen. To enter text, you can use a keyboard (**Figure 5-4**). An **on-screen keyboard** is displayed on the screen and includes keys for typing text, numbers, and symbols. Many on-screen keyboards assist you by predicting words and phrases you might want to type based on context, or by providing automatic

Figure 5-4: Sample Bluetooth and on-screen keyboards

Sorapop Udomsri/Shutterstock.com

Bluetooth keyboard

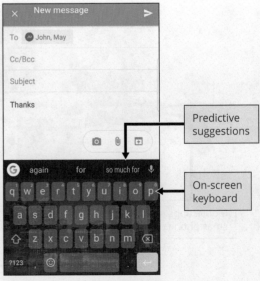

Predictive suggestions

On-screen keyboard

corrections. Some on-screen keyboards include voice recognition capabilities, so you can speak the words to be typed. Users who need to type significant amounts of information may opt for a portable keyboard that they can connect to their smartphones using Bluetooth.

Many mobile devices come pre-installed with apps for managing email, contacts, calendars, a photo gallery, a web browser, sending and receiving text messages, a camera, a voice recorder, mobile payments, and more. You can organize apps into groups by category, such as Games or Social Media, to make them easier to find.

Figure 5-5 shows how you might interact with mobile apps throughout your day.

Figure 5-5: Using mobile apps throughout the day

7:30 AM
While taking the bus to work, you use a calendar app to review your schedule for the day.

7:45 AM
You check your email with an email app.

8:00 AM
Walking to your first appointment, you consult a mapping app for directions.

11:00 AM
Hi. What's up?
Your appointment finishes early, so you send a text message to invite a friend to lunch.

12:30 PM
TRANSFERRING
CANCEL
You pay for lunch, using the mobile payment app on your phone.

6:45 AM
You wake up and use a weather app to see if you'll need a coat or umbrella today.

11:00 PM
LONDON
05:45 MONDAY
07:00
You use a clock app to set the alarm to wake you at 6:45 am.

6:30 PM
SCANNING
On your way home you see a billboard with a QR code and scan it for more information.

5:00 PM
MUSIC PLAYER
SONG NAME
You go to the gym after work and use a streaming app to listen to your playlists while working out.

12:45 PM
PHOTO
After lunch, you use a camera app to take a selfie with your friend.

Table 5-1 lists common mobile apps and the tasks they can help you accomplish.

Describe the Pros and Cons of Mobile Apps

Although mobile apps are popular and convenient, they have limitations, as described in Table 5-2.

Apps are represented by icons on your screen (Figure 5-6). Many mobile apps require the ability to connect to the Internet, either over Wi-Fi, or using your carrier's mobile network. Connectivity is crucial to today's mobile user; people want to stay connected to

Table 5-1: Popular types of mobile apps

Type of app	Helps you to	Examples
Banking and payment	Manage bank accounts, pay bills, deposit checks, transfer money, make payments	Your bank's mobile app, Venmo, PayPal
Calendar	Maintain your online calendar, schedule appointments	Google Calendar, Outlook Calendar
Cloud storage	Store your files in the cloud	Box, OneDrive, Google Drive, iCloud, Amazon Drive
Contact management	Organize your address book	Contacts
Device maintenance	Optimize storage, delete unused or duplicate files, optimize device performance	CCleaner, PhoneClean
Email	Send and receive email messages from your mobile device	Outlook, Gmail
Fitness	Track workouts; set weight-loss goals, review stats from fitness tracking devices	Fitbit, MyFitnessPal
Games	Play games on your mobile device	Candy Crush
Location sharing	Share your location with friends	Find My Friends, Find My Family, Google Maps
Mapping/GPS	View maps; obtain travel directions based on your location	Google Maps, Waze
Messaging	Send text messages, photos, or short videos, or make voice or video calls to your friends	Facebook Messenger, FaceTime, WhatsApp, GroupMe
News and information	Stay up to date on current affairs of interest to you	Flipboard, Google News, Weather Channel, CNN
Personal assistant	Search the Internet, set timers, add appointments to your calendar, make hands-free calls by speaking commands	Siri, Cortana, Google Home, Amazon Alexa
Personal productivity	View and make minor edits to documents received by email, or stored on your device or in the cloud	Microsoft Word, PowerPoint, Outlook, Excel, Gmail, Google Docs, Spreadsheets, Slides
Photo and video editing and sharing	Modify photos and videos by cropping, adding filters, adjusting brightness and contrast	Fotor, Canva, Adobe Lightroom
Shopping	Make online retail purchases	Amazon.com
Social media	Share status updates, photos, or videos on social networking sites or view friends' posts	Facebook, Instagram, LinkedIn
Travel	Make airline, hotel, and restaurant reservations; read and post reviews	Airbnb, Kayak, Priceline, Yelp, TripAdvisor
Web browsing	View websites on your mobile devices	Chrome, Edge, Firefox, Safari

Table 5-2: Pros and cons of mobile apps

Pros	Cons
Can be created quickly compared to native apps	Not as fast as and have fewer features than native web apps or desktop apps
You can access your information on the go	Poorly designed apps can turn people away
Voice input, touch screens, and smart on-screen keyboard simplify interactions	Typing using a small on-screen keyboard can be cumbersome

their office, home, and friends all the time, no matter where they are. Files that the apps use or create often are compatible between your desktop or laptop computer and your mobile device.

Most mobile apps are **platform-specific**, that is, designed for a specific operating system like Android OS or iOS. If you have an Android phone, you need to install the Android version of your app; if you have an iPhone, you need to download the iPhone version of your app. In most cases, the capabilities of different versions of the same app are comparable; each device's app has a consistent look and feel with that device's user interface and is built to run with that device's mobile operating system.

List Additional App Categories

In addition to productivity and graphics apps, which are covered in the next sections, there are many other types of apps that you can use.

Personal interest apps give you tools to pursue your interests. You might use travel, mapping, and navigation apps to view maps, obtain route directions, or locate points of interest. News apps gather the day's news from several online sources in one place, based on your preferences. Reference apps provide access to information from online encyclopedias, dictionaries, and databases. Educational apps provide training on a variety of subjects and topics. Entertainment apps include games, movie times, and reviews. Social media apps enable you to share messages, photos, and videos with your friends and colleagues. Shopping apps allow you to make purchases online.

Communications apps provide tools for sharing or receiving information. Using a browser, you can access webpages; with email apps you can send and receive electronic mail messages. Messaging apps share short messages, videos, and images, usually between mobile phone users. Video conferencing apps provide the ability to have voice and video conversations over the Internet. Other communications apps allow you to transfer files between your computer and a server on the Internet.

Device management apps provide tools for maintaining your computer or mobile device. With a file manager app, you can store, locate, and organize files in your device's storage or in the cloud. A screen saver shows a moving image after a period of no keyboard or mouse activity. Security apps will keep your computer or mobile device safe from malicious activity.

Figure 5-6: App icons and grouped apps

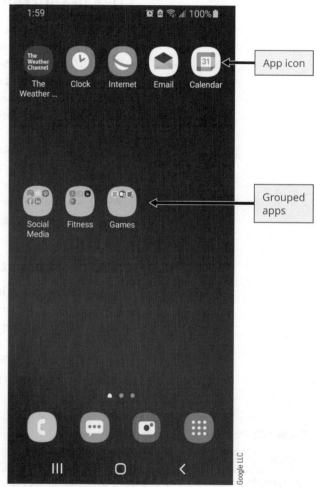

Google LLC

Use Common Features of Productivity Apps

Productivity apps are apps for personal use that you may use to create documents, develop presentations, track appointments, or stay organized. You use productivity apps when you are writing a letter or report, maintaining a budget, creating slides for a presentation, or managing the membership list for an organization. Productivity apps include word processing apps for creating documents, spreadsheet apps for creating worksheets, presentation apps for creating slides, and may include email, database, note-taking, and other apps for creating a variety of documents.

Use Productivity Suites

Many vendors bundle their individual apps into a **productivity suite**, or collection of productivity apps such as Microsoft Office 365, Apple iWork, G Suite, or Apache OpenOffice (**Table 5-3**). You can share text, graphics, charts, and other content among projects you create with individual apps and download additional templates for creating specialized projects. For example, you could include a chart created in a spreadsheet app as part of a slide in a presentation, or as a figure in a word processing document.

In addition to productivity apps that are part of a productivity suite, individual productivity apps are popular as well. For example, Prezi is an online presentation app that you can use to zoom in and out of parts of a canvas to create an online presentation. Zoho Writer is an online word processing app with additional features such as posting directly to popular online blogging platforms.

Use Collaboration Tools

By storing documents in the cloud, you can share documents with several people who can read, edit, and comment on the same document at the same time (**Figure 5-7**). If they are unsure of the edits, they can discuss the changes in comments and tracked changes to compare versions, without creating multiple copies of the same file. This process of collaboration is often more efficient than exchanging multiple versions of the same file by email, and then merging each person's changes together.

Table 5-3: Popular productivity suites

Suite	Available programs	Versions	Cloud storage
Microsoft Office	Word, Excel, PowerPoint, Access (database) Outlook (email), and OneNote (note taking)	Microsoft Windows and macOS, and as Office Online, a collection of web apps in a browser	Microsoft OneDrive
Apple iWork	iWork (word processing, spreadsheet, and presentations), Apple Pencil (drawing)	macOS and iOS	iCloud
G Suite	Docs, Sheets, Slides, Google Calendar, Gmail (email), SketchUp (drawing)	ChromeOS and as a web app, as well as mobile app for Android and iOS	Google Drive
Apache OpenOffice	Writer, Calc, Impress (presentations), Draw and Base (database)	Open source app downloaded from a website for free	

Figure 5-7: Creating, collaborating, and commenting on a shared document

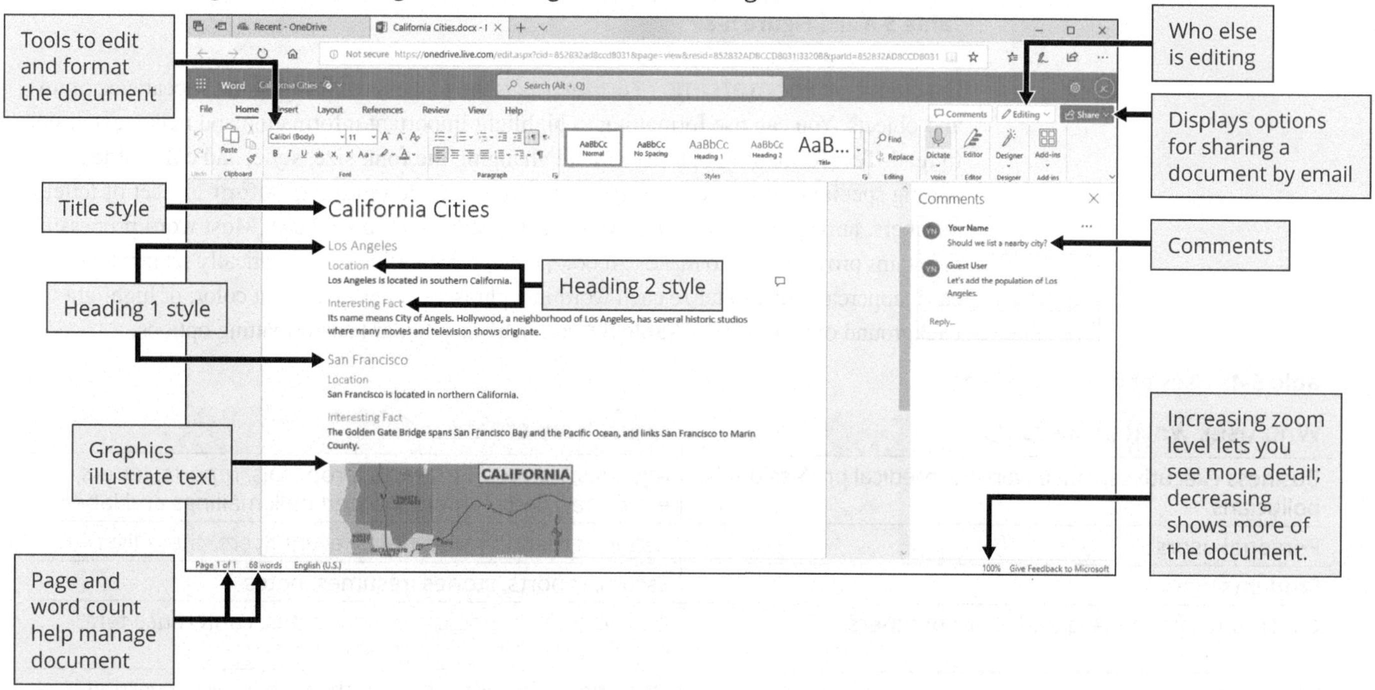

Tools to edit and format the document

Who else is editing

Displays options for sharing a document by email

Title style

Comments

Heading 1 style

Heading 2 style

Graphics illustrate text

Increasing zoom level lets you see more detail; decreasing shows more of the document.

Page and word count help manage document

California Cities

Los Angeles
Location
Los Angeles is located in southern California.

Interesting Fact
Its name means City of Angels. Hollywood, a neighborhood of Los Angeles, has several historic studios where many movies and television shows originate.

San Francisco
Location
San Francisco is located in northern California.

Interesting Fact
The Golden Gate Bridge spans San Francisco Bay and the Pacific Ocean, and links San Francisco to Marin County.

CALIFORNIA

Comments

Your Name
Should we list a nearby city?

Guest User
Let's add the population of Los Angeles.

Reply...

Messaging apps such as Slack and Microsoft Teams are used to send messages regarding work projects among colleagues. While they can have personal uses, they are widely used in business. Within these apps you can participate in video conferencing, store and share files, and chat with others. Microsoft Teams can be used with cloud-based versions of Microsoft Office to enable collaboration.

Use Word Processing Apps

Word processing is one of the most widely used types of apps. A **word processing app** includes tools for entering, editing, and formatting text and graphics. You can create documents and reports, mailing labels, flyers, brochures, newsletters, resumes, letters, and more. You can enhance your documents to look more professional, as well as share and collaborate with others.

Word Processing Features   All word processors share some common key features. The electronic files you create are called **documents**. A document can contain only one page or an unlimited number of pages. When you open a word processing program, a blank document opens on the screen. The screen displays an **insertion point**, a blinking vertical line that appears when you click the screen, indicating where new text or an object will be inserted. **Scroll bars** appear on the right edge (vertical scroll bar) and bottom edge (horizontal scroll bar) of a document window to let you view a document that is too large to fit on the screen at once. You can use scroll bars to navigate to view parts of a document that are too large to fit on the screen all at once.

With some word processing programs, you can speak the text into a microphone connected to your computer or mobile device, and the program will convert your speech to text and type it for you. As you type or speak text, when you reach the end of one line, the word processing software automatically "wraps" the words onto the next line. When the text fills the page, the new text automatically flows onto a new page.

Word processing programs have both business and personal uses, as summarized in **Table 5-4** and **Figure 5-8**.

Document Formatting   Formatting is the process of changing the appearance of text and objects. You can use formatting to highlight important information and make text easier to read. Text formatting options involve changing the font, size, style, and color of text and adding special effects such as reflection, shadows, and outlining. A **font** is a set of letters, numbers, and symbols that all have the same style and appearance. Most word processing programs provide tools to make text bold, italic, or underlined; automatically set text to lower-case, uppercase, or capitalize each word in a phrase; changing the font color; or highlight the background of text in color. **Table 5-5** summarizes popular text-formatting options.

Table 5-4: Uses of word processing

Who uses word processing	What they create
Business executives, office workers, medical professionals, politicians	Agendas, memos, contracts, proposals, reports, letters, email, newsletters, personalized bulk mailings and labels
Personal users	Letters, greeting cards, notes, event flyers, check lists
Students	Essays, reports, stories, resumes, notes
Conference promoters and event planners	Business cards, postcards, invitations, conference tent cards, name tags, gift tags, stickers
Web designers	Documents for publishing to the web after converting them to HTML

Figure 5-8: Word processing programs have both personal and business uses

Document for personal use

Document for business use

Table 5-5: Text formatting options

Format option	Description and use	Examples
Font type	Defines what characters look like. Some fonts have rounded letters; others are more angular. Some are formal; others are more casual.	Times New Roman Arial **Arial Black**
Font size	Determines the size of the character, measured in *points*; each point is 1/72 of an inch; change the title font to be bigger than the rest of your text or use smaller fonts for footnotes or endnotes.	This text is 12 points This text is 18 points
Font style	Adds visual effects features to text; bolding text makes it stand out on the page, shadow gives it depth, underlining, italicizing, and highlighting text provide emphasis.	**bold** shadow underline *italics* highlighting

You can format the layout of a document to improve its appearance and readability. Document formatting features include formatting in multiple columns, adding borders around text, adding a page break to specify a location for a new page to begin, and changing spacing between lines of text. You also can specify a document's margins and the **page orientation**, which is the direction in which content is printed on the page. **Portrait orientation** prints a page so that it is taller than it is wide. **Landscape orientation** prints a page so that it is wider than it is tall.

To give a document a professional appearance, you can specify styles for a document's title, headings, paragraphs, quotes, and more. A **style** is a named collection of formats that are stored together and can be applied to text or objects. For example, the Heading 1 style for a document might format text using Calibri font, size 16, blue text color, left justified. Any text in the document formatted with the Heading 1 style will have those characteristics. If you modify the characteristics of a style, all the format of text in that style will update to reflect the new characteristics.

Many productivity suites offer built-in templates for creating different kinds of documents. A **template** is a document that has been preformatted for a specific purpose (such as an invitation, a brochure, a flyer, a cover letter, or a resume). You can specify the content of your documents, but you do not have to develop a color scheme or design a layout.

In addition, you might make use of the features shown in **Table 5-6** when creating or editing a document.

Other tools include mail merge, which you can use to create and send customized letters or email messages that are personalized with the recipient's name and other information, and reference tools which you can use to create a bibliography containing citations to reference articles in a research paper.

Some word processing features are included in programs and apps for creating different types of documents. **Table 5-7** lists several examples.

Table 5-6: Additional document formatting options

Use this feature	When you want to
Alignment	Align paragraphs or lines of text at the left margin, right margin, or center of the page
Graphics	Add photos, pictures, logos, charts, or screenshots to your document to add visual appeal
Headers and Footers	Display information such as a document title, author's name, or page number at the top or bottom of each page
Hyperlinks	Direct readers to related documents, email addresses, or websites online
Line Spacing	Specify how much "white space" appears before, between, or after each line of text (measured in points)
Lists	Display a list of items preceded by numbers or a symbol called a bullet
Margins	Specify the region of the page where text will appear, measured from the left, right, top, and bottom edges of the page
Tables	Organize text in rows and columns

Table 5-7: Programs and apps for creating different types of documents

Related program	Function	Use to create
Desktop publishing	Combines word processing with graphics and advanced layout capabilities	Newsletters, brochures, flyers
Text / code editor	Creates webpages using HTML tags	Webpages
Note taking	Stores and accesses thoughts, ideas, and lists	Notes
Speech recognition	Enters text that you speak, rather than type	Documents

Document Management   **Document management tools** protect and organize files and let you share your document with others. Collaboration tools are an example of document management tools. You also can copy elements of a document, such as text and graphics from a word processing document or a chart from a spreadsheet, from one to another.

When sharing a document, you can restrict access to a document by providing view-only or read-only access. A **view-only link** is a link to content on a OneDrive or other online location that can be viewed by users. **Read-only access** offers a way to share files so others may read the file but cannot change it.

Use Spreadsheet Apps

You can use spreadsheet apps to manipulate numbers or display numerical data. Keeping to-do lists, creating a budget, tracking your personal finances, following the performance of your favorite sports teams, and calculating payments on a loan are all tasks you can accomplish using a spreadsheet. Businesses often use spreadsheets to calculate taxes or payroll.

A **spreadsheet** is a grid of cells that contain numbers and text (**Figure 5-9**). In Microsoft Excel, a spreadsheet is called a worksheet. You use spreadsheet software to create, edit, and format worksheets. A **worksheet** is a single sheet in a workbook file that is laid out in in a grid of rows and columns. A **workbook** is collection of related worksheets contained within a single file.

You can use spreadsheet apps to enter, create, and interact with numbers, charts, graphics, text, and data. Using a spreadsheet you can perform calculations on data stored in a grid of cells. If you enter new data that is used in a calculation, the spreadsheet recalculate values automatically.

Figure 5-9: Using spreadsheet software

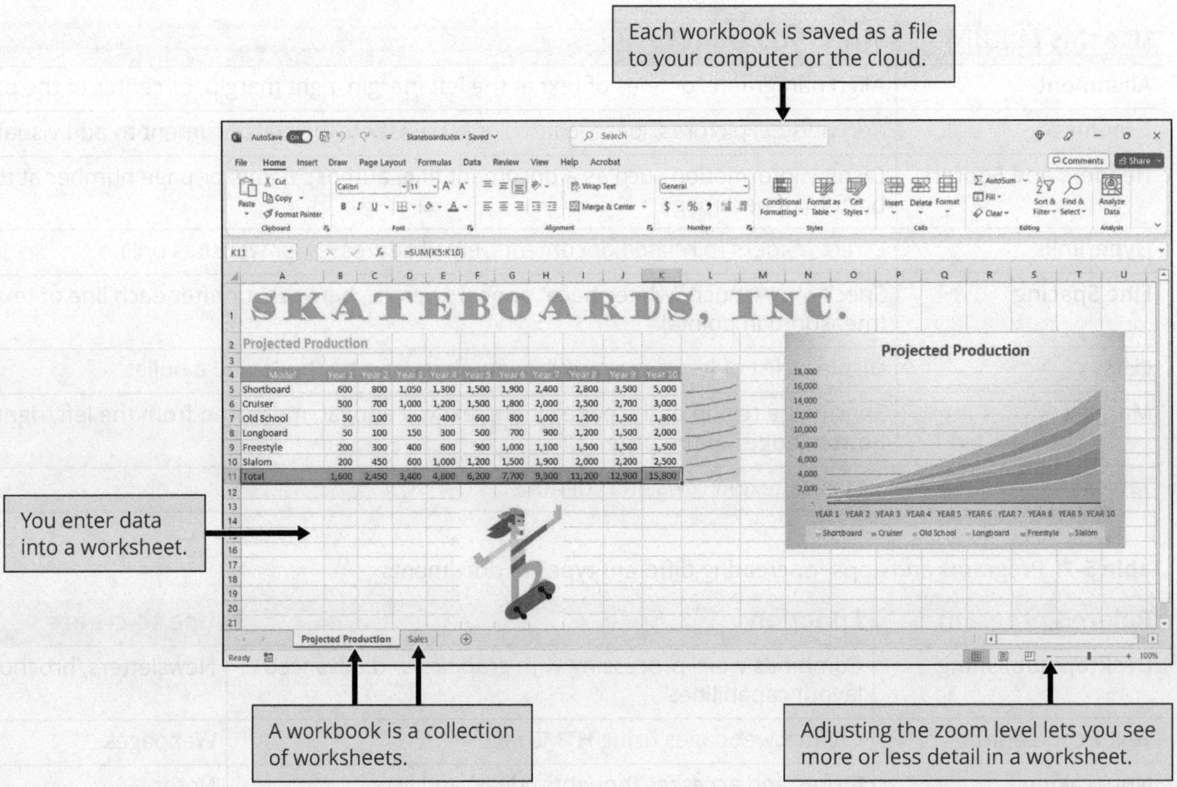

Each workbook is saved as a file to your computer or the cloud.

You enter data into a worksheet.

A workbook is a collection of worksheets.

Adjusting the zoom level lets you see more or less detail in a worksheet.

OpenClipArt

A **cell** is the box formed by the intersection of a column and a row. Worksheets use letters or pairs of letters, such as A or AB, to identify each column and consecutive numbers to identify each row. You can refer to a cell by its **cell address**, or location in the worksheet. For example, cell K11 is located at the intersection of column K and row 11. In **Figure 5-10**, cell K11 contains the number 11,800, which represents the number of total projected production of skateboards in Year 10.

Spreadsheets Features   Spreadsheet software often includes many additional features (**Table 5-8**).

You can automate your worksheets with **macros**, small programs you can create to perform repetitive tasks. For example, if your worksheet contains information for a sales invoice, you can create a macro to save it as a PDF file, centered on the page. By assigning these steps to a macro, you can perform this task with one button click.

Spreadsheet Formatting   You can change how a worksheet looks by using formatting features as well as by inserting elements such as graphics. Formatting highlights important data and makes worksheets easier to read; graphic elements enhance a worksheet. When you format a number, the value remains the same, even if the way it appears in a cell changes.

Figure 5-10: Basic features of spreadsheet software

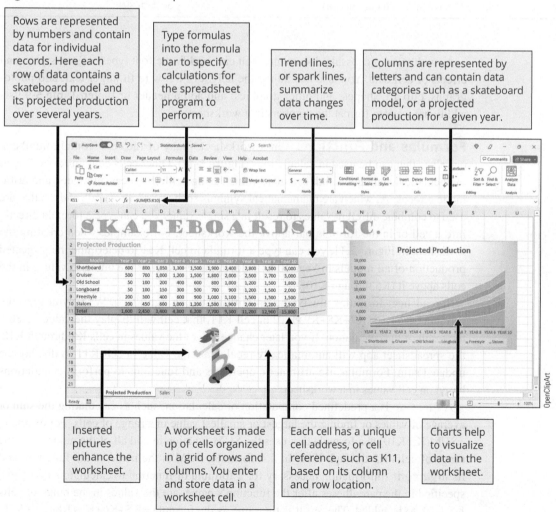

Rows are represented by numbers and contain data for individual records. Here each row of data contains a skateboard model and its projected production over several years.

Type formulas into the formula bar to specify calculations for the spreadsheet program to perform.

Trend lines, or spark lines, summarize data changes over time.

Columns are represented by letters and can contain data categories such as a skateboard model, or a projected production for a given year.

Inserted pictures enhance the worksheet.

A worksheet is made up of cells organized in a grid of rows and columns. You enter and store data in a worksheet cell.

Each cell has a unique cell address, or cell reference, such as K11, based on its column and row location.

Charts help to visualize data in the worksheet.

Table 5-8: Spreadsheet features

Feature	Use to
Formatting tools	Change a worksheet's appearance
Page layout and view features	Change the zoom level, divide a worksheet into panes, or freeze rows or columns, to make large worksheets easier to read
Printing features	Control whether you want to print entire worksheets or only selected areas
Web capabilities	Share workbooks online, add hyperlinks, and save worksheets as webpages
Developer tools	Add customized functions
Charts and graphs	Analyze data in a spreadsheet

Table 5-9: Formatting worksheet data

Formatting option	Use to	Examples
Currency	Identify currency value such as dollars, pounds, or euros	$4.50 or £4.50 or €4.50
Decimal places	Display additional level of accuracy	4.50, 4.500, 4.5003
Date or Time	Display dates or times while enabling them to be used in calculations	3/4/2027 or March 4, 2027 12:31:00 or 12:31 PM
Percentage or fraction	Display the results of a calculation	80% or 4/5

As with word processing documents, you can modify the font types, colors, styles, and effects of cell data. You also can adjust the height of a row to fit larger text; add photographs, clip art, shapes, and other graphics; and add a header or footer. **Table 5-9** lists additional ways to format the numbers in a worksheet.

Formulas and Functions In a worksheet, many of the cells contain numbers, or values that can be used in calculations (**Figure 5-11**). Other cells contain **formulas**, or mathematical statements that calculate values using cell references, numbers, and arithmetic **operators**, which are mathematical symbols such as "+", "−", "*", and "/" that are used to combine different values to result in a single value. You can type a formula directly into a cell or in the formula bar above the worksheet. For example, when creating the worksheet in Figure 5-11, you can type a formula in cell K11 to determine the projected production of all models in Year 10 by calculating the sum of the numeric values in the cells above it (K5 through K10).

Spreadsheet formulas always begin with an equal sign ("="). When you type the formula =K5+K6+K7+K8+K9+K10 in cell K11, that cell will display the value 15,800, the result of the calculation. If you later change any of the values in cells K5 through K10, the spreadsheet app will automatically recalculate the value in cell K11 to display the updated sum. Formulas use arithmetic operators and functions to perform calculations based on cell values in a worksheet.

A **function** is a predefined computation or calculation, such as calculating the sum or average of values or finding the largest or smallest value in a range of cells. For example, =SUM(K5:K10) is a formula that uses the SUM function to add all of the numbers in the range of cells K5 through K10. In this formula, SUM is the name of the function, and its **argument** (information necessary for a formula or function to calculate an answer), specified in the parentheses after the function's name, are the values in the range of cells K5:K10, to be added. The result is the same as the formula =K5+K6+K7+K8+K9+K10, but using the function is simpler, especially if you are adding values in many cells.

Figure 5-11: Working with charts

To create a chart, select a data range, and choose a chart type, layout, and location.

Chart tools help you design visually appealing charts.

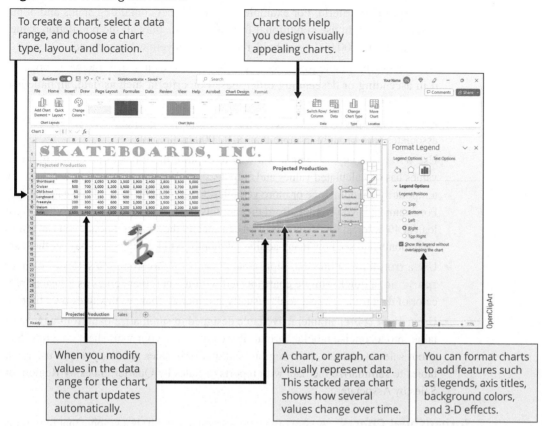

When you modify values in the data range for the chart, the chart updates automatically.

A chart, or graph, can visually represent data. This stacked area chart shows how several values change over time.

You can format charts to add features such as legends, axis titles, background colors, and 3-D effects.

Formula arguments can be values or cell references. An **absolute cell reference** is a cell reference refers to a specific cell and does not change when you copy the formula and paste it in a new location. A **relative cell reference** is cell address that automatically changes to reflect the new location when the formula is copied or moved. Relative references are the default type of referencing used in Excel worksheets.

Spreadsheet apps contain **built-in functions** to perform financial, mathematical, logical, date and time, and other calculations (**Table 5-10**). Many spreadsheet apps allow users to write their own custom functions to perform special purpose calculations.

Spreadsheet Data Organization and Analysis
Once you enter data into a worksheet, you can use several tools to make the data more meaningful.

Table 5-10: Common spreadsheet functions

Use these functions	To do this
SUM, AVERAGE, COUNT	Calculate the sum, average, or count of cells in a range
RATE, PMT	Calculate interest rates and loan payments
DATE, TIME, NOW	Obtain the current date, time, or date and time
IF, AND, OR, NOT	Perform calculations based on logical conditions
MAX, MIN	Calculate largest and smallest values in a group of cells
VLOOKUP	Look up values in a table

- Use **conditional formatting**, which is special formatting that is applied if values meet specified criteria. For example, in a worksheet containing states and populations, you might use conditional formatting to display all the population values greater than 10,000,000 using bold, red text with a yellow background.

- **Sort** data such as table rows, items in a list, or records in a mail merge, to organize it in ascending or descending order, based on criteria such as date, alphabetical order, file size, or filename.

- **Filter** data to specify a set of restrictions to display only specific data, such as sales associates who brought in more than $100,000 in a month.

- Use **what-if analysis**, which is a way to explore the impact that changing input values has on calculated values and output values. You can test multiple scenarios by temporarily changing one or more variables, to see the effect on related calculations. For example, if you cannot afford the monthly payment of $590.48 on a $20,000 car loan at 4% interest for 36 months, you can specify the smaller amount you can afford each month and see how many additional months will be required to pay off the loan.

- Use a **trendline**, a line that represents the general direction in a series of data, or **sparkline**, a quick, simple chart located within a cell that serves as a visual indicator of data trends. These tools visually summarize changes in values over time.

- Use a **pivot table**, an interactive table designed to summarize data from a range or table into a concise tabular format. For example, if your worksheet contains data about sales associates, their region, and quarterly sales results, you can use pivot tables to summarize the data with reports of Sales by Quarter, Sales by Region, or Sales by Associate.

Spreadsheet Charts   A **chart** (sometimes called a graph) is a graphic that represents data using bars, columns, dots, lines, or other symbols to make the data easier to understand and to make it easier to see the relationships among the data. You can visualize data using pie charts, bar graphs, line graphs, and other chart types. A line chart tracks trends over time. A column chart compares categories of data to one another, and a pie chart compares parts (or slices) to the whole. A stacked area chart illustrates how several values (projected production of various models of skateboards) change over time in the same graphic.

Use Presentation Apps

A **presentation app** lets you create visual aids for presentations to communicate ideas, messages, and other information to a group. You might create a presentation for work or school, show slides of photos from your vacation to friends, or create digital signs. Presentations can be printed; viewed on a laptop, desktop, or mobile device; projected on a wall using a multimedia projector connected to a computer; or displayed on large monitors or information kiosks.

With presentation apps you can create slides that visually communicate ideas, messages, and other information. A **presentation**, also called a **slide show**, is a document that lets you create and deliver a dynamic, professional-looking message to an audience in the form of a slide show. Each slide has a specific layout based on its content (such as titles, headings, text, graphics, videos, and charts), and each layout has predefined placeholders for these content items (such as title layout, two-column layout, and image with a caption layout).

As you work, you can display presentations in different views. Normal view shows thumbnails, or small images of slides, and an editing pane, where you can add or modify content. In Notes view, you can add speaker's notes with talking points for each slide when giving the presentation. You can insert, delete, duplicate, hide, and move slides within your presentation.

Figure 5-12: Creating a presentation

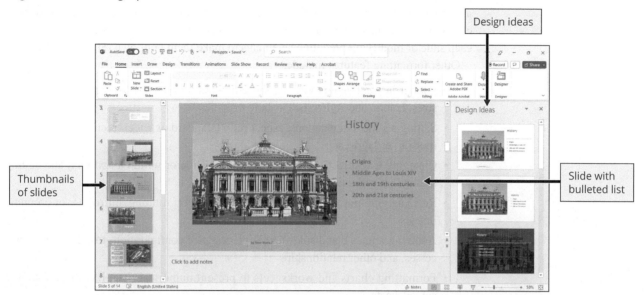

Presentation apps sometimes include a gallery that provides images, photos, video clips, and audio clips to give presentations greater impact. Some presentation apps offer a search tool to help you locate online images or videos to include in your slides. Some presentation apps even offer design ideas to give your slides a more professional appearance (**Figure 5-12**).

You can add main points to a slide as a bulleted list by typing them into a text box on the slide. You also can add graphics or images to illustrate your talking points. Presentation apps may also incorporate features such as checking spelling, formatting, researching, sharing, and publishing presentations online. Adding headers and footers lets you display the presentation title, slide number, date, logos, or other information on a single slide, or on all slides automatically.

There are many ways to present slide content so it appears in the clearest way for your audience (**Table 5-11**).

Table 5-11: Adding content to slides

Slide content	How to enter	Provides
Text in a paragraph or bulleted list	Click a placeholder and type, or copy and paste text from another file, or insert text from a document file.	Content; most programs offer a variety of bullet styles, including number and picture bullets
Graphics such as line art, photographs, clip art, drawn objects, diagrams, data tables, and screenshots	Click a content placeholder, draw directly on the slide, or copy and paste a graphic from another file.	Illustrations to convey meaning and information for the slide content
Media clips, such as video and audio, including recorded narrations	Click a content placeholder and choose a file, or insert the file directly onto a slide by recording it.	Media content to enhance a slide show
Links	Click content placeholder, copy and paste links from a website or type the link directly.	Links to another slide, another document, or a webpage
Embedded objects	Click menu commands or a content placeholder.	External files in a slide
Charts	Link or embed a worksheet or chart from a spreadsheet or create a chart directly within the presentation.	Graphic display of data to support your presentation

Presentation Formatting   Slides can contain text, graphics, audio, video, links, and other content. You can select the theme, or design, for the entire presentation by choosing a predefined set of styles for backgrounds, text, and visual designs that appear on each slide or modifying predefined elements to make them your own (**Figure 5-13**).

Other formatting features include:

- Formatting text using tools like those in word processing software to choose fonts, sizes, colors, and styles such as bold or italics
- Setting a slide's dimensions, aspect ratio (standard or widescreen), and orientation (portrait or landscape)
- Changing text direction, aligning text on a slide or within a text box, and adding shadows or reflection effects
- Resizing graphics to make them larger or smaller; rotating, mirroring, or cropping images
- Adding graphics that display text in predesigned configurations to convey lists, processes, and other relationships
- Formatting charts and worksheets to present numerical data, like those found in spreadsheets
- Moving objects to different locations on a slide, aligning objects, and grouping objects

Transitions, Animations, and Templates   A **transition** refers to the manner in which a slide appears on the screen in place of the previous slide in a slide show. For example, you can apply a push transition to "push" an existing slide off the right edge of the screen as a new one slides in from the left, or apply a cube transition that will make the new slide appear as if it was on the side of a rotating cube. You can set many options for transitions, such as sound effects, direction, and duration. You can set transitions for individual slides or for the entire presentation, to begin automatically after a preset amount of time, or manually with a screen tap or mouse click.

Figure 5-13: Formatting a presentation

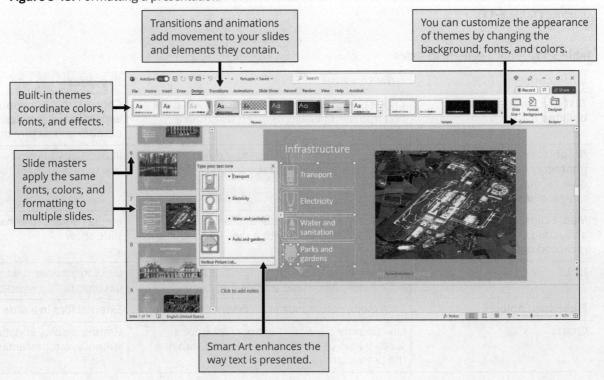

Animations are effects you apply to an object that make the object appear, disappear, or move. Presentation apps offer a variety of animations, such as entrance, exit, and emphasis, each with a variety of options. A photo can fade in as you display a slide, or an object can fly in from the edge of the slide. You can set animations to begin automatically when you advance a slide, or to start when you click or tap. Animations can move horizontally, vertically, or diagonally across the slide. You can set the order for multiple animations, such as displaying a bulleted list one item at a time, and then float in a graphic from the bottom edge of the slide.

Using a presentation template, you can add your content to a predefined design to create common presentations such as calendars, diagrams, and infographics. A **slide master** is the template for the slides in a presentation that contains theme elements and styles, text formatting, the slide background, and other objects that appear on all the slides in the presentation.

Share and Display Presentations   When giving a presentation to a large group, you often display the slides on a large monitor or project them to a screen as a slide show, so everyone can see them (**Figure 5-14**). You might print handouts from your slides so audience members can take notes or send a link to your slides by email so audience members can follow along during the presentation on their own devices. When presentations are stored in the cloud, others can access them online. You also can share them on a blog or website by a code provided by the presentation app's share option and pasting it into a blogpost or webpage.

Presentation Design and Delivery   When creating a presentation, it is important to communicate the content as clearly as possible. By following these tips, you can design effective presentations.

- Organize your presentation to have a beginning, a middle, and an end. Figure out how to visualize each of your topics.
- Your audience can read a slide faster than you can talk about it. Plan your presentation so you focus on one topic or item at a time. Be careful not to cram too much information on one slide. When including text on a slide, many people follow the 6×6 rule: no more than six bullets or lines of text with no more than six words per line. However, the clarity of your message is more important than word count on a slide.

Figure 5-14: Giving a presentation

Audience members can take notes, participate in a chat, or follow the presentation on their laptop or device.

A presenter can show a presentation on a large screen in a conference room.

Luthfi Syahwal/Shutterstock.com

- Choose appropriate backgrounds, colors, and fonts. Use large fonts (at least 20 point) so the audience can see your text from across the room. Be careful with your choice of font color: many people with color blindness cannot see the difference between red or green, so do not use these colors when formatting text to categorize items.

- Use graphics wisely, so they enhance the story your presentation is trying to convey. When searching online for graphics or images, look for public domain or Creative Commons-licensed content that you can modify, adapt, or build upon for use in your presentations. Verify that you have permission to use any image or photo you did not create yourself and provide attribution as necessary.

- Use animations carefully to enhance the presentation; too many transitions or animations can be a distraction. Pick one or two transitions and apply them to the entire presentation. You want your audience to focus on the slide's message, not the elaborate screen effects.

- Use the spelling and grammar features built into your presentation software. If your slides have spelling or grammatical errors, your content will lose credibility.

When delivering a presentation, follow these tips to keep your audience interested and engaged:

- Check your equipment in advance. If presenting to an in-person audience, be sure your laptop or mobile device is connected to the projector and perform a sound check if your presentation includes music or other audio, and make sure you can hear the audio through any connected speakers. If presenting over a web conferencing tool, make sure you have a steady Internet connection.

- Speak loudly and clearly, as if you are having a conversation with the audience. If the room is large, use a microphone so everyone can hear you. Consider muting the audience members in a web presentation to eliminate unnecessary noise.

- Don't read your slides when giving a presentation. Use as few words on your slides as possible. Instead, let the slides be reminders for you about what to talk about, and the images on the slide a backdrop as you tell your story and look at the audience.

- If in person, try not to stand behind a podium or only in one place. Moving around the stage or the room and interacting with audience members will keep their attention.

- Consider using technology to enhance your presentation. Use a laser pointer or other pointing device when explaining figures on your slides. Use a wireless remote control to advance your slides so you do not have to stand behind a podium computer. Use a tablet computer so you can write on slides with a stylus.

- To ensure accessibility for audience members with visual impairments, send an electronic version to them ahead of time so that they can follow along on a tablet or e-reader.

- Involve your audience. Ask a question and use an interactive polling tool or your web conferencing tool's chat or polling feature (**Figure 5-15**) to invite the audience to respond. Consider having a colleague monitor responses and other comments.

Figure 5-15: Collecting and displaying poll results during a conference

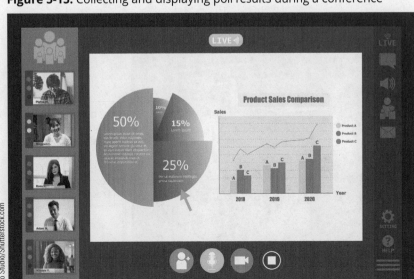

Platoo Studio/Shutterstock.com

- Practice beforehand to get a sense of how much time the presentation will take. If you give a short presentation, such as 5 minutes, you might consider creating a presentation with 20 slides and setting the timing so that slides advance automatically at preset intervals, such as 15 seconds apart. This technique allows the speaker to talk to the audience without having to advance the slides manually. It ensures the presentation will end on time, and the slides become a visual backdrop for engaging the audience with your message.

Use Database Apps

You can use database software to keep track of contacts, addresses, collections, and more. Large enterprises use databases to store vast quantities of data that enable us to shop online, execute web searches, or find friends on social media.

A **database** is a collection of data organized in a manner that allows access, retrieval, and reporting of that data. With database software, you can create, access, and manage a database by adding, updating, and deleting data; filter, sort and retrieve data from the database; and create forms and reports using the data in the database. To create reports from a database, you specify queries, or requests for information from the database.

Databases are used for many purposes. For example:

- Individuals use database software on a personal computer to track contacts, schedules, possessions, or collections.
- Small businesses use database software to process orders, track inventory, maintain customer lists, or manage employee records.
- Companies use databases to store customer relationship management data, such as interactions with customers and their purchases.

Database software provides visual tools to create queries. The database software represents a query in **SQL (Structured Query Language)**, a language that provides a standardized way to request information from a relational database system. Advanced users may type SQL commands directly to interact with a database.

Database software is available as a desktop, server, or web-enabled application. Desktop applications are designed for individual users to run on desktop or laptop computers. When a database has multiple users accessing it simultaneously, a server solution is usually the best. Products such as Oracle, Microsoft SQL Server, and MySQL allow you to organize large amounts of data, and have many users update it simultaneously.

Databases can be stored in a file on a hard disk, a solid-state drive, an external drive, or in cloud storage. Because many users may need to access a database at the same time, and databases can be quite large, enterprise databases generally run on a shared computer called a server. Data can be exported from a database into other programs, such as a spreadsheet program, where you can create charts to visualize data that results from a query. You also can export data from a database to other formats, including HTML, to publish it to the web.

A **relational database management system (RDBMS)**, or **relational database**, is a database that consists of a collection of tables where items are organized in columns and rows. A unique key identifies the value in each row. Common values in different tables can be related, or linked, to each other, so that data does not have to be repeated, making it less prone to error.

Microsoft Access is a popular relational database for personal computers. While Microsoft Access is geared toward consumers and small businesses, SQL Server and Oracle provide advanced database solutions for enterprise use.

Databases and spreadsheets both are used to store data. Database tables are similar to spreadsheets in that the data is stored in rows and columns and can be used in formulas and calculations. However, unlike a spreadsheet, you can establish relationships between data using a database. For example, you can use data from the same table in both a query and a report. If you update the data in the table, the query and report data are updated. Databases are better for storing large quantities of data in order to analyze it. **Big Data** refers to large and complex data sources that defy easy handling with traditional data processing methods.

After opening a database, you choose options to view tables, create queries, and perform other tasks. The software displays commands and work areas appropriate to the view for your task. You enter and edit data in some views. You design, modify, and format layouts of database objects such as tables, queries, reports, and forms in others. You can retrieve data using queries and print reports to see the results.

Database Tables   In a relational database, such as Microsoft Access, data is organized into tables and stored electronically in a database. A **table** is a collection of records for a single subject, such as all the customer records, organized in grids of rows and columns, much like worksheets in spreadsheet applications. Tables store data for the database. Columns contain fields; rows contain records. A database can contain one or more tables.

Records are rows of data in a table, representing a complete set of field values for a specific person, place, object, event, or idea. Each piece of data in a database is entered and stored in an area called a **field**, a column containing a specific property for each record, such as a person, place, object, event, or idea. Each field is assigned a **field name**, a column label that describes the field. Fields are defined by their data type, such as text, date, or number. The text data type stores characters that cannot be used in mathematical calculations. Logical data types store yes/no or true/false values. Hyperlinks store data as web addresses.

You can sort table data by one or more fields to create meaningful lists. For example, you might sort customer data by the amounts of their purchases in decreasing order, to see the customers with the largest purchases first. Filters let you see only the records that contain criteria you specify, such as purchases over $1,000. **Figure 5-16** shows a table in an Access database for an animal care center.

Database Queries   A **query** is an object that provides a spreadsheet-like view of data, similar to that in tables; it may provide the user with a subset of fields and/or records from one or more tables. Queries extract data from a database based on specified criteria, or conditions, for one or more fields. For example, you might query a sales database to find all the customers in Connecticut who made purchases of more than $1,000 in January and sort the results in decreasing order by the purchase amount. **Figure 5-17** shows a query on the animal care center database that returns the animal names in alphabetical order, with their owner's first and last names.

A query contains the tables and fields you want to search along with the parameters, or pieces of information, you want to find. You can use text criteria or logical operators to specify parameters. The query displays results in a datasheet, which you can view on-screen or print. You can save queries to run later; query results are updated using the current data in the tables each time you run the query.

You can build queries using a visual query builder tool, which converts your query specifications to SQL. SQL provides a series of keywords and commands that advanced users might type directly to create and run queries.

Database Forms   A **form** is an object that provides an easy-to-use data entry screen that generally shows only one record at a time. Like paper forms, database forms guide users to fill in information in specified formats. A form is made up of **controls**, which are elements such as labels, text boxes, or combo boxes. Controls specify where content is placed and how it is formatted.

You can use controls to reduce data entry errors. For example, a form might contain a text box in which a database user can type an email address. The form only would accept data that is in the format of a valid email address.

Figure 5-16: Tables, fields, records, and relationships in a database

Tables are related by common values. The OwnerID in the tblAnimal table refers to the owner information associated with the OwnerID in the tblOwner table.

Records can be sorted in ascending or descending order based on a field's value. In the tblAnimal table, records are sorted in increasing order of Owner ID values.

Field names often describe the field's contents.

A record is the set of field values for a single entity, such as an animal owner.

Fields can have different data types. The Animal Birth Date field has data type Date/Time; the other fields are have the Short Text data type.

A table is a collection of records.

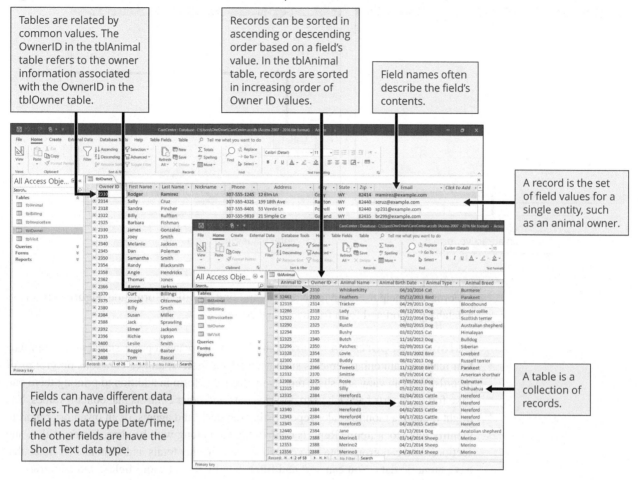

Figure 5-17: Creating and running a database query

Run the query to obtain the results.

Relationship between the tblOwner and tbleAnimal tables

Query results sorted by animal name

Query uses the animal names from the tblAnimal table and the owner name from the tblOwner table.

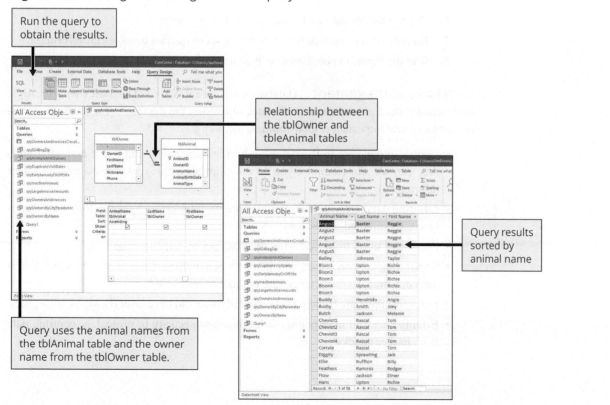

Figure 5-18: Creating and running a database query

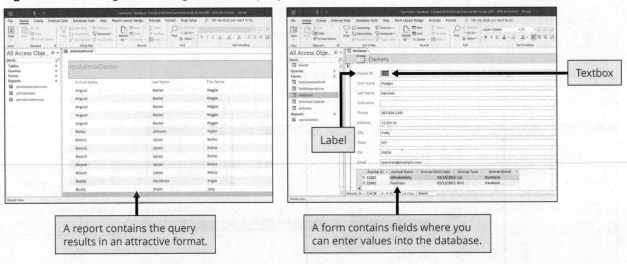

A report contains the query results in an attractive format.

A form contains fields where you can enter values into the database.

Forms also help users navigate records and find specific information. **Figure 5-18** shows a database report and form for the animal center.

Database Reports   A **report** is an object that creates a professional printout of data that may contain enhancements such as headers, footers, and calculations on groups of records. You can view and share reports in electronic form in addition to printing them out. Like forms, reports have labels to describe data and other controls that contain values. You might prepare a monthly sales report listing top deals and agents, or an inventory report to identify low-stock items. Reports contain the data along with headers, footers, titles, and sections. You can group data into categories and display totals and subtotals on fields that have numeric data. You can sort and filter data by one or more fields, and add graphics such as charts, diagrams, or a company's logo.

Follow these steps to create a report:

1. Specify the format and layout options for the report.
2. Identify data to include based on a data set or queries using specified criteria.
3. Run the report to populate it with data from the database.

Database Management   Databases are complex files. Databases with multiple users usually need a database administrator to oversee the database. A database administrator has several important responsibilities, including:

- Controlling access to the database by regulating who can use it and what parts they can see; for example, you do not want all employees to view private salary information
- Ensuring data integrity and minimizing data entry errors by controlling how data is entered, formatted, and stored
- Preventing users from inadvertently changing or deleting important data
- Controlling version issues, which arise when multiple users access the same data at the same time, so that changes are not lost or overwritten
- Managing database backup plans regularly to avoid or recover damaged or lost files
- Establishing and maintaining strict database security to protect susceptible data from hacker attacks

Recognize Graphics Apps

To create digital sketches, resize or add special effects to digital photos, or add titles and credits to a video, you will want to use graphics apps. Graphics apps include tools for creating drawings and three-dimensional objects and editing photos and videos. Graphics apps let you create multimedia to include in letters and reports, presentations, spreadsheets, and other documents.

Graphics and media apps allow you to interact with digital media. With photo editing apps, you can modify digital images, performing actions such as cropping, applying filters, and adding or removing backgrounds and shapes. With video and audio editing apps, you can arrange recorded movie clips, and add music, titles, or credits to videos. With media player apps, you can listen to audio or music, look at photos, and watch videos.

When you need a new banner image for your website, or you want to edit a digital photo, or create a logo for your business, you can use graphics software to accomplish the task. You can create, view, manipulate, and print many types of digital images using graphics programs and apps.

Digital images are stored either in bitmap, sometimes called raster, or vector format. Bitmap images, also called raster images, are based on a grid of square colored dots, called pixels (picture elements). A bitmap assigns a color to each pixel in a graphic. The large number and small size of pixels gives your eye the illusion of continuity, and results in a realistic looking image (see **Figure 5-19**). A high-resolution photo can contain thousands of pixels, so bitmap files can be large and difficult to modify. Resizing the bitmap image can distort it and decrease its resolution.

Vector graphics consist of shapes, curves, lines, and text created by mathematical formulas. Vector graphics are useful for images that can be shrunk or enlarged and still maintain their crisp outlines and clarity. Many company logos are designed as vector graphics because they need to scale to different sizes. They must look sharp when shrunk to fit on business cards as well as when they are enlarged to display on webpages or print on large signs.

Figure 5-19: Comparing vector and bitmap images

Vector graphics can be enlarged without losing quality.

Bitmap images can lose quality and appear pixelated when enlarged.

Table 5-12: Popular graphics formats

Name	Extension	Description
Bitmap	.bmp	Uncompressed file format that codes a value for each pixel. Files can be large.
TIFF (Tagged Image File Format)	.tiff	Large image format commonly used for print publishing because it maintains quality. Avoid using on webpages because of the large file sizes.
JPEG (Joint Photographic Experts Group)	.jpg	A compressed image file format usually used to save photos taken with digital cameras. Useful for images on webpages and in documents, because they have high quality and small file sizes.
GIF (Graphics Interchange Format)	.gif	A proprietary compressed graphics format that supports images with animation and transparent backgrounds.
PNG (Portable Networks Graphics)	.png	An open compressed format that has replaced GIF in many cases. Supports images with transparent backgrounds. Low resolution images that you can edit without losing quality. Great for use on webpages.
Raw data	.raw	Uncompressed and unprocessed data from a digital camera, usually used by professional photographers.

Most clip art images are stored as vector graphics. **Clip art** is a collective term for pre-made pictures and symbols you can use in electronic documents. Clip art libraries include images that are available sometimes for free, or for a small fee. Clip art is a quick way to add simple graphics to your work.

Graphics software programs use a variety of drawing and editing tools to create, modify, and enhance images. You can use tools to change the size, crop, rotate, and flip an image. Many programs have features to adjust the brightness, color saturation, and contrast of photos. Many graphics programs allow you to:

- Use a mouse or stylus to draw on the screen using a crayon, pencil, paintbrush, or calligraphy pen, and set the color and thickness
- Use shape tools to create lines, circles, rectangles, arrows, and callouts
- Use color palettes to specify colors for shapes, lines, and borders
- Add filters and effects to provide visual interest, and adjust brightness and contrast
- Add text to graphics using a variety of fonts, colors, sizes, and styles
- Crop or resize an image

When working with a graphics program, you can save images in a variety of file formats, as summarized in **Table 5-12**. Some of these formats compress images so they require less storage.

Describe Paint Apps

Paint apps are designed for drawing pictures, shapes, and other graphics with various onscreen tools, such as a text, pen, brush, eyedropper, and paint bucket (**Figure 5-20**). Some programs provide templates for adding graphics to popular documents such as greeting cards, mailing labels, and business cards. Some paint apps allow you to create 3D images and diagrams.

Figure 5-20: Using a paint program

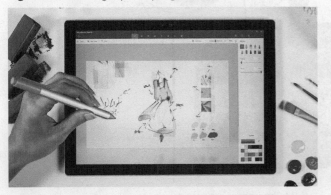

Microsoft Paint and Paint 3D are easy-to-use paint programs. GIMP is a free paint program you can download, and SumoPaint is a free web-based paint app with many features.

Describe Photo Editing Apps

Photo and image editing apps provide the capabilities of paint apps and let you enhance and modify existing photos and images. Modifications can include adjusting or enhancing brightness, contrast, saturation, sharpness, or tint (**Figure 5-21**).

Image editing software for the home or small business user provides an easy-to-use interface; includes tools to draw pictures, shapes, and other images; and provides the capability of modifying existing graphics and photos. Lightroom and Adobe Photoshop are popular image and photo editing apps. Word processing, presentation, and other productivity applications usually include basic image editing capabilities.

Before copying or downloading any image or photo you did not create, you need to find out its copyright status. You many need to purchase the image, or simply give credit to the owner. An image owner or creator may provide you with a license that specifies how you can use the image. Some images can be edited or manipulated, but others cannot. Before manipulating any image, even ones that you create or own, consider any ethical implications. If your edits make the image misleading or inaccurate and you are using it to support an argument, that may not be ethical. Also be aware of how any appearance changes to a person in your photo may be viewed by that person.

With photo management apps you can view, organize, sort, search, print, and share digital photos. Some photo management app services such as Google Photos will organize your photos for you based on the date, time, or location where they were taken. They use advanced image recognition techniques to search your photos for particular items, colors, people, or scenes.

Figure 5-21: Enhancing a photo using a photo editing app

Options for adjusting a photo's appearance include brightness, contrast, saturation, and sharpness.

Fotor app

Figure 5-22: Editing a video using a video editing app

Plays the video

Selects the clip to edit

Video editing options

Video editing apps, such as FilmoraGo, allow you to modify a segment of a video, called a clip. For example, you can reduce the length of a video clip, reorder a series of clips, or add special effects, such as a title at the beginning of the video, or credits that scroll up at the end (**Figure 5-22**). Video editing software typically includes audio editing capabilities. With audio editing apps, such as Audacity, you can modify audio clips, produce studio-quality soundtracks, and change the playback speed. Most television shows and movies and many online videos are created or enhanced using video and audio editing software. You can record audio or video using your mobile device, and use audio and video editing apps on your phone, tablet, or computer to edit these files.

Describe Drawing Apps

Drawing apps let you create simple, two-dimensional images. In contrast to paint apps, drawing apps generally create vector graphics. You can modify and resize vector graphics without changing image quality. Some drawing programs can layer graphics one on top of another to create a unique complex graphic or collage of images.

Drawing programs feature freehand drawing tools such as pens or brushes, as well as tools for drawing lines and shapes, and specifying their colors. You can use drawing programs to create logos, diagrams, blueprints, business cards, flyers, and banner graphics for your website. Popular drawing programs include Adobe Illustrator, CorelDraw, and OpenOffice Draw.

Module 5 Summary

The term software is often used interchangeably with apps and programs. While apps and programs mean the same thing, software is any set of instructions that tell the computer or device how to operate. Apps require end-user interaction.

Types of apps include native, web, mobile, and portable. Native apps are written for a specific operating system and installed on a computer or mobile device. Web apps are stored on the Internet and run from within a browser. Mobile apps are native apps that are downloaded and installed on a mobile device. Mobile web apps are stored on an Internet server and can be run entirely in a web browser using a smartphone or tablet. Portable apps run from a removable storage device. Some benefits of mobile apps include that they are easy to create, information can be accessed on the go, and the input methods simplify interactions. Downsides include a slower speed than native apps, and the challenges of typing on a small on-screen keyboard.

Other app categories include: personal interest (travel, news, reference, educational, entertainment, social media, and shopping); communications (browsers, messaging, and video conferencing); and device management (maintenance, file management, screen saver, and security).

Productivity apps are used for personal use to create documents, develop presentations, and stay organized. Many share features in common such as icons on a desktop you can use to open the app, and a window with menus and buttons you can use to access features or issue commands. Some vendors bundle apps into productivity suites you can use to share information between apps. Microsoft Office, Apple iWork, G Suite, and Apache Open Office are examples of productivity suites. You can use collaboration tools to share documents and communicate with colleagues.

Word processing apps enable you to create documents by adding and formatting text and graphics. Spreadsheet apps enable you to manipulate numbers or display numerical data.

You can use presentation apps to create visual aids for presentations, called a presentation or a slide show. When delivering a presentation, always prepare your equipment ahead of time, speak clearly, use technology, and involve the audience. Database apps enable you to store and work with large collections of data. A database can be quite large; enterprise databases generally run on a server. Big data refers to very large data sources that cannot be handled with traditional data processing methods.

In addition to productivity apps, you should be familiar with graphics apps, which allow you to interact with digital media, and include photo editing apps, video and audio editing apps, and media player apps. With graphic programs you can draw, use shape tools, apply color palettes, add filters and effects, add text, and modify images. Paint apps enable you to draw pictures, shapes and other graphics, and possibly 3D graphics. Photo and image editing apps are used to enhance and modify existing photos and images. You can use video editing apps to reduce the length of a video, reorder clips, or add effects. Drawing apps let you create simple, two-dimensional images.

Review Questions

1. A native app runs from _____.

   a. a web browser
   b. a USB flash drive
   c. the cloud
   d. the device upon which it is installed

2. When an app is available as both a web app and a native app, you can _____ the data and settings so that the app is set up the same way on all of your devices.

   a. synchronize
   b. paste
   c. analyze
   d. report

3. Canva is an example of a _____ app.

   a. personal productivity
   b. photo editing
   c. shopping
   d. messaging

4. (True or False) Mobile apps are not as fast as and have fewer features than desktop apps.

5. A screen saver appears _____.

   a. after a period of no keyboard or mouse activity
   b. when you restart the computer or device
   c. when you receive a notification from a messaging app
   d. during a transition between slides in a presentation

6. A named collection of formats that are stored together and can be applied to text or objects is called a _____.
   a. font type
   b. template
   c. style
   d. format

7. In a spreadsheet formula, characters such as "+", "−", "*", and "/" are called _____.
   a. operators
   b. functions
   c. arguments
   d. values

8. In a presentation, an effect that you apply to an object that makes the object appear, disappear, or move is called a(n) _____.
   a. animation
   b. transition
   c. format
   d. 3D image

9. In a database table, a row of data in a table is called a _____.
   a. field
   b. query
   c. form
   d. record

10. Most paint programs produce _____ images.
    a. bitmap
    b. vector
    c. photographic
    d. video still

11. Adobe Illustrator is an example of a _____ app.
    a. photo editing
    b. word processing
    c. drawing
    d. video editing

12. (True or False) Google Photos is an example of a photo management app.

Discussion Questions

1. Explain the differences between native apps and web apps. How can you ensure your settings and data from both types of apps will transfer between devices? Name one reason you would use a portable app. Have you ever had trouble getting your data to appear in both a web and native app? Do you prefer mobile apps or desktop apps? Why?

2. Define the terms read-only access and view-only link in terms of document management. In what other ways can you take advantage of document management tools? Have you ever collaborated on a document with others? For what purpose did/might you use collaboration tools?

3. Define the following database objects: tables, queries, forms, and reports. Come up with an example of a database, and explain how you might use each object within the database. Why is using a form important for data entry? Have you ever used a form on a website or other format to enter data?

4. Differentiate between vector and bitmap graphics. Why might you choose to create a vector graphic? Why might you choose to create a bitmap graphic?

Critical Thinking Activities

1. You teach a class at a community center in your city about technology. A common question you get from attendees of your classes is whether mobile apps are reliable and how to use them. List two pros and cons for using mobile apps. What is your experience with using mobile apps? Why did you choose a mobile app over a native app?

2. You have been asked to give a presentation at your company's annual meeting about the company's finances from the previous year. Name three features of presentation apps you will use for your presentation and why you would choose each. List three pieces of advice for delivering your presentation. As an audience member, what factors do you feel make a presentation successful?

3. You run a pet day care center. You need to keep track of contact information for your customers, their animals, the services provided (such as walking and grooming), and the staff who are assigned to care for them. You also must send out invoices for payment each month. What features of spreadsheet and/or database software might you use to facilitate your business? Explain your choices. Why might you choose a spreadsheet over a database? Do you prefer filling out paper forms over digital? Why or why not?

4. You are taking a class in graphic design and must select a graphics app to create your own project for your final project. Explain the differences between paint, photo editing, and drawing apps, and give an example of each. What ethical concerns do you have about enhancing or modifying graphics?

Apply Your Skills

Sara Jackson is starting her own interior design consulting firm. While she is based in the United Kingdom, her customers will be from all over the world. She will need to use a variety of apps to create presentations and drawings for customers and graphics for her firm's website. She will write work proposals and contracts using a word processing app, manage her firm's income and expenses in a spreadsheet, and track her customers in a database. Sara uses graphic software to adapt customers' photos and videos of their space to demonstrate how it would look with different furnishings.

Working in a small group or by yourself, complete the following:

1. Explain what additional app categories Sara might want to use for her business or personal use, and give an example of how she would use each. Have you used a tool to manage your device? For what purpose?

2. List two examples of how Sara would use each of the following app types for her business: word processing, spreadsheet, presentation, and database. Which of those have you used? For what purpose?

3. Explain what types of tools Sara may have used to create a logo for her business. Give an example of each. In what other ways could she use graphics apps? Why is it important to make sure to use Creative Commons content?

Cybersecurity and Safety

In This Module

- Determine the risks associated with cybersecurity attacks
- Describe the hazards associated with using technology
- Apply defenses to repel cyber attacks
- Use protective measures against technology hazards

iStock.com/Giulio Fornasar

Tony Blanco has been hired as an intern at a company that installs solar panels. Because he is completing his degree in cybersecurity at the local college, he works in the company's security operations center (SOC) assisting security managers and technicians who protect the company's computers and networks from cyberattacks. One of Tony's recent assignments was helping the technicians who monitor for signs of attacks and then take action to prevent the attacks from quickly spreading. Tony has begun offering Lunch-and-Learn sessions for employees with hands-on training on how to keep their devices safe.

Consider all the technology devices that you use every day: smartphone, laptop computer, smart watch, tablet, and voice assistant, just to name a few. You use these devices to exchange messages with friends and coworkers, search for a new restaurant, work on school assignments, play games, shop for clothes, and stream movies, among many other activities. But each of our devices has a darker side: as a pathway for attackers to steal our data, invade our privacy, empty our bank accounts, and turn our entire lives upside down in a matter of moments. These attackers, who may be in a coffee shop down the street or a basement halfway across the world, are constantly probing for the tiniest opening to invade our devices and wreak havoc.

In this module, you will examine the risks that come from cybersecurity attacks and the potential dangers associated with using technology. You'll discover strategies for protecting your devices and your personal information from attackers. You will also learn how to use protective measures against additional technology hazards, such as the risks associated with data collection and physical, behavioral, and environmental risks. As you reflect on what you learn in this module, ask yourself: Do you know the cyberattacks that your devices face daily? Have you ever suffered neck or arm pain from using your computer? Are you aware of how to harden your devices, to defend them from attackers? Do you want to lessen the environmental impact when disposing of old technology?

Determine the Risks Associated with Cybersecurity Attacks

Cybersecurity events have become commonplace, with stories such as "Hackers Exploit Gaping Loophole to Give Their Malware Access," "U.S. Government Agencies Earn a Grade of D For Cybersecurity," and "EV Charging Stations Are the Latest Targets of Attackers" hitting newsfeeds every day. What exactly is cybersecurity? Who are the attackers? By understanding the different types of attacks that can occur, you can begin to understand the importance of actively following proactive security recommendations.

Define Cybersecurity

The word "security," which comes from the Latin meaning freedom from care, means something that makes us safe. You take steps every day to stay safe: you press a button on a key fob to lock your car, you stay aware of your surroundings when walking at night, and you use a shredder to destroy documents that contain personal information.

Cybersecurity refers to the practices, processes, and technologies used to protect devices, networks, and programs that process and store data in an electronic form. In short, cybersecurity includes everything you do to keep your electronic devices and the data stored on them safe.

Figure 6-1: Attacker wants to steal your money

Sasun Bughdaryan/Shutterstock.com

Describe the Importance of Cybersecurity

Cybersecurity is important because the primary goal of cyber attackers is to make money from their attacks, often leaving us responsible to repay the stolen funds and spend hundreds of hours trying to resolve the situation (**Figure 6-1**). While at one time banks and financial institutions would absorb any financial losses that occurred due to a cyber event so that a customer would not be responsible, that is no longer the case.

One type of data that cyber attackers want to steal is your payment card numbers, such as debit cards, credit cards, or gift cards. Once the attacker has these numbers, they can use them to purchase thousands of dollars of merchandise online—without having the actual card—before you or your bank is even aware the number has been stolen.

Another type of data that attackers steal is your personal information, such as a Social Security number, which they then use to impersonate you for financial gain. The thieves may create new bank or credit card accounts under your name and then charge large purchases to these accounts, leaving you responsible for the debts and ruining your credit rating. This type of criminal activity is known as **identity theft**, using someone's personal information, such as their name, Social Security number, or credit card number, to commit financial fraud. A new victim of identity theft occurs every two seconds. Each year, losses from reported identity theft exceeds $3 billion. In one year, 47 percent of Americans experienced financial identity theft, and 30 percent have experienced identity theft more than once.

Explain the Difficulties of Cybersecurity

Why is it so hard to prevent attacks? Can't we just install a software program to thwart all attacks or add a hardware device to block any intruders? Unfortunately, there is no one-size-fits-all cybersecurity solution. Preventing attacks involves addressing a constantly evolving host of difficulties, which include:

- **Universally connected devices**. It is unthinkable today for any technology device—not only a laptop computer or tablet but also a smartphone, door lock, or doorbell camera—not to be connected to the Internet. Although this connectivity provides enormous benefits, it also makes it easy for an attacker halfway around world to silently launch an attack against any connected device.

Figure 6-2: Cybersecurity can be confusing

fizkes/Shutterstock.com

- **Increased speed of attacks**. Attackers can quickly scan millions and millions of devices to find weaknesses and then immediately launch attacks with unprecedented speed. And these attack tools will "scan and attack" completely on their own without any human help, thus increasing the speed at which users are attacked.

- **Greater sophistication of attacks**. Attacks are becoming more complex, making it difficult to detect and defend against them. Attackers today use common Internet communications and web applications to hide their attacks, making it more difficult to distinguish an attack from legitimate network traffic. Other attack tools even vary their behavior, so the same attack appears differently each time, further complicating detection.

- **User confusion**. The one factor that accounts for the greatest difficulty in preventing attacks is user confusion (**Figure 6-2**). For many years, end users have been called upon to make often difficult security decisions and then perform complicated procedures on their devices—often with little information to guide them. This is compounded even more by cybersecurity information circulated through consumer news outlets and websites that is often contradictory, inaccurate, or misleading, resulting in even more user confusion.

Catalog Types of Attackers

At one time the word "hacker" was used to refer to a person who had advanced computer skills that were used to attack computers. However, as cybersecurity attacks have changed, so too have the terms used to refer to attackers. Today, **threat actor** is the formal term used to describe an individual or entity responsible for launching cyberattacks. The informal or generic term is simply *attacker*.

Attackers are classified in distinct categories:

- **Cybercriminals**. The very first cyberattacks that occurred were mainly for the attackers to show off their technology skills (fame). However, that soon gave way to attackers with the focused goal of financial gain (fortune). A person who conducts cyber-related attacks for financial gain is a **cybercriminal**. Cybercriminals seek out not only individual users but also businesses and even government computers to steal data and make money.

- **Script kiddies**. **Script kiddies** are typically younger individuals who want to attack computers but lack the knowledge of computers and networks needed to do so. Script kiddies instead do their work by downloading automated attack software (scripts) from websites and using it to perform attacks acts (**Figure 6-3**).

- **Brokers**. Many software companies offer money to individuals who uncover vulnerabilities in their software and then privately report it so that they can be fixed. However, some individuals who uncover vulnerabilities do not report it to the software company but instead sell them to the highest bidder. Known as **brokers**, these individuals are willing to sell their knowledge of a hardware or software vulnerability to other attackers or even governments. The buyers are willing to pay a high price because this vulnerability is unknown to anyone else and thus is unlikely to be fixed until after new attacks based on it are already widespread.

Figure 6-3: Script kiddie web site

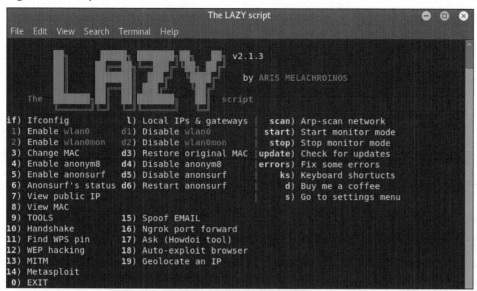

- **Cyberterrorists**. Terrorism today has expanded from planting bombs or other acts of violence against innocent civilians to cyberattacks on a nation's network and computer infrastructure, such as bringing down a power grid or crippling a water treatment plant. Known as **cyberterrorists**, the goal of these attackers are to cause disruption and panic among citizens and their motivation is ideological (relating to their principles or beliefs). Cyberterrorists are the attackers that are most feared, for it is almost impossible to predict when or where an attack may occur.

- **Hacktivists**. Another type of attacker who is strongly motivated by principles or beliefs is a **hacktivist** (a combination of the words *hack* and *activism*) who typically acts alone or in small groups and targets businesses or government agencies with which they disagree. For example, one hacktivist group disabled the website belonging to a bank because that bank had stopped accepting online payments that were deposited into accounts belonging to groups supported by hacktivists. Today many hacktivists work through "disinformation campaigns" by spreading fake news and supporting conspiracy theories.

- **State actors**. Instead of using an army to march across the battlefield to strike an adversary, governments are increasingly employing cyber attackers known as **state actors** to launch cyberattacks against the government's foes. Their foes may be foreign governments or even citizens of their own nation that the government considers hostile or threatening.

Contrast Different Cybersecurity Attacks

There are two types of cyberattacks, malware attacks and social engineering attacks.

Malware Attacks   Most successful attacks use **malware**, software that enters a device without the user's knowledge or permission and then performs a harmful action. The term combines two words, *mal*icious and soft*ware*, and refers to a wide variety of damaging programs.

Kidnapping is a crime that involves capturing a person and then holding them as a captive until a ransom is paid for their release. In a similar fashion, cyber attackers can perform a "kidnapping" of a user's device and hold it "hostage" until a ransom is paid. **Ransomware** is a type of malware that prevents a user's device from properly and fully

Figure 6-4: Ransomware message

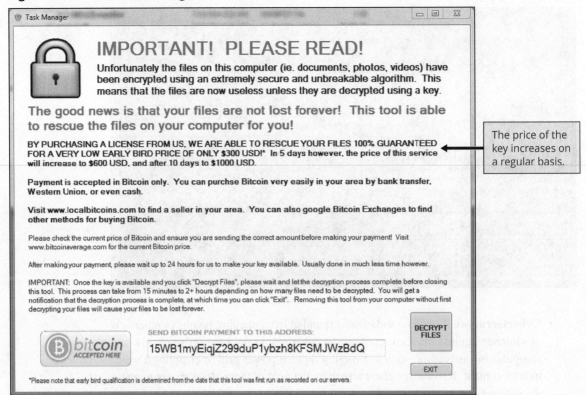

functioning until the user pays a fee. The ransomware embeds itself onto the computer in such a way that it cannot be bypassed, even by rebooting. For instance, a ransomware attack could lock a spreadsheet containing important financial data or a document of a research paper. After the files have been locked, a message appears on the screen telling the victim what has occurred and that money must be paid to receive a key to unlock the files (**Figure 6-4**). Usually, the message contains a warning claiming that the cost for the key increases every few hours, the goal being to increase the victim's sense of urgency and spur them to action. On some occasions, attackers will start deleting locked files and increase the number deleted each hour until they receive payment. And, if the ransom is not paid by a specific deadline, the key to unlock the files can never be purchased.

Another type of malware is a **keylogger**, which captures a user's keystrokes and may also capture screen images and other information without the user's knowledge. The attacker can then search the captured text for any useful information such as passwords, credit card numbers, or personal information. Keyloggers can go far beyond just capturing a user's keystrokes. These programs can also make screen captures of everything that is on the user's screen and silently turn on the computer's web camera to record images of the user (**Figure 6-5**).

According to ancient legend, the Greeks won the Trojan War by hiding soldiers in a large hollow wooden horse that was presented as a gift to the city of Troy. Once the horse was wheeled into the fortified city, the soldiers crept out of the horse during the night and attacked the unsuspecting defenders. A computer **Trojan** is malware that pretends to be a program performing a normal activity but also does something malicious. For example, a user might download what is advertised as a calendar program, yet when it is installed, in

Figure 6-5: Keylogger

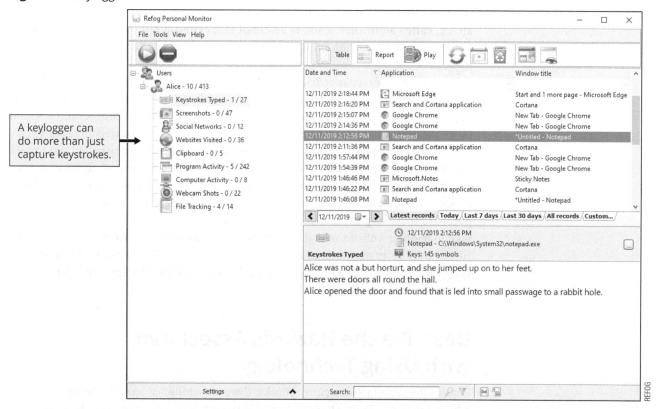

A keylogger can do more than just capture keystrokes.

addition to providing a calendar, it also installs malware that scans the system for credit card numbers and passwords, connects through the network to a remote system, and then transmits that information to the attacker.

A computer **virus** is a computer program designed to copy itself into other programs with the intention of causing mischief or harm, usually without the user's knowledge or permission. Each time the infected program is launched, or the data file is opened, the virus first unloads its payload to perform a malicious action (delete files, prevent programs from launching, steal data to be sent to another computer, cause a computer to crash repeatedly, turn off the computer's security settings, etc.). Then the virus reproduces itself by inserting its code into another file. When a user copies or emails an infected file to another computer, that device then becomes infected with the virus.

Social Engineering Attacks   Not all attacks rely on malware; in fact, many cyberattacks use little if any technology to achieve their goals. **Social engineering** is a category of cyberattack that attempts to trick the victim into giving valuable information to the attacker.

One of the most common attacks based on social engineering is **phishing**, which is sending an email or displaying a web announcement that falsely claims to be from a legitimate enterprise in an attempt to trick the user into giving private information. The word phishing is a variation on the word "fishing," with the idea being that bait is thrown out knowing that while most will ignore it, some will "bite." For example, a user may receive an email that looks like it came from their bank. They are directed to a website that looks like it is their bank's website where they must update personal information, such as passwords, credit card numbers, Social Security numbers, bank account numbers, or other information. However, the email is from an attacker and the website is an imposter site set up to steal information the user enters. Another type of phishing attack, called an invoice scam, is an email that claims a bill is overdue and demands immediate payment. The victim pays in haste but the funds go directly into the hands of the attacker.

If a threat actor cannot trick a user into visiting a malicious website through phishing, they may try a different type of social engineering tactic. Consider what happens when a user makes a typing error when entering a uniform resource locator (URL) address in a web browser, such as typing *goggle.com* (a misspelling) or *google. net* (incorrect domain) instead of the correct *google.com*. If the misspelled site name is one that's owned by an attacker, the false page will open instead of an error message alerting the user that they made a misspelling. This fake site may look closely enough like google.com that the user doesn't notice the error. Attackers deliberately purchase these slightly-off domain names as part of **typo squatting**, registering a fake look-alike website so that users who enter a misspelled URL are directed to that site. The fake site may pretend to be the legitimate site and trick the user into entering personal information, or simply display ads for which the attacker receives money for traffic generated to the site.

Describe the Hazards Associated with Using Technology

Besides the risk of cybersecurity attacks, there are additional hazards that are associated with using technology. These include the risk of data collection, as well as physical, behavioral, and environmental hazards.

Narrate the Risks of Data Collection

You and everyone else have a large amount of personal data: your name, where you live, your Social Security number, your school records, your health information, and on and on. Sometimes you are asked to give some of that personal data to another person or entity. For example, your physician may ask you to provide your address and mobile phone number because they have a legitimate business need for that information, and they openly ask you for that information.

However, increasingly your personal data is collected in a concealed and questionable way—concealed when it's done without your knowledge and express permission; and questionable when there is not a clear business case for gathering it.

Many organizations today take advantage of the fact that every time you use technology you leave behind a "data trail," which is a digital record of your activity. This includes obvious activities such as sending an email, browsing the Internet, and making a purchase. Yet it also includes any activity using technology.

Merchants collect digital data using tracking features, often known simply as trackers, that are embedded in virtually every app on your smartphone; in fact, the average app has six trackers. Trackers allow third parties to collect data from your interaction with the app along with exactly where you are located throughout the day. As people perform more and more everyday activities electronically, using more and more interconnected devices, the volume of data compiled on you grows exponentially.

Table 6-1: Risks of data collection

Risk	Explanation
The data is gathered and kept in secret.	You have no formal rights to find out what private information is being gathered, who gathers it, or how it is being used.
The accuracy of the data cannot be verified.	Because you do not have the right to correct or control what personal information is gathered, if it contains errors you cannot check and correct it.
Identity theft can impact the accuracy of data.	Victims of identity theft will often have information added to their profile that was the result of actions by the identity thieves with no right to see or correct the information.
Data is being used for important decisions.	Private data is being used on an ever-increasing basis to determine eligibility in significant life opportunities, such as jobs, consumer credit, insurance, and identity verification.

This data collection results in advertisements appearing in our web browsers and through email messages that we receive and is called **adware**. Adware itself is not considered harmful. Although some users find it annoying, other users like that the ads they receive are tailored to their interests. However, beyond adware there are serious risks with this secret collection and use of your private data, as described in **Table 6-1**.

Define Other Technology Hazards

"Warning: Using This Device Could Be Hazardous to Your Safety and Health" is a label you may never see on a computer. But using a computer can carry hazards that are more tangible than that of data collection, including physical, behavioral, and environmental.

Physical Hazards   Many users of technology devices report aches and pains associated with repeated and long-term usage of the devices, a hazard known collectively as **repetitive strain injury (RSI)**. Also called repetitive stress injury, RSI impacts your muscles, nerves, tendons, and ligaments, and most often affects the upper parts of the body, including elbows, forearms, hands, neck, shoulders, and wrists. It is usually caused by one or more of three factors, listed in **Table 6-2**.

Table 6-2: Causes and examples of RSI

Cause	Description	Example
Repetitive activity	Repeating the same activity over a lengthy time period	Typing on a keyboard for multiple hours every day over several years
Improper technique	Using the wrong procedure or posture	Slouching in a chair
Uninterrupted intensity	Performing the same high-level activity without frequent periods of rest	Working at a computer all day with no breaks

Figure 6-6: Incorrect posture while working on a computer

Face too close to the screen

Glare from window reflecting off the screen

Not sitting up straight in the chair

Africa Studio/Shutterstock.com

Many computer users suffer from RSI that is brought about through using an improper technique for sitting at a computer. Examples of incorrect posture while working on a computer include: the user is not sitting up straight in the chair, he is too close to the computer screen, and glare from the window behind him is reflecting off the screen (**Figure 6-6**). Being too close to a screen or looking at screens without regular breaks can cause eyestrain.

Behavioral Hazards   Just as there are hazards to physical health from using digital devices, there also are behavioral health hazards. These hazards are sometimes more difficult to observe but every bit as serious as RSI and other physical hazards.

One behavioral hazard is **technology addiction**, which occurs when a user is obsessed with using a technology device and cannot walk away from it without feeling extreme anxiety. Because near-constant use of technology has become the norm, technology addiction can be difficult to identify in a friend or companion, and in yourself. Some symptoms may include having significant mood swings, focusing exclusively on the Internet and digital media, being unable to control how much time they spend on technology, and showing withdrawal symptoms when not using the Internet or technology.

In addition to technology addiction, there are other behavioral risks associated with using technology, including:

- **Sedentary lifestyle**. Too much time spent using a technology device often results in too little time for physical activity and can contribute to an overall sedentary lifestyle.
- **Psychological concerns**. Excessive use of technology has been associated with several psychological mental health concerns such as poor self-confidence, anxiety, depression, lower emotional stability, and even lower life satisfaction.
- **Hindered social interaction**. Users who spend excessive amounts of time using technology often resist face-to-face interaction with others, and this may hinder social skill development or even cause social withdrawal.

Another risk that can result in serious emotional harm is a type of bullying, which is the act of using strength or influence to intimidate someone else. **Cyberbullying** is bullying that takes place on technology devices like smartphones, computers, and tablets using online social media platforms, public online forums, gaming sites, text messaging, or email. Cyberbullying includes sending, posting, or sharing negative, harmful, mean-spirited, and

Table 6-3: Harmful features of cyberbullying

Feature	Bullying	Cyberbullying
Seems to never end	A person may be bullied at school or work, but once the person goes home the bullying ceases.	Because cyberbullying comments posted online are visible all the time, to the victim the bullying never ends.
Everyone knows about it	Mean-spirited words spoken to a victim may be witnessed only by those who are nearby.	A cyberbully can post comments online that everyone can read.
May follow for a lifetime	Bullying usually stops when the person or victim leaves the school or organization.	Posted cyberbullying comments may remain visible online for years and even follow the victim through life, impacting college admissions and employment.

usually false content about another person. It can even include sharing personal or private information to cause embarrassment or humiliation to that person before others. Cyberbullying, once it begins, is difficult to control because it is done online and many web sites consider it as "free speech" that should not be censored. **Table 6-3** compares features of bullying to cyberbullying.

Figure 6-7: E-waste

Lucian Coman/Shutterstock.com

Environmental Hazards   What happens to an electronic device when it reaches the end of its useful life? It's estimated that only 12 percent of these unwanted devices are taken to an approved recycling center to be dismantled and the components reused, while the rest are thrown away. This results in large amounts of **e-waste**, or electronic waste, which is electrical or electronic equipment that no longer works or is no longer being used. Some of this equipment may be broken and cannot be repaired so it is thrown away as garbage. Other equipment may still work but the owner no longer wants it and just throws it away. About 40 million tons of e-waste are generated each year worldwide, through people throwing out devices (**Figure 6-7**). That's the equivalent of disposing of 800 laptop computers every second.

   E-waste is a hazard to humans. Computer parts contain harmful toxins including mercury, lead, cadmium, polybrominated flame retardants, barium, and lithium. Most e-waste is incinerated, which releases these toxins into the air. E-waste that is buried in landfills can eventually contaminate the ground and water supply, causing harm to the environment and all living beings.

Apply Defenses to Repel Cyber Attacks

As an informed computer user, you can apply defenses to block cyberattacks. To do so effectively, it's important to acknowledge a basic principle about the relationship between security and convenience: it is not directly proportional. That is, as security around your data and devices increases, convenience does not increase. Instead, this relationship is inversely proportional: as security increases, convenience actually decreases. In other words, the more secure something becomes, the less convenient it may become to use. In addition, increasing its convenience usually decreases its security (**Figure 6-8**).

Figure 6-8: Relationship of security to convenience

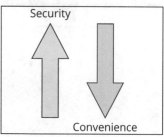

Security

Convenience

Consider accessing your bank's online website. While it would be quicker and easier for you not to enter a username and password, that extra protection is well worth the cost of the extra security that it gives. Security is often described as sacrificing some convenience for the sake of safety. When considering whether an extra security measure is worth the time or trouble, remember the consequences of not protecting your device. You can have money taken from your bank account, an imposter taking out a loan in your name, or any number of serious issues.

Use Strong Authentication

Authentication is the process of ensuring that the person requesting access to a computer or other resources is authentic, and not an imposter. There are different types of authentications or "proof of genuineness" that can be presented.

Passwords   Virtually all user technology devices rely on something that only the "real" user knows and an imposter does not know for authentication. This is done by entering a **password**, a string of uppercase and lowercase letters, numbers, and symbols that when entered correctly, allow you to open a password-protected device or account. A secret password serves as the key to unlock access to a device by proving you are the authentic user (**Figure 6-9**).

Despite their widespread use, passwords provide only weak protection. The weakness is due not to technology but to the frailties of human memory. First, the best passwords are long and complex, but these are difficult to memorize and then accurately recall. Second, because passwords should be unique for each device, users must remember multiple passwords for all their devices and accounts. These can include different computers and mobile devices at work, school, and home; multiple email accounts; online banking; Internet site accounts; social media accounts, and so on.

To make signing on easier, many users instead take shortcuts that make the process more convenient but much less secure. They may use a **weak password**, which is one that is short in length (less than 15 characters), and/or uses a common word as a password (princess), a predictable sequence of characters (abc123), or personal information (Braden). Another common shortcut is to repeat the same password on more than on device or account, which, if the password were discovered, would compromise not just one account but all accounts that use that same password. Weak and duplicate passwords make your devices and accounts vulnerable to an attacker.

The most important characteristic of a password that makes it resistant to attacks is its length and not its complexity. A longer password is always more secure than a shorter password, regardless of complexity. An easy way to remember this is "Long is strong." Most security experts recommend that a secure password should be a minimum of 20 characters in length.

A **strong password** is a password that is long and contains a mix of letters (both uppercase and lowercase), numbers, and symbols. Strong passwords should not use dictionary words or phonetic words; it should not repeat characters (xxx) or use sequences (abc, 123, qwerty); and it should not contain birthdays, family member names, pet names, addresses, or any personal information.

Figure 6-9: Password

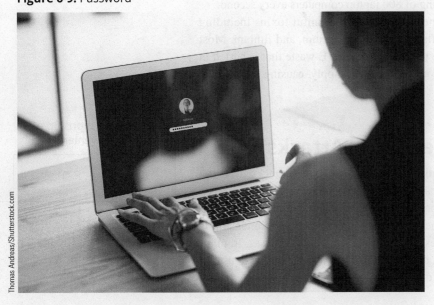

Thomas Andreas/Shutterstock.com

Figure 6-10: Password manager

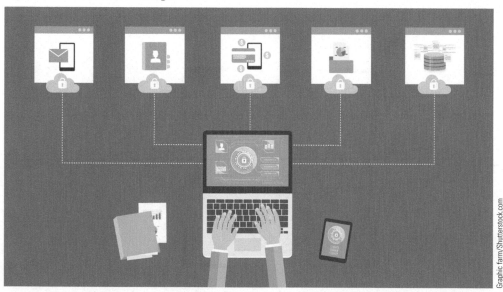

Graphic farm/Shutterstock.com

You may wonder, how can I possibly apply all these recommendations and memorize long, complex, and unique passwords for all my accounts? The simple answer is that you cannot. But instead of relying on your memory for passwords, you should use a **password manager**, which is a program or secure website in which you can create and store all your strong passwords in single user "vault" file that is protected by one strong master password. You can then retrieve individual passwords as needed from the vault file, thus freeing you from the need to memorize multiple passwords (**Figure 6-10**). The value of using a password manager is that unique strong passwords such as *WUuAôxB$2aWøBnd&Tf7MfEtm* can be easily created and used for any of your accounts.

Multifactor Authentication (MFA) Combining multiple types of authentication, known as **multifactor authentication (MFA)**, is a way to increase security when using passwords. The combination most often used is a password (something you know) and a smartphone (something you have). After correctly entering your password, a four- to six-digit code is sent to your smartphone. The code must then be entered as the second authentication method, proving that you are the genuine user (**Figure 6-11**).

Figure 6-11: Multifactor authentication (MFA)

Julia Tim/Shutterstock.com

Figure 6-12: Face recognition

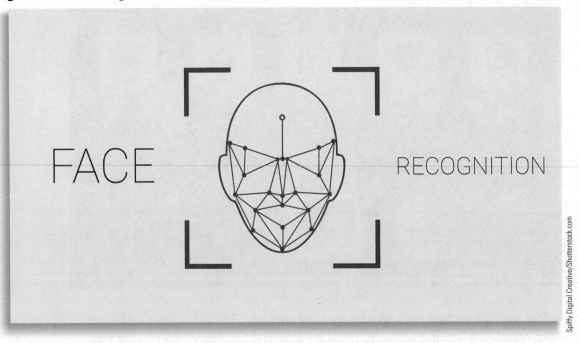

Spiffy Digital Creative/Shutterstock.com

Biometrics   Another increasingly common type of authentication uses **biometrics**, the unique characteristics of a body part for authentication. Compared to things that you *know*, such as entering a password or using two-factor authentication, biometrics rely on something you *are*—your unique fingerprint or face, for instance. The most common biometrics in use today are:

- **Fingerprint**. Your fingerprint consists of a unique pattern of ridges and valleys. A static fingerprint scanner requires you to place your entire thumb or finger on a window or button that takes an optical "picture" of the fingerprint and compares it with the fingerprint image on file.

- **Face**. A biometric authentication that is becoming increasingly popular on smartphones is facial recognition. Every person's face has several distinguishable "landmarks" called nodal points (**Figure 6-12**). Facial recognition software can measure these nodal points and create a numerical code (faceprint) that represents the face to compare it with the original code faceprint created.

- **Eye**. The human eye can also be used for biometrics. The iris, which is a thin, circular structure in the eye, is responsible for controlling the diameter and size of the pupils to regulate the amount of light reaching the retina. Eye recognition identifies the unique random patterns in an iris for authentication.

Manage Patches

A **patch** is a software "fix" for a vulnerability found in a program. Most major software companies create a patch and then either make it available on their website to download or "push" the patch out to your computer.

Both Microsoft Windows and Apple macOS distribute, or "push," patches out to your computer. Depending on how your computer is configured, you may receive a notification that a patch is available or has already been downloaded and installed on your computer or will be installed at a later time.

Promptly installing patches once they are available is the most important step to protecting your device. You can facilitate this by configuring your devices to automatically download and install patches when they become available. You may still have to confirm the installation or restart your computer, but the process is more streamlined than having to manually check for updates and hope that you don't forget.

Back Up Your Data

One of the most important defenses against ransomware and malware attacks, as well as a wide range of other threats, is frequently overlooked. A **data backup** is a copy of a file or message that is stored in another location for safekeeping. Data backups should be conducted on a regular basis. Data backups protect against cyberattacks because they can restore infected computers to their properly functioning state, and they can also protect against hardware malfunctions, user error, software corruption, and natural disasters.

The most comprehensive solution for most users is a continuous cloud backup. This type of backup occurs continually, without the user needing to intervene. Instead, software monitors which files have changed and automatically updates the backed-up files with the most recent versions. These backups are stored online in the cloud. There are several cloud-based services available that provide features such as:

- **Automatic continuous backup**. Once the initial backup is completed, any new or modified files are also backed up. Usually the backup software will "sleep" while the computer is being used and perform backups only when there is no user activity. This helps to lessen any impact on the computer's performance or Internet speed.
- **Universal access**. Files backed up through online services can be made available to another computer.
- **Optional program file backup**. In addition to user data files, these services have an option also to back up all program and operating system files.
- **Delayed deletion**. Files that are copied to the online server will remain accessible for up to 30 days before they are deleted. This allows a user to have a longer window of opportunity to restore a deleted file.

Recognize Social Engineering Attacks

There are two basic principles when combating social engineering attacks. The first principle is that attacks based on social engineering can come at any time without any advanced warning. The second principle is that the attacker presents themself as someone who can be trusted. This means that both of these principles must be counteracted: you must always be aware, and you must not automatically trust everything that you receive.

Table 6-4: Social engineering defenses

Social engineering attack	Secure action	Explanation
An email stating you have won a prize and you must send your bank account number for the money to be deposited.	Recognize scams.	Any offer for "easy money" that requires you to provide something should be rejected.
A text message that a friend vacationing overseas has lost her purse and needs you to immediately purchase gift cards or a money wire transfer to send funds to a foreign bank account.	Think before you click.	Attackers employ a sense of urgency to make you act now and think later, so action on any highly urgent or high-pressure messages should be paused until it can be verified through another method of communication different from the message itself (like calling the person if a text message was received).
An email from a company that says your credit card will be charged for a recent purchase, but you did not make the purchase; you are asked to open the email attachment for proof.	Research sources.	Always be careful of any unsolicited messages, and instead of responding through email or text call about it.
You receive an email from a friend that has an attachment with the subject line "I can't believe this is a picture of you doing this!"	Never download unexpected file attachments.	Always verify through a different channel (phone, text message, etc.) with the sender that the attachment is legitimate, especially if there is a sense of urgency with the message.
A text message asks you to make a donation to a disaster recovery effort due to a tornado that occurred last night.	Reject requests for help.	Perform research into the organization asking for funds.
An email says that you are eligible to apply for federal disaster relief and this company will assist you.	Deny unsolicited offers of assistance.	Go directly to the website that provides assistance and never give personal information through an email to an unknown sender.

Table 6-4 list several social engineering defenses.

Configure Your Web Browser Settings

Modern web browsers allow you to tailor settings based on your personal preferences. Beyond basic settings such as preferred home page and the size of displayed characters, browsers also allow you to customize cybersecurity settings.

However, the number of different options for customizing a secure web browser can quickly become overwhelming and even confusing. To address this, modern browsers now implement "modes" of cybersecurity that encompass multiple settings. This requires a user only to select an appropriate mode, such as Balanced or Strict, rather than sorting through multiple individual settings (**Figure 6-13**).

It is recommended that the highest level of security mode be turned on in a web browser. If this proves to be too restrictive, then exceptions can be made to this highest level. For example, in Microsoft Edge, an exception list can be made for accessing certain websites that are known to be trustworthy. If creating exceptions still impact the browsing experience, then the lower-level mode can be implemented.

Figure 6-13: Microsoft Edge security modes

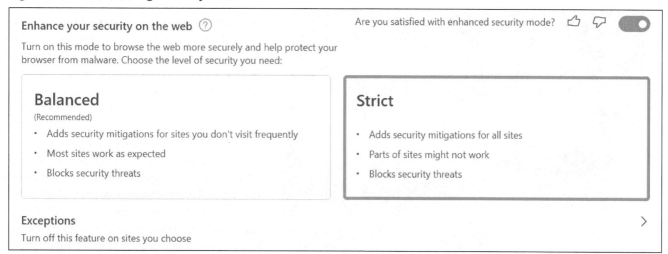

Use Antimalware Software

Antimalware software is software that can combat various malware attacks to protect files. One of the earliest antimalware software security applications was antivirus (AV) software. This software can examine a computer for any infections as well as monitor computer activity and scan new documents that might contain a virus. (This scanning is typically performed when files are opened, created, or closed.) If a virus is detected, options generally include cleaning the file of the virus, quarantining the infected file, or deleting the file.

At one time, running AV software was considered to be the primary—and often the only required—defense against attacks. However, it was later recognized that due to the many different types of malware, AV software, despite many user's perceptions, is not a complete security solution.

In addition to AV protection, modern antimalware software often includes the following:

- **Intrusion prevention**. The software analyzes information arriving from a network and blocks potential threats before they enter a computer.
- **Reputation protection**. Using information gathered from a global network, it is able to classify software application files as "dangerous," "risky," or "safe" based on their attributes.
- **Behavioral protection**. This monitors applications for suspicious behavior and automatically blocks the software if necessary.

Both Microsoft Windows and Apple macOS have built-in comprehensive antimalware software, Microsoft Defender Antivirus and Apple XProtect. Despite that fact that antimalware software is not perfect and does not provide absolute protection, it does provide a degree of protection that would be lacking if this software was not running. Without a valid reason, you should not turn off built-in comprehensive antimalware protection. However, antimalware software should be recognized as one tool but not the only tool that can be deployed to protect the integrity of files.

Use Protective Measures against Technology Hazards

There are several steps that can be taken to protect against technology hazards. These including securing your privacy, practicing good ergonomics, and protecting the environment.

Figure 6-14: Micro-cut shredder

Sarah Biesinger/Shutterstock.com

Secure Your Privacy

It is admittedly difficult to protect your data's privacy today. First, every time you use technology you leave behind a "data trail," which is a digital record of your activity. Second, despite the best intentions and diligent actions of users to protect the privacy of their data, sometimes nefarious actions by businesses can counteract these. One company agreed to pay a $150 million penalty for targeting ads at users by using their telephone numbers and email addresses that were collected from those users when they enabled multifactor authentication (MFA).

However, there are steps that can be taken to safeguard what you do have control over. To protect important information, consider the following privacy best practices:

- Do not provide personal information either over the phone or through an email or text message.
- Be cautious about what information you post on social networking sites and who can view your information. Show a reduced version of a profile to "limited friends," such as casual acquaintances or business associates.
- Use common sense: websites that request more personal information than would normally be expected, such as a username and password to another account, should be avoided.
- Be sure that strong passwords are used on all accounts and use multifactor authentication (MFA) when available.
- Shred financial documents and other paperwork that contains personal information before discarding it. There are three common types of shredders. The most secure is a micro-cut shredder device will shred documents into tiny pieces (**Figure 6-14**).
- Give cautious consideration before giving permission to a website or app request to collect data.
- Be sure that "https" appears at the beginning of a web address that asks for credit card numbers or other sensitive information. Do not provide any information if that is not present.
- Be cautious about surrendering personal information in exchange for a coupon or to enter a contest. Today brands are deploying an array of tactics to persuade users to surrender data to the brand itself through loyalty programs, sweepstakes, newsletters, quizzes, and polls. Resist the temptation to trade your personal information to enter a contest.
- Advocate for state and federal regulations that limit the collection and usage of private data.

Practice Good Ergonomics

To prevent RSI, you should arrange your workplace so that you are positioned ergonomically. **Ergonomics** is an applied science that specifies the design and arrangement of items that you use so that you and the items interact efficiently and safely. There are correct ergonomic posture and techniques for working on a computer (**Figure 6-15**). These include:

- **Arms**. The arms are parallel to the floor at approximately a 90-degree angle.
- **Eyes**. The distance to the screen is 18–28 inches (45–61 centimeters) from the eyes, and the viewing angle is downward at about 20 degrees to the center of the screen.

Figure 6-15: Correct ergonomics

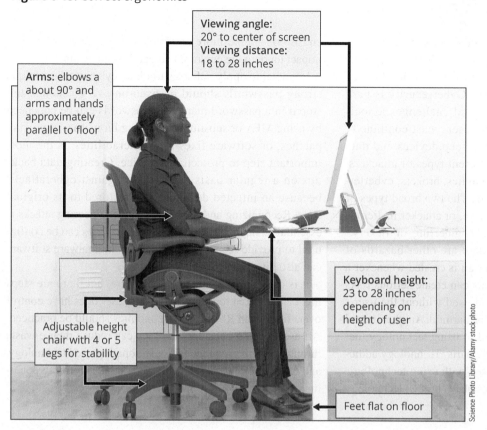

Viewing angle:
20° to center of screen
Viewing distance:
18 to 28 inches

Arms: elbows a about 90° and arms and hands approximately parallel to floor

Keyboard height:
23 to 28 inches depending on height of user

Adjustable height chair with 4 or 5 legs for stability

Feet flat on floor

Science Photo Library/Alamy stock photo

- **Feet**. The feet are flat on the floor. Use a proper chair with adjustable height and multiple legs for stability.
- **Back**. A lumbar support pillow for an office chair can provide back support.
- **Lighting**. The easiest way to reduce glare and screen reflections is to adjust the display's tilt and swivel mechanisms. You can also change the monitor's background and adjust the text colors. Light characters on a dark background will produce the minimal amount of screen glare, while dark characters on a light background can increase screen glare.

Reduce E-Waste

All users should consider how they can reduce their e-waste. An initiative called Sustainable Electronics Management (SEM) promotes the reduction of e-waste. **Table 6-5** outlines the action steps of SEM. As a security best practice, always remove any personal data before donating or recycling any device.

Table 6-5: Sustainable Electronics Management

Step	Action	Description
1	Buy green	When purchasing new electronic equipment, buy only products that have been designed with environmentally preferable attributes.
2	Donate	Donate used but still functional equipment to a school, charity, or non-profit organization.
3	Recycle	Send equipment to a verified used electronics recycling center.

Module 6 Summary

Cybersecurity involves the steps taken to keep electronic devices and the data stored on them safe. It is important for users to secure their devices due to the damage that can be inflicted by attackers. Cybersecurity is hard to achieve because there are several challenges associated with countering attacks, and users must continue to meet those challenges in order to keep devices and data safe. Potential threats include different types of attackers, including cybercriminals, script kiddies, brokers, cyberterrorists, hacktivists, and state actors. The two broad types of cyberattacks are those using malware, or attacker malicious software, and those based on social engineering, or trickery.

Besides attacks on devices, there are other hazards of using technology. Because a data trail is created whenever a user interacts with technology, this can create serious risks of private data being exposed and used without the user's permission and in ways that could be harmful. Another hazard is RSI, which is a physical hazard of using technology that causes physical discomfort in body parts. Technology addiction occurs when a user is obsessed with using technology. Cyberbullying is bullying that takes place through technology

and is considered more harmful. And e-waste can have an impact on both the environment and human health.

It is vital to apply defenses to block cyberattacks. Unique strong passwords should be used on every account and stored in a password manager. Passwords can be enhanced by using MFA or substituted by using biometrics. Applying patches, or software fixes for vulnerabilities, is the most important step to protecting a device. Creating data backups on a regular basis can protect against cyberattacks because an infected device can be restored to its original state. Recognizing and resisting social engineering attacks is essential to staying safe. Web browser settings can be configured to provide security, and installing antimalware software can also give a degree of protection.

It is difficult to protect personal data, but there are steps that can be taken to safeguard what a user does have control over. To prevent RSI proper ergonomics should be practiced. All users should consider how they can reduce their e-waste through buying green technology, donating used technology, and recycling (always removing personal data prior to donating or recycling).

Review Questions

1. Cybersecurity refers to protecting devices, networks, and programs with practices, processes, and _____.

   a. technologies
   b. people
   c. malware
   d. policies

2. An attack that occurs when an attacker steals your Social Security number and then uses that to impersonate you is called _____.

   a. data theft
   b. identity theft
   c. personal heist
   d. data scraping

3. The one factor that undoubtedly accounts for the greatest difficulty in preventing attacks is _____.

   a. universally connected devices
   b. increased speed of attacks
   c. user confusion
   d. decreased law enforcement

4. What category of cyber attacker sells software vulnerabilities to the highest bidder?

   a. Brokers
   b. Cyberterrorists
   c. Hacktivists
   d. State actors

5. Which of the following attacks locks down a user's device until a fee is paid?

   a. Kidnapping
   b. Keylogging
   c. Virus control
   d. Ransomware

6. A risk of data collection is that _____.

   a. the accuracy of the data cannot be verified
   b. it takes time for merchants to collect the data
   c. there may not be enough data collected for it to be worth the effort
   d. data can only be collected when a smartphone is in sleep mode

7. What is the name of the technology hazard that impacts your muscles, nerves, tendons, and ligaments?

   a. CSI
   b. SISI
   c. RSI
   d. KTI

8. (True or False) Data backups can protect you from more than just cybersecurity attacks.

9. The most important characteristic of a password that makes it resistant to attacks is _____.

   a. complexity
   b. length
   c. native language
   d. how quickly it can be memorized

10. What is the most important step to protecting a device?

   a. Using antimalware software
   b. Keeping your device turned off when not being used
   c. Backing up your data once per month
   d. Promptly installing patches

11. Which of the following is correct about antimalware software?

   a. You should always turn off built-in antimalware software because it can slow down your computer.
   b. Antimalware software is the only defense that you need on your computer to protect against cyberattacks.
   c. Antimalware software should be recognized as one tool for protection.
   d. Antimalware software should only be manually turned on when you are under attack.

12. (True or False) A recommended ergonomic practice is to have your arms parallel to the floor at approximately a 90-degree angle.

Discussion Questions

1. Why is it unrealistic to seek a one-size-fits-all cybersecurity solution to prevent all attacks? Identify at least three difficulties associated with cybersecurity.

2. What is the difference between bullying and cyberbullying? What forms does cyberbullying commonly take, and how do these types of actions intimidate the person they target? Why is cyberbullying difficult to control? Identify at least two differences between bullying and cyberbullying that make cyberbullying such a serious hazard.

3. Describe two or three shortcuts users commonly take when creating passwords and explain how these shortcuts result in weak passwords. Describe the most important characteristic of a strong password, especially as compared to a weak one.

4. What are the risks associated with data collection? What common activities leave a data trail for organizations who are seeking your personal data? How can this activity harm you?

Critical Thinking Activities

1. After the bank account of a friend was compromised by attackers, you learn that it was because of a weak password that your friend used on the account, a password they also used on several other of their accounts. You decide to review the passwords for your accounts to prevent any future vulnerabilities. List three items you would look for to identify weak passwords. Give each item a negative numeric value from −1 to −10 based on your estimate of the relative negative impact of this item to creating a weak password; that is, if X is the item that would have the greatest negative impact on a password, then you might assign it the value −10. Next, list three items that would make for a strong password. Rate those with a positive numeric value from +1 to +10, assigning the value +10 to the item you think would have the highest relative value in making a strong password. When you reflect on this list and think of the passwords you use for you own accounts, do you feel your passwords are strong enough, or do you think you may need to make some changes?

2. You are starting as an intern in the Marketing Department of a local bank. After several days on the job, you realize that the bank has been using personal information about its customers without their permission for advertising. At a meeting the director of the department has announced that they are finalizing a new smartphone app that will have six trackers installed to monitor the users' smartphone activity and will also start using this data in their marketing campaigns. None of the users will be asked for their permission to gather and use their personal data. What should you do? Should you speak up about the risks of using personal data? Or should you remain silent since many companies use this technique? If you were in this situation, would you speak out?

3. One evening your roommate is working on their laptop computer while sitting on the floor. They begin to complain about the chronic pain in their neck and how tired their eyes are. You suggest that the discomforts could be a result of where they are sitting and the lighting of the room. Your roommate asks if you could help them create a workspace that could prevent these pains. Create a checklist of correct ergonomic postures and techniques that could help your roommate work in a pain-free environment. As you consider your own computer use, do you experience any of these issues? If so, how do they impact your overall well-being?

4. While you are away on vacation you wake up to an unsettling email. The email is from your bank that says several days ago you used your credit card multiple times and one of the charges was for purchasing clothing that cost several hundreds of dollars. That now makes your balance above your credit limit and any future charges will be declined. Because your spending pattern while away on vacation has been very different, you cannot remember whether you made this purchase. You are depending on using your credit card to pay for your hotel room and to get back home, but if your card is now "frozen" you are unable to use it. The email from the bank includes an attachment for you to open that lists details about the charge. You are tempted to immediately open the attachment but are unsure if it may be a phishing attack. What process should you go through to determine if the email is legitimate? Have you ever been the victim of a phishing attack? How did you cope with it?

Apply Your Skills

Tony Blanco has been hired as an intern at a company that installs solar panels. Because he is completing his degree in cybersecurity at the local college, he works in the company's security operations center (SOC) assisting security managers and technicians who protect the company's computers and networks from cyberattacks. One of Tony's recent assignments was helping the technicians who monitor for signs of attacks and then take action to prevent the attacks from quickly spreading. Tony has begun offering Lunch-and-Learn sessions for employees with hands-on training on how to keep their devices safe.

Working in a small group or by yourself, complete the following:

1. Tony has been asked to give a Lunch-and-Learn session to new interns who are unfamiliar with social engineering attacks. What types of social engineering attacks should Tony discuss? Provide at least three examples he should cover.

2. Tony receives a text message from a new intern that says they are very concerned that their supervisor is exhibiting behaviors that shows they have technology addiction. The reasons given are the supervisor is always working on their computer throughout the day, they rarely leave their desk, the only conversations they have seem to be about the latest technology, and they constantly look at their smartphone while eating lunch. Is this technology addiction or is it the normal use of technology by a busy supervisor? Have you ever been concerned that you or someone close to you may be addicted to technology? How did you address the concern?

3. A recent data breach occurred in the company, and it was tracked down to an accountant who reused the same password on all their accounts, including social media and their work accounts. What are two solutions that Tony can give this accountant to help prevent this occurring again? In acknowledging that these solutions may decrease convenience around accessing accounts, do you feel that using them would be worth your time?

4. Several new interns have complained to Tony about their working conditions. The interns all share a cramped office that used to be a storage area and has very poor lighting. Instead of desks there are only two tables that all the interns must share as their workspaces, and because the chairs are not office chairs, they lack armrests and adequate back support. Use the Internet to research potential ergonomic products that Tony could recommend to create a better environment for the interns. For example, you might research ergonomic products such as desks, standing desks, office chairs, indirect lighting, copyholders, keyboard trays, elevated mouse pads, antiglare screen covers, footrests, and wrist rests, among other ergonomic tools. Based on your research, create a list of at least five potential products. Rank the five products from 1 to 5 in terms of their importance for creating an ergonomic environment, with 5 being the most important and 1 being the least.

Digital Media

In This Module

- Explain digital media technology concepts
- Describe uses for digital media
- Describe how to create digital media

Ninad uploads digital photos he takes using a digital camera or his smartphone on the cloud.

Ninad uses a variety of digital graphics and media apps in his work.

Andrey_Popov/Shutterstock.com

To prepare for a career in the video game industry, Ninad Patil took courses in graphic design, art, illustration, and animation. His courses enabled him to acquire technical skills and experience in creating and using digital media. He learned about digital video, 2D and 3D animation, computer graphics, and digital music and videos. In his free time, he streams movies and TV shows from his smart TV. He is also creating a video that compiles footage he shot during his two weeks in Paris, France last summer. He plans to submit the finished video to film festivals and use it to showcase his work to potential employers.

Digital media—including colorful images, animated effects, and realistic sounds—enhances your experiences when using your computer or device. You probably interact with digital media often to watch movies and videos, listen to music, play games, and share experiences with others. Digital media also is an essential part of most industries. Demonstrating skills and knowledge about digital media makes you a more attractive job applicant and valuable employee.

In this module, you explore and evaluate the technology behind digital media. You will learn how to use digital media for your own entertainment and for business. You will explore the tools and techniques required to create digital media and protect your work from copyright infringement. As you reflect on what you learn in this module, ask yourself: In what situations would you use a 2D rather than a 3D graphic or animation? How do I translate what I know about using digital media to meet my business needs? What skills do I need to create and protect original digital media?

Explain Digital Media Technology Concepts

Digital media is content you create, produce, and distribute in digital, or computer-readable, form (**Figure 7-1**). You likely are more familiar with reading, viewing, and listening to digital media as a consumer. If you are involved with efforts to promote a product, service, or yourself, you can use digital media to reach your audience and emphasize your message.

List Types of Digital Media

Websites, entertainment products, and business marketing efforts often use a combination of digital media to attract, inform, entertain, and persuade viewers and listeners. Types of digital media include graphics, animations, video and audio, and virtual reality.

Figure 7-1: Types of digital media

Listen to digital music.

Create and share digital photos.

Watch digital animated movies and TV shows.

Figure 7-2: Digital graphics

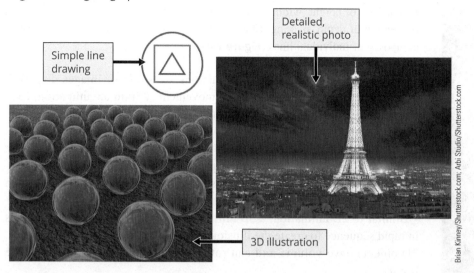

Table 7-1: 2D digital graphics types

Type	Description
Bitmap graphics	A grid of pixels that forms an image. The simplest bitmap graphic has only two colors, with each pixel being either black or white. Bitmaps become more complex as they include more colors. Bitmaps are appropriate for detailed graphics, such as photographs and the images displayed on a display screen.
Vector graphics	A vector graphic groups and layers simple objects to create an image. When you work with a vector graphic, you interact with a collection of lines, not a grid of pixels. Vector images are appropriate for simple drawings, such as line art and graphs, for fonts, and for animations.
Photos	Photographs or pictures taken with a digital camera or digitized by other methods. Photos with shading can have millions of colors, which increases file size.

2D and 3D Digital Graphics   Digital graphics are images you can see, store, and manipulate on a computer, tablet, smartphone, or other digital device (**Figure 7-2**). A 2D digital graphic can be a simple line drawing, or a highly detailed photo (**Table 7-1**). **2D** refers to the two dimensions of height and length.

Figure 7-3 describes the differences between bitmap and vector graphics.

Figure 7-3: Comparing bitmap and vector graphics

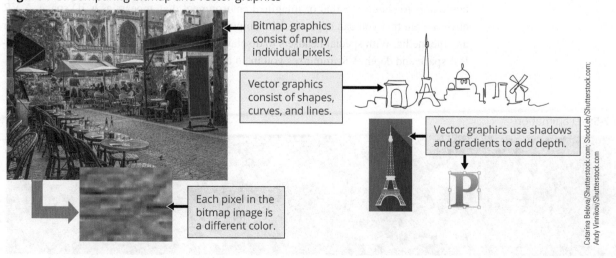

Figure 7-4: 3D wireframe

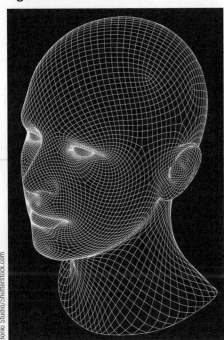

More complex skills are required to create 3D images. **3D** refers to the three dimensions of height, width, and length. A **3D image** portrays an image with a perception of depth, making it look real. A **wireframe drawing** is a 3D object composed of individual lines (**Figure 7-4**).

2D and 3D Animations

Animations are series of images displayed in sequence to create the illusion of movement. Within an animation, each individual image is called a frame. Instead of storing moving images, a digital animation stores data about the color and brightness of each individual frame. Films, games, training videos, business presentations, and websites are the most popular venues for animation. Like graphics, animations can be 2D or 3D.

A **2D animation** displays 2D images in rapid sequence to create the illusion of lifelike motion, as in a classic animated cartoon (**Figure 7-5**).

Similar to 2D animation, a **3D animation** displays 3D objects or models in rapid sequence to create the illusion of natural motion. Unlike 2D objects, 3D objects have volume and can rotate 360 degrees, making them more lifelike.

Another type of 3D animation is stop motion animation, which movies such as *Coraline* directed by Henry Selick and *Isle of Dogs* directed by Wes Anderson, use. With **stop motion animation**, animators move real-life objects through a sequence of poses and capture the movements one frame at a time; when you play the frames in sequence, the objects seem to move.

Although 3D animation is more complex and realistic than 2D animation, one form of animation is not necessarily better than the other. Each type produces a different effect, with 2D animation providing clear, simple expressions of concepts and stories, and 3D animation creating a more immersive, dynamic experience.

Digital Video and Audio

Like animation, a video is a series of still images played quickly enough to appear as continuous motion. While you typically create an animation by drawing illustrations, you create a **digital video** by capturing live footage using a video camera. While a video camera can be a standalone piece of equipment, many smartphones possess the capabilities to produce high quality videos. Some full-length films are entirely shot and edited using only an iPhone.

Digital video usually includes **digital audio**, sound that is recorded and stored as computer data (0s and 1s). Music, speech, and sound effects are types of digital audio.

Virtual Reality

Although digital video can be convincingly realistic, you still are aware of being a viewer watching the video content. **Virtual reality (VR)** is the use of computers to simulate a real or imagined environment that appears as a 3D space. A VR environment that you can explore and manipulate removes the barrier between the viewer and the media. With special headsets to display 3D images that create the illusion of limitless space and depth, VR immerses you in an artificial world (**Figure 7-6**).

Figure 7-5: 2D animation

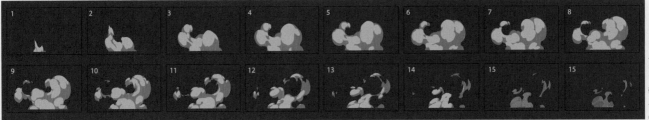

Figure 7-6: VR uses headsets to display a virtual world

Max kegfire/Shutterstock.com

Describe How Computers Represent Images

Bitmap graphics (also called raster graphics) assign colors to the smallest picture elements, or pixel. Each color is assigned a binary number. To a computer, a bitmap image is a list of the color numbers for all the pixels it contains, using RGB values, or the values assigned to red, green, and blue (**Figure 7-7**).

Vector graphics consist of shapes, curves, lines, and text created by mathematical formulas. Instead of storing the color value for each pixel, vector graphics contain instructions that define the shape, size, position, and color of each object in an image.

Figure 7-7: Selecting a color using binary numbers in Microsoft Paint

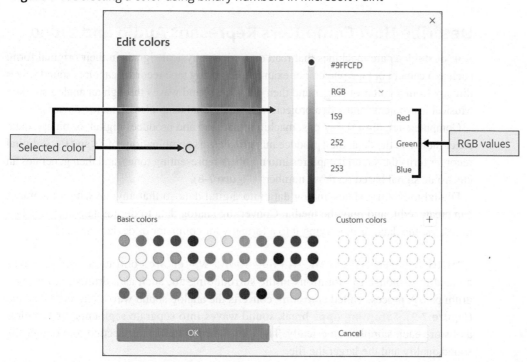

Data Representation   The binary number system is a two-digit system of 1s and 0s. All computer data is fundamentally composed of 1s and 0s, even movies with sophisticated special effects and musical recordings of full orchestras. Computers are binary machines because they are electronic devices, and electricity has two states: on and off. For instance, in most color systems black has the binary value 00 and white has a value of 11.

A bit is the smallest unit of information a computer handles. A bit can have the value of 0 or 1. Bits appear in groups of eight, called bytes. Bytes can represent letters, symbols, and numbers. Bytes are the basic building blocks of digitally representing sounds, colors, and other data.

Resolution and Compression   When using graphics in your work, you should be aware of how certain properties affect quality. **Resolution** refers to the clarity or sharpness of an image: the higher the resolution, the sharper the image and the larger the file size.

For example, if a photo has a resolution of 1500 × 1225, it has 1500 pixels across and 1225 pixels down the image, for a total of 1,837,500 pixels and 1.13 MB of data. If you are selecting images for a website, you want to use images with a file size small enough so they load quickly, but large enough so they appear sharp and clear.

Bitmap graphics are **resolution dependent**, which means image quality deteriorates as their dimensions increase. If you significantly resize or stretch bitmaps to fit a space they were not designed to fill, the images become blurred and distorted. Unlike bitmap graphics, vector graphics keep the same quality as their dimensions change.

On a digital camera, resolution is typically measured in **megapixels**, or millions of pixels. The higher the number of megapixels, the higher the resolution of your photos, and the larger the picture files. However, high-resolution photos and other complicated graphics can be difficult to copy, download, or send as email attachments, due to their large file size.

Compression is a space-saving technique used to store data in a format that takes less space. Compression makes digital media files smaller by reducing the amount of data in the files. **Lossy compression** is a method of reducing graphics file size in which some of the original file data is discarded. The effect of the lost data is generally not noticeable. **Lossless compression** is a method of reducing graphics file size in which none of the original file data is discarded. When opened and viewed, the files are uncompressed and contain all of their original data.

Describe How Computers Represent Audio and Video

Analog devices are machines that read or produce physical signals in their original form, such as a camera or tape player. For example, an analog tape recorder captures sound waves directly from a guitar or singer and then plays the sound waves through an analog speaker. Musical instruments and video projectors are additional examples of analog devices.

Computers are **digital devices**, machines that read and produces digital, or binary, data. After they read the data, they produce numeric data as combinations of 1s and 0s. A digital recorder turns the sound it captures into numbers representing tones, and then generates an electronic signal based on those numbers (**Figure 7-8**).

Digital media translates analog data into digital data so that anyone with a computer can create, edit, and play the media. Converting analog data to digital data is also called **digitizing** the data, or modifying it to a format your computer or device can read.

Sound Representation   **Analog sound waves** are continuous sound waves created in response to vibrations in the surrounding air, such as a drumstick hitting a drum pad. A process called **sampling** converts the analog sound waves into digital sound (**Figure 7-9**). **Sampling apps** break sound waves into separate segments, or samples, and store each sample numerically. The more samples taken per second, the higher the sound quality and the larger the file.

Figure 7-8: Converting analog sound into digital sound

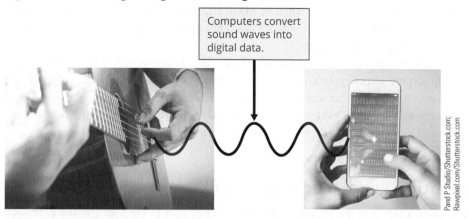

Figure 7-9: Sampling sound

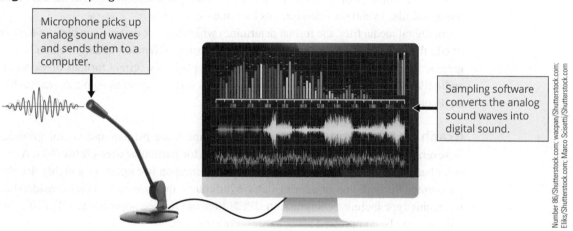

The quality of an audio file is also determined by its **bit rate**, which is the number of bits of data processed every second. Bit rates are usually measured as kilobits per second (kbps). As with the sampling rate, the higher the bit rate, the higher the sound quality and the larger the file.

Large files take longer to download from a website or load and play on a webpage. They also require more storage space than smaller files. If you are using an audio file in a project and can choose from varying bit rates (such as 128 kbps and 160 kbps) and sampling rates (such as 22,050, 44,100, and 88,200), choose a file that balances quality and size.

Video File Resolutions   Video file formats are one way to describe a video file. Resolution is another. If you've seen videos available for download on the web described as 720p, HD, or 4K, those descriptions refer to resolution.

Digital video resolution is given as width × height. The higher the resolution, the sharper the video, and the larger the file size. Video resolutions can be organized into three categories (**Table 7-2**).

Table 7-2: Video resolutions

Resolution type	Examples
Standard Definition (SD)	640 × 360 and 720 × 480
High Definition (HD)	1280 × 720 (called 720p) and 1920 × 1080 (called 1080p or Full HD)
Ultra High Definition (UHD)	The 4K standard provides a resolution of 3840 × 2160 (called 2160p), while the 8K standard provides a resolution of 7840 × 4320 (called 4320p)

Although 8K videos provide the highest resolution, that doesn't mean you should download the 8K version of a video when an SD or HD video is available. An 8K video file is 16 times larger than a Full HD video. Files that large take a long time to download and require significant storage space.

In addition, only some devices can play UHD files. If you want to watch a 4K video on a 720p display screen, your computer or TV converts the high-resolution video to 720p because that is the best the screen can offer.

In most cases, Full HD videos balance high-quality playback with smaller file sizes that download quickly, making them ideal for sharing and posting on websites.

Identify Digital Media File Formats

File format refers to the organization and layout of data in the file. The file extension, typically a three- to four-character prefix that appears after the file name, indicates the type of file format. For instance, files in the bitmap graphics format have the extension .bmp, and files in certain video formats have the extension .avi.

For digital media files, the format determines which apps or devices you can use to open or edit the file. For example, you need a paint app such as Windows Paint to edit a bitmap graphic. Digital media playback devices can often play only certain formats of video and audio files. For example, you can play older iTunes songs only on an Apple device such as an iPhone.

Graphics File Formats   You can create and store bitmap and vector graphics in several file formats. Each file format is suited for particular uses (**Table 7-3**). A two color button for a webpage, vacation photos for posting on Instagram, or a highly detailed photograph that will appear in print all have different requirements. Another consideration in graphic type includes compression. JPEG files use lossy compression. TIF, PNG, and GIF files can be compressed using lossless compression.

Table 7-3: Common graphics file formats

Graphic file format	File extension	Best use / Notes
Bitmap graphics		
GIF	.gif (Graphics Interchange Format)	Simple web graphics and short web animations Format is limited to 256 colors; supports transparency; small file size makes it good for websites
JPEG	.jpeg or .jpg (Joint Photographic Experts Group)	Photos on the web Images have rich colors, but discard some data to reduce file size, which can affect quality
PNG	.png (Portable Network Graphics)	Logos, icons, and illustrations Images have good quality even when highly compressed; supports 16 million colors; better quality and smaller file size than GIF
TIF	.tif or .tiff (Tagged Image File Format)	High-quality photos and printed graphics Large file size is better suited for print than web use
Vector graphics		
EPS	.eps (Encapsulated PostScript)	Logos and other illustrations that are frequently resized A standard format for exporting vector graphics without data loss
SVG	.svg (Scalable Vector Graphics)	Illustrations on the web Developed by the World Wide Web Consortium (W3C); allows interactivity and animation

Table 7-4: Common audio file formats

File format	File extension	Compression	Notes
AAC and M4P	.aac and .m4p	Lossy	Apple uses these formats for iTunes downloads
AIFF (Audio Interchange File Format)	.aiff or .aif	None	Files are large; good to excellent sound quality
MP3	.mp3	Lossy	Common format for music and audio books; most digital audio devices can play MP3 files
WAVE or WAV (Waveform Audio)	.wav	None	Files are large; good to excellent sound quality
WMA (Windows Media Audio)	.wma	Lossless	Played using Microsoft's Media Player; also copy-protected

Audio File Formats   As with graphics, you can store audio files in a variety of formats, each with a specific purpose. For example, some types of audio formats are for storing music, others are for audio recordings such as audio books, and others are for podcasts. Some formats use lossy or lossless compression to reduce file size. You can identify an audio file format by looking at the file extension (**Table 7-4**).

To create uncompressed audio files such as WAV and AIFF files, you convert real sound waves directly to digital form without additional processing, resulting in accurate sound quality, but very large files. Choose uncompressed audio files to capture and edit pure audio, and then save them in a compressed format.

Audio files lose data when they are compressed with lossy compression, giving up quality and fidelity for file size. However, most people cannot detect any difference between uncompressed and lossy compressed audio files. Choose audio files with lossy compression (MP3 or M4P) when you are listening to sound other than music or want to conserve disk space.

Audio files with lossless compression have good audio quality and smaller file sizes than uncompressed audio files, but still larger than files with lossy compression. Choose audio files with lossless compression (WMA) if you want to listen to music with accurate audio representation.

Video File Formats   Digital video files have two parts: a codec and a container. A codec (short for compressor/decompressor) is a device or app that encodes and usually compresses digital media data for storage and then decompresses the data for playback (**Table 7-5**). Video files typically use lossy compression.

Table 7-5: Common video codecs

Name	Compatible with	Best use / Notes
DivX	AVI video container	Commercial video production Provides the highest video quality at the expense of file size
H.264	MP4 video container	Playing on playback devices or streaming services Common, efficient codec; preferred for YouTube videos
H.265	MP4 video container	Very high resolution videos New video codec; also called HEVC
MPEG-2	MP4 and Quicktime containers	DVDs, Blu-ray discs, professional-grade cameras Not used for streaming services
MPEG-4	Wide range of compatibility	Online streaming services Common codec providing good quality

Table 7-6: Common video containers

Name	File size and quality	Best use / Notes
AVI (.avi)	Files are often larger than others	Videos to store on a computer One of the oldest and most accepted formats
MP4 (.mp4)	Relatively small files and high quality	Nearly universal Websites such as YouTube and Vimeo prefer MP4 files
Windows Media (.wmv)	Small file size with reduced quality	Sharing with others and posting on the web Developed by Microsoft

A video **container** is a wrapper that contains parts of a video file including the video, audio, and codec in a single package (**Table 7-6**). Most digital video file formats are named after their container. Video codecs are compatible with only some containers.

Describe Uses for Digital Media

There are many personal uses of digital media (**Figure 7-10**). Because digital media is so appealing, it is a major part of entertainment products such as games and movies. It also has uses in education and training. For example, digital videos and virtual reality create simulated experiences when direct training would be difficult or dangerous, such as when learning how to fly jets or perform brain surgery. Businesses of all kinds use digital media in advertising and product support.

Figure 7-10: Uses for digital media

Listen to a podcast.

Play an AR game.

Post an animated GIF of you doing a cartwheel.

Use speech-to-text apps.

Explain How to Use Gaming Systems

Today's video games use high-end graphics, powerful processors, and the Internet to create environments that rival physical reality and bring together players from around the world. Computer and video games include role-playing, action, adventure, education, puzzles, simulations, sports, and strategy/war games.

Figure 7-11: Gaming console with built-in speakers and game controllers

Saikorn/Shutterstock.com

Gaming Consoles   Most games are played on **video consoles**, which are hardware devices with special controllers that let you play video games. A popular choice for video gaming is a **game console**, which is hardware that allows you to play video games using handheld controllers as input devices. Examples include Xbox, Nintendo Wii, and Sony PlayStation. These systems use speakers (built-in or separate) and a television screen or computer monitor as output devices, a hard drive, and memory cards or cloud folders for storage (**Figure 7-11**).

On consoles that connect to the Internet, you can interact with other players online and watch TV or movies. Large-scale multiplayer games such as Halo, Overwatch, and Minecraft, operate on many Internet servers, with each one handling thousands of players.

For a more immersive experience, you can set up a **VR gaming system** using hardware necessary for playing virtual reality games. These systems run on special desktops optimized for game playing called consoles and include a headset such as the Oculus Go controller, and sensors to track your movements. The Oculus Quest and PlayStation VR are VR consoles that you can use instead of a PC. Popular VR games include Robo Recall and Skyrim.

Microsoft offers the HoloLens headset, though it calls the experience of using it mixed reality. **Mixed reality** is a hybrid of virtual reality and augmented reality and includes simulations that let you see the real world while interacting with realistic virtual objects. HoloLens headsets do not require separate sensors because they include cameras and sensors to track motion.

HoloLens headsets use **holograms**, projected images that appear 3D, to allow you to superimpose virtual objects and characters onto scanned images of real objects in the room, and then interact with the virtual and real objects. For example, in the game Fragments, you explore a virtual space to solve a crime, looking for clues and interacting with virtual characters who appear to be seated in the room.

Instead of purchasing special hardware for gaming, you can also play games on computers, tablets, or smartphones. Simple games may come with the operating system of a computer or mobile device; you can also download them from an app store. Many of these games use 2D animation.

People use game consoles for activities other than entertainment. For example, doctors can practice their fine motor skills on surgery simulators using motion-sensing game consoles, which allows players to interact with the system through body movements. Input is usually accomplished through a combination of spoken commands, natural real-world actions, and gesture recognition. Physical therapists use these consoles along with virtual reality gaming techniques to challenge and motivate patients doing rehabilitation.

Mobile Gaming   Some game consoles are self-contained devices that fit in one hand, such as the Nintendo Switch (**Figure 7-12**). These consoles are portable, have a small screen, use built-in controllers, and are designed for single-player or multiplayer video games. Many use memory cards to store games. Others use a cartridge or a cloud folder for storage.

Figure 7-12: Portable gaming console

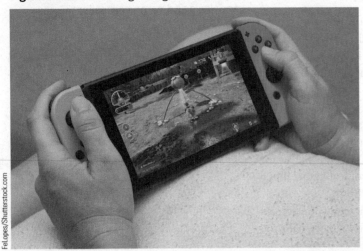

FeLopes/Shutterstock.com

Figure 7-13: Augmented reality

Shopping center 53-59M
★★★★★ 2741 votes

Coffee shop 50-55M
★★★★ 210 votes

Fashion shop 45-48M
★★★★ 881 votes

Zapp2Photo/Shutterstock.com

Mobile computing and smartphones put the world of gaming in the palms of your hands. Phones often come with scaled-down game versions to introduce them to new players. Other games, such as Words with Friends, are designed to be played by people on their mobile devices and can be played with others whose devices are not compatible with yours.

Mobile games were the first to popularize **augmented reality (AR)**, a type of virtual reality that uses an image of an actual place or thing and adds digital information to it, such as places to shop (**Figure 7-13**). **Augmented reality gaming** is a type of gaming that integrates visual and audio game content with your real environment. Unlike VR gaming, which often requires a separate room to create an immersive experience, AR gaming superimposes digital game elements in the real world, as with the breakthrough AR game Pokemon Go. You usually play AR games on smartphones, tablets, and portable consoles.

Virtual Worlds   Virtual reality apps simulate a real or imagined environment that appears as 3D space, also called a **virtual world**. When playing a VR game, for example, you wear a headset with built-in headphones to experience a virtual world, a 3D, 360-degree environment (**Figure 7-14**).

A virtual world is different from other simulations such as video games or movies because it is believable, interactive, and immersive. In a virtual world, a 3D computer model creates a convincing illusion of depth and space to make you feel you are part of a real scene you can explore. Sensors detect your movements and a head-mounted display adjusts what you see and hear. For example, if you are visiting a virtual version of Paris and enter a café, the sights and sounds in the virtual world change as you move, just as they would in the real world.

Figure 7-14: Robo Recall virtual reality game

In a VR game with a virtual world, you are a character in a 3D, 360-degree environment.

Interact with objects and other characters.

Oculus VR

A virtual world is also different from augmented reality, mixed reality, and some types of virtual reality. If you had an augmented reality app on your phone, for example, and were roaming real-world Paris, you could point the phone at a landmark to display an image of the landmark overlaid with details about it, including its name and history. The app enhances, or augments, the reality, while a virtual world replaces it.

Like augmented reality, mixed reality maintains a connection to the physical world. The goal of mixed reality is to produce an environment where physical and digital objects interact.

Many games such as flight and racing simulators have elements of virtual reality. For example, you could use a wide screen, headphones with surround sound, and a realistic joystick in a flight simulation game to experience piloting a jet. However, the game doesn't fully immerse you in a virtual world. If you turn your head away from the screen, you break the illusion of flying a plane.

Explain How to Use Animations

Although you might think the main purpose of animation is entertainment in films and games, animation has other uses. For example, animation can teach medical students a procedure or novice pilots how to maneuver through bad weather. **Simulations** are sophisticated computer animations that are useful for training and teaching in many fields, particularly in areas in which learning can be dangerous or difficult (**Figure 7-15**).

A popular use of simple animations is in PowerPoint or Google Slides presentations, in which you can animate slide text and objects. PowerPoint transitions, the way one slide moves to another, are a type of animation.

Web Animations   Ads, films, TV shows, computer games, and promotional videos use 2D animation. Websites frequently use it to enhance content. One popular animation method on the web is an **animated GIF**, a series of slightly different GIF images displayed in sequence to achieve animation effects.

For many years, people used Adobe Flash to create static or animated graphics in the SWF format, which was designed for web use. But Flash required users to download a **plug-in**, a component added to your browser, to play videos. Flash also became a target for malware developers. For these reasons, Flash is no longer used.

Figure 7-15: Using animation in training

aapp/Shutterstock.com

Figure 7-16: Real-time 3D animation

Electronic Arts

Currently, most web animations are created with **HTML5**, the latest version of the Hypertext Markup Language that is built into browsers. HTML5 features high-quality playback without the need for additional plug-in apps and is the standard for web animation development. Adobe Flash has been replaced by Adobe Animate CC, which incorporates HTML5.

Animation Use in Entertainment
The most popular uses of 3D animation are in ads, films, and computer games. 3D animation in films is done during the production phase, while the film is being shot, and then incorporated into the final footage.

In computer games, the 3D animation is called **real-time animation**, as it is produced as you're playing because you are in control of the characters' movements (**Figure 7-16**).

Real-time animation consumes an incredible amount of computer resources. At 60 frames per second, your computer must handle more than 1 billion bits of information every second to display a 3D image. The computer also has to track the movements of each player, using even more resources. Because of these requirements, you need a computer with a powerful processor to play games with 3D animation.

Explain How to Use Graphics

You can use graphics to improve your work by adding dramatic or informative photos to reports and articles. Select illustrations and drawings that reflect the ideas and concepts you want to communicate. On the job, you use **logos**, recognizable symbols that identify a person, business, or organization. Logos are used on business documents and websites to increase brand awareness. In digital content, you might use graphical buttons and icons to trigger actions such as displaying a menu or navigating to a new page. A **meme** is a video clip, animated GIF, or digital image, often with humorous text added, that are spread by Internet users (**Figure 7-17**).

Figure 7-17: Using animation in training

YOU USED AN IMAGE WITHOUT PERMISSION?

Gabriela Popa/Shutterstock.com

You can obtain graphics from external sources such as the web, or you can create your own. Before you can use graphics that you did not create on your social media page or in a presentation, you need to acquire them. While some images are widely available and may be considered fair use, you always should check before using someone else's work, especially for business purposes.

If you want to add a picture to a document or presentation to illustrate a key point, you can **download** it, which is the process of transferring (copying) a file from a server, computer, or device to another computer or device. Before you download any graphic from an external source, be sure to read the license and follow restrictions on using the image. The Internet provides rich sources for graphics, including the Creative Commons website. Online **stock photo galleries** are websites that maintain an inventory of photographs and other graphics and makes them available for download. Services such as Shutterstock and openclipart.org maintain large inventories of photographs and other graphics, which you can download, usually for a fee.

Search engines such as Google and Bing help you find websites containing graphics relating to specific topics. To help you find images that you can use legally, Google and Bing let you search using a **license filter**, which is a search engine tool that lets you search for pictures that you can use, share, or even modify for personal or commercial use.

Explain How to Play Digital Media

To watch videos or listen to audio such as audio books, podcasts, and music on your computer, you can download the media files the same way you download graphics files. When downloading, you must transfer the entire video or audio file to your computer, which can take a long time and a lot of storage space. As an alternative, you can **stream** the media, which is a way of receiving audio and video content on your computer or smart TV that lets you watch or listen to the content as it arrives.

On-demand content is media such as radio or TV shows where the original media file is stored on the media distributor's server and is sent to your computer for viewing. If you subscribe to the streaming service, it sends the media to your computer for viewing. Because the file is stored online, you can watch it more than once. Examples of subscription video streaming services include Netflix, Hulu, and YouTube. With **live video streaming**, streaming video content is transmitted live as it happens, and you can view the media as it arrives. Live video streaming often is available only once and frequently is used for sports events.

Streaming Video   In addition to viewing streaming video on your computer or mobile device, you can view it on your television set. A **smart TV** is a television that can connect to the Internet and stream TV shows and movies from subscription streaming services. Smart TVs use your Wi-Fi network connection. If you don't have a smart TV, you can connect hardware to your television, such as a TV stick or set top box. A **TV stick** is a device, usually the size of a USB drive, that connects to a television to provide access to the Internet and to streaming apps (**Figure 7-18**). A **set top box** is a device that allows you to view streaming media on your TV set. Examples of set top boxes include Apple TV, Roku, and Google Chromecast.

Because streaming video is more convenient and less expensive than traditional cable and satellite television content, many people no longer subscribe to cable

Figure 7-18: TV stick

Picturesque Japan/Shutterstock.com

and satellite television stations. Instead of watching scheduled content, you can create a personal entertainment hub with a smart TV and streaming video service to watch your favorite shows, movies, news, and sports at your convenience.

Streaming Audio
You also can stream digital audio in the form of audio books, using sites such as Audible, and as audio podcasts, which may include news stories, music, lectures, or radio shows. To stream music, you can use a music streaming service such as Pandora, Spotify, or SoundCloud. Some streaming services are free and others are paid. Free services usually feature advertisements. As with streaming video, streamed music is not stored on your computer.

You can play audio directly from the Internet by connecting to a **live audio feed**, which is audio transmitted live, as it happens. Live audio feeds often are used for live sports events, shows, or even police, fire department, and air traffic control feeds using a web browser or a media player.

Video Hardware and Apps
To watch video on a computer, you need special hardware and apps. The hardware is built into computers, tablets, or smartphones and includes a screen, speakers, and a video card—a circuit board that lets your device process video.

You also need a **media player**, which is an app that lets you play audio and video files. Most laptops, tablets, and smartphones come with media players. Video technology changes so quickly that you may need to update your media player and related apps frequently. Many people watch videos using the YouTube or Vimeo app on mobile devices.

Videos on the Web
Fast Internet connections have made watching videos on computers and mobile devices as easy as watching programs on a television. You can find videos on many websites, whether the videos are posted by individuals, by web developers, or as advertising. People use websites such as YouTube, Vimeo, and Instagram to share personal videos; you can also watch commercial movies and TV through YouTube. If you post a video or other content that is shared millions of times over social media in a short period, it is said to have gone **viral**.

A **Video conference** is a meeting among several geographically separated people who use a network or the Internet to transmit audio and video data (also called a web conference). These face-to-face meetings using computers are increasingly used on the web as a way of reducing business travel costs and bringing friends and family together over long distances. Microsoft Teams, Zoom, Facetime, and Slack offer video conferencing capabilities.

Describe How Businesses Use Digital Media

Businesses use digital media in marketing and advertising to attract and interact with customers by sharing it on social media, sending in a link in a text message or email, or posting it to their website. Careers in digital media might focus on creating media, selling media, or coming up with strategies to best use media to increase business.

In addition to marketing and advertising, many industries use digital media as a central part of their products and services. Entertainment and technology companies create and sell digital media content. Education uses videos to communicate information and enhance learning. Healthcare, military, and transportation organizations use VR for training purposes. Technology manufacturers can upload videos to depict highly detailed features of new hardware or apps.

Collectors and creators of digital graphics have contributed to a growing market of NFTs that can be sold or traded to others. A **non-fungible token (NFT)** is a digital identifier assigned to one file or version of a digital graphic and is used to claim ownership and certify authenticity (**Figure 7-19**). An NFT cannot be copied or substituted for another. NFT uses a technology called blockchain. In simple terms, a **blockchain** is a database that includes a list of ordered records, called blocks, which are encrypted and linked. Blocks contain information about the NFT, including ownership, certification, timestamp, and transaction data.

Figure 7-19: Creating an NFT for sale

Regardless of how a business uses digital media, the following strategies are important to consider:

- Make sure that the content is accessible to all. If sharing a video, include captions for users with audio impairments. Include alternative text with image files and text transcripts of audio files.

- Optimize the content for playback. Ensure that it is compatible with multiple devices, or offer alternative formats. Consider the resolution or quality of the media, and use the format that will allow the best quality with the smallest size for streaming or downloading.

- Ensure you have the legal rights to publish the media and all of its components.

Computer-Aided Technology   In fields such as manufacturing, interior design, and architecture, people use computer-aided technology to bring their products or designs to life. Computer-aided technology involves using computers to help design, analyze, and manufacture products.

Architects, scientists, designers, engineers, and others use **computer-aided design (CAD) apps** to create highly detailed and technically accurate drawings that can be shared, modified, and enhanced with speed and accuracy (**Figure 7-20**).

Interior designers use CAD apps to model proposed room designs. Clothing designers can experiment with fabrics and patterns. Architects use CAD to prototype buildings and create floor plans. Engineers and scientists use **3D CAD apps** to create wireframe drawings of objects, which they can rotate to view from many angles.

Increasingly, CAD is using **artificial intelligence (AI)**, the technological use of logic and prior experience to simulate human intelligence, to help automate design tasks, such as creating precise shapes. In broad terms, AI lets computers perform tasks that require

Figure 7-20: Designing using CAD

human-level intelligence. **Machine learning (ML)** is a branch of AI that uses statistics to help machines learn from data, identify patterns, and make decisions to progressively improve their performance without much human intervention. Engineers can use CAD apps with built-in machine learning tools to discover quicker production methods, evaluate the results of using different materials or changing a product's features, and produce design options based on goals and constraints.

Describe How to Create Digital Media

Besides downloading or streaming digital media, you can create graphics and animations, record audio, develop original videos, and edit your digital media files. Each of these tasks requires apps that range from basic to highly sophisticated (**Figure 7-21**). For example, if you want to remove some background from a photo, you can modify it in Windows Paint, which comes pre-installed on Windows computers. If you want to blend images or correct color in a photo, you need a more feature-rich app, such as Adobe Photoshop.

Explain How to Create Graphics and Animation

If you can't find a graphic or animation you need online, you may need to create it yourself using hardware or an app. Some hardware devices are specifically designed to aid graphic and animation creators.

Graphics Hardware
You can capture images using hardware devices such standalone digital cameras, a smartphone's digital camera, a graphics tablet, or a scanner (**Figure 7-22**).

A digital camera creates a digital image of an object, person, or scene. Almost all smartphones contain high-quality digital cameras for taking digital photographs. The latest smartphone cameras have 12-megapixel resolution, include a built-in gyroscope for image stabilization, and work well in low-light settings. Digital cameras also can identify a picture's geographical location, a feature known as **geotagging**, and can automatically post photos to online locations, such as your social media or a cloud folder. High-end digital cameras have these features and more.

You can use a **graphics tablet**, which is a hardware device used to create drawings with a pressure-sensitive pen. Architects, mapmakers, designers, and artists use specialized graphics tablets. General-purpose tablets also let you draw and edit graphics but

Figure 7-21: Editing digital media

Make basic changes in graphics software such as Paint.

Make advanced edits in photo-editing software such as Photoshop.

kenkuza/Shutterstock.com; Adobe.com

Figure 7-22: Hardware for creating digital graphics

Billion Photos/Shutterstock.com; Kaspars Grinvalds/Shutterstock.com; StockPhotosArt/Shutterstock.com; Kaspars Grinvalds/Shutterstock.com

have fewer capabilities. In addition, your operating system may come with a drawing app. Many laptop computers have touch screens, enabling you to draw on the screen with a digital pen or your fingertip.

A scanner converts an existing paper image into an electronic file that you can open and work with on your computer. Scanners work by dividing the image into a grid of tiny cells and assigning colors to each cell. Scanners vary in size and shape and include flatbed, sheet-fed, pen, and handheld types.

Graphic and Media Apps

You can use graphic and media apps to create, view, manipulate, and print digital images such as photos, drawings, clip art, and diagrams. You can create bitmap images with painting apps using brush tools and paint palettes that simulate watercolors, pastels, and oil paints. **Image-editing apps** let you open and modify existing images. For example, you can rotate an image on its axis, change its colors, or modify lines and other shapes. At sumopaint.com, you can edit images online free of charge.

Drawing apps let you create simple 2D images, which are often vector graphics. In some apps, you layer graphics to create collages. You can use more advanced apps such as Adobe Illustrator to create sketches, logos, typography, and complex illustrations for web or print use.

You can use photo-editing apps, such as Adobe Photoshop, to enhance and retouch photographs. For example, you can add special effects such as reflections or sepia tones, correct problems such as red-eye or poor lighting, or remove unwanted parts of an image. You can also edit photos on a smartphone using free mobile apps such as Snapseed, VSCO, and Adobe Lightroom. While editing photos can be fun and artistic, you should consider whether your editing choices are ethical. Some individuals and organizations have raised concerns about misuse of photo-editing apps, especially when the intent is to mislead the audience. For example, magazines that make a model appear thinner or insert a person into a photo where they were not present, can cause confusion over what is real and what is not.

Figure 7-23: 3D rendering

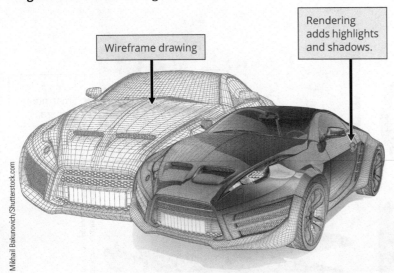

Wireframe drawing

Rendering adds highlights and shadows.

Mikhail Bakunovich/Shutterstock.com

Animation Apps   To create a 2D animation, you draw one image in a frame, followed by another in a slightly different pose and so on until the motion is complete. **In-betweening**, often shortened to betweening or tweening, is an animation technique using a sequence of images, in which one or more objects are changed slightly between each image. You can create the in-between images manually or let a computer create them. A 2D animated video requires 24 frames per second (fps).

3D animation is more complex than 2D animation because you must first create the 3D graphic and then create 24 to 60 versions of the graphic for each second of animation. A 3D animation in a computer game or film displays 24–60 fps.

To create a 3D animation, you create a digital 3D object, ranging from a simple ball to a complex character, and then add shadows and light. You define the texture of each surface on the object, which determines how it reflects the light. One way to create a solid 3D image is to apply highlights and shadows to a wireframe drawing (a 3D object composed of individual lines), a process called **rendering** (**Figure 7-23**).

After creating a 3D object, you define how it moves. For example, a ball compresses slightly when it bounces. To make the object move, you set its starting position in a **keyframe**, a location on the editing timeline that marks the beginning of the movement. For example, frame 1 of the animation might be a keyframe. Move the object to a later position on the timeline, such as frame 100, which becomes the next keyframe. You use animation apps to generate images of the changes in the object as it transitions from one keyframe to the next, creating the illusion of movement.

Figure 7-24: Text animation

Use animation software to add animated text to videos and other digital content.

jörg röse-oberreich/Shutterstock.com

Figure 7-25: Blender animation software

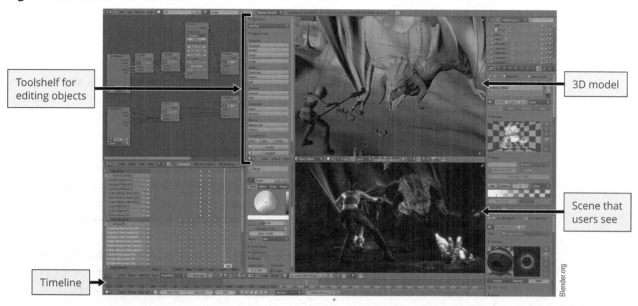

Toolshelf for editing objects

3D model

Scene that users see

Timeline

Blender.org

With a personal computer and readily available apps, all you need is a little training and some skill to create animations. **Animation apps** let you create animations to give objects the appearance of motion or activity. Adobe After Effects, Adobe Animate CC, and Blender are examples of animation apps. After Effects is designed to add animation to digital graphics and videos. For example, you can add a simulated snowfall to a skiing video, create scrolling 3D titles, animate a logo or character, or 3D text you created and animated with After Effects to show the text sinking in the water (**Figure 7-24**).

With Adobe Animate CC, you create animated content, including cartoons, ads, and games, from scratch or by adapting images provided with the app. You use Blender to create high-quality 3D animations (**Figure 7-25**). Professional-level animation apps such as Autodesk Maya and LightWave 3D is expensive and has a steep learning curve. Film studios and special effects departments use apps such as Maya and LightWave 3D to animate movies, TV shows, and games.

HTML5 supports creating and displaying animation for webpages and is being used by Apple on its iPhone, iPad, and other products.

Explain How to Record and Play Sounds and Music

You may want to record yourself performing a song, creating a podcast episode, or reading a **voice-over**, which is voice narration that can accompany a slide presentation or other video. To record voice-overs and save the recordings for playback on a computer, you need the following hardware and apps:

- An **audio input device**, such as microphone or headset, that lets you enter sound into a computer. A headset includes one or more headphones for output, and a microphone for input.
- **Sound recorder apps** can capture sound from an audio input device such as a microphone or headset.
- Apps that can digitize the captured sound or convert it to a format your computer can read.

Many smartphones have built-in sound recording tools, including microphones and apps, for capturing your own voice memos and narrations or the speech of other people.

After you capture and digitize sound, you can save it as an audio file and then play it back or add it to a video or presentation, for example. To play music files you download or record yourself, you also need special hardware and apps, including a **sound card**, a circuit board that gives a computer the ability to process sound.

Speakers play sound and can be built-in or attached as peripheral hardware to your device, either by a cable or wirelessly. Add-on speakers, which often offer higher-quality sound than built-ins, used to have bulky profiles. Today's portable **micro speakers** can be as small as an inch or two in height and width. They connect to your smartphone, tablet, or other devices using a wireless Bluetooth connection, and can double as speakerphones for phone calls or similar audio communications. If you're in an environment such as an office or library, where speakers are not practical, you can use a headset or headphones to keep the sound private.

You also need an app to play sound. **Audio apps** are included on portable media players including smartphones, and often offer features such as file-shuffling and volume control; some audio apps even have **skins**, visual images created by audio player apps to go along with the sounds being played.

When playing certain types of audio files on a desktop or laptop, such as MP3 files, you need a **stand-alone player**. For Windows computers, you can use apps such as Media Player or YouTube to play stand-alone audio files such as downloaded songs.

Synthesized Music
Some digital audio files are recordings of actual sounds converted to a digital format. Another type is **synthesized music**, which is created as a digital file from the start using electronic instruments called synthesizers, or synths for short. Musicians play synthesizers, which look like piano keyboards, to mimic sounds from acoustic or electric instruments or to produce unusual sounds that other instruments cannot generate (**Figure 7-26**).

To play a synthesizer, you press a key on the keyboard, generating an electrical current that becomes sound when it passes through an amplifier and speakers. A technology called **MIDI (Musical Instrument Digital Interface)** is a standard music file protocol used by a variety of electronic musical instruments, computers, and other related devices to connect and communicate with one another. MIDI converts the electric current to digital form so that you can store and play the synthesized music on a computer or mobile device.

In addition to synthesizers, you can create MIDI files using other instruments connected to a computer, such as guitars, violins, and drums. MIDI files do not contain sound; rather, they contain instructions for generating the components of sounds, including pitch, volume, and note duration.

MIDI technology also lets synthesizers and other electronic musical instruments communicate with each other. For example, you can play a certain note on a MIDI synthesizer to trigger a beat on a drum machine. If you are a solo performer, you can use connected MIDI devices to produce the effect of a larger musical ensemble. Because the music you create is digital audio, you can edit the files to change the key or tempo, reorder sections, and add instrumentation, meaning you can produce, record, and modify synthesized music in a home studio.

Figure 7-26: Synthesizer

stockphoto-graf/Shutterstock.com

Speech and Voice Recognition Apps
Speech recognition is a technology that enables a computer to understand and react to spoken statements and commands. Using speech recognition apps, you can talk to your laptop to have the words appear on the screen, speak commands that your device performs, and even write a report by speaking into the microphone on your device.

Basic or older speech recognition apps have a limited vocabulary and are usually accurate only if you speak very clearly. More advanced apps such as Apple Siri and Amazon Alexa can understand natural speech and can be trained to interpret your words more accurately over time.

Speech recognition is part of most new computers and mobile devices, making the app easy to access and use. The drawbacks include dropping spoken words because of variations in pronunciation and difficulty screening out background noise. Most speech recognition apps understand English but not many other languages.

Digital assistants such as Siri and Alexa are so appealing because they use AI to bring humanity to speech recognition technology. They use machine learning to overcome the drawbacks of varied pronunciations and background noise. At the same time, these technologies also bring concerns about data collection and privacy.

Voice recognition once meant the same thing as speech recognition but is coming to mean speaker recognition, or determining who is speaking rather than what is being said. Voice recognition apps are used as a security measure to allow access only to authorized people the app recognizes by voice.

Synthesized Speech   Where speech recognition apps translate spoken words into text a computing device can understand, by contrast, **text-to-speech apps** accept text as input and then generate sounds from phoneme sequences to create synthesized speech. Text-to-speech also is called read aloud technology. It works by breaking words into individual sound units called phonemes and then stringing them together to create words and phrases, or **synthesized speech**. A digital assistant such as Siri uses synthesized speech to respond to your questions.

Businesses and call centers use synthesized speech for routine communications. Assistive apps use synthesized speech to narrate on-screen text, making computers accessible to people with low vision. Applications are increasingly using this technology to provide read aloud features for all users. For example, Google has a tool for apps developers called Cloud Text-to-Speech. Developers can include the code in their app to synthesize speech in 30 voices, including multiple languages.

You can also use text-to-speech apps to type text into an application, create a sound file, and then play it back, post it on a website as a podcast, or email the sound file.

Explain How to Develop Original Videos

You probably use video often for entertainment, school, and work, especially on a mobile device. You can capture video using a smartphone or digital video camera and stream it live (**Figure 7-27**), play it back on a computing device, post it on a video-sharing website.

Video Capture   You can use a digital video camera or smartphone to capture full-motion images and store them in a file on the camera or phone. Action video cameras are compact, waterproof, and weather-resistant, making them ideal for live action. You might use them for activities such as sailing, surfing, skiing, and extreme sports.

Digital video files are large: when you transfer a video from a digital video camera to your computer or storage media, you need 1 to 30 GB of storage for each hour of video, with HD video requiring storage space on the upper end of that range.

Figure 7-27: Streaming live video

Chay_Tee/Shutterstock.com

A webcam is a type of digital video camera that captures video and still images as well as audio input and often is built into a desktop, laptop, or tablet computer. You typically use a webcam for video communications with apps such as Skype or Zoom. The video sessions can be recorded and saved for later playback in order for those who might have missed the session to view it or to generate notes or meeting minutes.

Explain How to Edit Digital Media Files

After you capture video, you can use video editing apps to modify a segment of a video, called a clip. Video editing apps also can be used to enhance and customize the video. Most video editing apps show the video as a timeline with separate tracks for video and sound (**Figure 7-28**).

Lightworks and Filmora are popular personal video editing apps. More fully featured video editing apps include Apple Final Cut Pro and Adobe Premiere Pro. You can also edit video on your smartphone using apps such as GoPro App, Bluebeam Revu for Apple devices, and Magisto for Android smartphones. With some apps, you can delete unwanted footage or rearrange and copy scenes to produce a professional-looking video. You can also add voice and music to narrate a scene or create a mood.

You can edit, copy, and share digital audio files with **audio capture and editing apps** such as Audacity, Adobe Audition, and Acoustica. Use these apps to enhance audio by removing background and other unwanted noises or pauses, deleting or reordering entire sections, and adding special effects.

Music production apps such as Apple GarageBand and Logic Pro X let you record, compose, **mix** (combine), and edit music and sounds (**Figure 7-29**). Create sounds of multiple instruments, change tempos, add notes, or rearrange a score to produce a unique arrangement.

While many music production apps are geared toward consumers, full-featured audio apps such as Adobe Audition let professionals edit sound for commercial websites, podcasts, presentations, and even TV shows and movies.

Audio-editing apps and features are often integrated into video editing apps because sound tracks are integral to video.

Figure 7-28: Editing video

Editing tools

Playback controls

Video appears on a timeline.

Source: Adobe, Inc.

Figure 7-29: Editing audio

Gorodenkoff/Shutterstock.com

Describe Ways to Protect Your Digital Media Content

Many creators of digital media content offer their work for sale. Some upload pictures of physical work to purchase, such as a framed print or a mug with artwork on it. Others sell a high-resolution version of the digital content itself, such as an image or video for others to use in their work. Digital media creators must have a balance between sharing previews of their digital media to customers and the risk of people downloading or accessing media without permission.

For instance, to protect your digital video from being illegally copied or downloaded, you can include hidden information to track the video, and add your copyright information to the video. To protect your digital content from illegal copying or downloading, upload only low-resolution versions of the work and offer the high-resolution only to buyers. You also should make your contact information available and easy to find so that interested parties know how to make purchases or ask questions.

You also should prevent your content from being able to have a **screenshot** (an image of a computer screen or an active window) taken, or enabling someone to copy and paste your work. To do this you can include a **watermark**, semi-transparent text or a graphic that appears behind or in front of the image. Often artists use their logo or their copyright information as a watermark (**Figure 7-30**). **Tile** the image by uploading pieces of the image separately and then putting them back together on your website so that someone would have to download each individual piece of the image to achieve the same effect.

Figure 7-30: Watermarks can protect digital photos

Cameo Photos© ← Watermark

sun ok/Shutterstock.com

Although your work is protected as your own intellectual property from the moment it is created, in order to effectively protect your artwork, you can register a copyright for it. There often is a fee associated with official registration, but it may be worth it if you find out your work has been illegally copied or downloaded and you have to take legal action. Laws, including the Digital Millennium Copyright Act (DMCA), have been passed and updated to try to keep up with the changing technology. However, many of the laws quickly are outdated and can be unclear or controversial. The best thing to do is to follow the steps above, keep digital records of your work in the stages of creation to prove you were the creator, and to register your work for copyright protection.

Module 7 Summary

Digital media is content created, produced, and distributed in computer-readable form, and includes graphics, animations, video and audio, and virtual reality. All digital media is composed of 1s and 0s. Digital media digitizes, or converts, analog data such as the sound waves produced by a person's voice to digital data so that it can be used on a computer. Digital media file format determines the apps or devices which you can use to open or edit the file.

Individuals use digital media for entertainment, gaming, creating, and more, and business create and incorporate digital media as part of their marketing and core offerings. Computers and video games include role-playing, action, adventure, education, puzzles, simulations, sports, and strategy. Games can be played on video consoles, which include the hardware and controllers necessary to participate in the game. Some game consoles connect to the Internet, enabling you to interact with other players online. VR players use headsets, controllers, and sensors to track their movements. Mixed reality includes simulations that let you see the real world while interacting with virtual objects. Some games also can be run on a computer or mobile device. Game consoles have practical uses as well, such as doctors practicing surgery. Some games use augmented reality, which is a type of virtual reality that uses an image of a place or thing and adds digital information to it. Virtual worlds in games use 3D computer models to create an illusion of depth and space. Simulations can be used for training and teaching, such as training pilots to navigate in bad weather.

Graphics, including logos, can be used to add dramatic or informative photos to reports or articles. A meme is a video clip, animated GIF, or digital image, often with text, spread by Internet users. Before you use any graphics, you need to acquire it or check to see if it is fair use.

A smart TV connects to the Internet using Wi-Fi and can be used to stream content from subscription services.

Streaming audio can include audio books, podcasts, or music. Live audio feeds are transmitted as they happen. Hardware and apps required to watch a video on your computer or device include: a screen, speakers, a video card, and a media player app. A viral video is one that has been shared millions of times over a short period of time. Video conferencing is a meeting among several people over a network or the Internet.

Businesses use digital media as a marketing and advertising tool, often over social media, on a website, or by sending a text or email message. Digital media careers include creating and selling media or coming up with strategies for its use. An NFT is a digital identifier used to certify authenticity and ownership of a digital graphic. Businesses should ensure their content is accessible, optimized for playback, and acquired legally. Computer-aided design (CAD) technology is used by architects, scientist, designers, and engineers. To create graphics and animation, you need hardware, such as a digital camera, graphics tablet, or scanner. Graphics and media apps include paint apps, image-editing apps, and drawing apps. Animation apps use in-betweening, which is a technique that uses a sequence of images that each are changed slightly. A keyframe is the starting position of a 3D object in a 3D animation. HTML5 supports the use of animations on websites.

To record sounds you need an audio input device, sound recorder app, and an app that digitizes the sound. To play audio, you need a sound card and speakers. Audio apps are used to play sounds. MIDI is the protocol used by electronic musical instruments to connect and communicate with each other. Speech recognition apps enable you to talk to your device to have the words appear on a screen or complete a command. Voice recognition is used to identify the speaker, not what is being said. Text-to-speech apps create synthesized speech.

Digital video cameras, smartphones, and action video cameras capture full-motion images. Video editing apps typically show the video as a timeline, with separate tracks for video and sound. You can use audio capturing and editing apps to enhance audio, delete or reorder sections, and add special effects. Music production apps can be used to record, compose, mix, and edit music and sounds.

Digital media creators protect their work from illegal copying or downloading by including hidden information to track the videos and adding their copyright information. Your work is protected as intellectual property from the moment you create it. You also can register a copyright for it, which is helpful if you have to take legal action to protect it. Laws to protect digital media can be controversial and also often go out of date quickly.

Review Questions

1. A 3D object composed of individual lines is called a _____ drawing.

   a. wireframe
   b. keyframe
   c. rendered
   d. sampled

2. A bitmap graphic's quality deteriorates as its dimensions increase because it is _____ dependent.

   a. compression
   b. data
   c. resolution
   d. format

3. A process called _____ converts analog sound waves into digital sound.

   a. sampling
   b. augmenting
   c. in-betweening
   d. simulating

4. All of the following are types of bitmap graphics except for _____.

   a. GIF
   b. JPEG
   c. PNG
   d. EPS

5. A projected image that appears 3D and allows you to superimpose virtual objects onto real objects is called a(n) _____.

   a. hybrid
   b. hologram
   c. simulation
   d. animation

6. A video clip, animated GIF, or digital image, often with humorous text added, which is spread by Internet users is called a(n) _____.

   a. virtual image
   b. hologram
   c. meme
   d. NFT

7. (True or False) Watching video content as it arrives is called streaming.

8. NFTs store information such as ownership and certification using a technology called _____.

   a. big data
   b. blockchain
   c. CAD
   d. codec

9. The animation technique that uses a series of images in which one or more objects are changed slightly between each image is called _____.

   a. sampling
   b. transitioning
   c. in-betweening
   d. rendering

10. (True or False) MIDI is a file protocol used by a variety of digital video cameras.

11. Logic Pro X is an example of a(n) _____ app.

   a. music production
   b. animation
   c. photo-editing
   d. video creation

12. Semitransparent text or a graphic that appears behind or in front of the image is called a _____.

   a. logo
   b. tile
   c. timestamp
   d. watermark

Discussion Questions

1. List three types of 2D graphics. Explain what each is used for. What is the main difference between 2D and 3D graphics? Do you have the skills needed to create 2D or 3D graphics? If not, what skills do you need to acquire?

2. What is the difference between analog and digital sound? What does the sampling process do? Do you play a musical instrument that you have used to record digital media? Describe the experience, and/or list equipment and technology you would/did use to do so.

3. What is the difference between voice and speech recognition technology? List uses for speech recognition. Do you find apps such as Siri or Alexa helpful? Why or why not? Do you have any security concerns about having such a device in your home? Explain your answer.

4. Photo-editing apps have become so sophisticated, they can alter images convincingly, such as by placing people in locations they've never been or making models look like they have flawless skin. Do you think the practice of modifying photos is ethical? Why or why not? In what situations would you strongly discourage it?

Critical Thinking Activities

1. Differentiate between virtual, augmented, and mixed reality. How do they differ from a virtual world? Describe a situation not referred to in this module in which VR could be used practically. Do you enjoy, or think you would enjoy, immersing yourself in a virtual world? Why or why not?

2. Explain how compression and resolution affect file size and quality of digital media. Why is this important to know if you pursue a career in digital media? Have you ever had trouble accessing digital media because of issues with the file size? Describe how this did/would make you feel as a consumer.

3. Explain steps a digital creator can take to protect their work. Why do you think laws have trouble keeping up with the changing technology? As a digital citizen, what is your responsibility to only use work that you have acquired permission for? Have you ever knowingly or unknowingly accessed media for which you did not have permission?

4. What career opportunities are there in digital media? Describe how businesses use digital media in marketing and advertising. Explain how digital media impacts your purchasing decisions. Describe a situation in which you did/could be persuaded positively or negatively to buy or not buy something based on the digital media provided by the company.

Apply Your Skills

To prepare for a career in the video game industry, Ninad Patil took courses in graphic design, art, illustration, and animation. His courses enabled him to acquire technical skills and experience in creating and using digital media. He learned about digital video, 2D and 3D animation, computer graphics, and digital music and videos. In his free time, he streams movies and TV shows from his smart TV. He is also creating a video that compiles footage he shot during his two weeks in Paris, France last summer. He plans to submit the finished video to film festivals and use it to showcase his work to potential employers.

Working in a small group or by yourself, complete the following:

1. Ninad needs a high-quality version of his video to submit to film festivals. What codec and container would you recommend? What would you recommend if he plans to post a smaller version that loads quickly on a social media site?

2. What does Ninad need to stream digital video from his smart TV? To enable his roommate's older TV to be able to stream digital video, what hardware might Ninad purchase? Do you rely on streaming services, or do you subscribe to cable or satellite TV stations? Why, or in what circumstances, would you cancel your cable or satellite subscriptions and rely only on streaming services?

3. Ninad uses a variety of graphics and media apps. List two types and describe their purposes. Explain what hardware Ninad might need to complete his video project. Have you used a free version of any of these apps or services provided by your operating system or device or found on the web? What limitations, if any, did you encounter?

App Development

In This Module

- Categorize development roles and methods
- Identify development phases
- Describe development tools and strategies
- Explain how to sell apps

Ji-Woo uses a code editor to view and edit her students' code.

Ji-Woo considers UX when selecting colors for her app.

Ji-Woo uses an app on her tablet to manage her sales in the app store.

iStock.com/Nattakorn Maneerat

Ji-Woo Yoon is an experienced app developer. She also is a computer science graduate student teaching a course in app development. Her students need to know the different types of app development methods, strategies, and tools. Students in her class develop an app during the semester, from the planning phase through the support and security phase. Currently they are working on a plan to distribute the app and monetize their efforts. She uses her expertise to help her students to plan, program, test, protect, and sell their apps.

App developers create apps that users can buy or acquire to accomplish tasks on computers and mobile devices. There are many methods and tools to developing apps. Knowing the basics of development can help you to understand and make choices if you decide to learn how to create your own apps. Even if this is not your goal, you still should understand the steps involved in development.

In this module, you will learn about types and methods of app development, as well as tools and strategies critical to development. You also will learn the different ways you can sell or distribute it. As you reflect on what you learn in this module, ask yourself: What development role best suits your interests? What would be the consequences if any phase in the development life cycle was skipped? How does a developer use an integrated development environment? What are the consequences of illegally downloading or using an app?

Categorize Development Roles and Methods

Development is the process of creating apps from the idea stage to distribution to users. Along the way, many steps and people are involved in planning, designing, programming code, and testing the app. App development can be as simple as creating a store's app that tracks users' purchases, coupons, and reward points. Other development projects may be complex systems that provide infrastructure to large enterprises. Whatever the scope, similar roles and methods are present in development.

List Development Roles

The **programmer**, the person who creates app code, might be the first person who comes to mind, but there are many roles that need to be filled during development. Depending on the project, some people may take on multiple roles, while other tasks might be so large as to require many individuals to complete.

Development should involve representatives from each department in which the proposed system or app will be used. This includes both nontechnical users and IT professionals. For each project, an organization usually forms a project team to work on the project from beginning to end. The **project team** consists of users, the systems analyst, and other IT professionals (**Figure 8-1**).

As app technology evolves, so do the roles and tasks involved in development, but the same general responsibilities of those involved remain (**Table 8-1**).

During development of large information systems, a systems analyst meets and works with a variety of people. A **systems analyst** is responsible for designing and developing an information system. The systems analyst is the users' primary contact person. Depending on the size of the organization, the tasks performed by the systems analyst may vary. Smaller organizations may have one systems analyst or even one person who assumes the roles of both systems analyst and developer. Larger organizations often have multiple systems analysts who discuss various aspects of a development project with users, management, other analysts, database analysts, database administrators, network administrators, web developers, software developers, and vendors.

Figure 8-1: A project team consists of analysts, programmers, and testers

Blue Planet Studio/Shutterstock.com

Project Leadership   The goal of project management is to deliver an acceptable system to the user in an agreed-upon time frame, while maintaining budgeted costs. In smaller organizations or projects, one person manages the entire project. For larger projects, the project management activities often are separated between a project manager and a project leader. In this situation, the project leader manages and controls the budget and schedule of the project, and the project manager controls the activities during system development. Project leaders and/or project managers are part of the project team. The systems analyst either acts as the project manager or works closely with the project manager.

To plan and schedule a project effectively, the project leader identifies the following elements:

- **Scope** (a project's goals, objectives, and expectations)
- Required activities
- Time estimates for each activity
- Cost estimates for each activity
- Order of activities
- Activities that can take place at the same time

After these items are identified, the project leader usually records them in a project plan, often using project management software.

Table 8-1: Common roles and responsibilities of the development team

Role	Duties
Project manager	Coordinates project components and ensures that each member is progressing as planned. Oversees the product's team, budget, and schedule. Reports to the development company's management.
Designer	Develops the program's user interface, including colors, fonts, and layout, keeping in mind how the user will interact and respond to the design.
Programmer	Writes code or uses a product development app to create the program's specifications.
Tester	Reviews every aspect and functionality of a program to ensure it works as intended. Often projects will have multiple testers at each phase of the project.
IT department	Interacts with customers and users of the product to assist them with any issues that arise.

Describe Components of the Development Process

User Experience (UX) refers to the focus on the user's reaction to and interaction with a product, including its efficiency, effectiveness, and ease of use. UX comes into play during all aspects of the development process. During the analysis phase, the needs of the customer help decide the scope of the project. A designer takes into account how the user will interact with the program to come up with a design that is appealing and easy to use. Programmers and testers work together to recreate and troubleshoot potential issues or areas of confusion. Designers use **wireframes**, which are blueprints of different aspects of the program that also indicate how a user gets from one area of the program to another (**Figure 8-2**).

Developers follow three general guidelines:

- Group activities into phases, such as planning, analysis, design, implementation, security, and support.

- Involve users for whom the program is being developed. Customers, employees, data entry specialists, and accountants all are examples of users.

- Define the standards, or sets of rules and procedures, the developers should all follow to create a product with consistent results.

Reasons for Development   App developers usually focus on a new or developing need or service (such as ride sharing), or extending a product or company's existing offerings (such as providing users with an app from which they can shop a website's products or order from a restaurant).

A user may request a new or modified information system for a variety of reasons. The most obvious reason is to correct a problem, such as an incorrect calculation or a security breach. Another reason is to improve the information system. Organizations may want to improve hardware, software, or other technology to enhance an information system.

Sometimes, situations outside the control of an organization require a modification to an information system. Corporate management or some other governing body may mandate a change. Mergers, reorganizations, and competition also can lead to change.

Figure 8-2: Wireframes help plan user interaction and experience

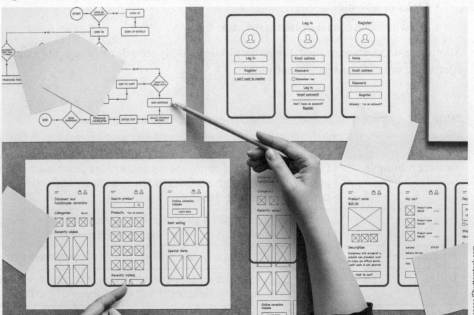

maicasaa/Shutterstock.com

To start the development process, users write a formal request for a new or modified information system or app, which is called a project request or request for system services. The project request becomes the first item of documentation for the project. **Documentation** is a collection and summary of the data, information, and deliverables specific to the project. Documentation should occur during all phases, and should reflect decisions, approvals, and notes. At the end of a project, all documentation is compiled and organized. A **deliverable** is any tangible item, such as a chart, diagram, report, or program file. The developer can be involved in the request for development or be asked to take on the project after the request is made.

Change Management

After a project's features and deadlines have been set, the developer, acting as the project leader, monitors and controls the project. Some activities take less time than originally planned; others take longer. The developer may realize that an activity is taking excessive time or that scope creep has begun. **Scope creep**, also called **feature creep**, occurs when one activity has led to another that was not planned originally; thus, the scope of the project now has grown.

Project leaders should use **change management**, which is the process of recognizing when a change in the project has occurred, taking actions to react to the change, and planning for opportunities that may arise because of the change. For example, the project leader may recognize the team will not be able to meet the original deadline of the project due to scope creep. Thus, the project leader may extend the deadline or may reduce the scope of the system development. If the latter occurs, the users will receive a less comprehensive system at the original deadline. In either case, the project leader revises the first project plan and presents the new plan to users for approval. It is crucial that everyone is aware of and agrees on any changes made to the project plan, especially when it involves changes in features, costs, or delivery dates.

Explain How to Evaluate Vendor Proposals

After the project is approved, the systems analyst begins the activity of obtaining additional hardware or software from a vendor, or evaluating cloud service vendors that offer the services to meet the organization's needs. The systems analyst may skip this activity if the approved solution does not require new hardware or software. If this activity is required, it consists of four major tasks: (1) identify technical specifications, (2) solicit vendor proposals, (3) test and evaluate vendor proposals, and (4) make a decision.

Technical Specifications

The first step in acquiring necessary hardware and software is to identify all the hardware and software requirements of the new or modified system. To do this, systems analysts use a variety of research techniques. They talk with other systems analysts, visit vendors' stores, and search the web. Many trade journals, newspapers, and magazines provide some or all their printed content online.

After the systems analyst defines the technical requirements, the next step is to summarize these requirements for potential vendors. The systems analyst can use three basic types of documents for this purpose: an RFQ, an RFP, or an RFI (**Table 8-2**).

Table 8-2: Vendor proposal types

Request type	Description
Request for quotation (RFQ)	Identifies the required product(s). With an RFQ, the vendor quotes a price for the listed product(s).
Request for proposal (RFP)	The vendor selects the product(s) that meets specified requirements and then quotes the price(s).
Request for information (RFI)	A less formal method that uses a standard form to request information about a product or service.

Vendor Proposal Requests   Systems analysts send the RFQ, RFP, or RFI to potential hardware and software vendors. Another source for hardware and software products is a value-added reseller. A **value-added reseller (VAR)** is an organization that purchases products from manufacturers and then resells these products to the public—offering additional services with the product.

Instead of using vendors, some organizations hire an IT consultant or a group of IT consultants. An **IT consultant** is a professional who is hired based on technical expertise, including service and advice.

Vendor Proposal Testing   After sending RFQs, RFPs, or RFIs to potential vendors, the systems analyst will receive completed quotations and proposals. Evaluating the proposals and then selecting the best one often is a difficult task.

Systems analysts use many techniques to test the various software products from vendors. They obtain a list of user references from the software vendors. They also talk to current users of the software to solicit their opinions. Some vendors will provide a demonstration of the product(s) specified. Others supply demonstration copies or trial versions, allowing the organizations to test the software themselves.

Vendor Proposal Decisions   Having rated the proposals, the systems analyst presents a recommendation to the committee or person in charge of making a decision. Typically, those with decision-making responsibilities are part of an organization's management team and are in charge of setting a company's priorities and goals, securing funding, and ensuring that projects have the support that they need. The recommendation could be to award a contract to a vendor or not to make any purchases at this time. The recommendations should include information about the process taken in the first three steps, including the top proposals (if any) and reasons for making the recommendation.

If it is decided that a project will go forward, the development team will then start the technical work of coding and creating the project using a programming language and development tools.

Identify Development Phases

A project starts with a request or need for a new app or enhancements to a current one. In many instances, developers have to get approval to create or improve the app. The approval can come from a manager, a board of directors, or other stakeholders in the company that weigh the costs of development with potential revenue. Once the idea of a project is formed and approved, the development can start. The set of activities used to build a program is called the **software development life cycle (SDLC)**. The "S" in SDLC also can stand for "systems" when the SDLC phases are used to create a large information system, such as a company network. Each activity, or phase, is a step in the life cycle. There are multiple approaches to the SDLC.

Discuss the Phases in the SDLC

The goal of the SDLC is to produce the fastest, least expensive, and highest quality product. The steps can vary, and sometimes overlap, but most development processes include most or all of the following phases: planning, analysis, design, implementation, and support and security (**Figure 8-3**). To give context to each phase, consider the example of building a virtual reality app for firefighters to simulate fighting a fire in a high-rise building.

Figure 8-3: The SDLC

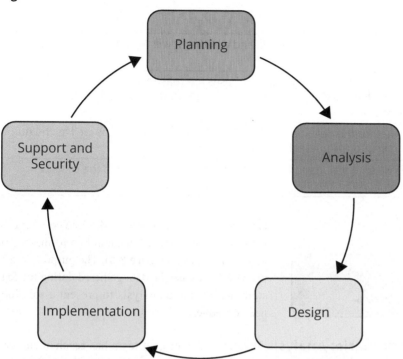

Planning Phase   A project begins with a request for the project. The request might come to a committee that authorizes development, that may consist of business managers, managers, and IT professionals. The **planning phase** is the initial phase of the SDLC, and includes reviewing and approving requests for the project, allocating resources, and forming a project team (**Figure 8-4**).

Figure 8-4: The planning phase of the SDLC

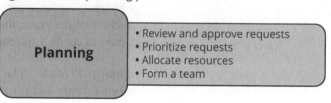

Case Scenario: Planning Phase   The request for a new app comes in from an association of fire chiefs in large cities. They have seen a need to safely train newer firefighters with techniques needed to fight fires in larger buildings. They prioritize their needs by asking for one type of building at first—a twelve story older brick building filled with apartments. They have received a grant that will cover the costs of creating this app. You form a development team that includes designers, programmers, and testers, as well as several fire chiefs to review the product during each phase.

Analysis Phase   The **analysis phase** of the SDLC includes conducting a preliminary investigation and performing detailed analysis. The preliminary investigation sometimes is called a feasibility study. The goal of this part of the phase is to determine if the project is worth pursuing. **Feasibility** is a measure of the suitability of the development process to the individual project at any given time. This is a critical phase, as it provides the customer or client with a clear-cut plan for achieving the goals. If a program gets developed without a feasibility study, the work you put into development could be wasted if stakeholders are not happy with the final product. There are four general factors that determine a project's feasibility (**Table 8-3**).

Analysts conduct studies to reach a conclusion about whether or not the project should continue. This study might include interviewing the person(s) who submitted the initial request, reviewing existing documentation, and more. Detailed analysis produces an overview of the users' wants, needs, and requirements and recommends a solution.

Table 8-3: Factors that determine feasibility

Factor	Purpose
Operational	Measures how well the app will work, and whether it will meet the requirements of the users.
Schedule	Determines if the deadlines for project phases are reasonable. Issues with schedule feasibility might lead to the project's timeline being extended, or the scope of the apps features to be scaled back.
Technical	Measures whether the developers have the skills and resources, as well as the number of programmers, to complete the features of the app.
Economic (cost/benefit)	Determines whether the benefits (profits) of an app will outweigh the costs of developing and supporting it.

Figure 8-5: The analysis phase of the SDLC

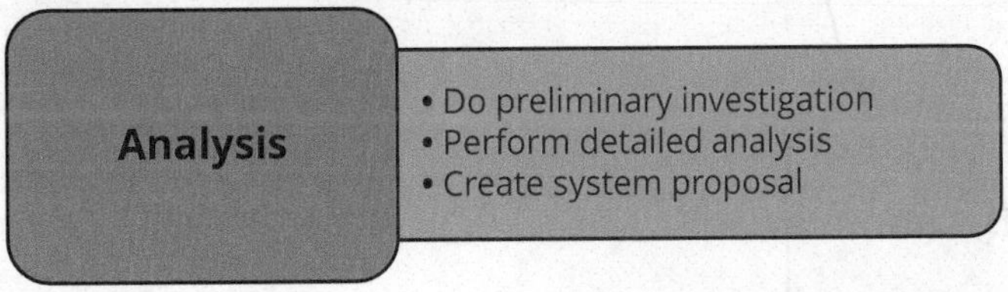

Analysis
- Do preliminary investigation
- Perform detailed analysis
- Create system proposal

Once these steps are completed, if the committee or analysts determine the project should go forth, they produce a system proposal (**Figure 8-5**). The purpose of a **system proposal** is to use the data gathered during the feasibility study and detailed analysis to present a solution to the need or request.

Case Scenario: Analysis Phase   The project team has reached an agreement on the scope and requirements with the fire chiefs consulting on the project. The team next determines the feasibility of the project. The developers have created similar apps before, so they meet the technical feasibility of the project. The timeline is to have a product available for use before the winter, as more fires occur in those months. Because of the grant, the project is economically feasible. The team uses all of these factors to create a system proposal.

Design Phase   The **design phase** is when the project team acquires the necessary hardware and programming languages/tools, as well as develops the details of the finished product (**Figure 8-6**). A **programming language** is a set of words, abbreviations, and symbols, which a programmer or developer uses to create instructions for an app.

During the first part of the design phase, all technical specifications are determined, evaluated, and acquired. The team produces a list of requirements and sends out requests for solutions from potential vendors. Vendors submit back to the team proposals that include all estimated costs, as well as a timeline for completion. The team then makes decisions about how best to meet the technical needs of the project and accepts the proposals from vendors that meet those requirements.

The second phase outlines the specifications for each component in the finished project. This includes all input and output methods, as well as the actions a user can perform. During this phase, the analyst or developer will create charts and designs that show a mockup of the sample product. Other decisions that get made during this part of the phase include media, formats, data validation, and other factors developers use to create a prototype of the final product. A **prototype** is a working model that demonstrates the functionality of the app.

Figure 8-6: The design phase of the SDLC

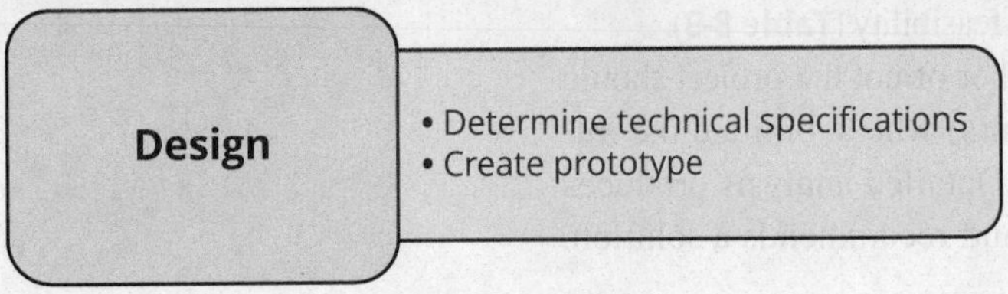

Design
- Determine technical specifications
- Create prototype

Case Scenario: Design Phase   During this phase, the team working on the fire safety app chooses a designer from a short list of vendors who can meet the schedule and budget. The developer presents a chart of all of the options and navigation methods of the training, as well as the technical specifications to complete the tasks. The team considers UX when coming up with a prototype that includes the format, media, and sample data.

Figure 8-7: The implementation phase of the SDLC

Implementation	• Development • Install and test the product • Train users

Implementation Phase   The purpose of the implementation phase is to build the new app and deliver it to users. During this phase, the development team performs three major activities (**Figure 8-7**):

- Develop the app using programming tools or languages.
- Install and test the product, including each individual component and how it works with other apps.
- Train users to use the new product, including one-on-one or group sessions, web-based tutorials, and user manuals.

In the case of an app that will be used on a network or system, such as a database, the final step in the implementation phase is to convert to the new system. Conversion can happen all at once, in phases, or as a pilot program in one location or department (**Table 8-4**).

Case Scenario: Implementation Phase   The developers create the first versions of the finished app using programming tools. They install and test the product on the fire chiefs' devices, then gather and incorporate their feedback. Then they test the app with a wider audience, and train firefighters to use the app. The team also creates a user manual that is accessible from the app.

Support and Security Phase   During the support and security phase the app receives necessary maintenance, such as fixing errors or improving its functionality. Analysts also monitor the performance to ensure the efficiency of the app (**Figure 8-8**).

One of the most important parts of any app's development is ensuring its security. All elements of the app must be secure from hacking, or from unauthorized collection of data of its users. Security concerns are addressed through each phase of development, and apps are tested for reliability.

Table 8-4: Conversion options

Conversion type	Description
Direct	The user stops using the old product and begins using the new product on a certain date. The advantage of this strategy is that it requires no transition costs and is a quick implementation technique. The disadvantage is that it is extremely risky and can disrupt operations seriously if the new product does not work correctly the first time.
Parallel	Consists of running the old product alongside the new product for a specified time. Results from both products are compared. The advantage of this strategy is that you can fix any problems in the new product before you terminate the old product. The disadvantage is that it is costly to operate two products or systems at the same time.
Phased	Each location converts at a separate time. For example, an accounting system might convert its accounts receivable, accounts payable, general ledger, and payroll sites in separate phases. Each site can use a direct or parallel conversion. Larger systems with multiple sites may use a phased conversion.
Pilot	Only one location in the organization uses the new product so that it can be tested. After the pilot site approves the new product, other sites convert using one of the other conversion strategies.

Figure 8-8: The support/security phase of the SDLC

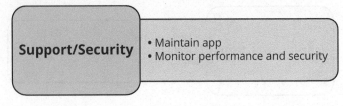

One of the ways developers ensure that their products work as intended is to test them thoroughly. The **testing** phase of the SDLC involves providing necessary maintenance for a program or app, such as fixing errors or improving functionality; also includes monitoring performance to ensure efficiency. Testing starts at the first phases of development and continues throughout. **Quality assurance** testers perform the testing and report any issues to the developers.

Testers and developers include documentation in the code. In addition to the data, information, and deliverables specific to the project, documentation involves adding notes to the code that explain and outline the intended function of sections or lines of code. During development, project members produce documentation. It is important that all documentation be well written, thorough, consistent, and understandable. Project managers distribute documentation guidelines to all project members to ensure that the documentation each produces will be complete and consistent.

Documentation reflects the development process in detail. Developers should produce documentation during development, not after, in order to ensure its accuracy and thoroughness. At this phase, the documentation is compiled and distributed. Documentation also can be used as the basis for user manuals and instructions that help you learn how to use all features of the app. Reputable developers include both testing and documentation for all of their products.

Case Scenario: Support and Security Phase   The team continues to add different firefighting and emergency scenarios to the app, increasing the knowledge that can be gained by using it and ensuring the scenarios represent real-world issues the firefighters might encounter. Each new scenario is thoroughly tested before its release. The team also addresses any security issues that arise.

Differentiate Between Development Methodologies

Several methodologies exist to guide the SDLC process, but all fall within one of two main categories. **Predictive development** uses a linear, structured development cycle. One example of predictive development is the waterfall method. The **waterfall method** takes each step individually and completes it before continuing to the next phase (**Figure 8-9**).

Agile development, also called **adaptive development**, incorporates flexibility in the goals and scope of the project. Agile projects may evolve in phases, releasing components as they are finalized, and adding functionality as it is needed or requested by users (**Figure 8-10**). Agile development incorporates testing and feedback from users and stakeholders at all phases of the process, making it more responsive to rapidly changing technologies and markets.

Rapid application development (RAD) uses a condensed or shortened development process to produce a quality product. The team involved must be highly skilled at programming and development to ensure the quality of the code and instructions. RAD development is best for projects with a clear goal and limited scope. RAD projects can be lower in cost because of the shortened process, and work well for time sensitive programs.

The **DevOps** method encourages collaboration between the development and operations, produces programs quickly, and then offers continuous updates to increase the functionality

Figure 8-9: The waterfall method

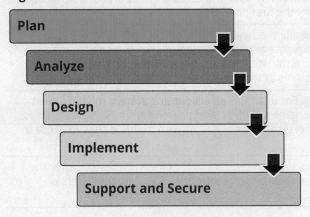

Figure 8-10: Agile development

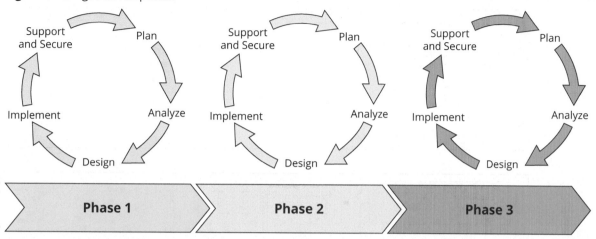

| Phase 1 | Phase 2 | Phase 3 |

of the program. While DevOps ensures frequent releases of fixes and enhancements, some users prefer to have a complete product from the start, without needing continuous updates.

The methodology chosen depends on several factors. If the project is based on previous successful projects, predictive methods may be the best choice. For projects without a clear goal or whose scope may change, agile development works best.

Describe Development Tools and Strategies

During system development, members of the project team gather data and information. They need accurate and timely data and information for many reasons. They must keep a project on schedule, evaluate feasibility, and be sure the system meets requirements. Learning about programming languages and tools can help you select the best options for your project. As technology evolves, so do trends in app development.

Explain Project Management Techniques

One aspect of managing projects is to ensure that everyone submits deliverables on time and according to plan. Charts can help to create schedules and assign tasks. Developers also use **project management apps** to assist them in planning, scheduling, and controlling development projects (**Figure 8-11**). **Project management** is the process of planning, scheduling, and then controlling the activities during system development.

Figure 8-11: Project management apps track the status of tasks

Andrey_Popov/Shutterstock.com

Figure 8-12: Sample Gantt and PERT charts

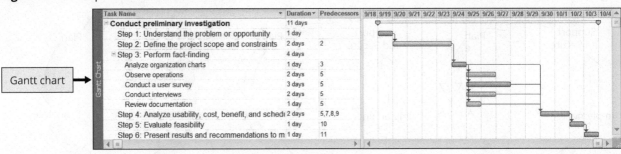

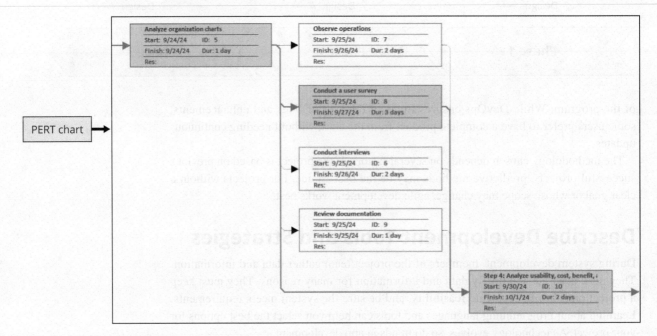

Gantt and PERT Charts   Popular tools used to plan and schedule the time relationships among project activities are Gantt and PERT charts (**Figure 8-12**).

- A **Gantt chart** shows project schedule timelines. Developed by Henry L. Gantt, they show project phases or activities using a bar chart with horizontal bars. The left side, or vertical axis, displays the list of required activities. A horizontal axis across the top or bottom of the chart represents time.
- Developed by the U.S. Department of Defense, a **PERT chart**, short for Program Evaluation and Review Technique chart, analyzes the time required to complete a task and identifies the minimum time required for an entire project.

PERT charts, sometimes called network diagrams, can be more complicated to create than Gantt charts, but are better suited than Gantt charts for planning and scheduling large, complex projects.

Project Management Apps   Several project management programs and apps are available, some for free while others are fee based. These programs and apps are designed for projects of specific sizes, so be sure to research the various programs and apps on the market and choose one that best suits your needs. To manage a project using project management software, follow these steps:

1. Make sure you understand the project in its entirety, as well as the steps you must take to bring the project to completion.

2. Determine the date by which the project must be completed.

3. Verify you have the appropriate resources (people and materials) to complete the project. If you do not have the necessary resources, obtain them, if possible.

4. Determine the order of the steps that must be taken to bring the project to completion. Identify steps that must be taken before other steps, as well as steps that can be completed at the same time as other steps.

5. Verify the feasibility of the plan.

6. During the project, update the progress and possibly adjust dates as necessary to reflect actual deliverable dates. Communicate changes to the project and its dates to the entire project team.

Data and Information Gathering Techniques   Systems analysts and other IT professionals use several techniques to gather data and information, as follows:

- **Review documentation:** By reviewing documentation, such as organization charts, memos, and meeting minutes, systems analysts learn about the history of a project. Documentation also provides information about the organization, such as its operations, weaknesses, and strengths.

- **Observe:** Observing people helps systems analysts understand exactly how they perform a task. Likewise, observing a machine allows someone to see how it works.

- **Survey:** To obtain data and information from a large number of people, systems analysts distribute surveys.

- **Interview:** The interview is the most important data and information gathering technique for the systems analyst. It allows the systems analyst to clarify responses and probe during face-to-face feedback.

- **Schedule JAD sessions:** Instead of a single one-on-one interview, analysts often use joint-application design sessions to gather data and information. A **joint-application design (JAD) session**, or **focus group**, consists of a series of lengthy, structured group meetings in which users and IT professionals work together to design or develop an application (**Figure 8-13**).

Figure 8-13: Focus groups enable people to work together

REDPIXEL.PL/Shutterstock.com

- **Research:** Newspapers, technology magazines and journals, reference books, trade shows, the web, vendors, and consultants are excellent sources of information. These sources can provide the systems analyst with information, such as the latest hardware and software products and explanations of new processes and procedures. In addition, systems analysts often collect website statistics, such as the number of visitors and most-visited webpages, etc., and then evaluate these statistics as part of their research.

Determine How to Select Languages and Tools

One of the most important decisions a programmer or developer can make is the language and tools to use. Knowledge of types of tools and programs available can help them make this decision. Training and courses exist online, using books, and at institutions such as community colleges to teach individual tools and programming languages.

When determining which language or tool to use, developers rely on the following guidelines:

- Determine the device(s) on which the app will run. Some platforms, such as Apple devices, have limited languages and tools available.

- Explore the capabilities of each language or tool, as they vary greatly.

- Consider the speed at which apps developed with a certain language or tool will run.

- Determine the type of environment the program or tool offers. Some rely only on text editors. Others provide graphical interfaces as well as text editors.

Differentiate Among Programming Languages

Several hundred programming languages exist today. Each language has its own rules, or **syntax**, for writing instructions (**Figure 8-14**). Syntax uses colors, indentations, and punctuation as some of the methods for distinguishing and categorizing codes and establishing hierarchies within code. Some languages are designed for a specific type of application. Others can be used for a variety of apps. Since each language has its strengths and features, often developers use more than one language during development.

Figure 8-14: Syntax methods includes colors, indentations, and punctuation

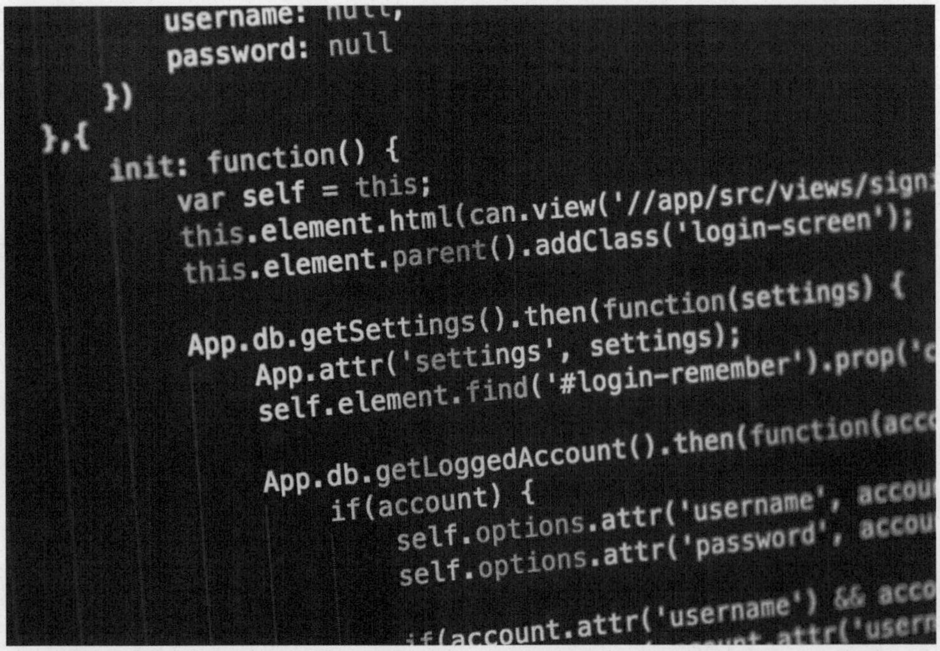

photovibes/Shutterstock.com

Figure 8-15: Translating text into binary code

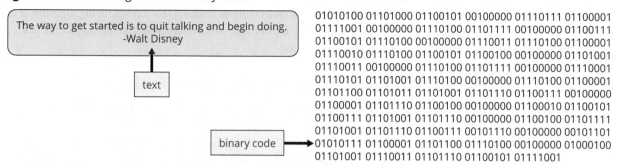

With each generation of programming languages, the process became easier and more human-like. This progress has enabled high-quality programs to be developed in a shorter amount of time and with fewer errors. The first languages that were developed are considered low-level languages. Two types of low-level languages include machine and assembly languages. **Machine languages** are first generation, low-level languages; their instructions use a series of binary digits (0s and 1s) (**Figure 8-15**). Coding in machine language is tedious and time consuming. Assembly languages are the second generation of languages. With an **assembly language**, the programmer uses symbolic instruction codes, such as A for add, M for multiply, and L for load. These languages are difficult to learn. Procedural languages such as C and Fortran are the third generation of languages, and are considered high-level languages. **Procedural languages** use a series of English-like words to write instructions, such as ADD for addition, or PRINT for printing.

Fourth generation languages, or **4GLs**, provide a graphical environment in which the programmer uses a combination of English-like instructions, graphics, icons, and symbols to create code. Examples of 4GLs include Python, SQL, PHP, and Ruby. 4GLs reduce development time, and increase productivity of the programmers. Many database programmers use 4GLs to save time, as they can use sample code provided to create the necessary functionality of the database. **Table 8-5** lists popular programming languages.

Table 8-5: Commonly used programming languages

Language	Description
C	Stable language that uses the Unix environment. Developed in 1972, but still in use today.
C++	Developed in the 1980s as an alternative to C. Flexible language that includes predefined classes.
C#	High-level language with English-language commands used to create apps for Microsoft platforms.
HTML	The standard language used to create websites; HTML uses tags to instruct the browser. Sometimes considered strictly a markup language, not a programming language, as it deals with the layout and specifications of content rather than determining actions.
Java	Flexible OOP language commonly used to create apps for servers, as well as video games and mobile apps.
JavaScript	Essential tool for creating interactive features to add to websites.
PHP	Flexible language used by WordPress and other platforms to add functionality to websites and connect them with databases.
Python	Interpreted, OOP language commonly used to create scientific modeling apps, as well as data mining.
Ruby	Object-oriented language known for using English-language commands to create apps quickly, including those for simulations and 3D modeling.
SQL	Used to manage, access, and search for database content.
Swift	Open-source language developed by Apple for use in creating apps for iOS.

Fifth generation languages, or **5GLs**, provide a graphical environment in which artificial intelligence attempts to solve problems without human intervention, using algorithms and predictions. This has proved difficult to implement; many 5GLs on the market are actually 4GLs that include some automation.

Differentiate Among Programming Tools

Application development tools provide a user-friendly environment for building apps. These languages provide methods to create, test, and translate apps.

A **source code editor** is a text editor designed for programming. When you enter code in a source code editor, the editor adds color coding to highlight syntax to differentiate between types of code, indentation for substeps, autocomplete of common instructions, and the automatic addition of braces and other punctuation that separates code.

Programmers also use **debuggers** to test code in one section, or an entire program, to determine any errors and provide suggestions to fix them. Debuggers often will stop running the code when an issue is detected in order to highlight exactly where in the code the error occurs. Some allow you to step through the code one instruction at a time to ensure each phase works as intended.

Assembly and procedural languages produce a program's source code. In order to run the app, the source code must be translated into machine language, the 0s and 1s of binary code. The two tools that assist in translation are compilers and interpreters.

- A **compiler** is a separate program that converts the entire source program into machine language before executing it. The output from a compiler is the object code, which the compiler stores so that the app can be run. The compiler also produces a list of errors in the source code.

- An **interpreter** translates and executes one statement at a time. Interpreters do not produce or store object code. Each time the source program runs, the interpreter translates instructions statement by statement.

Programmers might use separate tools for each of these, or use an IDE. An **integrated development environment (IDE)** is an application that provides multiple programming tools in one environment. The benefit of an IDE is that you become familiar with one interface, and the tools can work together to automate and perfect your program. Examples of IDEs include Microsoft Visual Studio, Oracle NetBeans, and Eclipse.

To make creating apps even easier, IDEs that use 3D environments such as Unity (**Figure 8-16**) enable developers to create and add code and visualize the effects at the same time. These environments combine code editors, graphical previews, and an engine that allows the program to run on multiple platforms.

Code repositories are another web-based tool programmers use to archive and host source code. Repositories are often used by open source projects so that developers can access the parts of the code they want to modify. Many code repositories include social aspects that enable programmers to connect with each other, comment on, and share code. Examples of code repositories include GitHub and SourceForge.

Define Object-Oriented Programming

A common method of programming is **object-oriented programming (OOP)**, which focuses on objects and the behavior and data associated with those objects. An **object** is an item that can contain both data and the procedures that read or manipulate that data. An object represents a real person, place, event, or transaction. A **class** is a type of object that defines the format of the object and the actions an object can perform. Each object in a class has the same format and can be used in the same way. A **method** is an action that an object can perform. Developers use OOP tools to implement objects in a program.

Figure 8-16: Unity 3D game development environment

Unity Technologies

For example, consider a program developed for a human resources department. You might have a class called Employee, with specific instances or objects called partTime and fullTime. The Class (Employee) would define the format of each object (works more than or less than 30 hours per week) and the associated actions (tax status, benefit accrual, etc.). Each object would contain data and operations pertaining to the individual object. One benefit of OOP is the ability to reuse and modify existing objects. For example, once a developer creates a fullTime object, it can be used by both the payroll program and the health benefits program. Developers can create apps faster, because they design programs using existing objects. Java, C++, and Visual Basic are examples of pure OOP languages.

Summarize Trends in App Development

Technology evolution not only affects how apps are developed, but what types of apps and what capabilities they have. With the growth and popularity of mobile devices, today more people access apps on mobile devices than on laptop or desktop computers. This increased usage requires designers and developers to design apps with mobile devices in mind first, and to take advantage of the connectivity and new business opportunities that mobile devices enable.

Mobile first design means that designers and developers start building apps to work on mobile devices first because these typically have more restrictions than a tablet or desktop computer, such as smaller screens. Then, they develop expanded features for a tablet or desktop version. This approach causes app designers and developers to prioritize the most important parts of their websites and apps and implement them first. Mobile first design requires designers to streamline how people interact with their apps by placing content first and providing a simplified user experience.

By using **cross-platform** development tools, developers can build apps that work on multiple platforms, rather than writing different code for Android or iOS devices. iOS developers write apps in Swift or Objective-C, and Android developers write apps in Java. Some cross-platform development tools rely on HTML5, JavaScript, and CSS to create a common web app that runs on multiple platforms. Other cross-platform development tools provide a compiler that can translate code into the different native formats for iOS and Android devices.

Figure 8-17: Wearable device apps can sync with mobile or other apps

App designers are influenced by new technologies and are encouraged to include them in development to keep current and enhance users' experience. Some technologies influencing app development include:

- **Artificial intelligence (AI):** Enabling apps to create output such as text or images based on user input.
- **Predictive technologies:** Using past customer behavior to build a profile of preferences and customize the user's app experience.
- **Internet of Things (IoT):** Allowing users to monitor home systems remotely in order to control appliances, heating/cooling systems, and security systems.
- **Wearable devices:** Creating versions of apps that run on a wearable device and enable the user to sync or download the data, such as fitness tracking or communications (**Figure 8-17**).
- **5G networks:** Taking advantage of high-speed connectivity to facilitate communications or streaming.
- **Beacons:** In-store technology allowing stores to compile and analyze customers' movements to better streamline services.

Explain How to Sell Apps

When you sell or distribute an app, you are giving users the right to use the product according to terms specified in the license agreement. A **license agreement** identifies the number of devices on which you can install the product, any expiration dates, and other restrictions. While you can offer an app for download and payment using your company's website, you likely will register your app with an app store. **App stores** help you to locate and download apps for your mobile device (**Figure 8-18**). It is important to determine users' rights and limits when using apps. You also should know how users install apps and what tools are available for users to troubleshoot them.

Typically, apps are developed to provide income generation by one of three methods: selling the app, enabling in-app purchases, or selling advertising to other companies. When you register with an app store, you select which money-generating methods you will use, if any. The app store takes fees or percentages of the sales, and may help you enable ad sales within the app based on partnerships it has with advertisers.

Determine How to License Your App

Figure 8-18: App store icons

When you create an app, you are protected under copyright laws, even before you apply for them. Apps are considered the intellectual property of the creator(s). As part of development, you should consider the type of license(s) you want to offer, or whether to distribute the app as open source. **Table 8-6** lists different types of license agreements.

Websites exist that help developers acquire trademarks and copyrights, often for a fee. You also should secure a domain name for your company or product so that you can ensure you have a website to sell, market, and support the app. You may want to consider hiring an attorney who specializes in digital copyrights in order to protect against piracy and to develop your license agreements.

Table 8-6: Types of license agreements

Type	Description
Single user or **End user license agreement (EULA)**	Grants permission for one installation
Multiple-user license agreement	Lets a specified number of users access the app
Site license	Allows an organization to provide access to as many users as they want, either by individual installations or providing network access or Internet passwords

Piracy   A common infringement on copyrights is **piracy**, where people illegally copy apps, movies, music, and other digital materials. Piracy is common in software, where the code and files are digital. Piracy is illegal, and users can be fined or otherwise punished if they purchase or sell pirated apps. Fines typically are assigned for each act of piracy—illegally copying or distributing hundreds of digital materials may result in fines of thousands of dollars for each item. Piracy affects the pricing and availability of apps to the everyday user who follows the rules. Developers put in time and money to produce, market, and distribute apps. They expect to profit from each program or license sold. When you purchase or use pirated apps, the developer does not get any money, and they may be forced to discontinue or increase the price of the app. Piracy also impacts innovation in program development. If a developer does not make all expected profits, they are not motivated to keep creating new products.

To ensure you are not contributing to piracy, buy only from legitimate resellers or directly from the manufacturer, register your product to ensure it cannot be installed on another device without your knowledge, and report any illegal sale or purchase of programs or apps. As a developer, registering your product with an app store and determining license and copyright protections can help prevent and prosecute piracy.

Free Apps   Freeware, shareware, and public domain apps are available at little or no cost. **Freeware** apps are copyrighted and provided at no cost, but the developer retains all rights to the product. **Shareware** is copyrighted and distributed for free for a trial period, after which users must send payment to continue using the program. Public domain apps are available and accessible to the public without requiring permission to use, and therefore not subject to copyright. Intellectual property, including apps, is considered restricted by copyright laws, even if the author has not applied for legal protections, unless the author or creator expressly disclaims protection. Lack of a patent, copyright, or trademark does not mean a program is public domain.

Public domain programs differ from freeware and shareware. Freeware and shareware still are protected by copyright laws. The creators of freeware maintain copyrights, but do not restrict installation or use, or charge a fee to use. Shareware creators distribute apps for little or no cost, or for a brief trial period. Shareware creators intend to make a profit, either by charging to purchase or subscribe to the product, or by including advertisements.

Explain How Users Acquire and Manage Apps

When you register your app in an app store you determine whether the app will be free or will cost to download. App fees typically vary between $1 and $5. iPhone users can obtain apps from Apple's App Store; Google Play and Amazon's App Store are popular app stores for Android users.

An app store typically enables users to apply automatic updates and fixes to apps they download to their mobile devices. **Updates** change an app to prevent or repair problems, enhance the security of a device, or improve performance. Mobile apps typically update automatically, without any action on a user's part. Programs that run on a desktop or laptop may require users to download updates from the manufacturer's website. Some SaaS programs allow you to turn on automatic updates. Updates that address a single issue are called **patches**. A **service pack** is a collection of updates combined in one package. **Upgrades** are new releases of the app, and may require an additional fee to enable the upgrade to install. Upgrades might include additional features not available in the version you currently are running.

App Installation   Installing is the process of setting up the app to work with a user's computer, mobile device, and other hardware such as a printer. During installation, the app stores all of the files it needs to run on a user's computer or device, including any files that interact with the operating system.

During installation of an app or before the first use, you can program the app to ask users to register and/or activate the program. **Registration** typically is optional, and usually involves submitting the user's name and other personal information to the manufacturer or developer. One benefit of registration is that if the app runs on multiple devices, users can sync their account to each, enabling them to access the same data, information, documents, etc. from each device.

Activation is a technique that some manufacturers use to ensure that users do not install the app on additional devices beyond what they have paid for. Activation usually is required upfront, or after a certain trial period, after which the app has limited functionality or stops working. In order to continue with the app, or access data they have entered into it, users must activate the product.

Troubleshooting Tools   Knowing how to fix issues can save not only frustration, but time and money. A **crash** occurs when the app stops functioning correctly. This can be caused by an issue with the hardware, the software, a virus or other malware, or using invalid data or commands. Recovery from a crash can be as simple as rebooting your computer or device. Many resources exist online, such as Help forums or free IT support chat rooms. **Troubleshooting** refers to the steps you take to identify and solve a problem, such as a crash.

Many tools exist to help you troubleshoot issues with apps:

- **Process managers** track the memory usage, status, and errors of currently running apps.
- **System information lists** keep track of license numbers and installation keys in case you need to reinstall apps.
- **Auditing tools** analyze security, performance, and network connections.
- **Patch finders** compare the app versions you are running with the latest versions available on the developers' websites, and identify any updates, or patches, you need to install.
- **Restorers** allow you to restore your computer or software settings. These are helpful if you made an update that seems to have caused issues with your system or a specific program.

Module 8 Summary

Many people are involved in developing apps from the idea stage to distribution to users. Roles include the programmer, who creates app code, and representatives from departments that will be using the system or app. A project team consists of users, the systems analyst, and others, including the project manager, designer, programmer, tester, and IT department.

During app development, UX is the focus on the user's reaction to and interaction with a product, including efficiency, effectiveness, and ease of use. If any hardware or software is required for development, a systems analyst researches the best solutions and requests vendor proposals. Instead of sending proposal requests directly to vendors, some development teams use value-added resellers that sell products and offer support services or use IT consultants to come up with solutions. Typically, selection decisions are made by a management team.

The SDLC (software/system development life cycle) consists of five phases: planning, analysis, design, implementation, and support/security. The phases may overlap. There are many approaches to the SDLC, including predictive (linear) development, such as the waterfall method, and agile or adaptive development, in which the project evolves in phases. Rapid application development (RAD) uses a shortened process. RAD is best when the teams are experienced and the project has limited scope.

Project management apps can be used to ensure timely and accurate submission of project deliverables. Project management is the process of planning, scheduling, and controlling development activities. Gantt and PERT charts are two tools used in project management. To use project management apps, make sure to know the scope of the project, including order of steps to be taken, feasibility, and more. When IT professionals gather and analyze data, they may review documentation, observe users, create surveys, interview users, conduct JAD sessions or focus groups, and do research.

Each programming language has its own syntax, or rules, such as color, indentations, and punctuation, used for writing instructions. Each programming language generation has evolved to make it easier to code. First generation languages used machine language (0s and 1s). Assembly languages are the second generation, which used symbolic instruction code. Third generation languages include C and Fortran, high-level languages that use words to write instructions. Fourth

generation languages provide a graphical environment in which the programmer uses instructions, graphics, icons, and symbols. 5GLs in theory use artificial intelligence, but in reality because of technological difficulties, usually are 4GLs with automation.

Programming tools include source code editors (text editors), debuggers (to test sections of code), and compilers and interpreters to convert source code into machine language. An integrated development environment (IDE) provides multiple tools at once. When determining which language or tool to use, determine the device on which the app will run, capabilities of each language/tool, speed of development, and environment type. App development trends are influenced by technological advancements.

Object-oriented programming focuses on objects, which represent people, events, or transactions, and the behavior and data associated with the object. A class is a type of object that defines its format and actions. A method is an action that an object can perform.

App users are given a license agreement that specifies the terms under which they can use the app. You can register your app in an app store for mobile devices. App income generation typically comes from selling the app, in-app purchases, and selling ads. Apps are considered intellectual property and are protected by copyright laws. You can determine which type of license agreement to provide: single- or end-user, multiple user, or site license. Piracy impacts not only the developer, who doesn't get paid for their efforts, but also development innovation, because it limits developers' enthusiasm if they are not getting paid. Free apps include freeware (free to use, but all rights retained by developer), shareware (free for a trial period, but costs to use beyond that), and public domain (no permission needed to use and not subject to copyright).

App stores enable users to download automatic updates and fixes. A patch addresses a single repair issue, and a service pack is a collection of updates. Upgrades are new releases of an app. When a user installs an app, they typically must register (submit information about the user) and/or activate it (a technique that ensures the device is not installed on more devices than were licensed).

Troubleshooting can help solve problems, such as a crash, which occurs when the app stops functioning. Tools to troubleshoot apps include process managers, system information lists, auditing tools, patch finders, and restorers.

Review Questions

1. During development, the person responsible for developing the program's user interface is the _____.
   a. designer
   b. programmer
   c. IT department
   d. project manager

2. A project's goals, objectives, and expectations make up its _____.
   a. shareware
   b. creep
   c. interface
   d. scope

3. RFP stands for request for _____.
   a. program
   b. proposal
   c. package
   d. price

4. During which phase of the SDLC does the feasibility study take place?
   a. Planning
   b. Design
   c. Analysis
   d. Implementation

5. (True or False) The waterfall method is an example of agile development.

6. A JAD session is another term for a _____.
   a. focus group
   b. vendor proposal
   c. project team
   d. Gantt chart

7. In OOP, the element that defines the format of an object and the actions the object can perform is the _____.
   a. class
   b. method
   c. interpreter
   d. source

8. Procedural languages are the _____ generation of programming languages.
   a. first
   b. second
   c. third
   d. fourth

9. (True or False) An interpreter translates and executes one statement at a time.

10. In-store technology allowing stores to compile and analyze customers' movements to better streamline services is called _____.
    a. IoT
    b. embedded computers
    c. assembly language
    d. beacons

11. A program that is copyrighted and provided at no cost, but the developer retains all rights to the product, is referred to as _____.
    a. shareware
    b. freeware
    c. open source
    d. public domain

12. An upgrade that addresses a single issue is referred to as a(n) _____.
    a. service pack
    b. update
    c. patch
    d. debugger

Discussion Questions

1. Describe the process of change management. Define scope creep and explain how it relates to change management. Have you ever worked on a project that could have benefited from applying change management techniques? What did you do or what could you have done to solve the problem?

2. List each phase of the SDLC and describe what happens during each phase. Come up with a sample development project for an app you think would be interesting or useful. List one task that must be completed for each phase. Which phases might overlap? Explain your answer.

3. Explain the mobile first development strategy. List three app development trends. Which of these trends have you seen in apps that you use? What other trends do you think impact app development?

4. Define piracy as it applies to apps. What are the downsides to piracy? Have you ever used an app illegally? Would you do it again? Why or why not?

Critical Thinking Activities

1. List and define the types of vendor proposals. Explain how proposals are tested and what goes into the decision-making process. Which type of proposal would you use as a project manager? Why?

2. Differentiate between predictive and agile development methods. Explain when and why a project team might use the strategy. If you were developing an app that was likely to change in response to new stakeholders weighing in on the progress and priorities for the app, which type of development method would you prefer to use? Why?

3. Describe OOP and how objects, classes, and methods are used. How would a developer determine which OOP language or tool to use? Which type of language or tool would you prefer to use? Why?

4. Differentiate among freeware, shareware, and public domain apps. If you were a developer, which would you want to register your apps as? Why?

Apply Your Skills

Ji-Woo Yoon is an experienced app developer. She also is a computer science graduate student teaching a course in app development. Her students need to know the different types of app development methods, strategies, and tools. Students in her class develop an app during the semester, from the planning phase through the support and security phase. Currently they are working on a plan to distribute the app and monetize their efforts. She uses her expertise to help her students to plan, program, test, protect, and sell their apps.

Working in a small group or by yourself, complete the following:

1. Ji-Woo asks her students to come up with a reason for developing a new app. Assume you are one of her students. What app would you develop for her class? What reason would you give for developing your app?

2. Ji-Woo assigns you to list a task that you would complete during each phase of the SDLC. Explain what other roles you might need to involve during each phase. What role(s) would you like to take on? Why?

3. List programming tools you might use to create the app for Ji-Woo's class. Explain why a program uses a compiler or interpreter. What happens during these processes? What is the difference between each? What tool(s) and languages would you prefer? Why?

4. After the app has been developed, Ji-Woo asks you to create a plan for selling or distributing your app. Explain why you might choose to put your app in an app store. Would you require users to register your app? Why or why not?

Web Development

In This Module

- Compare the roles of HTML5, CSS, and JavaScript when developing websites
- Describe strategies for creating and publishing websites
- Manage websites using data tools and analytics
- Build a website from code

Leo needs to upload content to a web server so visitors can see important information on his website.

Leo is coding a website using HTML5, CSS, and JavaScript.

iStock.com/Vladans

Leo Francisco helps run a community volunteer group called Parks Unlimited. He wants to create a website to share information about the group, upcoming park beautification projects, city park locations, and contact details. Leo will need to register a domain name and set up web hosting, as well as determine whether to code the website by hand, or make use of a content management system to publish the website online. He also wants to track usage data from visitors to the volunteer group's website.

Many factors influence how you might develop a personal or professional website. If your site does not need frequent updates, you might code it directly with HTML; if your site is more complex or you want to develop it quickly, you might use a website builder or content management system to assist in designing and developing it. Once a website is published online, you can use analytics tools to monitor visitor behavior on the website.

In this module, you will learn how HTML, CSS, and JavaScript can be used to describe the content, appearance, and behavior of webpages. You will follow an example that develops a simple webpage as you learn about the roles of various web technologies; compare strategies for designing, publishing, and managing websites; and use code to add images, text, hyperlinks, and paragraphs while specifying fonts, colors, and styles to build webpages that are visually appealing. As you reflect on what you learn in this module, ask yourself: What website technologies would help you build websites more effectively? What types of website building tools will work best for your interests and skills? How do website data tools help improve your experience of the websites you visit most often? How can an understanding of webpage code help you imagine possibilities for websites you might want to build?

Compare the Roles of HTML5, CSS, and JavaScript When Developing Websites

When developing a website, you must consider what content the site will contain, what it will look like, and how users will interact with it. Regardless of how simple or complex a website appears, three technologies describe the site's content, appearance, and behavior:

- **HTML (HyperText Markup Language)**, a collection of symbols called tags, to specify the content within a webpage, such as headings, paragraphs, images, and links
- **CSS (Cascading Style Sheets)**, to specify the format and appearance of content on a webpage, such as fonts, colors, borders, backgrounds, and alignment
- **JavaScript**, a language for writing scripts that run in your browser to control a webpage's behavior, such as checking if values on a form are blank, performing calculations, or dynamically changing content, which often makes it interactive

Explain How to Use HTML

A webpage is a document that contains codes called **tags**, written in HTML, to identify or "mark up" the content in a webpage. For example, the `<p>` and `</p>` tags can surround text to format the beginning and ending of a paragraph. Webpages can contain headings, paragraphs, hyperlinks, lists, images, videos, forms, buttons, and other elements. HTML has evolved since it first was introduced; the current version is HTML5.

Figure 9-1: A webpage and its source code

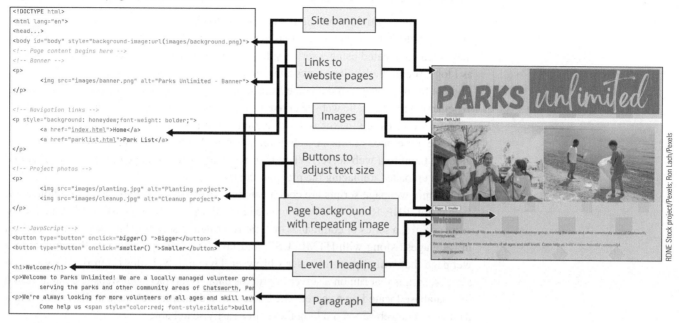

You can create webpages for a website by writing HTML code by hand or by using tools to assist you in this process. After creating or modifying a webpage, you must publish the page and any multimedia content it contains to a web server so visitors can access it on the Internet.

In many web browsers, you can display the underlying HTML, CSS, and JavaScript code for a webpage by right-clicking on the page and selecting the View Source or View Page Source option. **Figure 9-1** compares a webpage as it appears in a browser, and the corresponding HTML5, CSS, and JavaScript source code.

Explain How to Use CSS

CSS (Cascading Style Sheets) describes how content on a webpage will be displayed in a browser. Web developers use CSS to specify colors, position, alignment, fonts, background images, and other features. By using CSS, you can define styles for your webpages to specify how they will appear on devices with different screen sizes, including smartphones, tablets, laptops, and desktop computers.

Explain How to Use JavaScript

JavaScript is a popular language for writing **client-side scripts**, that is, scripts that run in your browser to control a webpage's behavior and often make it interactive. When you complete a form in a browser, code written in JavaScript can check to make sure you did not miss any of the required values. When a webpage displays a slide show of photos or images, JavaScript code probably controls it. When you can click a button to display the text on a webpage in a larger or smaller font size, or when a webpage displays the current date and time, JavaScript enables these features.

Describe Strategies for Creating and Publishing Websites

Considering how often you will need to update a website, the number of people who will add content to it, and the types of devices that will access it can influence how you choose to develop it.

Explain When to Use Static and Dynamic Websites

Static websites provide content that is unlikely to change frequently. **Dynamic websites** provide content that changes often as you interact with it or that is unique to each user; they often are created using a server-side scripting language. More complex websites such as blogs, social media sites, news sites, and online shopping or travel sites, are dynamic. Content for these pages might come from several sources or change as you interact with it. Whether to create a static website or a dynamic website depends on various factors.

Static websites are inexpensive to maintain and perfect for small companies looking to create a presence online. A web developer usually codes the pages in HTML and then uploads them to a web server. When making changes to the page content, new or edited files are uploaded, replacing the previous content.

Dynamic webpage scripts are coded using a **scripting language** such as Python, Java, JavaScript, PHP, Ruby, or C# (pronounced "C-sharp"). These websites combine one or more **scripts**, a series of commands or actions written in scripting language and embedded in webpages. Along with HTML, CSS, and JavaScript, scripts generate the content of a webpage that will appear in a user's browser. Dynamic websites often run **server-side scripts**, scripts that run on a server to process data, to interact with website content stored in a database located on a server. The content of a dynamic website usually is stored in a database on a web server, making these sites easily searchable.

A **web address** is the unique address on the Internet where a webpage resides, also called a URL (Uniform Resource Locator) of a webpage. When you type a web address in your browser's address bar, the browser requests the page from a web server, and the web server locates the page based on its unique address. If the page contains only HTML and client-side scripts, the web server sends back the page content to render, or display, according to the HTML tags on the page. If the page contains a server-side script, the server runs the script and returns its results as HTML for a browser to display.

For example, think about what happens when you enter your user name and password on a form to sign in to a website. After you enter your credentials, you press a Submit button on the form that causes the webpage to send the information to a web server on the Internet. A server-side script might compare the values for the user name and password you entered with those stored in a user database, which is located either on the server or somewhere the server can access it (such as another server or a cloud-based authentication service). If they match, you will be able to access the website. If not, the website will display the login page again (**Figure 9-2**) or an error message.

Figure 9-2: How a server-side script runs

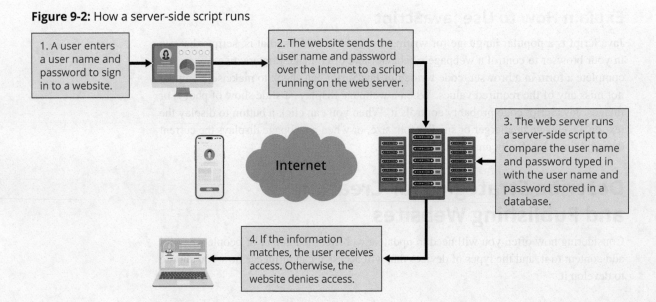

1. A user enters a user name and password to sign in to a website.

2. The website sends the user name and password over the Internet to a script running on the web server.

Internet

3. The web server runs a server-side script to compare the user name and password typed in with the user name and password stored in a database.

4. If the information matches, the user receives access. Otherwise, the website denies access.

Explain the Importance of Responsive Design

Figure 9-3: Responsive design

Many websites are designed to appear correctly on any device, regardless of its screen size. Pages with responsive design automatically adjust the size of their content to display appropriately, relative to the size of the screen of the device on which it is displayed. When webpages are responsive, users do not have to scroll from left to right or resize the graphics or text to read them on a mobile device with a small screen. Because more people interact with webpages on smartphones than on desktop or laptop computers, creating pages that are responsive is important to improve the user's experience. **Figure 9-3** compares a webpage with responsive design, displayed in browsers on a desktop, laptop, tablet, and smartphone.

Compare Tools for Creating Websites

If you are coding or designing a website from scratch, you might use a text editor or Integrated Development Environment (IDE) to enter the HTML5, CSS, and JavaScript code.

If you don't have the time or technical skills to create a website from scratch, you can save documents created using Microsoft Office apps in HTML5 format to publish online. For example, you could create a Microsoft Word, PowerPoint, or Excel document and use the tools in these apps to generate a webpage HTML5 file and related files that you can display in a browser or publish online. You also can use Microsoft Sway, an app in Microsoft Office, to create and share interactive reports, stories, and presentations, and publish them online.

To create a more complex website quickly without coding HTML, you can use a website builder or content management system (CMS). These tools are useful to create a personal blog or website, or a website for an organization or small business. They provide many templates or themes to design your website and a visual editor, like a word processor, to enter site content. Many templates incorporate responsive design and allow you to preview your site as it will appear on a mobile device.

Many website builders and CMSs are web applications that present webpages containing forms where you can enter website content and settings. A database located on a server stores the structure, appearance, and content of a website. The application obtains this information from its database, and then assembles it to provide the code for a browser to display.

Website Builders   A **website builder** is a tool used to create professional looking websites by dragging and dropping predefined elements to their desired locations on a page without coding, though some website builders allow you to adjust the underlying code directly if you wish. You do not need to install or configure any software to use a website builder. Website builders provide a simple drag-and-drop editor, predesigned layout options, and business capabilities such as shopping carts, online payments, product catalogs for online stores, photo galleries, and video libraries. Some may offer apps for updating a website using your mobile device. Website builders often show sample demonstration sites to give ideas of how to design your own website. Many website builders include search engine optimization (SEO) capabilities, so search engines can better find or index your website.

Because websites created with a website builder are stored in a database on the web host's server, moving the site later to a different web host or platform can be difficult. Often, you are limited to the templates provided when selecting a design or layout for your site. Many website builders offer basic free hosting and services that are adequate for most personal sites, with advanced capabilities (such as using a custom domain name or increasing the amount of storage for site content) available for a fee.

Google Sites is an easy-to-use website builder from Google, often used for personal or small websites. It integrates with Google apps and services. Wix and Weebly are popular website builders to create websites for individuals and small businesses. Both include hosting services, an easy-to-use drag-and-drop interface, and a variety of responsive themes and templates so your site will look good on any device. They also support online stores, SEO tools, adding your own domain name, and creating email marketing campaigns.

To create a website using a website builder:

1. Sign up for the service on the provider's website.
2. Select a template, or design, for your website.
3. Choose your site's domain name.
4. Set up SEO and other site options.
5. Customize the website design, and enter website content using a drag-and-drop interface and visual editor.

Figure 9-4 gives an example of designing a website using Wix.

Content Management Systems   If you need to create a more complex website with several contributors, you might opt to use a **content management system (CMS)**, a type of software that lets a group of users maintain and publish content of all kinds, but especially for websites. Many CMSs are open-source applications and offer regular updates, enhancements, plug-ins, and themes for download, often at no cost. A plug-in is a third-party program that extends the built-in functionality of an application or browser. Plug-ins for CMSs add capabilities such as providing a contact form, accepting online payments, tracking website traffic, or adding website security features.

CMSs require you to obtain web hosting services, set up a domain name for your website, and manage the content, contributors to the website, and their roles. You can sign in to your website on your browser and access the CMS through a dashboard page. The dashboard has options to add new pages, blog posts, images, and other content.

Figure 9-4: Creating a website using the Wix website builder

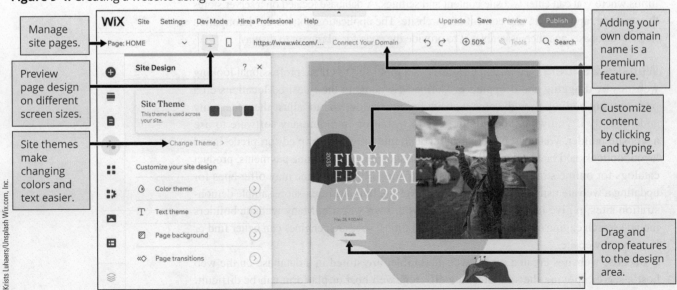

When working on websites with hundreds or thousands of pages, you often share the process of entering or updating content with others who are responsible for managing different pages of a website. Using a CMS, you often can restrict access to certain capabilities based on a contributor's role when working on the website. For example, an editor might be able to add or update content, while an administrator also might be able to add or remove users and change the site's theme.

WordPress is a popular, user friendly, open-source CMS often used as a blogging platform and tool for creating small to medium sized sites. WordPress has many plug-ins and themes available free or for purchase from third-party developers, and the software has frequent updates.

For easy setup, you can subscribe to free or paid service plans from WordPress, offering various features, storage, hosting, and customization capabilities. Advanced or professional users can install and configure the WordPress software on their own web servers. Many web hosts offer automatic installation tools to simplify the process of installing WordPress and creating its database.

Many large organizations use Drupal, another powerful open-source CMS, for developing their websites. When designing a website using a CMS, you can select a theme, specify site navigation menus, and identify content to appear in the sidebars, header, or footer of each page (**Figure 9-5**).

To create a website using the WordPress CMS:

1. Select a theme for your website.

2. Set up the theme in the dashboard, specifying fonts, colors, menu items, page header and footer content, and other settings.

3. Set up website options, including site name, description, and format of links.

4. Install plug-ins for SEO, site maintenance, managing access, and other functions.

5. Enter website content using a drag-and-drop interface and visual editor, or edit the HTML code for page content.

Figure 9-5: Creating a website using the WordPress CMS

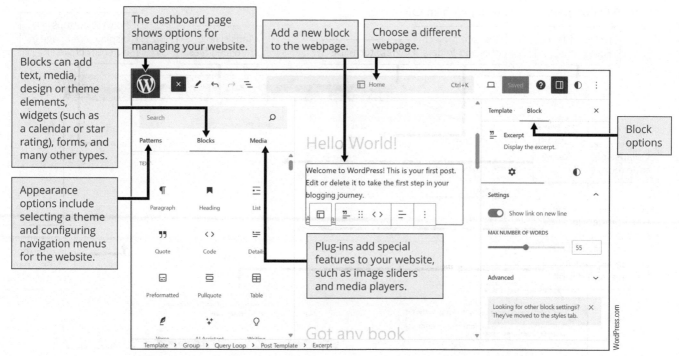

Table 9-1: Comparing website builders and content management systems

	Website builder	**Content management system**
Examples	Google Sites, Wix, Weebly	WordPress, Drupal
Popular uses	Small businesses, personal websites, online stores	Blogs, websites for large businesses or organizations, online stores
Collaboration	Few contributors	Few or many contributors
Setup required	Little to none; can get a website up and running quickly	If self-hosted, need to manage and configure a web server and install software before designing the website, or use a fully hosted version for easier setup
Templates and themes	Available from provider	Available from provider or third-party designers free or for purchase
Ease of use	Enter content in a visual editor	Enter content in a visual or HTML editor
Customer support	Paid subscriptions provide tech support through chat or online forums	Self-hosted CMS users rely on a community of enthusiasts and online resources for assistance

Table 9-1 summarizes features of website builders and content management systems.

Text Editors and IDEs   You can use a **text editor**, an app such as Notepad in Windows or TextEdit on a Mac, to enter the programming code for your website. A text editor is like a word processing app, but it lacks most text formatting features, such as fonts, colors, margins, and paragraphs. If you are using a Mac, you might need to set preferences in TextEdit to save files containing HTML code in a text format. A browser interprets the text file containing the marked-up content for a page and displays it according to the tags specified in the file.

Rather than use a text editor, many people find it easier to use an Integrated Development Environment (IDE) when coding a website. An IDE combines advanced code editing tools, debugging tools, file management tools, and publishing tools to simplify the process of developing websites and applications. Some IDE tools are also available online, as web apps. **Figure 9-6** compares a text editor with an IDE.

Figure 9-6: Comparing a text editor with an IDE

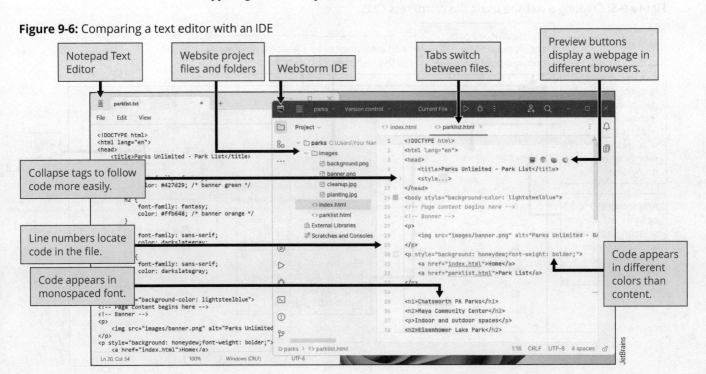

IDEs have built-in features to help you code a website, such as automatically displaying HTML tags in a different font color than the rest of the page to make them easier to see, providing suggestions and assistance when entering tags and styles, automatically indenting and formatting code, and making sure the code you type follows HTML specifications. Most IDEs contain a **code editor**, a type of text editor that has additional features to help write code accurately and efficiently. An IDE stores the files and folders relating to a website being developed in a **project**.

Some professional web developers use Adobe Dreamweaver, an IDE integrated with the Adobe Creative Cloud suite of apps and resources for creating and editing websites, audio, video, and graphics. Many IDEs, such as Visual Studio Code (VS Code) by Microsoft or WebStorm by JetBrains, are open source or have versions that you can download and install at no cost. To find information about obtaining a free educational license for WebStorm, search online for "WebStorm student license" and look for results from the JetBrains site. WebStorm has versions available for Windows, macOS, and Linux operating systems. Many of the code screenshots in this module show code in the WebStorm IDE.

Describe How to Host and Publish a Website

You need to host your website on a web server on the Internet so that other people can access it. Your college or university might give you space on one of their web servers to host a website for your classes; when creating a personal or professional website, you can purchase hosting services from a web host.

You also will need to select a domain name for your website so visitors can locate your site easily. Your web host might provide or allow you to specify a web address at their domain that you can use for personal sites or while your site is under development; for a more professional website, you will need to purchase a domain name from a **domain registrar**, an organization that sells and manages web domain names, such as GoDaddy. You can reserve the use of a domain name for periods from one to several years. When choosing a domain name, select one that is descriptive of your website's purpose or reflects your business name. If a domain name is not available, you will need to select a different one. Some people who want to protect their brand will purchase a top-level domain name (such as example.com) and several variations with different extensions (such as example.org and example.net).

Several factors are important to consider when selecting a web host:

- **Determine the amount of disk space needed.** If your website will contain many photos or videos, you will need a significant amount of disk space to store these files. If the web host provides storage on a server with a solid-state drive, the website performance might be faster than if storage is on an older hard disk drive.
- **Determine the amount of bandwidth needed.** If you expect lots of traffic to your website, you might want to go with a plan that offers unlimited bandwidth.
- **Be sure the operating system is compatible with software you want to host on the server.** Many web hosts offer servers running Windows or Linux operating systems.
- **Check the host's reliability.** **Uptime** is a measure of the percent of time a website is "up" or online; checking this helps you determine a web host's reliability. It could be costly to you if your website goes down due to an issue with your hosting provider; many hosting companies will claim to offer 99% or 99.999% uptime. These uptimes can be compared by the number of nines, such as two nines (99%) or five nines (99.999%), with more nines indicating better uptimes.

Basic hosting packages are very affordable and might include space on a shared server for one website along with websites from other customers, and limited disk space for file and data storage. Higher-end packages are good choices for businesses and websites

Figure 9-7: Managing a website through the web host's control panel

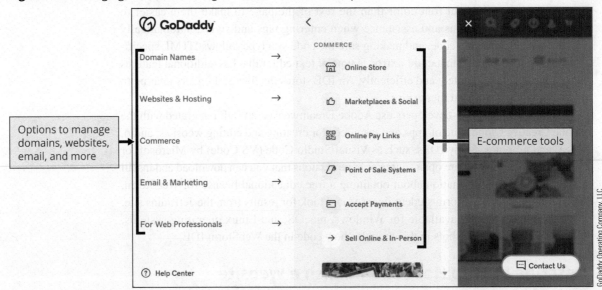

Options to manage domains, websites, email, and more

E-commerce tools

GoDaddy Operating Company, LLC

requiring additional bandwidth, processing, and speed for their websites, and storage on a dedicated server that they can administer themselves. Hosting data on a dedicated server also provides additional security. Read online reviews and do your research to find a hosting service that meets your needs.

Web hosts provide a control panel where you can access online services including managing domains, installing WordPress or other software, setting up email, and billing and account information (**Figure 9-7**).

Manage Websites Using Data Tools and Analytics

Website analytics provide a set of measurements that help you to understand how people use your website. Analytics data can include the number of visitors online and where they are located geographically, what link brought them to your site, which pages are visited the most, how long a visitor stays on each page, the devices and browsers they use, and the paths they follow to explore content on your site.

Often, this data can be displayed on a dashboard. The dashboard might contain charts, like pie charts or line charts, to show how the data changes over time. It might also contain indicators for when a certain threshold is crossed, such as an indicator that users are experiencing a high number of errors. Most data analytics dashboards can be customized according to what information you find most valuable.

Explain How to Track Website Usage with Analytics Tools

Website owners use analytics data to understand who their visitors are, where they are coming from, and how they interact with the site:

- **Site organization:** By learning how visitors explore a website, businesses can reorganize information and website content so the most requested information is easy to locate.
- **Site performance:** Tracking site performance data such as pages visited and how long it takes them to load can help determine when to increase bandwidth or other hosting requirements.

- **Traffic sources:** Identifying the most common ways site visitors find your site, such as Google search results or advertising on other sites, can help companies decide where to invest marketing funds.
- **Site design:** Determining the length of time visitors stay on the site and what parts of the site they interact with the most can help inform future site design decisions.

Clicky is a powerful tool for capturing and reporting website analytics data, and it is free for sites with less than 3,000 page views per day. **Figure 9-8** displays information about number of pages visited, number of new and returning visitors, their locations, and devices used. One attractive feature offered by Clicky is a heat map, which shows locations on pages that are clicked most often by visitors.

To set up Clicky on your website:

1. Create an account on the Clicky website at clicky.com.
2. Register your website's web address (URL) with Clicky to record usage data.
3. Set up reports to generate, such as number of visitors from a region or on a given day, or number of visitors per hour.
4. Add a tracking code to your website so you can collect analytics data. Clicky provides HTML code that you can include in your website, or you can use a plug-in with a CMS, such as WordPress, or properties of your website builder, such as Wix, to configure the tracking code.
5. After configuring Clicky, check back periodically to review the usage data that Clicky captures.

Describe the Use of XML to Update and Structure Data

While HTML provides a way to describe the content of a webpage, **XML (Extensible Markup Language)**, an open-source markup language, provides a way to classify data and share it between a wide range of applications. XML uses customized tags to describe data. Usually, XML code is generated by exporting data from one application, such as a database, into a text format that can be shared with other applications.

Figure 9-8: Clicky captures and reports website traffic

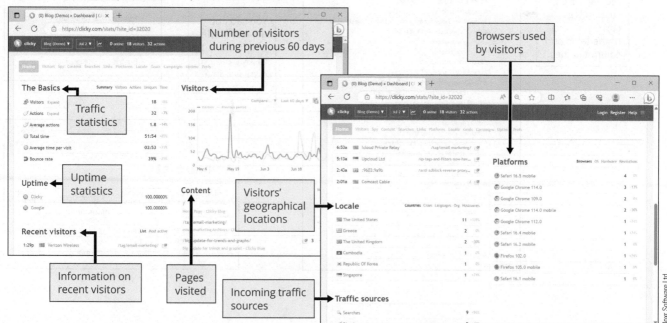

Roxr Software Ltd

Many e-commerce websites rely on XML-formatted data. When you visit an online shopping site, you easily can compare products from different vendors. When suppliers provide descriptions of their products in XML format using a set of standardized XML tags, the e-commerce site can display comparison information from many products to help you make your purchasing decisions. XML provides a standard way for suppliers to represent their products, so that buyers can compare products from many vendors.

Some organizations use XML-structured data to update the content of their webpages without having to reformat each item when displayed in a webpage or report. In **Figure 9-9**, a Microsoft Access database contains information about animals and their owners at a pet daycare center. After exporting the data to an XML file, a web developer can combine data from an XML file with instructions on how to place it on a webpage or report (such as in headings, paragraphs, lists, or tables) and how to style it (with fonts, colors, bold, or italics).

When animals enter or leave the pet daycare center, the pet daycare center can update the data in its database and export the data to a new XML file. The webpage containing the animal and owners report will update automatically with the current day's data. By applying different styles to the same data, the pet daycare center can present the information in different formats, such as in a list or table.

Table 9-2 compares features of HTML and XML.

Figure 9-9: XML makes it possible to export and share data with applications or webpages

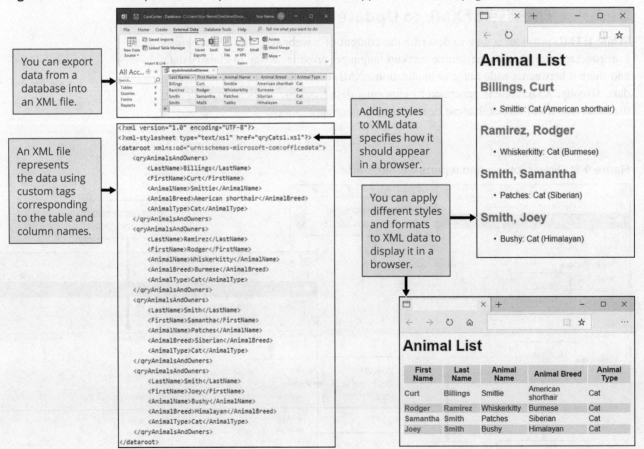

Table 9-2: HTML compared to XML

HTML	XML
Describes content and how to present it in a browser	Describes data without specifying how it will be presented
Stores layout information in a text format for a browser to interpret	Stores data in a text format to share between applications
Predefined tags describe placement of content on a webpage as paragraphs, links, headings, images, and other elements	Customized tags describe data in context (LastName, FirstName, AnimalName, AnimalBreed, AnimalType)

Build a Website from Code

Website builder apps and content management systems are popular tools for building websites because they do not require significant coding skills. All website builders and content management systems generate HTML, CSS, and JavaScript code. Sites that use predefined templates likely have a similar look and feel. Individuals or businesses that want their content and sites to stand out and reflect their unique brand will want to have a customized appearance.

Learning to code can give you finer control over how content appears on your website, whether you use a visual editor within a website builder or CMS, or you design your website or your own template using code. In this section, you can follow along with an example using HTML, CSS, and JavaScript to code a simple website for Parks Unlimited, a local volunteer group that helps with community park maintenance and upgrades. To learn to code a website, download the WebStorm IDE and perform the steps described as part of the Case Study that follows.

The website W3Schools.com is an excellent online reference with tutorials and examples for coding websites using HTML, CSS, and JavaScript (**Figure 9-10**).

Figure 9-10: W3Schools is a leading website for website developers

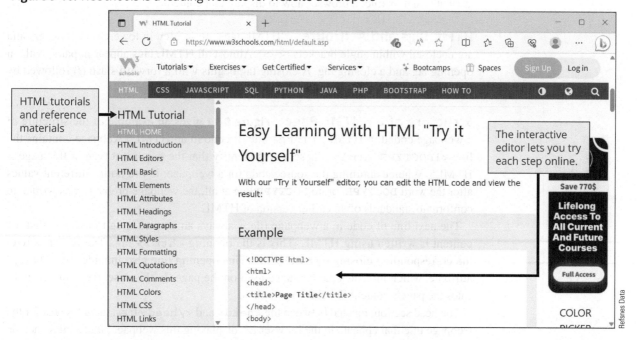

Describe the Steps for Coding and Publishing a Website

Follow these steps to code and publish a website:

1. Arrange and configure web hosting (if you are not using your school's web server).
2. Design the website (layout, navigation, content).
3. Create or obtain graphics and multimedia. Resize large images so they download quickly for site visitors.
4. Code each page.
5. Preview the website in several browsers and devices with screens of various sizes to make sure the appearance and behavior are correct.
6. Publish updated website files to a server with FTP.
7. Display the published version of your website in one or more browsers to verify that all the files were updated correctly.
8. Repeat Steps 4–7 as you add more content to your website.

When you have finished testing the pages in your website, you are ready to **publish** the website—that is, to post it to a web server online so anyone can access the site from a device connected to the Internet. Websites published on a web server are accessible on a network, such as the Internet. You can use an **FTP (File Transfer Protocol) client**, an app for uploading or downloading files between your local computer and a remote web server, to post the files. FTP specifies rules for transferring files from one computer to another on the Internet. Although it is possible to enter FTP commands in a command window to transfer files to and from a server, downloading and using a free FTP application with a graphical user interface, such as FileZilla or CuteFTP, is much easier. Many IDEs also include built-in FTP capabilities so you can publish your website to a web server without having to use a separate application.

Write Code for a Webpage

A webpage's source code contains text marked up with HTML tags and associated attributes that instruct a browser how to display that content.

HTML Tags and Attributes   HTML tags are written in lowercase characters and are enclosed within angle brackets (`< >`). Almost all HTML tags appear in pairs, with an opening tag and a closing tag. A closing tag begins with a forward slash (/) followed by the tag name.

Structure of an HTML Page   **Figure 9-11** gives an example of the structure of a webpage coded in HTML. The first line of code in an HTML5 webpage contains the line `<!DOCTYPE html>`. These words identify that the document type of this page is HTML5. When examining the source code for a webpage, if you notice different values after the word **DOCTYPE**, or no **DOCTYPE** line at all, the webpage probably was written to conform to standards of an earlier version of HTML.

The next line of code in a webpage file is always an `<html>` tag to indicate that the content is written using HTML. This is the opening `<html>` tag. The file ends with the corresponding closing `</html>` tag. This opening line also includes the `'lang'` attribute, which indicates the language used on the page. In this case, the value **en** indicates the page's content is written in English.

The head section, located between the `<head>` and `</head>` tags, includes tags for the webpage title that appears in the browser tab displaying this webpage; it also may include styles and JavaScript. The body section, located between the `<body>` and `</body>` tags, contains the content of the webpage marked up with HTML tags.

Figure 9-11: Structure of a webpage coded in HTML

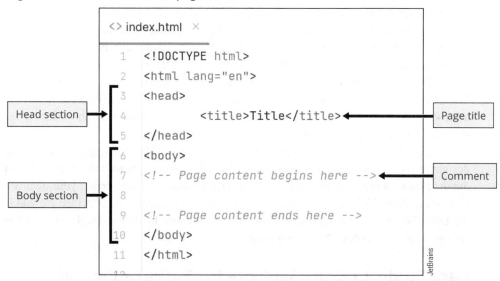

When tags enclose several lines of content, you might indent content between the opening and closing tags so they line up. This makes it easier to follow the HTML code when developing the webpage.

The content of a webpage is placed between the **<body>** and **</body>** tags. In Figure 9-11, this area is marked with comments to indicate where the page content begins and ends. Comments look similar to HTML tags, except they have an exclamation point and two dashes (**!--**) after the opening bracket and two dashes (**--**) before the closing bracket. The dashes are not required, but they help improve readability. Including comments makes it easier to understand the HTML code as you work on it, or if you need to make changes or troubleshoot problems later.

An opening tag contains the tag name followed by any **attributes**, or additional information needed to completely specify the tag. For example, the **lang** attribute in the html tag specifies the page's language. **Figure 9-12** illustrates the **<a>** (anchor) tag, used to indicate a hyperlink on a webpage. Each attribute is followed by an equal sign (=) and the attribute's value in quotation marks. Within the opening **<a>** tag are two attributes: **href** (hypertext reference) to specify the web address for the page to load when you click the link and its value, **"http://google.com"**; and **target** and its value, **"_blank"**, to specify that the page should open in a new browser tab. The link text, Google, appears between the opening and closing tags.

Figure 9-12: Syntax of the <a> (anchor) tag

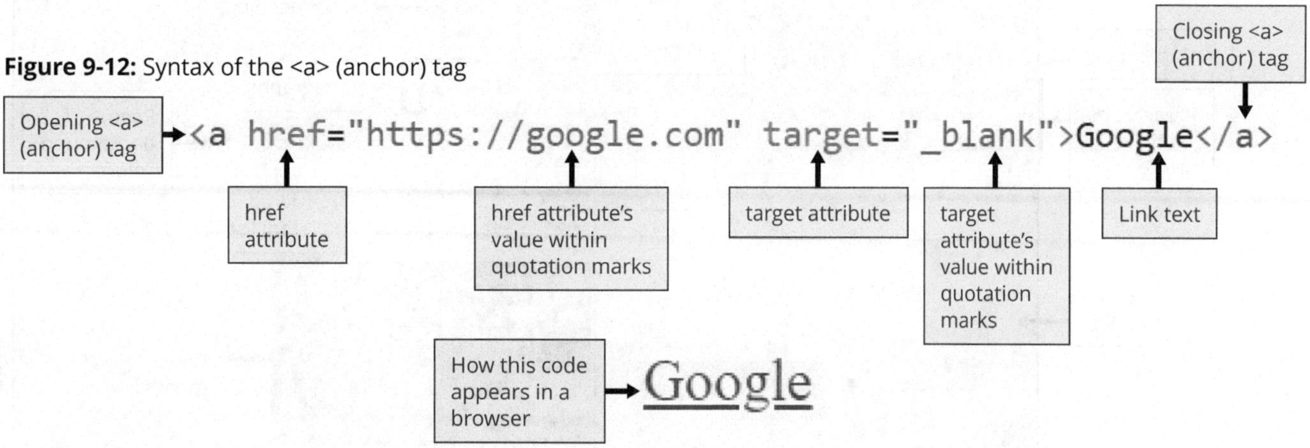

Opening <a> (anchor) tag → `<a href="https://google.com" target="_blank">Google</a>` ← Closing <a> (anchor) tag

href attribute

href attribute's value within quotation marks

target attribute

target attribute's value within quotation marks

Link text

How this code appears in a browser → Google

Webpage File Names   When you save the code for a webpage as a text file, choose a short but descriptive file name for the page. A good practice is to use lowercase letters, numbers, and underscores in webpage file names. Avoid using special characters or spaces in webpage names. The file extension for webpage files is usually .html. The .html file extension indicates to the browser that the file stores HTML code.

The file name containing the content of a website's home page usually is named index.html. You often can omit index.html when entering the address of a website's home page in a browser. Web servers automatically will look for a page named index.html if no page name is specified as part of a web address entered in a browser.

In the next section, you will learn how to use basic HTML, CSS, and JavaScript in designing and developing the Parks Unlimited website. You might read the steps to follow the development process, or type the code yourself using an IDE to create your own version of the Parks Unlimited website. The images for the website are provided for you in the Data Files folder for this course. Save the files to your hard disk, OneDrive, or other storage location to access them when needed.

Case Study: Create a Website for Parks Unlimited

Parks Unlimited is a local volunteer group that helps with community park maintenance and upgrades. To advertise their work and recruit new volunteers, the group needs a new website (**Figure 9-13**).

Figure 9-13: Parks Unlimited website (a) home page and (b) park list page

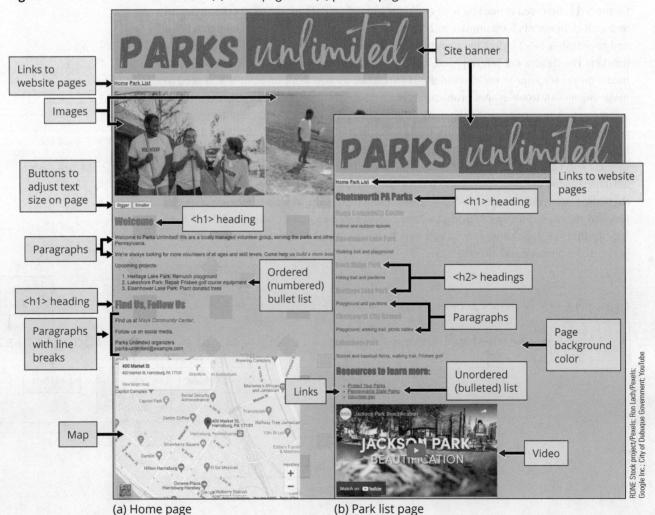

(a) Home page

(b) Park list page

RDNE Stock project/Pexels; Ron Lach/Pexels; Google Inc.; City of Dubuque Government; YouTube

The volunteer group wants a simple, static website with these specifications:

- The site's home page will contain two photos from previous projects, information about the group's projects, and a map showing the organization's home office location at one park.
- A parks page will display a list of parks, links to other resources, and a helpful video.
- Each page will contain a banner graphic and links to each page of the website.
- Visitors to the home page will be able to click buttons to display the text in larger or smaller font sizes.

To get started creating the Parks Unlimited website:

1. Download and install an IDE such as WebStorm, or choose a text editor that you will use to create and edit the website files.
2. Create a folder or directory named parks that will contain all the files and folders used in the Parks Unlimited website project. Note that, although some platforms use the term directory instead of folder, folders and directories are essentially the same thing.
3. Open the text editor or IDE, locate the project folder, and create a new HTML file inside your parks folder; name the file index.html.
4. Copy and paste, or type, the home page text (**Figure 9-14a**) between the `<body>` and `</body>` tags.
5. Save the file.
6. Create a new HTML file inside your parks folder; name the file parklist.html.
7. Copy and paste, or type, the park list page text (**Figure 9-14b**) between the `<body>` and `</body>` tags.
8. Save both pages and display them in a browser. Notice that each page includes one long paragraph of text with no structure.

Figure 9-14: Text of the Parks Unlimited (a) home page and (b) park list page

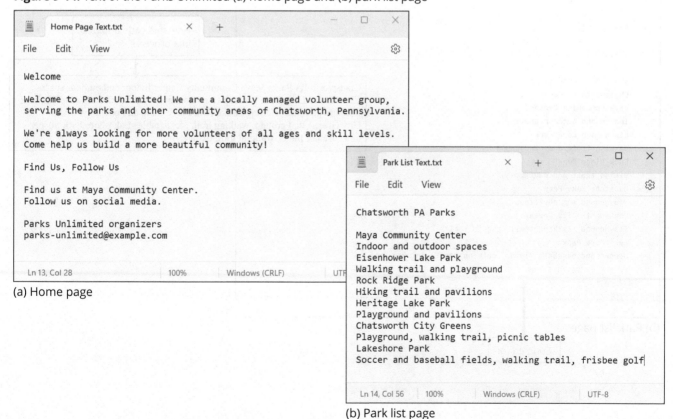

(a) Home page

(b) Park list page

After entering the text in a text editor and saving the index.html and parklist.html files, the Home and Park List pages should appear in a browser (**Figure 9-15**).

The sections that follow describe general features and elements you will need to finish coding the Parks Unlimited website, followed by Case Study sections that give step-by-step instructions for implementing those features.

Figure 9-15: Parks Unlimited (a) home page and (b) park list page without any markup

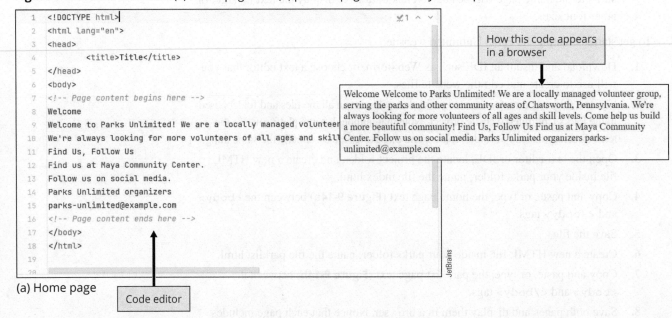

(a) Home page

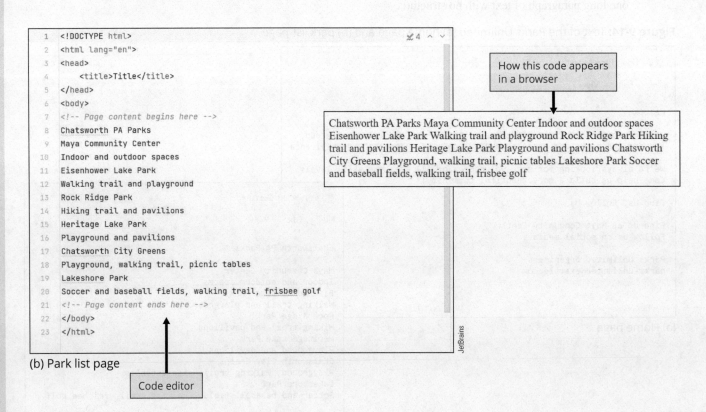

(b) Park list page

Add Titles, Headings, Paragraphs, and Line Breaks

Unformatted text in a website is not very useful or appealing. You need to organize and format it to convey the information you desire, starting with titles, headings, paragraphs, and line breaks.

Figure 9-16: Heading tags display headings in different text sizes

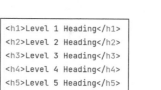

HTML tags for headings

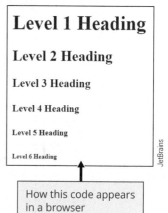

How this code appears in a browser

Titles   Each webpage needs a descriptive title. The webpage's title identifies the page, and appears in a browser tab. When you bookmark a favorite webpage, the browser will identify the bookmark by the webpage's title. A descriptive webpage title can help you locate it among other open pages in a browser. Search engines also index webpages based on their titles.

Headings   Headings indicate the different sections of a webpage. HTML5 supports six levels of headings, identified by the following tags: `<h1>`, `<h2>`, `<h3>`, `<h4>`, `<h5>`, and `<h6>`. The `<h1>` tag displays text in the largest font size, and the `<h6>` tag displays text in the smallest font size (**Figure 9-16**).

Paragraphs   In addition to a title and headings, you need to identify paragraphs. The `<p>` and `</p>` tags identify the beginning and ending of paragraphs. If you have several paragraphs of text on your webpage, these tags will inform the browser to insert additional line spacing above and below the paragraph so the text is easier to read. Because the browser ignores line breaks and line spacing in the HTML file, it is important to properly define the paragraphs using the `<p>` and `</p>` tags.

If you display the code in the index.html file in a browser before adding paragraph tags, the browser will display it as one long paragraph, even though the HTML file appears to have several paragraphs in the body text. To display the text correctly in a browser, place `<p>` and `</p>` tags around each paragraph.

Line Breaks   Add a `<br>` tag when you want to break a line with no white space before or after it. The `<br>` tag does not have a corresponding closing tag.

Case Study: Add a Title, Headings, Paragraphs, and Line Breaks to the Parks Unlimited Home Page

To add a title, headings, paragraphs, and a line break to the Parks Unlimited home page, edit the index.html file as follows:

1. Type `Parks Unlimited - Home` between the `<title>` and `</title>` tags in the head section to set the title of the page. Delete any placeholder text as necessary.

2. Type `<h1>` and `</h1>` tags around the lines `Welcome` and `Find Us, Follow Us;` and type `<p>` and `</p>` tags around the remaining paragraphs. You can press Enter to break lines that are too long in the code editor.

3. Type `<br>` after the first line of the Parks Unlimited contact information at the bottom of the page.

4. Save the file and preview it in a browser.

Figure 9-17: Parks Unlimited home page after adding a title, headings, paragraphs, and line breaks

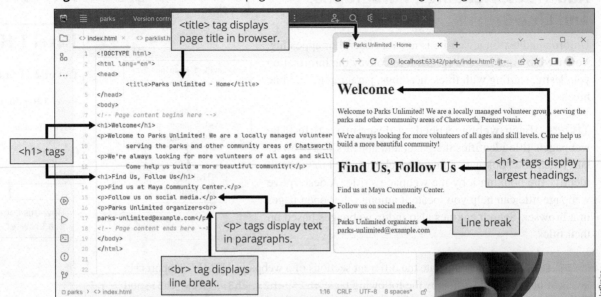

After adding the title, paragraphs, and headings, the home page should match **Figure 9-17**. Edit the parklist.html page as follows:

1. Type **Parks Unlimited – Park List** between the **<title>** and **</title>** tags in the head section to set the title of the page.

2. Type **<h1>** and **</h1>** tags around the line **Chatsworth PA Parks**.

3. Type **<h2>** and **</h2>** tags around the lines **Maya Community Center**, **Eisenhower Lake Park**, **Rock Ridge Park**, **Heritage Lake Park**, **Chatsworth City Greens**, and **Lakeshore Park**.

4. Type **<p>** and **</p>** tags around the descriptions of each park.

5. Save the file and display it in a browser.

After adding the title, paragraphs, and headings, the park list page should match **Figure 9-18**.

Figure 9-18: Parks Unlimited park list page after adding a title, headings, and paragraphs

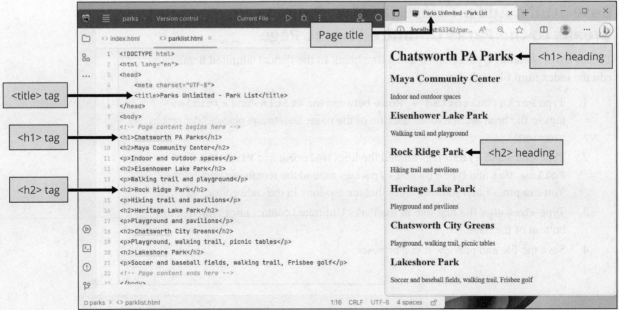

Add Images

Images on a website can capture the attention of your website's visitors. Some websites include a **banner**, a graphic that identifies the website, often placed at the top of each page so visitors will recognize the website easily. Photos and graphics can make a website more attractive or help to deliver its message, but not all visitors may be able to see them. Visitors to your page who are visually impaired or visitors whose browsers are configured not to display images may be unable to view images on a page.

When identifying images to include on a webpage, choose images with appropriate dimensions for the webpage and relatively small file sizes. Images load at the same time as the webpage, so pages with several large images might cause the page to take a longer time to load, which can be annoying to users. Most browsers can display images stored in JPEG, GIF, or PNG format (identified with .jpg, .gif, or .png file extensions).

If you are trying to display photos from a digital camera or smartphone, you should use image-editing software to shrink the photos to an appropriate size, such as 300×400 pixels for a small image or 600×800 pixels for a medium-sized image, to display in a browser. The size, or resolution, of a photo taken with an 8-megapixel camera can be approximately 2448×3264 pixels, which is larger than the resolution of the screens on many devices or monitors. Full-sized images can take a long time to load, which might impact the performance of your website.

Be careful when you include images or other content from another website on your own website, as it is possible that such content might not be displayed correctly. If the owner of the other website modifies the location or removes the content entirely, the image will not appear, or a broken link will result on your website. You should have permission to use images that you find online and provide a reference if they are not your own. Many online photos are published with a Creative Commons license, which describes conditions the owner sets to permit its reuse in other projects, such as with or without attribution, or whether you can adapt or modify the image. Search for royalty-free images or Creative Commons licensed images if you are looking for images to reuse on your website.

The `<img>` tag specifies information about an image to display on a website. You must include attributes to specify the location of an image file, and alternate text (alt text) to describe the image. **Table 9-3** summarizes common attributes for the `<img>` tag. When coding a website, a good practice is to store its images in a folder separate from the webpages so that you can locate them easily.

The `<img>` tag is one of several HTML tags that do not have a corresponding closing tag. When no additional information is required between an opening tag and its closing tag, HTML5 omits the closing tag. In this case, the image is specified entirely by its attributes, so HTML5 does not specify a tag to close the `<img>` tag. HTML5 tags that do not require a closing tag are sometimes called **one-sided tags**. Other one-sided tags include `<br>` (line break) and `<hr>` (horizontal rule).

Table 9-3: Common attributes for the `<img>` tag

Attribute	Meaning	Description
`src`	source	Location of the image file. Can be within the images folder or the web address of an image online.
`alt`	alt text	Text to describe the image. Some browsers will display alt text if the image is not set to load automatically, or if the file containing the image is not found. Website readers read the alt text aloud to assist visually impaired users in identifying the purpose of each image. The alt attribute is required when using the `<img>` tag in HTML5.

Figure 9-19: The <img> tag and its common attributes

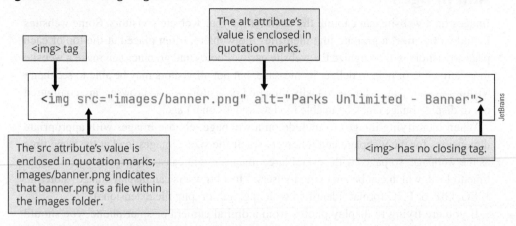

The alt attribute's value is enclosed in quotation marks.

<img> tag

```
<img src="images/banner.png" alt="Parks Unlimited - Banner">
```

JetBrains

The src attribute's value is enclosed in quotation marks; images/banner.png indicates that banner.png is a file within the images folder.

<img> has no closing tag.

Figure 9-19 analyzes sample code for an `<img>` tag.

Case Study: Add a Banner and Images to the Parks Unlimited Website

The Parks Unlimited website will contain four images: a banner graphic to identify the website, two photos of park work projects to add to the site's visual appeal, and a background image (**Figure 9-20**). All four images are provided to you in the Data Files folder for this course.

Figure 9-20: Images used in the Parks Unlimited website include (a) a banner, (b) photos of park volunteers, and (c) a background image

RDNE Stock project/Pexels; Ron Lach/Pexels

The website stores the images in a folder called images, within the website folder (**Figure 9-21**).

To add the banner graphic and two photos to the home page for the Parks Unlimited website:

1. Create a folder called images, located in your parks folder that also contains the index.html file.

2. Place the four image files (banner.png file, cleanup.jpg, planting.jpg, and background.png) in the images folder. You can find these files in the Data Files folder for this course, which you may have saved on your hard disk, OneDrive, or other storage location. You may want to copy these files to the images folder rather than moving them, to leave the originals untouched.

Figure 9-21: The images folder

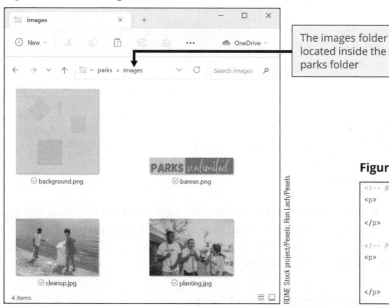

Figure 9-22: Home page image code

```
<!-- Banner -->
<p>
        <img src="images/banner.png" alt="Parks Unlimited - Banner">
</p>

<!-- Project photos -->
<p>
        <img src="images/planting.jpg" alt="Planting project">
        <img src="images/cleanup.jpg" alt="Cleanup project">
</p>
```

3. Enter the code displayed in **Figure 9-22** into the index.html file just above the **<h1>** welcome line, so the images appear at the top of the webpage. This code displays the banner in its own paragraph, and the two images in a separate paragraph. Comments identify the banner and project photos in the page content's code.
4. Save the file and display it in a browser.

Figure 9-23: Park list page image code

```
<!-- Banner -->
<p>
        <img src="images/banner.png" alt="Parks Unlimited - Banner">
</p>
```

To add the banner image to the park list page:

1. Type the code displayed in **Figure 9-23** to add the banner graphic in the parklist.html file just above the **<h1>** heading, so the image appears at the top of the page.
2. Save the file and display it in a browser.

After adding the images, the Home and Park List pages should appear in a browser as illustrated in **Figure 9-24**.

Figure 9-24: Parks Unlimited website with images added to the (a) home page and (b) park list page

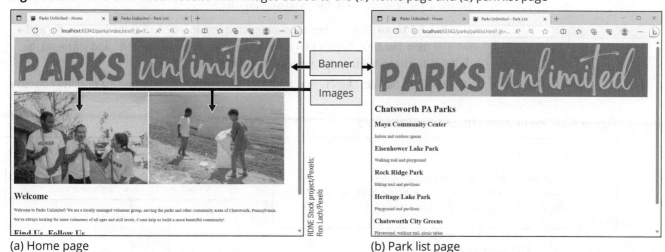

(a) Home page

(b) Park list page

Figure 9-25: Code and results for unordered and ordered lists

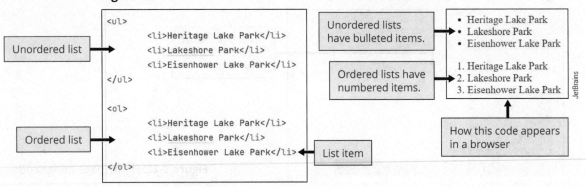

If the images do not appear when you preview the page in a browser, check that you correctly typed the code referencing the images and that the images exist in the location you specified (in this case, the images folder). Be sure that you saved the code files after adding the images, before reloading the page.

Add Unordered and Ordered Lists

Two types of lists that HTML supports are unordered lists and ordered lists. Unordered lists display a collection of items in a list format, with each list item preceded by a bullet symbol. Ordered lists, by default, precede each list item with a number. Displaying information in an unordered or ordered list makes it easier to follow than if it appeared in one long, multi-line paragraph.

The `<ul>` and `</ul>` tags surround list items for an unordered list and precede each list item with a bullet. The `<ol>` and `</ol>` tags surround list items for an ordered list and precede each list item with a number. For both list types, specify each item between `<li>` and `</li>` tags. **Figure 9-25** compares the code for ordered and unordered lists.

Case Study: Add Lists to the Parks Unlimited Website

To add an ordered list to the index.html file:

1. Add the upcoming projects as an ordered list, inserted just before the "Find Us, Follow Us" heading. Type `<li>` and `</li>` tags around each project, and surround the list items with `<ol>` and `</ol>` tags (**Figure 9-26**).
2. Save the file. Display it in a browser and verify the ordered list displays correctly.

To add an unordered list to the parklist.html file:

1. Add outside resources as an unordered list, inserted after the list of parks and a new heading. Type `<li>` and `</li>` tags around each item, and surround the list items with `<ul>` and `</ul>` tags (**Figure 9-27**).
2. Save the file. Display it in a browser and verify the unordered list displays correctly.

Figure 9-26: Home page with ordered list added

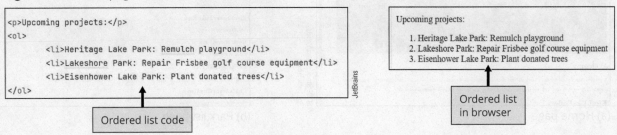

Figure 9-27: Unordered list on Park List page

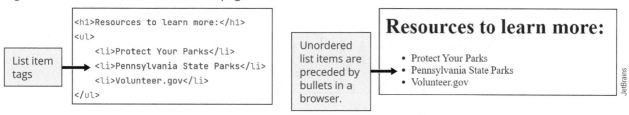

Add Links

A link, or hyperlink, can be text or an image in a webpage that you can click to navigate to another webpage, download a file, or perform another action, such as sending an email message.

Including links to all the pages in your website makes it easy for visitors to navigate your site. In addition to providing links to pages in your website, you also can provide links to other websites, called **external links**. Webpages always are stored as separate files, and hypertext references to the files appear in the HTML code using the `<a>` (anchor) tag. The `<a>` tag's `href` (hypertext reference) attribute often refers to the location of the file or webpage that you want to display or download.

The `<a>` (anchor) tag specifies information about hyperlinks to display on a website. You must provide an attribute to reference the location of the linked page or document, and optionally can specify in which browser tab to display it. **Table 9-4** summarizes common attributes for the `<a>` tag.

Absolute Web References and Relative Web References   The `href` attribute's value references a resource (usually a webpage, image, or file) using either a relative web reference or an absolute web reference. A **relative web reference** identifies the location of webpages and files in the current website. An **absolute web reference** identifies the location of webpages and files stored on other websites. An absolute web reference requires the full file path, including the protocol and domain name containing the webpage.

If your website has a broken link, the desired webpage, image, or file will not load correctly. Common causes of broken links include:

- The http:// or https:// protocol prefix is missing from an absolute web reference.
- You did not upload a webpage, image, or file to the web server.
- You made an error when typing the resource referenced in the `href` attribute.
- The webpage, image, or file is not located in the directory referenced in the `href` attribute.

Table 9-4: Common attributes for the `<a>` tag

Attribute	Meaning	Description
`href`	hypertext reference	Location of the image file. Can be within the images folder or the web address of an image online.
`target`	target	Browser tab or window in which to open the new page. Use the value `_blank` to open the linked document or page in a new tab, or omit this value to open the link in the current tab.

Figure 9-28: Code for hyperlinks with absolute and relative web references

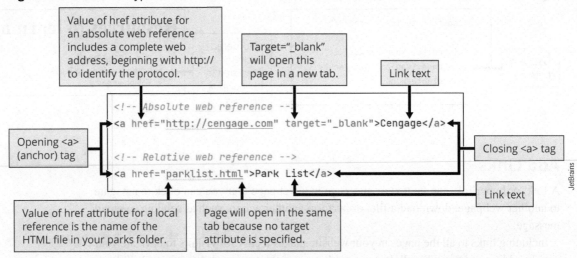

Although an absolute web reference must include http:// or https:// (for the secure version of HTTP), some browsers might not display the http:// or https:// prefix in the address bar when navigating to a webpage. Most websites will open links to pages on other websites in a new browser tab or window to indicate that you are leaving the website you are visiting currently.

Figure 9-28 compares hyperlinks with absolute and relative web references.

You also can use absolute and relative web references in an `<img>` tag with the `src` attribute to specify the location from where a browser should access an image to display on a website. In the HTML code, `<img src="images/banner.png" alt="Cafe Unlimited - Banner">`, the `src` attribute references a file named banner.png located in the images folder, and the images folder is in the same folder as the current file (index. html, in this case). This is a relative web reference, as the location is given relative to the location of the file requesting the resource.

To display an image stored on another website, specify an absolute web reference, including the http:// or https:// protocol, as part of the `src` attribute. For example, if you add the code, `<img src="https://www.w3.org/html/logo/downloads/ HTML5_Logo_512.png" alt="HTML5 Logo">` to a webpage, the page will display the HTML5 logo stored on the website w3.org. The image is not located in your website's images folder because it is stored on the website specified in the absolute web reference of the web address. If the location of that file at w3.org ever changes, or if the file is removed, the image will not display on your website.

Case Study: Add Links to the Parks Unlimited Website

The home page of the Parks Unlimited website will contain links as listed in **Table 9-5**.

Table 9-5: Links in the Parks Unlimited website

Hypertext reference	Description	Web reference type
`index.html`	Parks Unlimited – Home page	Relative
`parklist.html`	Parks Unlimited – Park List page	Relative
`https://education.nationalgeographic .org/resource/protect-your-parks/`	Protect Your Parks	Absolute
`https://www.dcnr.pa.gov/StateParks/ Pages/default.aspx`	Pennsylvania State Parks	Absolute
`https://volunteer.gov`	Volunteer.gov	Absolute

The two relative links refer to pages in the website. The absolute web references will each open in a new browser tab.

To add navigation links to pages in the Parks Unlimited website:

1. In the index.html file, at the line below the banner graphic, and above the project photos, type the code in **Figure 9-29** to create relative web links for both the index page and the park list page.
2. Repeat Step 1 to add the same navigation links to the parklist.html file.
3. Save both files.
4. Preview index.html in a browser. Click the Park List link, and make sure the park list page displays. On the Park List page, click Home link to make sure the index.html (home) page displays. You should be able to switch between the pages by clicking their links. The results should match **Figure 9-30**.

Figure 9-29: Navigation link codes

```
<p>
        <a href="index.html">Home</a>
        <a href="parklist.html">Park List</a>
</p>
```

Figure 9-30: Parks Unlimited website with navigation links added on the (a) home page and (b) park list page

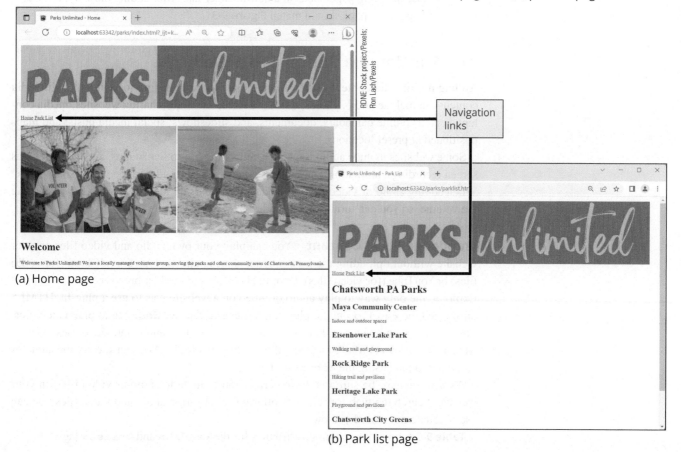

(a) Home page

(b) Park list page

Figure 9-31: Parks Unlimited Park List page with external links added

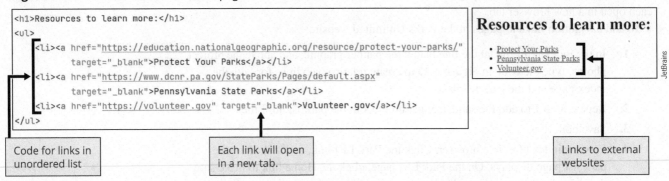

To add links to external sites in the parklist.html file:

1. Change the Protect Your Parks text to

   ```
   <a href="https://education.nationalgeographic.org/
   resource/protect-your-parks/" target="_blank">Protect
   Your Parks</a>
   ```

   so it appears as a hyperlink. Be sure to use the attribute `target="_blank"` to load the external website in a new browser tab.

2. Type similar code to create hyperlinks so the text Pennsylvania State Parks will load the website, `https://www.dcnr.pa.gov/StateParks/Pages/default.aspx`, and the text Volunteer.gov will load the website `https://volunteer.gov`, each in a new browser tab.

3. Save the file. Display it in a browser; click each external link to make sure the corresponding page opens in a new browser tab. After adding these hyperlinks, the park list page should match **Figure 9-31**.

Add Multimedia Content to a Webpage

Adding multimedia content makes your website more engaging to visitors. Multimedia content can include audio, photos, or videos stored on media sharing websites; media content, such as online calendars, documents, and slideshows; social media posts; and maps positioned at preset locations.

Some websites include audio, such as speech, music, or other sounds, and video, such as screen recordings, animations, and videos recorded with a video camera on a smartphone. When adding audio or video to a site, many developers include controls to adjust or mute the volume, so you can turn off the sound, if necessary.

Embedded Local Content   You can play your own audio and video files on your website without uploading them to a media-sharing site such as SoundCloud (for audio files) or YouTube (for video files). Prior to HTML5, and in older browsers such as Internet Explorer, the only way to play audio or video on a website was to use a plug-in. HTML5 introduced the `<audio>` tag to play audio files and the `<video>` tag to play video files. Similar to storing images in their own folder, you can store audio and video files for your website in a separate folder located within your parks folder. You can specify the audio or video file to play using the `<source>` tag.

As with images, be sure you have permission to include audio or video files on your website. Search the web for websites offering royalty-free audio and video files you can use if you do not record you own.

Table 9-6 summarizes common attributes for the `<audio>` and `<video>` tags.

Table 9-6: Attributes for the `<audio>` and `<video>` tags

Attribute	Description
`autoplay`	Include this attribute to play the audio or video automatically when the page loads (might not work on mobile devices).
`controls`	Include this attribute to display audio or video controls, such as play, pause, and volume. If you do not include this option, the only way to stop playing the audio is to close the page.
`width`	Define width of video player in pixels.
`height`	Define height of video player in pixels.

Figure 9-32: Webpage with an audio file and a video file

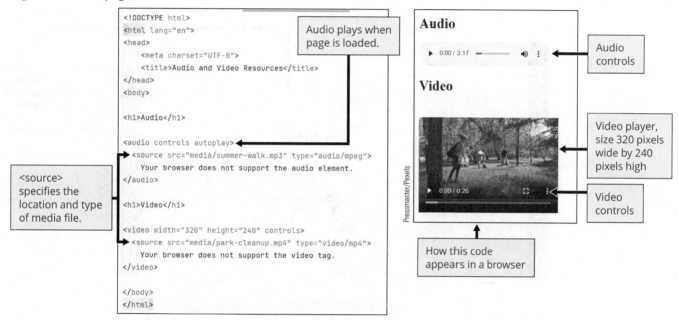

Figure 9-32 provides an example of code for adding an audio or video file to your website. In this example, the audio file, summer-walk.mp3, and the video file, park-cleanup.mp4, both are stored in a folder named media located within the parks folder.

Embedded External Content   Most media sharing sites, such as SoundCloud, YouTube, and SlideShare (for sharing presentations), as well as mapping sites such as Google Maps and social media sites such as Instagram, allow you to embed content posted on their website, on your own website. Look for a Share icon or an option often labelled Share or Embed. When you click Share, the webpage will display HTML code, usually containing an `<iframe>` tag, that you can copy and paste into your HTML file at the location where you would like the media to appear.

Case Study: Add a Map and a YouTube Video to the Parks Unlimited Website

Follow these steps to add to the Parks Unlimited website a map showing the location of the community center and a video.

To add a map to the index.html file of the Parks Unlimited website:

1. Open a new browser tab and open a mapping site such as Google Maps.
2. Search for the location 400 Market St, Harrisburg, PA, to display on the map.

3. **Figure 9-33** includes the embed code for adding a Google map to a website. Click the Share icon or link, and then click the Embed button or link. Click COPY HTML to copy the embed code to your clipboard.

4. Paste the embed code copied from the mapping site to the index.html file just below the email address.

5. Save the file. Preview it in a browser to make sure the map displays correctly. After adding the map, the Home page should match **Figure 9-34**.

Figure 9-33: Google Maps provides code to embed a map on a website

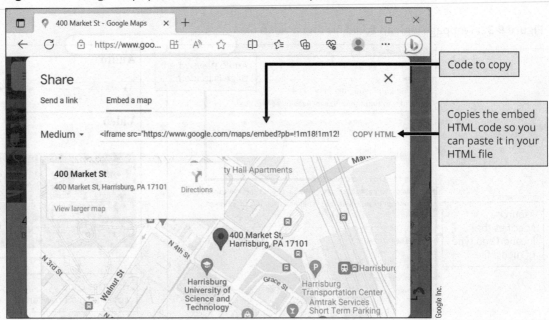

Figure 9-34: Parks Unlimited home page with a map

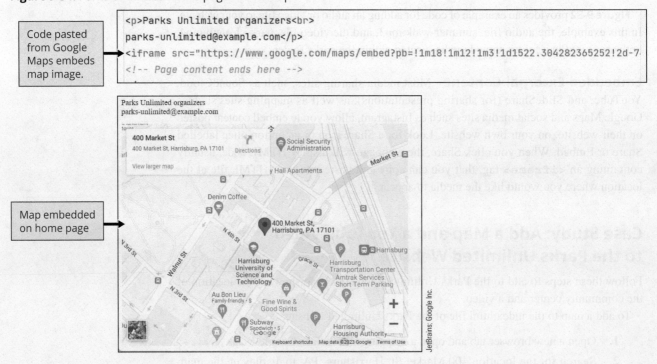

To add a YouTube video to the index.html file of the Parks Unlimited Park List page:

1. Open a new browser tab and open a video sharing site, such as YouTube.

2. Type park beautification in the site's search box to find a video about park improvement projects.

3. **Figure 9-35** includes the embed code for adding a YouTube video to a website. Click the Share icon or link, and then click the Embed button or link. Click the Copy button to copy the embed code to your clipboard.

4. Paste the embed code copied from the video sharing site to the end of the parklist.html file, just after the unordered list.

5. Save the file. Preview it in a browser to make sure the video displays correctly.

After adding the video, the Park List page in a browser should include a video player with a preview of the video (**Figure 9-36**).

Figure 9-35: YouTube provides code to embed videos on your website

Figure 9-36: Parks Unlimited Park List page with a YouTube video

Validate HTML Code

The World Wide Web Consortium (W3C) oversees the specification of HTML standards, and as HTML evolves, the W3C identifies some tags as obsolete, or **deprecated**, which describes technology that developers are discouraged from using because a newer technology has been created to take its place. Deprecated features can still be used, rather than being removed instantly, while users adapt to newer techniques developed to accomplish the same tasks. For example, in earlier versions of HTML, you could use the **<font>** tag to specify the font or color of text on a webpage. With the development of CSS, the W3C has deprecated the **<font>** tag. Although the **<font>** tag still may display text in a font correctly in some browsers, the preferred way to display text in a specific font is using CSS. When developers learn of deprecated features, they should begin to update webpages to follow the new standard. Deprecated features will still work in some browsers, but eventually might be unsupported.

The WebStorm IDE notifies you if you use a deprecated tag (**Figure 9-37**). You can then accept suggested edits, make your own edits, or leave the code as is.

The W3C also provides an HTML5 validator web app to ensure that a webpage's code follows the specifications, or rules, for HTML5. When coding a webpage by hand, using a validator ensures that the code complies with HTML5 standards and that the page displays correctly in all HTML5-compliant browsers. The HTML5 validator will identify any deprecated tags, required attributes that are missing, or other errors (**Figure 9-38**).

The code provided when embedding a map, video, or other online content sometimes contains an **<iframe>** tag. A validation service might issue a warning message when it recognizes code containing the **<iframe>** tag.

Figure 9-37: You can replace many deprecated tags with CSS

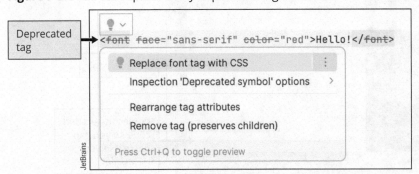

Figure 9-38: Use a code validator to make sure your code follows HTML5 specifications

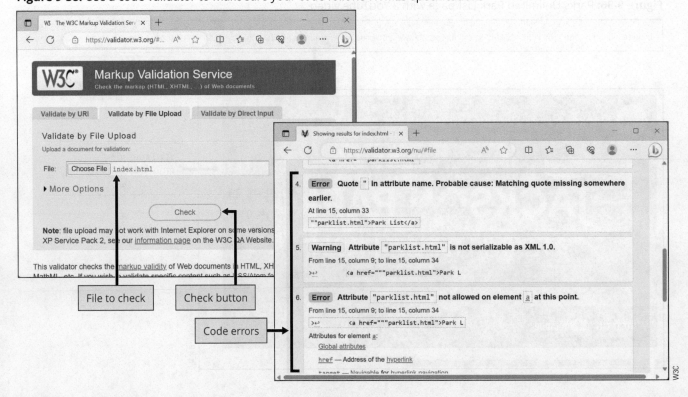

Case Study: Validate Your HTML Code for the Parks Unlimited Website

To check your HTML code using the W3C HTML5 Validation Service:

1. Locate the W3C Markup Validation Service webpage using a search engine.
2. Select the File Upload option, and then upload the index.html file for your website from your computer to the Validation Service page. Click the Check button to check your code.
3. Review the output to determine any code you need to fix for the page to pass inspection.
4. Repeat Step 2 for the parklist.html page.

Figure 9-38 provides examples of some possible results of validating the index.html page of the Parks Unlimited website when there is an error in one line of code.

Publish a Website Online

When you are ready to share your website online so others can access it, you can use an FTP client to transfer the files. This section describes how to set up FileZilla, a free FTP client, to transfer files between your computer and a web server (**Figure 9-39**).

The computer that you use to edit your website is called your **local computer**; this is the computer storing the files you will publish to an FTP server using an FTP client app. To transfer the files from your local computer to a **remote web server** (a web server on the Internet), you will need to connect to the remote web server using an FTP client.

You also will need an account on a web server in order to publish a website. If your school provides you with space to host a website, ask your instructor for the settings to connect to your account on the school's web server. In general, you will need to know the host or web server name and your user name and password to publish the files. You should publish only those files related to your website assignment on your school's web server.

Figure 9-39: Using FileZilla to upload website files to a web server

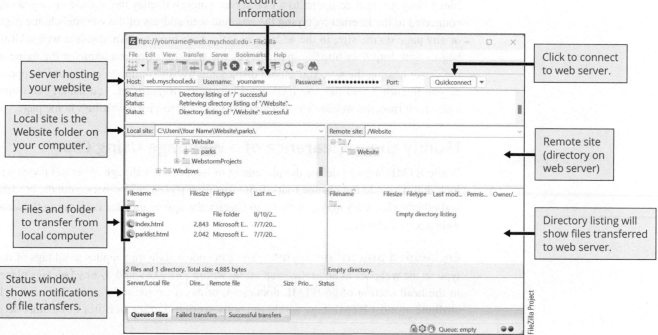

After the file transfer completes, check the time, date, and size of the files on the server. The sizes should match the sizes of the files on your local computer. A file's time and date show the time and date that the web server received the file.

Display the website by entering the web address of the website's home page (on the server) in the browser's address bar to verify the files uploaded correctly.

Case Study: Publish the Parks Unlimited Website Files to a Web Server

To connect to a remote web server using FileZilla, an FTP client:

1. Type the host name (the name of the web server) and the user name and password for the account or set up a profile containing this information using an FTP application. Click the Quickconnect button to connect to the server, as displayed earlier in Figure 9-39.

2. In the Local site section of the FTP application, navigate to the website folder containing the HTML, images, and other files for the website. In the remote site section of the FTP application, you should find the contents of your account on the web server. This area will contain an empty file directory listing until you upload files to the server.

3. Select the files or folders stored on your computer from the Local Sites section. To upload these files to the server, choose the transfer option, or drag these files to the Remote site section of FileZilla. The transferred files will appear in the directory listing section of the Remote site.

Each time you modify or add files or images to the website, you must upload the changes to the web server so visitors can access them. After uploading the files, make sure it looks correct by visiting the site and entering the absolute web address in your browser's address bar. Click through the site's links to ensure everything displays as you intended.

Display a Webpage Online

Uploading webpages to a web server allows anyone connected to the Internet to display them by entering their web address in a browser. When you have finished transferring the files from your local computer to a web server, you can display the website on any device connected to the Internet by typing the absolute web address of the website's home page, or any page on the site, in the address bar of a web browser. An absolute web address begins with http:// or https:// and includes the website's domain name or the name of the server hosting the site. You should display the website online to make sure it appears as you intended, and that the links work correctly. Remember, you usually can omit index.html from the website's web address if you want to visit a website's home page.

Modify the Appearance of a Webpage Using CSS

While HTML helps to define the placement of items on a webpage, your webpages will look dull if you do not change fonts, font sizes, font styles, colors, backgrounds, borders, and other styles. CSS makes it easier to specify the appearance for each tag in the same webpage or website.

Embedded and Inline Styles   You can code a style that applies to all tags of one type on the webpage as an **embedded style**, within `<style>` and `</style>` tags placed in the head section of an HTML document, or as an **inline style**, specified as a style attribute of most HTML tags within the body section. Larger websites often store style information in external files called **style sheets** to create a consistent appearance across all pages in the website. Individual webpages can reference a common style sheet, which helps ensure this design consistency.

The selector indicates the HTML tag being styled. A style declaration contains the style name followed by a colon, followed by the value for the style. If more than one style is used, separate each style with a semicolon. **Figure 9-40** compares an embedded style and an inline style.

When you create an inline style, the style must be associated with a tag. If you are applying a style to a small section of a document that is not surrounded by its own tag, such as a few words or phrases, surround that content with **<span>** and **</span>** tags, and specify the style using a style attribute within the **<span>** tag. **Figure 9-41** provides an example.

Figure 9-40: Comparing embedded and inline styles

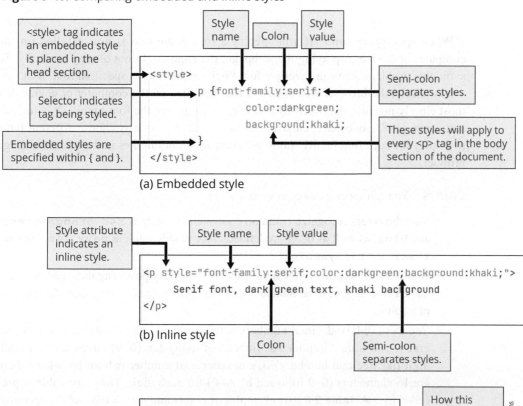

Figure 9-41: Using the <span> tag

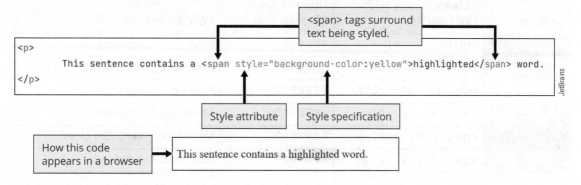

Table 9-7: Various font families displayed in a browser

Code	Edge
`<p style="font-family:serif">Hello!</p>`	Hello!
`<p style="font-family:sans-serif">Hello!</p>`	Hello!
`<p style="font-family:monospace">Hello!</p>`	Hello!
`<p style="font-family:cursive">Hello!</p>`	Hello!
`<p style="font-family:fantasy">Hello!</p>`	**Hello!**

When specifying fonts, if you specify a font name that is not installed on the computer or device displaying the webpage, the page might not display correctly. To avoid this problem, you can specify a font family rather than a specified font. By using a font family, the browser will choose a font installed on the computer or device that most closely matches the specified font family. Values for the font-family style include serif, sans-serif, monospace, cursive, and fantasy. Browsers may choose different fonts to display for each font family. **Table 9-7** compares font families in the Microsoft Edge browser.

Colors You can specify colors in several ways:

- Most browsers recognize common color names, such as **red**, **orange**, **green**, and **blue**, as well as other predefined color names, such as **navy**, **limegreen**, **khaki**, and **papayawhip**.
- You can use the **rgb()** function to specify colors by providing their **red**, **green**, and **blue** components as numbers between 0 (absence of a color) and 255 (fullness of a color).
- You can use hexadecimal numbers between 00 and FF to specify a color's red, green, and blue components. Instead of using ten (0–9) characters for each digit like decimal numbers do, a hexadecimal number is base 16, where there are 16 characters (0–9 followed by A–F) for each digit. The color value is preceded by a #. **Table 9-8** lists examples of colors and their RGB and hexadecimal color values.

Table 9-8: Color names with RGB and hexadecimal values

Color name	Sample	Values to use with rgb function	Hexadecimal color value	Comments
`black`		`rgb(0, 0, 0)`	`#000000`	Black is the absence of color
`gray`		`rgb(128,128,128)`	`#808080`	Same red, green, and blue values
`white`		`rgb(255, 255, 255)`	`#FFFFFF`	White is fullness of color
`red`		`rgb(255, 0, 0)`	`#FF0000`	All red, no green, no blue
`navy`		`rgb(0, 0, 128)`	`#000080`	No red, no green, 50% blue
`magenta`		`rgb(255, 0, 255)`	`#FF00FF`	Combines red and blue

The WebStorm IDE provides coding assistance with a popup menu showing color names, or you can use a Choose Color dialog box to select a color (**Figure 9-42**).

Figure 9-42: Choosing colors in the WebStorm IDE

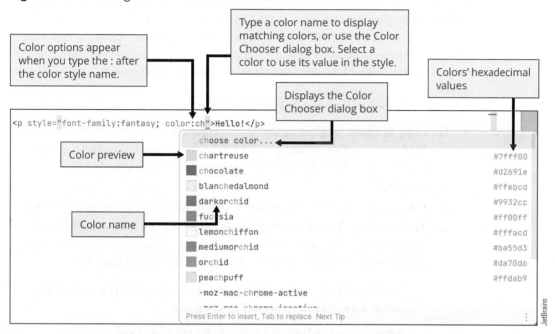

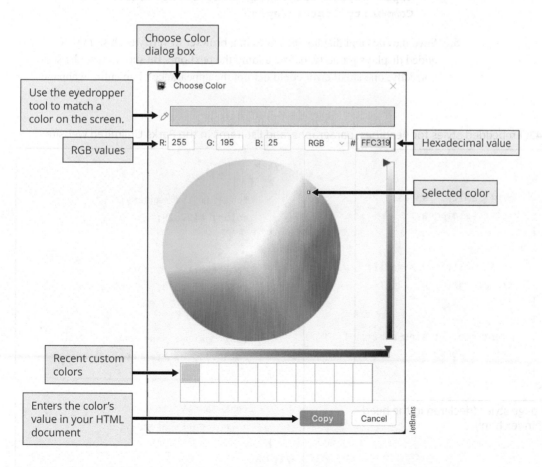

Case Study: Add Styles to the Parks Unlimited Website

Figure 9-43 provides embedded styles for the Parks Unlimited home page and park list page. The `p` and `li` styles on the home page both show the color `navy`; the `p` style specifies it using the `rgb` function, and the `li` style specifies its hexadecimal value.

The styles for `h1` and `h2` on the park list page use hexadecimal values. As explained by the CSS comments in between `/*` and `*/`, `h1` is the green color of the website banner, and `h2` is the orange color of the website banner. The semicolon after the last style in a series is optional.

To add embedded styles to the Parks Unlimited website:

1. Copy and paste, or type, the styles text (**Figure 9-43**) into the corresponding head sections of the index.html and parklist.html files. Traditionally, the styles text goes after the `<title>` tags; however, this is not required.

2. Save the files.

3. Display the pages in a browser and verify they display properly (**Figure 9-44**).

4. The home page uses inline styles for the phrase *build a more beautiful community*, and the phrase *Maya Community Center*. Replace those phrases with the corresponding code to make these phrases red and italic (**Figure 9-45**):

   ```
   <span style="color:red; font-style:italic">build a
   more beautiful community</span>

   <span style="color:red; font-style:italic">Maya
   Community Center</span>
   ```

5. Save the files and display the pages in a browser to verify each style you added displays properly, before adding the next one. Be sure to type the styles correctly; one small error could disrupt the appearance of an entire webpage.

Figure 9-43: Embedded styles for headings, paragraphs, and list items in the Parks Unlimited website

```
<style>
    h1 {
        font-family: fantasy;
        color: slategray;
    }
    P {
        font-family: sans-serif;
        color: rgb(0, 0, 128);
    }
    li {
        font-family: sans-serif;
        color: #000080;
    }
</style>
```

(a) Home page styles (declared in the head section of index.html)

```
<style>
    h1 {
        font-family: fantasy;
        color: #427d29; /* banner green */
    }
    h2 {
        font-family: fantasy;
        color: #ffb648; /* banner orange */
    }
    P {
        font-family: sans-serif;
        color: darkslategray;
    }
    li {
        font-family: sans-serif;
        color: darkslategray;
    }
</style>
```

(b) Park List page styles (declared in the head section of parklist.html)

JetBrains

Figure 9-44: Parks Unlimited home and park list pages with embedded styles added

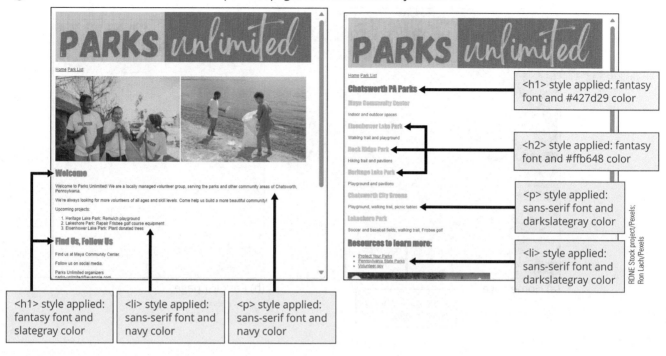

RDNE Stock project/Pexels; Ron Lach/Pexels

<h1> style applied: fantasy font and #427d29 color

<h2> style applied: fantasy font and #ffb648 color

<p> style applied: sans-serif font and darkslategray color

<li> style applied: sans-serif font and darkslategray color

<h1> style applied: fantasy font and slategray color

<li> style applied: sans-serif font and navy color

<p> style applied: sans-serif font and navy color

Figure 9-45: Parks Unlimited home page with inline styles added

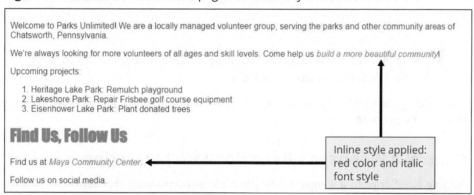

Inline style applied: red color and italic font style

You can change the background of the page to show a background color or a background image. Specify each as an inline style of the **<body>** tag. If an image is small, it will tile and appear as a repeating pattern in the browser window. You also can change the background color of text on the page using styles.

To change the background of the page or text on the page:

1. Make sure the background.png file is stored in the images folder.

2. To display a background image on the index.html page, add this style to its **<body>** tag:

   ```
   style="background-image:url(images/background.png)"
   ```

   This will tile the page with the background image named background.png stored in your images folder.

3. To display a background color on the parklist.html page, add this style to its **<body>** tag:

   ```
   style="background-color: lightsteelblue"
   ```

Figure 9-46: Parks Unlimited (a) home page and (b) park list page after backgrounds added

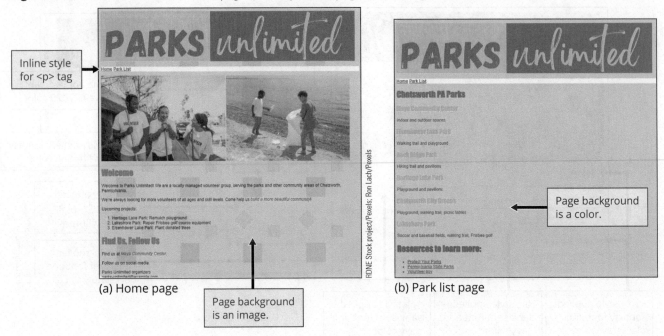

Inline style for <p> tag

Page background is an image.

(a) Home page

Page background is a color.

(b) Park list page

RDNE Stock project/Pexels; Ron Lach/Pexels

4. To display the navigation links on both pages with a light-colored background and bolder font, add this style to the **<p>** tag containing the links on each page:

```
style="background:honeydew;font-weight: bolder;"
```

5. Save the files, and then upload the changed files and images to a web server using FileZilla or another FTP client.

After adding these styles, the home page and park list page should appear in a browser as shown in **Figure 9-46**.

Control a Webpage's Behavior with JavaScript

Adding JavaScript to a webpage lets you code how you want the website to behave. JavaScript can perform simple actions, such as displaying an alert box if a required form field is empty or retrieving and displaying the current date and time, to more complex actions, such as performing calculations. In many cases, the JavaScript code appears between opening and closing **<script>** tags in the head section of an HTML document. In the body section, you can reference the JavaScript code to run. You can read more about JavaScript on W3Schools.com.

Some websites allow visitors to display the text on a webpage in a larger font size to make it easier to read, or a smaller font size to fit more information on the screen. Though this may sound complicated, all that is required to change the font size is to create a button that will reset the font-size value of the **<body>** tag's style attribute. JavaScript lets your website visitors change the webpage's font size with the click of a button.

Case Study: Add JavaScript to Change the Font Size of the Parks Unlimited Home Page

To add code so a visitor can change the font size of text on the Parks Unlimited home page:

1. Copy and paste, or type, the JavaScript code (**Figure 9-47**) into the head section of the index.html file, just below the **<title>** tag.

Figure 9-47: JavaScript code to offer visitors the option to change font size

```
<script>
        no usages
        function bigger(){
                document.getElementById('body').style.fontSize='x-large';
        }
        no usages
        function smaller(){
                document.getElementById('body').style.fontSize='medium';
        }
</script>
```
JetBrains

Figure 9-48: Code to create buttons, which will use the bigger and smaller scripts

```
<button type="button" onclick="bigger() ">Bigger</button>
<button type="button" onclick="smaller() ">Smaller</button>
```
JetBrains

Figure 9-49: Parks Unlimited home page with buttons to change the size of the text

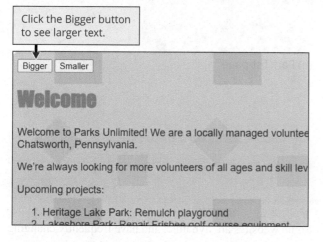
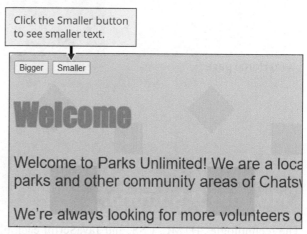

2. Type the attribute **id="body"** within the **<body>** tag to identify the tag to which the JavaScript code applies.

3. Copy and paste, or type, the **<button>** code (**Figure 9-48**) into the body section of the index.html file where you would like the buttons to appear, just below the two images.

4. Save the index.html file. Display the page in a browser. Click the Bigger and Smaller buttons to verify they work as expected.

After adding the JavaScript and button code, the new buttons on the home page should match **Figure 9-49**.

Figure 9-50 displays the completed home and park list pages for the Parks Unlimited website.

Figure 9-50: The completed Parks Unlimited (a) home page and (b) park list page

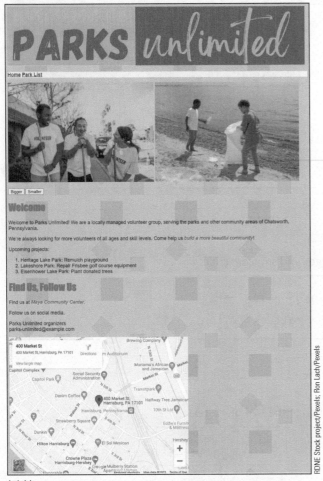

(a) Home page

(b) Park list page

RDNE Stock project/Pexels; Ron Lach/Pexels

City of Dubuque Government; YouTube

Module 9 Summary

The technologies HTML, CSS, and JavaScript each play an important role in the design of a website. HTML specifies the content of webpages, CSS specifies the formatting and appearance of the webpage content, and JavaScript provides scripts to control a webpage's behavior and add interactivity. Website builders and content management systems simplify the process of creating personal and professional websites. You can export data as XML to share with other applications or present the data in different ways.

When building a professional website, you need to register a domain name and obtain web hosting services so you can publish the site online. Using analytics tools, you can track data about visitors to your website, such as their locations, devices, and number of page views.

Some websites are dynamic, and have frequently changing content, while others are static. Many websites incorporate responsive design so they display correctly on computer screens and mobile devices. You can embed multimedia content from other websites on your own website.

Web developers use a text editor or an IDE when creating code, and an FTP client to transfer files from their local computer to a web server. You can include titles, paragraphs, headings, links, lists, images, audio and video, and other content on webpages. You can add styles to change the color, background, font, style, border, and other features. Embedded styles apply to all tags of a particular type on a page, while inline styles apply only to the tag in which they appear. With JavaScript, you can make a webpage interactive or change its behavior by displaying dynamic content.

Review of HTML Tags and Styles

Table 9-9 summarizes several HTML5 tags described in this module and provides notes about their usage. When a tag takes an attribute, the format is each attribute name followed by an equal sign (=), followed by its value in quotation marks, as in `<a href="http://www.google.com" target="_blank">Google</a>`, where `<a>` is the tag and `href` is its attribute.

You can find complete documentation for these tags on W3Schools.com. You can add a style attribute to many of these tags.

Table 9-9: Selected HTML5 tags

Tag(s)	Example	Description
`<!-->`	`<!--This is a comment. -->`	Comment from web developer, ignored when page is rendered
`<a>`	`<a href="https://www .cengage.com" target="_blank">Cengage</a>`	Anchor tag, specifies a link; specify **href** (hypertext reference) attribute **target="_blank"** to display the page in a new tab
`<body>`	`<body style="background-color:yellow">`	Body section of a webpage, styled to have a yellow background
` `	`Parks Unlimited ` `617-555-1234 `	Line break; **` `** has no closing tag
`<h1> - <h6>`	`<h1> This is a heading.</h1>`	Headings; **`<h1>`** is largest, **`<h6>`** is smallest
`<head>`	`<head> ... </head>`	Head section
`<hr>`	`<hr style="background-color:rgb(192,192,192);">`	Displays a horizontal rule (line) across the page to separate sections of content; optional style attributes may specify the background color of the line; **`<hr>`** has no closing tag
`<html>`	`<html> ... </html>`	Starts an HTML document

`<iframe>`	`<iframe`
	`  src="http://cengage.com"`
	`  width="600"`
	`  height="400">`
	`</iframe>`
		Embeds content from another website, such as a webpage or an online video; **height** and **width** attributes specify the size, in pixels, of the iframe container

`<img>`	`<img src="images/cat.jpg" alt="My cat">`	Image tag; **src** attribute specifies the source or location of the image, **alt** attribute (required in HTML5) provides an alternate description of the image, **height** and **width** specify the display size of the image in pixels; **`<img>`** has no closing tag

`<ol>, <ul>` `<li>`	`<ol>`
	`  <li>Item 1</li>`
	`  <li>Item 2</li>`
	`</ol>`
		Ordered (numbered), or unordered (bulleted) list; surround each list item with **`<li>`** ... **`</li>`** tags

`<p>`	`<p>This is a paragraph.</p>`	Paragraph
`<script>`	`<script> ... </script>`	Identifies JavaScript code; located in **`<head>`** section

`<span>`	`This text is`
	`<span`
	`  style="color:red;`
	`  font-weight:bold"`
	`>red and bold. </span>`
		Identifies section of content to apply a style

(Continued)

Tag(s)	Example	Description
`<style>`	```<style> h1 { font-family: serif; color: blue; } </style>```	Identifies embedded styles for tags; located in `<head>` section
`<title>`	`<title>My Website</title>`	Title of a webpage that appears in a browser tab; located in `<head>` section
`<audio>`, `<video>`	```<video controls height="300" width="400"> <source src="media/myvideo.mp4"> Video Not Supported </video>```	Audio or video tag, displays a player for an audio or video file stored in your media folder; the `controls` attribute adds play and pause buttons and other controls; if included, the `autoplay` attribute causes the file to start playing automatically when the page loads. Displays "Video Not Supported" if using an older browser that does not support the video tag.

Styles may appear in the `<style>` section or as part of a style attribute in almost all HTML tags. Websites with many pages may place styles in an external style sheet so each page can access the same set of styles. The format for a style declaration is the style name, followed by a colon, followed by the value for the style. If more than one style is used, separate each style with a semicolon. You can add styles for background colors and images; font families, sizes, and styles; border styles and thickness; left, right, or center alignment, and more. **Table 9-10** shows examples of several styles and code examples. Visit the W3Schools website for examples of these and other styles.

Table 9-10: Style examples

Style	Example	Description
`background-color`	`background-color:yellow;`	Specifies the background color of elements, such as `<p>`, `<h1>`, and `<body>`
`background-image`	`background-image: url ("images/stripes.jpg")`	Sets the background image of a `<body>`, `<p>`, `<h1>`, and other elements to the file whose path is given in the `url()` function
`border`	`border: 3px dashed red;`	Specifies a dashed border that is 3 pixels thick; border styles can be `solid`, `dashed`, `double`, or `dotted`
`color`	`color:blue;`	Colors can be a web color name, a hexadecimal value such as `#0000FF,` or an rgb value such as `rgb(0,0,255)` that specifies the red, green, and blue components of the color
`float`	`float:left;`	Specifies whether to place an element to the left or right relative to text; often used to position an image to the left or right of text
`font-family`	`font-family:serif;`	Specifies the font family for text. Font family names include `serif`, `sans-serif`, `cursive`, and `monospace`
`font-size`	`font-size:10px;`	Specifies font size in pixels

Style	Example	Description
font-style	font-style:italic;	Specifies font style; use **normal**, **italic**, or **oblique** as the value for this style
font-weight	font-weight:bold;	Specifies the font weight for a paragraph, heading, or other text element; use **bold** for thick characters, or numeric values **100** through **900**, in increments of 100; **400** is the same as **normal**, **700** is the same as **bold**
text-align	text-align:left;	Often aligns headings or paragraphs; values include **left**, **center**, **right**, or **justify**

Review Questions

1. To insert a hyperlink in a webpage, you can use HTML _____.

    a. scripts
    b. tags
    c. browsers
    d. websites

2. CSS lets you change the _____ of a website.

    a. behavior
    b. structure
    c. speed
    d. appearance

3. Which of the following tasks on a webpage is likely performed using JavaScript?

    a. Centering text on a page
    b. Displaying a slideshow of images
    c. Creating a hyperlink
    d. Displaying an image as the background of a webpage

4. Which of these websites is most likely an example of a static website?

    a. A website for purchasing an airplane ticket
    b. A website for making reservations at a local restaurant
    c. A website for learning about a local barbershop's hours and services
    d. A website for creating and sharing vacation photos

5. (True or False) Responsive design is intended to improve the web developer's experience of the website.

6. If you want to build a personal website without doing any HTML coding, you should probably use a(n) _____.

    a. website builder
    b. CMS
    c. plug-in
    d. IDE

7. To see if the URL you want for your website is available, check with a(n) _____.

    a. domain registrar
    b. search engine
    c. web host
    d. web developer

8. (True or False) A website analytics tool can collect information on how visitors found the website and how long a visitor stays on each page on average.

9. For what reason would you most likely create an XML file?

    a. To provide scripts for a website to run
    b. To transfer data between systems
    c. To define content for a webpage
    d. To define consistent style formatting for all of a website's pages

10. To upload webpage files from your computer to a web server, you should use a(n) _____.

    a. text editor
    b. website analytics tool
    c. website builder
    d. FTP client

11. When coding an image into a webpage, HTML5 requires you to _____.

    a. specify `height` and `width` attributes

    b. specify descriptive alternative information

    c. place the image in an images folder

    d. obtain all images from the same source

12. When older HTML tags are replaced with newer ways to accomplish the same task, they are _____.

    a. discontinued

    b. depreciated

    c. deprecated

    d. defunct

Discussion Questions

1. Is it necessary to know HTML, CSS, or JavaScript to create a website? Which of these tools do you think would be most important to learn if you were building your own website?

2. What decisions do you think should be made before starting to build a website? How would these decisions help you choose which tools to use during the build process?

3. What steps do you need to take to track user behavior on your website? Should your website include a statement informing visitors that your website is tracking user behavior?

4. What is the difference between tags and information included in the head section of a webpage, and tags and information included in the body section of a webpage? How can you help yourself remember which information goes where?

Critical Thinking Activities

1. You've developed your hobby of painting abstract art to the point people are asking how to purchase your paintings. You want to create a personal website to display and sell your artwork. You also need to show the location of your studio and add a video of your painting process. What features might you want to add to your website? What technologies will you need to build the website's content, styles, and scripts?

2. You work as a librarian at a community library, and you want to create a website for your library to promote events, featured books, and the site's contact information. You want the workers at the library to be able to post book reviews on the site frequently. Many of the library workers are not tech savvy, but they do know how to post updates on Facebook. How should you create the website to include these features and enable these non-technical employees to add new content regularly? Why do you think this approach will work well?

3. You run a cooking blog where you post a new recipe each day. You want to get a sense of where your visitors are from so you can choose recipes from the areas where your website visitors live. What other types of site usage information might you be able to gather using analytics tools that you could display on a dashboard? How can you use this information to improve the cooking blog for your visitors?

4. You work for a small café, which already has a plain website advertising its hours and menu. You want to spice up the website with some photos, graphics, and a couple of videos. What are some good sources for finding attractive, quality photos? How should you handle copyright issues for these photos? How would you feel if you learned that strangers were using your own art or photos for commercial purposes without your permission?

Apply Your Skills

Leo Francisco helps run a community volunteer group called Parks Unlimited. He wants to create a website to share information about the group, upcoming park beautification projects, city park locations, and contact details. Leo will need to register a domain name and set up web hosting, as well as determine whether to code the website by hand, or make use of a content management system to publish the website online. He also wants to track usage data from visitors to the volunteer group's website.

Working in a small group or by yourself, complete the following:

1. So far, the Parks Unlimited website contains only static content. What is a page you might add to the Parks Unlimited website that would contain dynamic content? What changes would you have to make to the website developed in this module to support this content? If you were building your own website, would you choose a static or dynamic website, and why?

2. The Parks Unlimited volunteer group has no budget for advertising but wants to do a better job of marketing their services. What other website analytics could be helpful for finding out how visitors are using the site and providing more targeted services? How do you feel about data being collected on your activity when visiting other websites?

3. The Parks Unlimited website needs some new graphics for a logo and some visual elements. What kinds of tools and resources could you use to develop visual elements for a website? What features would you need these tools to have so the graphics will be usable for the site? Identify at least two additional types of media the website could include, such as audio files. Thinking of your favorite websites, what kinds of features or tools do you find most helpful for navigating those sites and accessing the information you want quickly?

Networking

In This Module

- Describe key features of connected networks
- Connect to different types of networks
- Discuss issues of network security

Lilya is using multiple connected devices to perform her daily job functions.

iStock.com/PeopleImages

Lilya Baran is starting an entry-level position at a local company providing Internet, phone, and television services to home and business customers in Wyoming. Lilya has limited knowledge regarding how to set up a home wireless network, so she'll need to learn more. She eventually will be responsible for installing and configuring small networks for homes and small businesses, as well as educating customers about how to connect devices to and secure their networks. She'll also share tips about how to keep their data and information safe.

Wherever you go, you most likely will encounter and interact with some type of network. Whether it be a network that supports your cell phone, a wireless network at home or in a coffee shop that lets you browse the web and check your email, or an enterprise network connecting thousands of users, all networks have the same basic characteristics. Because you're working with technology that connects devices to one another, it's important to understand the security implications of using a network and how to safeguard your data and information.

In this module, you will learn about the key features of connected networks and explore how connections between networks are made. You'll also learn how to connect to different types of networks, and you will explore issues of network security in a connected world. As you reflect on what you learn in this module, ask yourself: What are the key features of a network that allow devices to communicate with each other? How are devices connected to different kinds of networks? What issues should you consider to keep your devices and your data safe when you use a network?

Describe Key Features of Connected Networks

Connected networks, regardless of size, have some of the same basic characteristics. Once you understand these foundational concepts of how a network works, you can apply this knowledge to many types of networks.

Explain How a Network Operates

A network is a system of two or more devices linked by wires, cables, wireless signals, or a telecommunications system. Networks allow computers to share resources, such as hardware, software, data, and information. A network requires a combination of hardware and software to operate. Smaller networks usually require simple hardware and can rely on the connected devices' operating systems' features to connect to other devices on the network, while larger networks typically require more sophisticated hardware and software.

Some networks provide connections to the Internet, which requires the services of an Internet Service Provider (ISP). When a network is connected to the Internet, it enables the network to communicate with other networks that are also connected to the Internet (**Figure 10-1**).

Define the Elements of a Network

Devices on a network, also called nodes, might include computers, tablets, mobile phones, printers, game consoles, and smart home devices. Most networks also include additional components such as switches and routers. These devices help connect multiple devices together and facilitate the connections among the devices that are communicating.

Figure 10-1: Networks can share resources and data

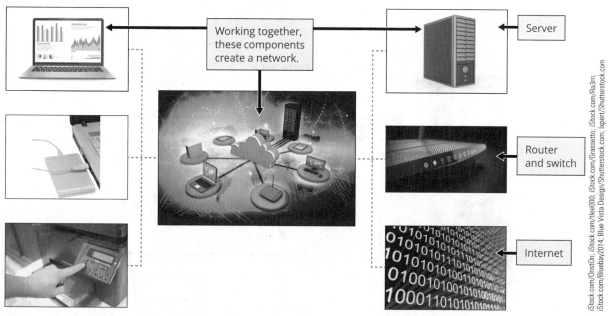

A **network switch** is a device that connects two or more computers to a network by providing a central point of connection for cables in a network. Although all the cables connect into the switch, it transfers data only to the intended recipient.

A **router** is a device that connects two or more networks and directs, or routes, the flow of information along the networks. Routers can also be used to connect computers to the Internet, so that multiple users can share an Internet connection.

Many routers used at home, called home routers, combine switch and router features along with wireless connectivity, which provide wireless network access to compatible devices. You might have a home router combination device installed at your house to which all devices connect.

The home router is typically connected with a wire or cable to a device called a modem, which provides Internet connectivity. A modem is a communications device that connects a communications channel such as the Internet to a sending or receiving device such as a computer or home router. The modem connects your network to the Internet through an Internet Service Provider (ISP), such as AT&T or Comcast. Most ISPs offer broadband connectivity, which is capable of transmitting large amounts of data at high speeds.

One way to categorize networks is by their size and typical uses, which gives two main categories: home networks and business networks. **Figure 10-2** illustrates a typical home network.

Home networks, which often exist in a single structure and are easy to install and configure, provide home users with the following capabilities:

- Multiple users can share a single Internet connection.
- Files on each computer, such as photos, can be shared.
- Multiple computers can share a single hardware resource such as a printer.
- Game consoles can connect to the Internet to facilitate online gaming.
- Voice over IP (VoIP) phone service provides voice communication without the need for traditional, copper telephone lines.
- Smart home devices such as thermostats, light switches, smart speakers, and personal assistants can connect to the Internet and apps on your smartphone.

Figure 10-2: Typical home network

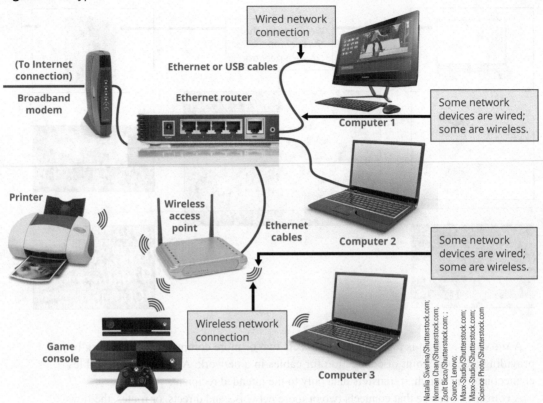

Business networks can be small or large and can exist in one or multiple buildings. Networks provide the following advantages to businesses:

- Facilitate communication among employees.
- Share hardware such as printers and scanners.
- Share data, information, and software with one another.
- Centrally store and back up critical information.

Identify Devices That Make a Network Work

Creating a network requires two or more devices capable of connecting, a technology that defines how they can communicate, and the infrastructure necessary to facilitate the communication. For a computer to connect to a network, it must have a network interface card. A **network interface card (NIC)** is a circuit board that connects a computer to a wired or wireless network. NICs often are internal to the device. Some NICs can connect a computer to a wired network, while other NICs can connect a computer to a wireless network. Some wireless network interface cards have a visible antenna that is used to better communicate with a wireless network.

As mentioned previously, a modem connects a network to the Internet. Most of today's modems are digital, which means they send and receive data to and from a digital line. Cable and DSL are two common types of digital modems. A **cable modem** sends and receives digital data over a cable TV connection. The cable modem might be part of a set-top cable box, or it might be a separate device. A **DSL modem** uses existing standard copper telephone wiring to send and receive digital data. The type of modem required for your network will depend on your ISP and the available wiring to your location.

Some modems also function as a wired and/or wireless router. For example, if you have a cable modem that you connect to your home's cable television lines, you might also be able to connect multiple wired and wireless devices if the cable modem also functions as a home router. **Figure 10-3** gives an example of a cable modem and a wireless router.

Figure 10-3: Cable modem and wireless router

Explain Network Design

Networks can be defined by how the devices are arranged (the network topology) and by their logical structure (network architecture). They can also be defined by their geographic reach.

Network Topology   The physical arrangement of computers and devices on a network is referred to as the **network topology**. Common network topologies include bus network, ring network, star network, and mesh network, as described in **Table 10-1**. Each topology has its own advantages and disadvantages. Some topologies are more appropriate for small networks, while others might be more appropriate for large networks. In addition to the four topologies identified below, networks might incorporate a combination of two or more topologies.

Table 10-1: Network topologies

Topology	Details	Network arrangement
Bus network	All devices attach to a central cable, called a bus, which carries the data. If the bus fails, the devices on the network will no longer be able to communicate.	
Ring network	Data travels from one device to the next in a sequential fashion. If one device on the network fails, communication on the network could cease to function. Ring networks are no longer common.	
Star network	Each device on the network is attached to a central device such as a server or switch. If the central device fails, the other devices will be unable to communicate. If a connected device fails, all other devices will still be able to communicate. Two or more star networks may be joined together using a bus to form a tree topology. Tree topologies often are used in schools and businesses.	
Mesh network	All devices interconnect with each other. If a single device on the network fails, the rest of the network will continue to function by communicating via an alternate route. Two types of mesh topologies are a full mesh topology (each device on the network is connected to every other device on the network) and a partial mesh topology (each device may or may not be connected to all other devices on the network).	

Figure 10-4: Typical client/server network

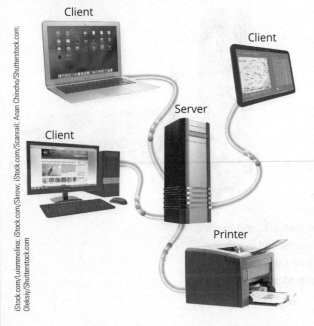

Figure 10-5: Peer-to-peer (P2P) network

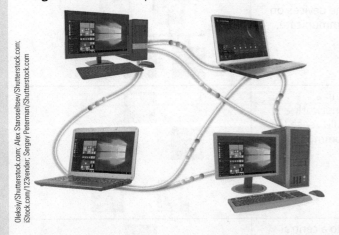

Network Architecture

While the network topology defines the physical arrangement of devices on a network, the **network architecture** determines the logical design of all devices on a network. Two common network architectures are client/server networking and peer-to-peer (P2P) networking.

On a **client/server network**, one or more computers act as a server and the other computers on the network request resources from the server (**Figure 10-4**). A **server** is a computer on the network that controls access to hardware, software, and other resources. The server can also provide a centralized storage location that other computers on the network can access. A **client** is a computer or mobile device on the network that relies on the server for its resources. Clients on a client/server network often do not have equal permissions; that is, one client might be able to access certain files or resources on the server, while other clients might not have access to those same resources. Client/server networks often are controlled by a network administrator. An example of a client/server network might be in an organization where employees all have one or more computers or mobile devices that connect to one or more servers for the purpose of sharing files and other resources.

A **peer-to-peer (P2P) network** is a network architecture that typically connects a small number of computers (typically fewer than 10). With this type of network, computers communicate directly with one another and can share each other's resources. For example, one computer can use a printer connected to another computer, while also requesting and downloading a file stored on a third computer. Because all computers on a peer-to-peer network are treated equally, a network administrator often is not required. **Figure 10-5** illustrates an example of a peer-to-peer (P2P) network.

Note that the mesh network pattern in the figure refers only to the logical connections between these devices where each device communicates with certain other devices on the network. Physically, the computers might still be connected to a central device, such as a switch, in a star network design.

An **Internet peer-to-peer (Internet P2P) network** is a type of P2P network where users share files with each other over the Internet. The files in an Internet peer-to-peer network transfer directly from one user's computer to the other, without first being stored on a server. Although Internet peer-to-peer networking is legal, it is illegal to share files or other resources that are protected by copyright.

In addition to sharing files using network architectures such as client/server or peer-to-peer (P2P) networking, cloud computing also supports file sharing. When you store files using cloud computing, you are said to be storing files "in the cloud." Files stored in the cloud are stored on one or more servers in different locations, and backup copies may or may not be stored locally on your computer or mobile device. Cloud computing offers advantages for storing files that include the following:

- Files can be stored and accessed from any computer or mobile device with an Internet connection.
- Files are stored on remote servers and will remain intact should anything happen to your computer or mobile device.
- Files do not necessarily take up space on your computer or device because they are stored in the cloud.
- You can easily share files with others and control who has access to each file.
- You can configure your computer or mobile device to automatically back up certain files to the cloud.

In addition to the many advantages cloud computing offers, there are also some disadvantages, including:

- The potential for unwanted individuals accessing your files if you do not carefully manage who can access them
- The inability to access your files if you lose your Internet connection

Geographic Reach   Networks come in all sizes and can be defined by not only the number of devices they connect or their physical/logical arrangement, but also by their geographic footprint. These networks include local area networks (LANs), wide area networks (WANs), metropolitan area networks (MANs), personal area networks (PANs), and body area networks (BANs).

- A **local area network (LAN)** connects computers and devices in a limited area, such as a home, a school building, or a small office complex, so they can share hardware and software resources.
- A **wide area network (WAN)** is a network that connects devices in a large geographic region, such as a school with buildings in different cities, a retail chain, or a multinational company. The Internet is classified as a WAN.
- A **metropolitan area network (MAN)** is a type of wide area network that is operated by or within a city or county. For example, an ISP might establish a metropolitan area network for companies located in close proximity, such as a downtown area.
- A **personal area network (PAN)** connects personal digital devices within a range of approximately 30 feet, such as a printer or smartphone connected to your laptop. Devices on a personal area network often are connected via the short-range wireless technology Bluetooth.
- A **body area network (BAN)** is a form of personal area network that consists of small, lightweight biosensors implanted in the body or worn on the body, such as a smartwatch. These biosensors can monitor an individual's health or activity, and possibly report statistics and results to a medical professional.

Figure 10-6 illustrates the relative size differences between these network types.

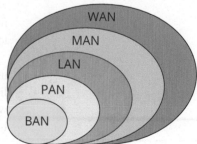

Figure 10-6: Relative network sizes

Table 10-2: Additional network types

Network type	Description
Wired network	Sends signals and data through cables, which may have to travel through floors and walls to connect to other network devices. Wired networks tend to be more secure and transmit data faster than wireless networks.
Wireless network	Sends signals through airwaves, and usually does not require cables. Wireless networks tend to be more convenient and easier to set up than wired networks, but can be less secure. Wireless networks make it possible to connect devices in locations where physical wiring is not possible or is difficult.
Intranet	A private network for use by authorized individuals. Organizations use intranets to communicate internally and can allow users to use a web browser to access company data posted on webpages. Intranets are preferable when the data being transferred should not necessarily reach the Internet.
Extranet	Allows outsiders (such as customers, vendors, and suppliers) to access some of an organization's network resources. For example, an extranet might be used if a supplier needs to check a customer's inventory levels before deciding whether to ship additional product.
Virtual private network (VPN)	A private, secure path across a public network that allows authorized users secure access to a company or other network. A VPN can allow an individual to access an organization's network by using encryption and other technologies to secure the data transmitted along the path.

Compare Types of Networks

Various types of networks exist, as well as several network topologies and network architectures. **Table 10-2** lists additional network types and their descriptions.

Connect to Different Types of Networks

Different general types of networks exist, such as home networks, corporate networks, wireless networks, wired networks, and cellular networks. For any device to communicate on a network, you must first connect it to the network. In addition, the computer or device must be capable of communicating with the network using predefined standards and protocols. By gaining an understanding of network standards and protocols, you'll be better prepared to work with the many types of networks you may encounter.

Explain the Purpose of Network Standards and Protocols

Computers and devices communicate on a network using a common language. **Network standards** specify the way computers access a network, the types of hardware used, data transmission speeds, and the types of cable and wireless technology used. For computers and devices to successfully communicate on a network, they must support the same network standards.

The most common standard for wired networks is **Ethernet**. This standard controls how network interface cards (NICs), routers, and modems share access to cables and phone lines, as well as dictates how to transmit data. The Ethernet standard continues to evolve, with new standards supporting faster data transfer rates at longer distances. **Table 10-3** lists other common network standards and how they are used.

Internet Protocols   Computers and devices communicating with each other on a network must do so while following a common set of rules for exchanging information, which is called a **protocol**. One common family of protocols is **TCP/IP (Transmission Control Protocol/Internet Protocol)**, a set of protocols that is used by all computers and devices on the Internet. TCP establishes conversations between two devices, and IP defines how data is routed through a network between these devices. To do this, IP specifies that all computers and devices connected to a network have a unique IP address.

Table 10-3: Network standards

Network standard	Common use
Ethernet	Most wired networks
PoE (Power over Ethernet)	Devices requiring both network connectivity and power to be supplied by the network, such as security cameras
Phoneline/HomePNA (Phoneline Networking Alliance) or Powerline	Networks using telephone lines or electrical wiring to connect computers and devices
Wi-Fi (wireless fidelity)	Wireless connections for home and business networks
LTE (Long Term Evolution) and 5G (5th generation)	Voice and data transmission on cellular networks

Two types of IP addresses exist: IPv4 (Internet Protocol version 4) and IPv6 (Internet Protocol version 6). IPv4 was the standard Internet protocol in use for many years, but the vastly growing number of computers and devices connected to the Internet demanded support for more IP addresses. As a result, the IPv6 protocol was developed. The IPv4 protocol supports nearly 4.3 billion unique IP addresses, while the newer IPv6 protocol supports more than 340 undecillion (3.4×10^{38}) addresses. That is about 340 trillion trillion trillion addresses. One researcher, Richard Olsen of the Teracom Training Institute, calculated that this number equates to approximately 664 billion IP addresses per grain of sand on the planet Earth.

Wireless Protocols   In addition to network protocols for LANs, WANs, and MANs, there are other, wireless protocols that support close-distance communication. **Table 10-4** lists these common wireless protocols.

Table 10-4: Close-distance, wireless network protocols

Network protocol	Common use
Bluetooth	Devices communicating with each other over a short range (usually less than 30 feet/9 meters)
RFID (radio frequency identification)	Radio signals transmitted through antennas, often found in tollbooth transponders or embedded chips in animals
NFC (near field communication)	Used in credit cards, smartphones, and event or service tickets to facilitate close-range communication
IrDA	Remote controls or other data transmission within close proximity

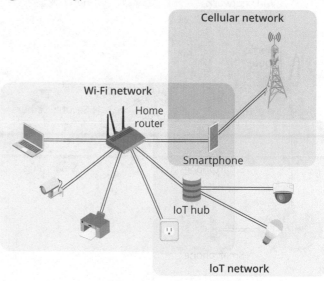

Figure 10-7: Types of wireless networks

Describe Wireless Network Types

Although perhaps not obvious to the typical user, there are many types of wireless networks. Each type uses different radio technologies and provides different capabilities, such as network speed and distance of reliable connections (**Figure 10-7**). Understanding the differences between these wireless network types will help you make more informed decisions when subscribing to services, purchasing devices, and troubleshooting problems.

Wi-Fi Networks   Many homes and businesses use Wi-Fi networks to provide network and Internet connectivity to computers and devices. These Wi-Fi networks

Figure 10-8: Available wireless networks

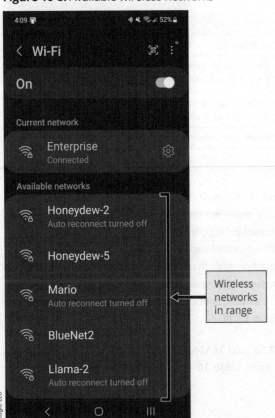

typically connect to the Internet through a wired connection and a modem, and then a wireless antenna broadcasts the Wi-Fi signal in a close area. When a device that supports Wi-Fi is within range of one or more wireless networks, you can view the list of networks and choose the one to which you want to connect. In **Figure 10-8**, a list of wireless networks appears on a smartphone using the Android operating system.

One significant difference between types of Wi-Fi networks is the radio frequency used to connect devices on the network. Most Wi-Fi networks today use either a 2.4 GHz signal or a 5 GHz signal. **Table 10-5** compares some of the differences between these options.

Table 10-5: Wi-Fi frequencies

2.4 GHz	5 GHz
Reaches longer distances.	Limited to shorter distances.
More resistant to obstacles. This means the signal is more likely to hold a reliable connection even through obstacles, such as walls and windows.	More sensitive to obstacles. This means the signal is less reliable if there are obstacles between the sender and receiver, such as walls or windows.
Carries data at a slower rate. This means users might notice slower uploads and downloads, such as when streaming a movie or playing a game.	Carries data at a faster rate. So long as the sending and receiving devices are close together, this frequency will provide the best user experience with data transfer speeds.

IoT Networks   Wi-Fi networks can provide Internet connectivity for other wireless networks, too. Internet of Things (IoT) networks use various wireless technologies, such as Bluetooth and RFID, to connect smart devices with a central hub device. The hub provides a bridge of communication between the IoT smart devices and the Wi-Fi network and on to the Internet. From there, the user can control IoT smart devices through an app on their smartphone. **Figure 10-9** illustrates these connections.

In the diagram, one smartphone is connected to the Wi-Fi network. From this point, it can, for example, turn on or off the smart bulb (**Figure 10-10**) or display a video feed from the security camera (**Figure 10-11**). Similarly, the smartphone on the Internet can also control the IoT network devices. The capability to control smart devices over the Internet allows you to control smart devices in one location from anywhere in the world. For example, you might want to check your security camera feeds at home while you are on a business trip.

When setting up an IoT network, there are a few pointers to keep in mind:

- Some IoT smart devices require a central hub device while others do not. Read the manufacturer instructions to know if a hub is required. If the IoT smart devices connect to a hub, only the hub needs to connect to your home network. Hubs sometimes provide additional features, such as local storage space for security videos, or the ability to extend your network's reach so devices can be positioned farther away.

Figure 10-9: IoT device connections

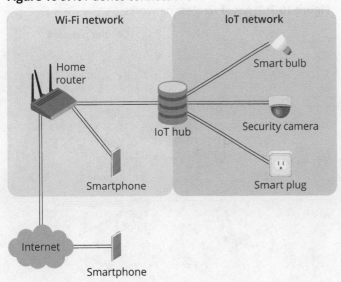

Figure 10-10: Smart bulb with smartphone app

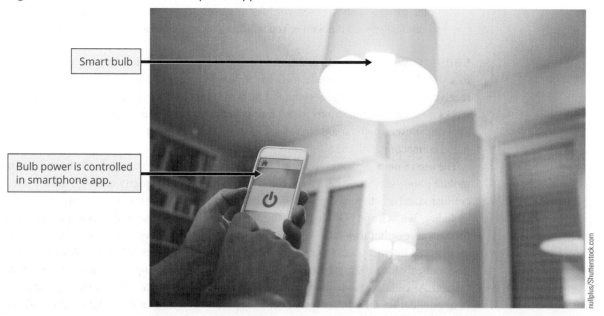

Smart bulb

Bulb power is controlled in smartphone app.

Figure 10-11: Security camera's feed on smartphone app

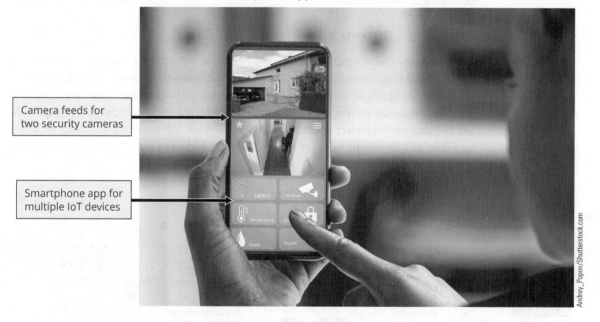

Camera feeds for two security cameras

Smartphone app for multiple IoT devices

- When IoT devices need to connect directly to your home network, most of these devices can only connect to a 2.4 GHz Wi-Fi network. When choosing IoT devices, first check your home router's supported Wi-Fi frequencies and ensure 2.4 GHz is an option.
- If an IoT device (such as a smart car, dashcam, or smartwatch) has the ability to connect to a cellular network, then that device does not need a Wi-Fi hot spot to connect to the Internet. However, in most cases, the connection to a cellular network requires a monthly payment to the cellular provider.
- When shopping for IoT devices, also consider whether the device is battery-powered or requires a wired power connection. In some cases, if the device connects to your network with a wired Ethernet connection, you can also provide power to the device through the network cable using Power over Ethernet (PoE).

- Make sure to implement any security features available on each IoT device. For example, use a strong password for any user account in an IoT network's app, and enable encryption if possible. You will learn more about encryption later in this module.

Cellular Networks   In addition to using computers and devices that are connected to a wired or wireless network, billions of people use their mobile phones to make and receive voice calls and to access the Internet. Although users experience these cellular networks as wireless connections to the Internet (that is, no wired connection is required for the typical user), cellular antenna towers are typically connected to the Internet through a wired connection.

The use of mobile phones to access the Internet has become so popular that providers of mobile phone services continuously must expand network capacity and support the latest cellular standards to keep up with demand. There are various types of cellular networks, including 3G, 4G, and 5G. Most 3G (third generation) cellular networks could provide basic Internet access, but they have been phased out by cellular providers. 4G networks provide widespread Internet access to cellular customers, while 5G networks provide higher speed data transmission, making them more appealing to those requiring access to high-bandwidth content. As cellular standards evolve, it is increasingly likely that home users may use a cellular provider for their Internet service, as opposed to relying on wired connections offered by cable and DSL providers. **Figure 10-12** gives examples of the wide variety of devices that depend on cellular networks..

Connect Network Devices

Computers and devices require specific hardware and software to connect to a network and must be capable of communicating via the appropriate network protocols. In addition to having the proper hardware and software, you must have an Internet Service Provider (ISP) to provide the Internet service. Most ISPs charge a fee for Internet connectivity and require the use of a modem to connect your network to the Internet. ISPs use hardware such as cables, satellites, and fiber-optic lines for these connections. Most of today's Internet connections

Figure 10-12: A wide variety of devices depend on cellular networks

AUTONOMOUS VEHICLES

IOT DEVICES

5G

CLOUD COMPUTING AND DATA CENTER

UTILITIES AND INFRASTRUCTURE

AR / VR EXPERIENCES

SMART HOME AND CITY

LAPTOPS AND SMARTPHONES, WEARABLES

MEDICAL DEVICES

VectorMine/Shutterstock.com

are broadband connections, which can transmit tremendous amounts of data across the network. Broadband connections usually are "always-on" connections, which means the computers and devices on the network are always connected to the Internet. Because of the risks associated with constant Internet connectivity, you should turn off computers and devices on your network when you are not using them for extended periods of time.

Home Wireless Networks The steps required to install a home wireless network may vary depending on factors such as the type of wireless network hardware you purchase, the size of your home, and the devices you want to connect to the wireless network. The following general steps describe how to set up a home wireless network.

1. Purchase a modem or separate wireless router and connect it to your home's Internet service.
2. Review the documentation that came with your wireless modem or router to perform the following tasks:
   a. Enable the wireless network.
   b. Configure a name for the network.
   c. Configure a wireless network key.
3. For each device you want to connect to the wireless network, perform the following tasks:
   a. Enable the device's wireless functionality.
   b. Search for and connect to the name of the wireless network you specified in Step #2b.
   c. Enter the wireless network key you set in Step #2c.

Figure 10-13: The password is required to connect

Wi-Fi Hot Spots You may sometimes need to connect to a Wi-Fi hot spot, a wireless network available in a public place. To do so, first select the name of the network. If you are connecting to a hot spot in a restaurant or hotel, for example, verify the name of the wireless network with an employee to make sure you are connecting to the correct network. Verifying the network name will help prevent you from inadvertently connecting to a fraudulent network.

After you have selected the network you want to connect to, tap or click the appropriate button or link to connect to the network. If you are connecting to a secure network that requires a wireless network key or authentication with a user name and password, you will be prompted to enter the required information (**Figure 10-13**). A **wireless network key** is a series of numbers and/or letters, sometimes referred to as a network security key, used to validate a user's request to join a network. Once the correct information has been supplied, you should automatically be connected to the wireless network. Some wireless networks in public places require you to open a web browser and agree to terms of service before connecting you to the Internet.

Mobile Hot Spots If you need to connect to the Internet where no Wi-Fi hot spots are available, you can consider using a mobile hot spot. Because a mobile hot spot uses your phone to create a Wi-Fi hot spot, you can then connect a phone, computer, or other device to the Internet through your phone's cellular network (**Figure 10-14**). Recall that a cellular network accesses the Internet through a wireless connection to a cellular provider's large antenna towers. These towers, then, connect to the Internet through a high-bandwidth, wired connection on fiber cable.

Figure 10-14: Mobile hot spot on a smartphone

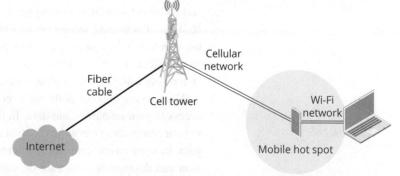

Figure 10-15: Mobile hot spot device

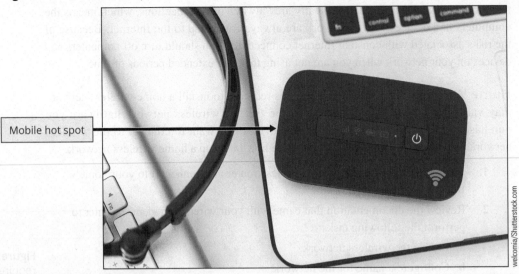

Mobile hot spot

welcomia/Shutterstock.com

Many smartphones contain mobile hot spot functionality, although cellular service providers might charge an extra fee to use it, and any data transmitted or received through the hot spot might be added to your overall data usage or might be subject to volume or bandwidth caps that limit the amount of data or the speed of the data. In addition, separate hot spot devices, about the size of a deck of cards, can provide Internet connectivity to computers and devices using the cellular network.

The mobile hot spot creates a wireless, Wi-Fi network to which nearby computers and devices can connect. The mobile hot spot will display the name of the wireless network, as well as the wireless network key (if necessary) you should enter to connect. If you are using a mobile hot spot in a busy location, you can also monitor the number of devices that are connecting. If you notice connections that you did not initiate, you should consider changing the wireless network key. Internet connections using a mobile hot spot typically are not as fast as home or business Wi-Fi networks. **Figure 10-15** illustrates an example of a mobile hot spot device.

Discuss Issues of Network Security

Communicating with others and using resources on a network can present some issues related to safety and security. By understanding the risks and benefits associated with using a connected network, you can better protect data transmitted over a network.

Identify Risks and Benefits Associated with Using a Network

Connecting to networks provides users with the ability to share resources such as hardware and software, as well as visit webpages and send and receive email. Connected networks facilitate this sharing among devices that are located in close geographic regions, or even thousands of miles away. Networks also facilitate easier, higher-quality, and less costly communication between individuals in different locations. In addition to the benefits associated with using a connected network, there are also many risks to consider.

When your computer or device is connected to a network, others might be able to gain access to your resources and data. In many cases, individuals called hackers can connect to your computer or device and obtain data without your knowledge for their own personal gain. In some cases, malware (malicious software) can install itself without your permission and damage or steal data on your computer or device. Malware typically installs

Figure 10-16: Distributed denial of service attack

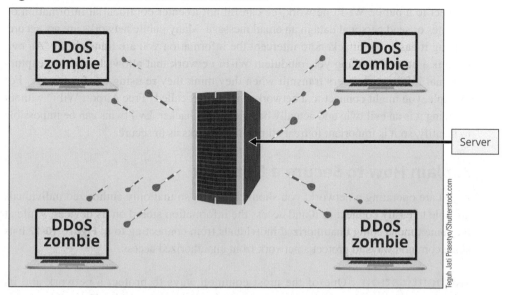

itself on your computer when you download infected files from the Internet or open email attachments from an unknown source. Malware can also install a **rootkit**, which is a type of software tool that gains administrator-level, or root-level, access to a computer or network without the system or users detecting its presence.

In addition to malware that could be installed on your computer or other device, there are additional risks to consider when using a network. For example, if hackers gain access to your personal data, they can steal credit card numbers, bank account information, personally identifiable information (such as your name, address, and Social Security number), medical records, and other data you might not want exposed. With this information, hackers can steal your identity and open credit cards in your name, purchase items online, and potentially cause great damage to your credit rating. One way hackers do this is through the use of **spyware**, which is software that tracks and transmits personal information from your computer or device without your knowledge. It might also change your computer settings without your consent.

Additionally, attackers can use network resources for their own purposes, or interfere with the functioning of network resources. For example, a **denial of service (DoS) attack** is a type of attack, usually on a server, that is meant to overload the server with network traffic so it cannot provide necessary services. If a server responsible for hosting websites is the recipient of a denial-of-service attack, it might be unable to display websites for visitors attempting to view them. These attacks can originate from one source, or they can originate from multiple sources. A **distributed denial of service (DDoS) attack** is when an attacker uses multiple computers to attack a server or other network resource. **Figure 10-16** illustrates multiple computers attacking a single server in a distributed denial of service attack.

In many cases, the attacking computers in a DDoS attack are attacking without the owner's knowledge, because they are under the control of malware or another attacker. A device infected with malware that an attacker uses to control the device remotely is called a **zombie**.

Explain Risks of Unauthorized Network Access

When hackers can connect to the same network as the computers or devices they wish to target, it is easier for them to obtain information being transmitted on the network. If you have a network set up at your home or place of employment, you should make sure to send and receive personal information only if the network is secure. Securing a network is discussed later in this section.

Your data also might be exposed by connecting to a fraudulent network. When you connect to a public Wi-Fi network, be careful not to enter confidential information on websites or send personal data in an email message. Many public networks are not secure, making it easier for attackers to intercept the information you are transmitting. An **evil twin** is a normal-looking yet fraudulent Wi-Fi network that allows hackers to capture personal information users transmit when they think they're using a safe network. For example, you might connect to a network at an airport called "Free Airport WiFi" without realizing it is an evil twin and actually being run by a hacker. Evil twins can be impossible to identify, so it is important to treat all public networks as unsecure.

Explain How to Secure a Network

If you are operating a network, you should secure it so that only authorized individuals are able to easily connect to it and access the information stored on its devices, while at the same time keeping unauthorized individuals from connecting to it. **Figure 10-17** lists some common ways to protect a network from unauthorized access.

Authentication   One of the most common ways to protect a network and its resources is by authenticating the users connecting to it—that is, identifying the users to the network. The most common form of authentication is providing a user name and password. However, additional forms of authentication exist, such as using biometric devices to scan physical characteristics. Windows Hello is a feature in Windows that authenticates users by scanning a user's fingerprint, face, or iris. Biometric devices can also authenticate based on characteristics such as a person's handprint, voice, or signature. For example, many smartphones use a fingerprint sensor that enables you to unlock it by scanning your fingerprint. Multi-factor authentication (MFA) can provide stronger security because requiring two or more authentication methods poses a greater challenge to hackers.

Figure 10-17: Network security

Encryption scrambles or codes data as it is transmitted over a network.

Authentication identifies you to the network. The most common type of authentication is providing a username and password.

Username
mkwatt

Password
Vi15820!

Login   remember me

Firewalls create a blockade between corporate or personal networks and the Internet.

Biometric devices authenticate identity by scanning your physical characteristics, such as a fingerprint.

chaoss/Shutterstock.com; bofotolux/Shutterstock.com; Nelia Sapronova/Shutterstock.com; ymgerman/Shutterstock.com; beboy/Shutterstock.com

If you are using a user name and password for authentication, always use a strong password, a long combination of letters, numbers, and/or symbols. A longer password is always more secure than a shorter password, regardless of complexity. Passwords should be changed frequently and never should be written in places where they can easily be obtained and identified by others.

Firewalls   In addition to using authentication to make sure only authorized individuals access the network, you can install a firewall to keep out unauthorized traffic. A **firewall** is a protective barrier between a computer or network and others on the Internet. It inspects data being transmitted to or from a network to prevent unsolicited data exchanges. There are two types of firewalls: hardware firewalls and software firewalls. Hardware firewalls are physical devices, often used on larger, corporate networks, that block unauthorized traffic and intruders from accessing the network (**Figure 10-18**). Software firewalls, also called local firewalls, are installed on your computer or device and block unauthorized communication to or from the network. Software firewalls often are built into the computer's operating system. Some Internet Service Providers also might provide software firewalls for you to install and use.

Figure 10-18: How a firewall might work

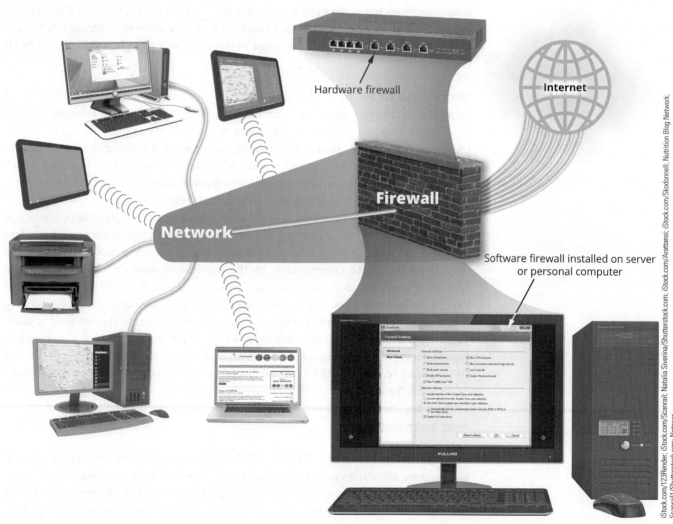

Hardware firewall

Internet

Firewall

Network

Software firewall installed on server or personal computer

Network Data   Because data and information stored on computers or devices connected to a network may be accessible by other computers and devices on the network, it is important to secure the data to prevent access by unauthorized individuals. One way to store data on a network is by using network attached storage. **Network attached storage (NAS)** devices consist of one or more hard drives that connect directly to a network and provide a centralized location for storing applications and data on large and small networks. On a home network, you might store family photos and videos so they are accessible to all members of your family. On a larger, more complex network, you might store important company files that require accessibility by multiple employees.

When you store files on a network, you might have the ability to specify users who can view the files, as well as users who can also make changes to the files or, if needed, delete files. For example, if a company's employment benefits documents are stored on a network, you might choose to let all company employees view the documents, but only allow executives and accounting personnel to make changes to the documents. Be careful not to grant individuals more permissions than necessary, as this inadvertently can lead to undesired changes to files or sensitive data shared outside the company.

Explain How to Secure a Wireless Network

Wireless networks require a slightly different approach to security because these network communications travel through the air rather than through physical cables. These signals can be detected outside of the physical buildings where the network is intended to be used. Due to this added vulnerability, data must be protected both when it is stored and when it is transmitted.

Encryption to Secure Wireless Traffic   Not only should you secure data stored on a network, but you also should turn on network encryption so that information from files being transmitted on the network cannot be intercepted by others. **Encryption** is the process of "scrambling" data so it is unrecognizable when it is transmitted on a network or stored on a storage device, except to users who enter the correct "key" to unlock it back to a readable format. If you are connected to a wireless network, make sure the network supports encryption so your data cannot be intercepted easily by others.

Encrypted wireless networks often use a version of the wireless network key to encrypt data sent between devices. Before you are able to use an encrypted wireless network, you must first enter the correct key. Both the sending and receiving device must know the key to communicate on the wireless network. When you attempt to connect to a wireless network requiring a wireless network key, you will be prompted to enter the key when you initiate the connection. If you connect to a wireless network that does not require a wireless network key, this often means the network is insecure, and you should avoid transmitting any type of private information. One common type of encryption on home routers is WPA (Wi-Fi Protected Access), where version 2 (WPA2) and version 3 (WPA3) are advanced enough to provide recommended levels of security. You can specify the type of encryption, as well as the desired wireless network key, through the wireless router's configuration utility that is often accessible using a web browser.

Safety Precautions on Wireless Networks   As discussed throughout the module, there are many risks to consider when using a connected network. Arguably, wireless networks can be the most vulnerable because it is easier to connect to wireless networks than wired networks. If you have set up a wireless network at your home, consider taking these safety precautions to keep it as secure as possible. Wireless network settings usually can be changed by accessing the wireless router with a web browser. Review the manual for your home router for more information on changing settings.

- Change the password required to access the administrative features on your wireless router. If a hacker connects to your network and attempts to access the configuration settings, they will most likely try the factory-supplied default password.

- Change the name of the wireless network (referred to as the Service Set Identifier, or SSID) from the factory-supplied default. The name you choose should be generic, and not contain information such as your name, address, or model of your home router.

- Enable encryption, such as WPA3, on the wireless network, and choose a secure wireless network key that is difficult to guess.

- Regularly change your wireless network key.

- If possible, regularly review the number of devices that are connected to your wireless network. If the number of connected devices exceeds what you are expecting, you might need to change the wireless network key.

- Enable and configure the Media Access Control, or MAC, address control feature. A **MAC address** is a unique hardware address identified for your computer or device, and the MAC address control feature specifies the MAC addresses of computers and devices that can (or cannot) connect to your network.

- Choose a secure location for your wireless router so it is not easy for unauthorized individuals to gain physical access to it.

- Regularly check for and perform updates to your router's software (also called its firmware) to make sure you benefit from all security improvements and feature enhancements.

Module 10 Summary

Networks allow computers to share resources. In addition to hardware required for a network to operate, software running on a computer or device also facilitates network communication. A connected network is comprised of various physical elements, including switches, routers, and modems. Creating a network requires devices such as network interface cards (NICs) for computers and devices to connect to the network. Modems, such as cable modems and DSL modems, are used to connect a home or small business network to an Internet Service Provider (ISP). The arrangement of physical devices on a network, as well as how they are connected to one another, is referred to as a network topology. Common network topologies include bus networks, ring networks, star networks, and mesh networks. Common types of networks include local area networks, wide area networks, metropolitan area networks, personal area networks, and body area networks. Other types of networks include wired networks, wireless networks, intranets, extranets, and virtual private networks (VPNs).

Different types of networks use various network standards and network protocols. Network standards specify the way computers and devices access a network, while network protocols specify how computers and devices communicate on a network. Various wireless technologies are also needed to support different types of wireless networks, including Wi-Fi networks, IoT networks, and cellular networks. Devices use different methods to connect to various types of wireless networks, including home wireless networks, Wi-Fi hot spots, and mobile hot spots.

Networks can provide many services and conveniences, but at the same time there are risks associated with using networks. When networks are accessed and used by unauthorized individuals, your personal information stored on network devices is put at risk. Securing wireless networks and maintaining wireless network security helps protect the data and the devices hosted on those networks. To protect a network from unauthorized connections, consider requiring some form of authentication such as a user name and password or biometric authentication, and installing a firewall. In addition to securing a network as well as the data stored on the network, consider encrypting the network using a wireless network key. When a network is encrypted, it disguises all network traffic so that it is unrecognizable to individuals who might attempt to intercept the traffic.

Review Questions

1. What is the minimum number of devices required for a network?

   a. One
   b. Two
   c. Three
   d. Four

2. (True or False) A switch is a communications device that connects a communications channel such as the Internet to a sending or receiving device such as a computer.

3. Which of the following devices can be used to access the Internet over a building's existing telephone lines?

   a. Home router
   b. Network interface card
   c. Cable modem
   d. DSL modem

4. Which of the following is a logical network architecture?

   a. Bus network
   b. Star network
   c. Client/server network
   d. Mesh network

5. A private network used by organizations to communicate internally is called a(n) _____.

   a. intranet
   b. Internet
   c. extranet
   d. virtual private network

6. Your smartphone can connect to a cell tower using _____.

   a. PoE
   b. Ethernet
   c. LTE
   d. Wi-Fi

7. If you park a smart car at the airport while you are on vacation, this IoT-enabled vehicle can communicate with the Internet and give you status updates using _____ networking technology.

   a. cellular
   b. Bluetooth
   c. Wi-Fi
   d. RFID

8. When your smartphone hosts a small Wi-Fi network, it is called a(n) _____ hot spot connection.

   a. Internet
   b. ISP
   c. cellular
   d. mobile

9. If a(n) _____ accesses your personally identifiable information, they might impersonate you and access your bank accounts or borrow money in your name.

   a. zombie
   b. malware
   c. hacker
   d. evil twin

10. When connecting to public Wi-Fi, be careful to avoid a normal looking, yet fraudulent, Wi-Fi network, which is called a(n) _____.

    a. DDoS
    b. firewall
    c. zombie
    d. evil twin

11. Which of the following is an advisable practice for securing data stored on a network?

    a. Store all data on network attached storage.
    b. Allow all network users access to all data.
    c. Only grant access to data to those with a legitimate need.
    d. Store data on a separate storage device instead of on one that is connected to the network.

12. (True or False) Encryption converts unrecognizable data into recognizable data.

Discussion Questions

1. Identify two or three networks you interact with on a regular basis. How do these networks benefit you personally or professionally? What factors do you think were considered in the design of these networks?

2. Choose three wireless technologies and explain how you use them. What is a situation when you might need a wired connection to the Internet or another network instead of a wireless connection?

3. When you are looking for Internet connectivity in various locations, you might choose to connect to any available wireless networks that are within range and do not require a wireless network key. Just because a wireless network is within range and does not require a wireless network key, is it okay to connect to that network? Why or why not?

4. When you set up a home or small business network, you might use wireless technology instead of a wired network because wireless networks are easier and often less expensive to install. What are some situations where setting up a wireless network might be risky? What measures could you take to reduce these risks?

Critical Thinking Activities

1. You were just hired by a small accounting firm to set up a computer network in their new office. The accounting firm has ten employees, and each employee uses either a desktop or laptop computer. Based on your knowledge from this module, would you recommend setting up a client/server network or a peer-to-peer (P2P) network? Justify your recommendation using the concepts you have learned in this module.

2. You have installed a wireless network at your house, but suddenly your computers and devices are unable to connect to the network. What steps might you take to troubleshoot the problem and correct it so that connectivity is restored? How do you think these steps will help you identify the problem?

3. You work with a home assistance company that helps homebound patients organize their environments to accommodate their physical needs. Your manager has asked you to research IoT technology that could help your company's patients. What IoT devices would you recommend for homebound patients to help enable their independence? How do you think these devices would help? Do you use any IoT devices currently? What IoT devices do you think would be especially useful in your everyday life?

4. You are helping to set up a website your team will use to store files and other data for a critical company project, launching soon. It is your responsibility to ensure the data and files will be kept safe. However, you also need to give your team readily available and convenient access to this storage site. What type of authentication should you choose, both to protect the sensitive data and to ensure each team member can access what they need? Why do you think this authentication method is a good fit? What weaknesses or problems should you anticipate with this method?

Apply Your Skills

Lilya Baran is starting an entry-level position at a local company providing Internet, phone, and television services to home and business customers in Wyoming. Lilya has limited knowledge regarding how to set up a home wireless network, so she'll need to learn more. She eventually will be responsible for installing and configuring small networks for homes and small businesses, as well as educating customers about how to connect devices to and secure their networks. She'll also share tips about how to keep their data and information safe.

Working in a small group or by yourself, complete the following:

1. Even before learning how to install networks, Lilya will need to be ready to answer common questions from customers. How can Lilya explain the differences between a network's physical architecture and its logical topology? What is an analogy Lilya might use to compare these two concepts? What other kinds of questions about how networks work should Lilya anticipate getting from her customers?

2. When Lilya is traveling, she will need to connect her own devices to multiple networks so she can stay in touch with her customers and her employer. What considerations should she keep in mind when choosing a Wi-Fi hot spot to connect to? When should she consider using her cellular network and her phone's mobile hot spot to connect her laptop to the Internet, instead of using a free Wi-Fi hot spot? Have you ever been in a situation where you had to choose between using free Wi-Fi vs. your own mobile hot spot? How did you decide which was the best solution for the situation?

3. When setting up a customer's home network, what setting changes should Lilya make sure to configure on the home router to secure the customer's wireless network? What tips should Lilya give the customer to ensure they can keep their home network safe? If you have a home network, have you ever allowed others to use your network? Now that you know more about home network security, what concerns might you have in the future about sharing a home network with other people? If a customer asks Lilya's opinion about whether to use a wireless network key, should Lilya advise that customers allow other people to use their wireless network, or suggest that customers lock their wireless networks from other users?

Digital Communication

In This Module

- Compare popular digital communication tools
- Use digital communication tools
- Evaluate the impact of digital communication on everyday life

Jordan uses multiple devices to keep in touch with colleagues, business partners, students, and friends.

iStock.com/Brothers91

Jordan Kinthe is a "digital nomad." Jordan works as a project coordinator for a nonprofit organization that partners with schools to help at-risk students and travels to various schools. When traveling, Jordan uses their laptop in shared office spaces, uses car- and bike-sharing when possible, participates in audio and video conferences with the nonprofit's home office, keeps up with the news using podcasts, and offers their condo as a short-term rental while they're on the road. Jordan contributes to a professional blog designed to help students and keeps in touch with family and friends using instant messaging. When communicating with digital tools, Jordan is careful to abide by the rules of netiquette to protect their professional and personal reputation.

Just today, you might have received an email from a potential employer, entered a status update on social media, or sent a text message to a friend or family member. In the past week, you might have sent an email, read a blog, or participated in a video conference. Whenever you perform these activities, you are using digital communication.

In this module, you will learn about the many types of digital communication and how they impact your personal and professional life every day. You also will learn how to develop an online presence that adheres to standard Internet etiquette guidelines to help ensure your safety and enhance your employability. As you reflect on what you learn in this module, ask yourself: What kinds of digital communication tools are available? How might you use these tools in your personal and professional life? What impact do these tools have on the way you interact with others, both personally and professionally?

Compare Popular Digital Communication Tools

When you send a photo and text message to a friend from your smartphone, add a restaurant review to a rating site, or learn how to improve your business writing while attending a webinar (an online educational web conference), you are using digital communication. **Digital communication** is the transmittal of data, instructions, and information from one computer or mobile device to another, often via the Internet (**Figure 11-1**).

In the last 25 years, the rise of digital communication has transformed the ways people work, interact, and spend leisure time. Paper communications such as memos, letters, and reports have given way to emails and other electronic documents. Voice communication via telephone and face-to-face interaction is often accomplished instead via electronic messages, video chats, and online conferencing. Many people prefer online books and other publications to physical books and magazines. Traditional telephones and cell phones have been replaced by multipurpose smartphones. Practically all business transactions, including orders, invoices, contracts, meetings, and presentations, are now performed almost solely using digital communication. Social media and social networking have transformed cultures worldwide. People in many geographical areas, even those that were once isolated, can now use mobile phones to follow and participate in worldwide events.

The speed, efficiency, and immediacy of digital communication in personal and business interactions have become the norm, so it's important to understand the types of digital communication, their purpose, as well as the basics of how to use each one.

Identify Key Netiquette Principles

When you're meeting friends, interacting with family, and working with colleagues, you're guided by rules for socially acceptable behavior, or *etiquette*. Even if much of your communication is now online, you still are encouraged to follow similar dos and don'ts

Figure 11-1: Some forms of digital communication

KULLAPONG PARCHERAT/Shutterstock.com;
Quora, Inc.; Google LLC; one photo/Shutterstock.com

that help make your online interactions civil and productive. As you use digital communications of any kind, it is vital that you follow the rules of Internet etiquette, known as **netiquette**, to protect yourself, your family, and your career.

The Internet is full of stories about people who made poor decisions in their digital communications and suffered drastic consequences in their lives as a result:

- Some have discovered that personal photographs and videos transmitted via email or other electronic means are likely to be shared in unexpected locations, causing untold loss of reputation, personal privacy, and employment.

- Numerous people have posted unflattering, false, or confidential comments about their employers and have lost their jobs as a result when the employer found the post.

- Others whose electronic missteps "went viral" have had their personal information spread online and had to relocate.

Individuals and businesses have values to protect and generally will not risk their reputations due to the bad choices of their friends or employees. Public shaming by ordinary citizens can spread quickly, and such damage can be difficult or impossible to undo. One poor decision can affect an entire lifetime.

Throughout this module, you'll learn guidelines for using digital communication tools and platforms. It is in your interest to follow such guidelines to protect your reputation and your future.

Explain How Email Works

For businesses and organizations, email is the standard for written communication and has largely replaced paper letters, memos, and reports. One of the earliest forms of digital communication, email (short for electronic mail) is a system used to send and receive messages and files using the Internet. You might use email to correspond with your manager, coworkers, friends, and family. A product manager who needs to send company newsletters, launch an online marketing campaign, or send project specifications to a team will likely use email to communicate that information.

According to Statista, a company that publishes market and consumer data, the number of email users worldwide will grow to over 4.5 billion people by 2025, which is about half of the world's population; the number of emails sent and received per day is expected to reach over 375 billion.

Email Communication Process
Every time you send or receive an email, your messages undergo a similar set of steps to get them from the source email account to the recipient's email account. Once sent, an email message can arrive at any destination in the world within seconds.

An email message can consist of only text or it can include an attachment, such as a document, a picture, or an audio or video file. **Figure 11-2** gives an example of an email message in the Microsoft Outlook application. A file, such as a photo or document, that you send with an email message is called an **email attachment**. If you receive a message with an attachment, you can save the attachment on your computer or open it to view its contents.

Any computer or mobile device that can access the Internet can connect with an email system, which consists of the computers and software that provide email services. The main computer in an email system is an **email server**, which is a computer server that routes email messages through the Internet or a private network. **Figure 11-3** illustrates how email is routed.

Figure 11-2: An email message in the Microsoft Outlook app

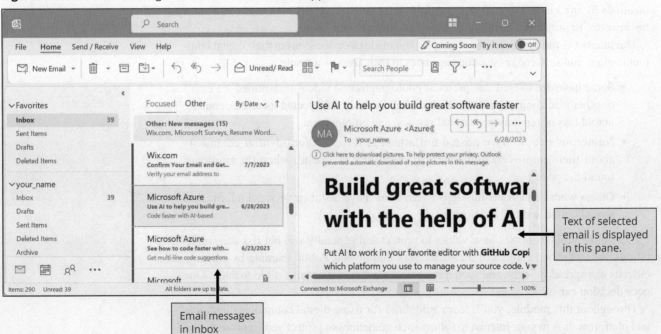

Figure 11-3: How an email travels from sender to receiver

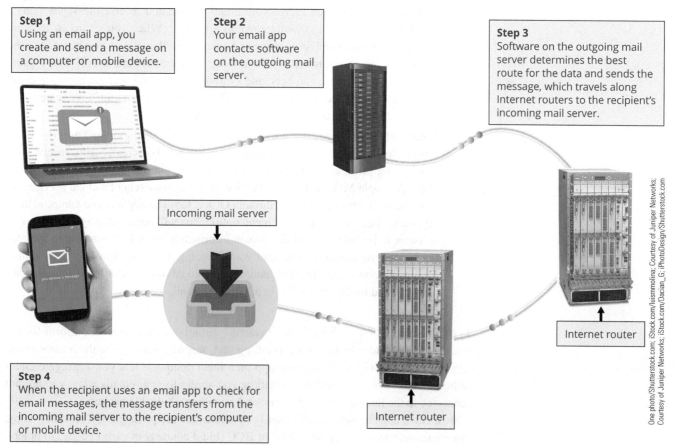

Step 1
Using an email app, you create and send a message on a computer or mobile device.

Step 2
Your email app contacts software on the outgoing mail server.

Step 3
Software on the outgoing mail server determines the best route for the data and sends the message, which travels along Internet routers to the recipient's incoming mail server.

Incoming mail server

Internet router

Internet router

Step 4
When the recipient uses an email app to check for email messages, the message transfers from the incoming mail server to the recipient's computer or mobile device.

One photo/Shutterstock.com; iStock.com/luismmolina; Courtesy of Juniper Networks; Courtesy of Juniper Networks; iStock.com/Dacian_G; iPhotoDesign/Shutterstock.com

Email Addresses   You can choose your own email address, with certain restrictions. An **email address** is a unique combination of a user name and a domain name that identifies a specific user on a network so that user can send and receive email messages. The user name is followed by an "at" (@) sign, followed by a domain name that specifies the Internet location of the recipient's email provider. The **email provider** is the company that provides the email server, the host computer for the email account. Common domains include gmail.com and outlook.com.

Figure 11-4 illustrates an example of an email address. Your user name must be unique for the chosen domain. For example, if you are setting up an example.com account and want to choose the address chris_smith@example.com, you might find the user name chris_smith is already taken. You then would have to try adding characters to make it unique, such as chris_smith386@example.com. Choose a user name that is easy to communicate to others verbally and that's easy to remember. For instance, you could easily verbalize the above address as, "Chris underscore Smith three eight six at example dot com." Do not choose a humorous or offensive user name; assume that your email communications will be used to communicate with potential employers and other professionals.

Figure 11-4: Example of an email address

Your_name@example.com

User name   @ sign   Domain name

Email Requirements   To send and receive email messages, you need:

- **An email account:** The email provider that you choose reserves an electronic mailbox for you. To sign up for an email account, you contact an email provider, which might be your Internet service provider (ISP), a school, an employer, or a website such as iCloud. You can also set up an account through an online service such as Gmail, and then access your email to send and receive messages using a web browser, an email system known as **webmail**. When you set up an account, you choose your unique user name and a password that allows you access to your account. Your password should be at least 12 characters and a difficult-to-guess combination of letters, numbers, and symbols. Your email account provider might enforce additional requirements. Never share your password with anyone else, and make sure to store your password in a safe place.

- **Email software:** If you are not using webmail, you need to install an **email app** (also called an **email client**), an application that lets you create, send, receive, forward, store, print, and delete email messages. Popular email apps include Gmail, Outlook, Apple Mail, and private services, such as your school's email services, or network email services, such as through Office 365. The app lets you compose messages and click a Send button or menu option. You will need to configure your email software to include your email account information, so it knows where to look for your incoming messages and send your outgoing messages. Email programs may run on Windows, macOS, iOS, and/or Android devices, and often offer calendar, contacts, and to-do capabilities in addition to email.

Typical Features of Email Software   Email software provides a form for the message and includes buttons for formatting text, setting a priority for the message, and attaching files. Using a client email app on a local computer lets you aggregate email addresses and store email offline, providing you access to your emails when you are not connected to the Internet or email server, and providing a valuable backup.

Most email apps let you send an email to the intended recipient and CC (courtesy copy, sometimes referred to as carbon copy) or BCC (blind courtesy or carbon copy) to others. All recipients can see those who are CC'd on an email, but only the sender can see the addresses that received a BCC. When you send an email message, your email address is included as the return address so your recipients can respond to your message by using the Reply or Reply All feature. Reply sends a response only to the original sender, while Reply All sends a response to the sender and anyone who received courtesy copies, but not blind courtesy copies. Use care when choosing a reply type. You might accidentally send a reply to a long list of recipients whom you don't want to receive your message. It's considered unprofessional to Reply All when the email contains a long list of recipients but only one or a few need the reply. After you receive an email message, you can forward it and its attachments to other recipients.

Email software also includes built-in folders for managing messages. For example, the Inbox folder is for messages you have received, and the Sent Items folder is for messages you have sent. Most email software also provides a Trash or Deleted Items folder for storing messages you want to delete. To prevent the accidental loss of important messages, the messages in the Trash folder might remain available until you permanently delete them. You also can create your own folders to help organize messages by topic, project, or sender.

If you want to remove older messages without deleting them, you can archive the messages. **Archiving** is the practice of moving email messages, usually those older than a specified date, to a file or folder separate from your active email.

Define Common Types of Written Digital Communication

Beyond email, there are many types of digital communication that rely on written material, including blogs, wikis, and electronic messaging.

Blogs   Traditionally, a news writer could tell the world about events using a newspaper or television broadcast; an author would communicate content through a book printed and distributed by a publishing company; and an academic writer would publish articles in a professional journal. Today, these writers have options for publishing their work directly to their audience. One of these options is to use a blog. A blog (short for web log) allows a writer to upload and publish text, images, or other content directly to an audience in a less formal way. Blogs are informal websites consisting of date- or time-stamped articles, called **posts**, in a diary or journal format. Blogs can contain text, photos, video clips, and links to additional information. **Figure 11-5** gives an example of a corporate blog for instructors.

A blog is more efficient than older publishing forms because a writer can communicate directly and immediately with an audience, without traditional expenses or gatekeepers who select and edit content. The audience for a public blog needs only its web address to access it. For a private blog, the audience also needs permission from the **blogger**, the author of the blog, to read entries. Visitors often can read and comment on blog entries, but they cannot edit them.

Businesses use blogs, along with email and other forms of social media, to build their online presence and increase sales. They also use blogs to communicate with employees, customers, and vendors.

- A sales department might encourage blog readers to sign up for a free product to develop sales leads.

- A corporate blog might show the company's expertise in their subject area, such as an employment firm creating a blog post on tips for job interviewing.

- A large company might use a blog to publicize its corporate mission and values, as well as its products.

Figure 11-5: Blog with text, images, and links

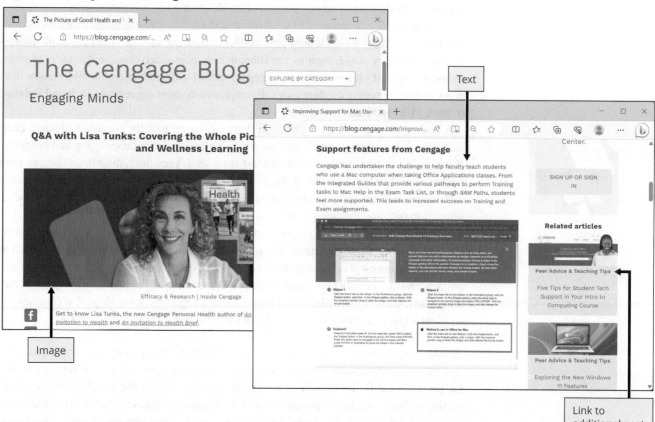

Figure 11-6: News aggregator Flipboard

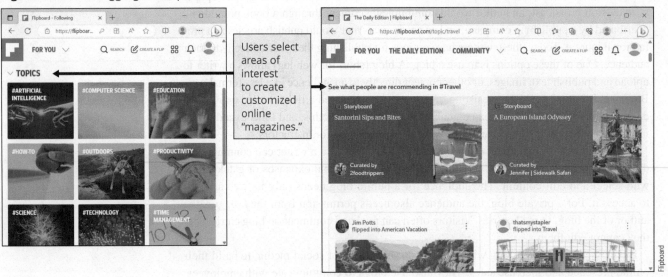

Users select areas of interest to create customized online "magazines."

Flipboard

Popular business blogs include the news blog Buzzfeed, technology and digital culture blog Mashable, and the technology blog TechCrunch.

For individual bloggers, the most popular blog creation site is WordPress, a free, easy-to-use site that lets you create a blog containing text and media, and even a complete website. In contrast, a **blogging network** is a blogging site that uses the tools of social networking. For example, Tumblr lets users post not only text but also photos, quotations, links, audios, and videos. Bloggers can tag their entries and chat with other bloggers. Bloggers can share each other's posts on Tumblr or on other social networks.

The worldwide collection of blogs, known as the **blogosphere**, varies by media, length, and purpose. Many blog authors post entries consisting of mostly text, though authors of video blogs, or **vlogs**, such as YouTube, mainly post video clips, and authors of photo blogs mainly post photos. Content aggregator sites locate and assemble information from many online sources, including blogs. Examples of content aggregators include Flipboard (**Figure 11-6**) and Reddit.

A **microblog** allows users to publish short messages, usually just a few hundred characters long, for others to read, making it a combination of text messaging and blogging. News media use microblogs to broadcast short messages, including headlines, to their readers. Cities and other municipalities use microblogs, wireless emergency alerts through cell phones, and community information services such as Nixle to send alerts about traffic, severe weather, and missing persons, such as Amber Alerts.

Businesses create blogs to communicate with employees, customers, and vendors. Personal blogs often focus on family life, social life, or a personal interest or project, such as building a house or planting a garden. Other blogs can include commentary on news and politics, and are an outlet for citizen journalists, members of the public who report on current events. Citizen journalists often produce **live blogs**, which are blogs that comment on an event while it is taking place, usually in the form of frequent, short updates.

Wikis   While many websites make large amounts of information available to the general public, and blogs allow people to comment on their contents, it's not always possible for users to modify the website or blog content itself. That is the job of a wiki, a collaborative website that lets users create, add to, change, or delete content using their web browser. A wiki (from the Hawaiian word for "quick") can include articles, documents, photos, or videos.

Figure 11-7: Wikipedia website

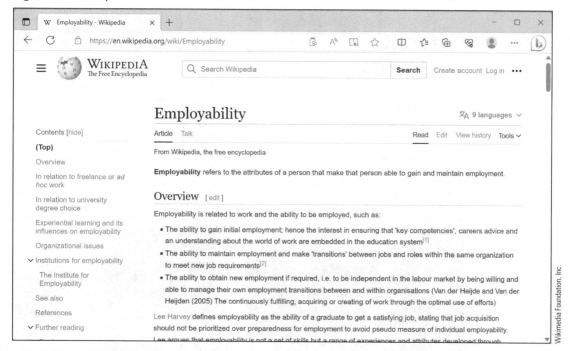

As with blogs, people use wikis to share their knowledge, experience, and points of view. Contributors to a wiki typically must register before they can edit content or add comments. Wikis can include articles, documents, photos, or videos. Some wikis are public, accessible to everyone, such as Wikipedia (**Figure 11-7**).

If you've ever used a search engine to look up a definition of a term or the meaning of a phrase, you've probably visited Wikipedia, one of the largest wikis on the web. Wikipedia is a free, online encyclopedia with millions of articles. Thousands of users regularly contribute to Wikipedia by writing, editing, and reviewing articles. You can edit articles by creating a Wikipedia account and then signing in.

Anyone can edit Wikipedia entries or add new ones. Although Wikipedia rates well on many surveys of accuracy, it is possible for inaccurate content to be posted, in spite of its quality standards and the efforts of its volunteer editors. When reading or using Wikipedia content, check its sources carefully.

Other wikis are private so that content is accessible only to certain individuals or groups. Many companies, for example, set up wikis as an intranet (an internal network) for employees to collaborate on projects or access information, procedures, and documents. Wikis are useful in education for students working together on projects; they can post online portfolios, share research notes, and give feedback to group members. Researchers use wikis to share findings, offer and receive suggestions, and test their work.

Businesses also use wikis, especially when employees are not all in the same physical location. Businesses use wikis in the following ways:

- **Distribute information:** Departments that make company-wide policies, such as human resources, can use wikis to make policies and updates available company-wide at any time.

- **Provide a central repository of information:** Project teams that are geographically isolated can access schedules, specifications, and procedures posted on a company wiki to ensure consistency throughout all stages of a project.

- **Enable communication:** Employees at all levels can contribute to a wiki, making it a useful way to exchange ideas and encourage participation from people in all departments and positions.

Figure 11-8: Types of electronic messages

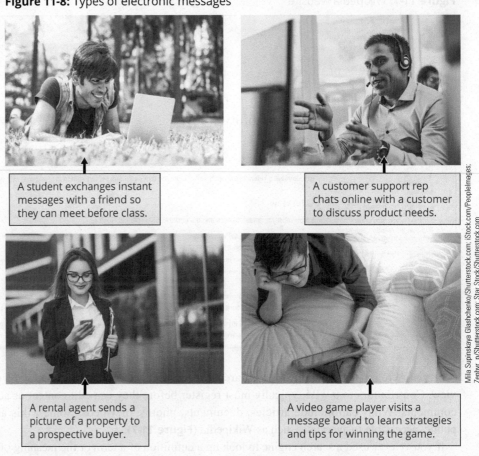

A student exchanges instant messages with a friend so they can meet before class.

A customer support rep chats online with a customer to discuss product needs.

A rental agent sends a picture of a property to a prospective buyer.

A video game player visits a message board to learn strategies and tips for winning the game.

Messaging Applications   Many business communications are short, such as changing an appointment time, verifying a fact, or confirming a project detail. **Electronic messaging** (**Figure 11-8**) is a popular technology for communicating with others, especially when exchanging short messages.

Electronic messaging technology can be part of larger applications such as Facebook, part of webpages, or separate applications. Popular messaging apps include WhatsApp, Skype for Business, and Slack. Most messaging apps, whether on smartphones or Internet-connected computers, include the following features, which allow for a variety of communication types:

- **Text messaging**, or sending short text messages, usually over cellular networks using mobile phones. This feature allows you to send messages to a person or group quickly. Participants do not have to be online at the same time.

- **Chatting**, or holding real-time typed conversations through the Internet between two or more people who are online at the same time.

- **Multimedia messaging**, or sending photos, videos, or links to websites using desktops or mobile devices, allowing participants to quickly share content. Messaging apps can even include custom animated characters you create using apps such as the Apple feature called Animoji, which uses face-tracking technology to apply your voice and facial expressions to animated characters. These are best used in personal rather than business communications.

- **Voice messaging**, or recording and posting digital audio messages for another person. One form of voice messaging is **voice mail**, which is a short audio recording made using digital technology and sent to or from a smartphone or other mobile device when the recipient did not answer a phone call. Once digitized, the voice mail is stored in the phone's voice mailbox. With visual voice mail, users can view message details, such as the length of a call and a time stamp showing when the message arrived (**Figure 11-9**). Another form of voice messaging is **voice notes**, or **voice memos**, which is a short audio recording created in a messaging app, such as WhatsApp or Android's Messages app, instead of sending a text message.

- **Voice-to-text** (also called speech-to-text), or converting incoming or outgoing voice messages to written text, for use in situations where typing messages is impractical and hands-free operation is required. Voice-to-text technology can also be used in visual voice mail, where it can translate voice messages into typed text.

Figure 11-9: A message in visual voicemail

Define Common Types of Audio and Visual Digital Communication

Some types of digital communication, such as podcasts and online conferencing, are focused less on text and more on audio or visual media.

Podcasts   If you miss a lecture or your favorite business news program, or if you're just looking for entertainment, chances are you'll find what you need on a podcast, a popular way to distribute audio or video content on the web. A **podcast** is recorded media that users can download or stream to a computer or mobile device and listen to at any time. Examples include lectures, radio shows, news stories, and commentaries. Podcasts are also useful tools that can help you learn more about practically any field, such as sports, music, politics, personal development, or investments.

A **video podcast** is a file that contains video and audio; it is usually offered as part of a subscription to a podcasting service. In **Figure 11-10**, a Duolingo Spanish podcast is playing.

VoIP Calls   **Voice over Internet Protocol (VoIP)** refers to voice communications over the Internet and is sometimes called **Internet telephony**. In the past, voice communications travelled only along phone lines. Communications or telephone companies charged for phone calls. With the Internet, voice can travel through the same network lines that carry webpages and other Internet services. Many Internet service providers (ISPs) now offer phone services; if you have a phone number through your ISP, you are using VoIP.

VoIP providers include Vonage, Skype, Grasshopper, Google, and others. Often, calls from one country to another are included in your monthly Internet fee. VoIP allows you to receive calls on your computer from business, home, or cell phone numbers and to place calls from your computer to these numbers. You can use different devices to make VoIP calls, including home phones, smartphones, laptops, tablets, and even desktop computers. If you have a webcam, VoIP technology might include the ability to add video to your calls.

Video Chats   Talking over a live video connection with a person at another physical location previously existed only in futuristic science fiction. Today, video chat commonly is used in businesses and education for **webcasts** (video broadcasts of an event transmitted across the Internet). Video chat, also called **video calling**, is a face-to-face conversation

Figure 11-10: Podcast on a smartphone

Figure 11-11: Video chatting

iStock.com/Tolgart

held over a network such as the Internet using a webcam, microphone, speakers, display device, and special software. It is also a popular way for people to stay in touch with friends and relatives who live far away (**Figure 11-11**).

You can use smartphones for video chatting as well as desktop, laptop, and tablet computers with an Internet connection, microphone, and webcam. Video chatting software lets you control the images that appear onscreen, voice and sound volume, and other features. Chatters without a webcam can participate in the chat but won't be seen on screen by other chatters.

Some video chat applications are now going beyond flat 2-D displays to develop holographic images, using beams of light to create patterns that appear as 3-D images. Such advancements will bring the tools of virtual reality into everyday communications.

Popular video chat apps include Skype, FaceTime, Facebook Messenger, WhatsApp, and Amazon Alexa. Some apps also allow **video messaging**, in which you can leave a video message for a recipient to pick up later.

Online Conferences   Suppose you're working on a business project with a team that includes people in different cities or countries. To collaborate on the project, you can have a **web conference** (also called a video conference), a meeting among several geographically separated people who use a network or the Internet to transmit audio and video data (**Figure 11-12**).

Web conferences typically are held on computers or mobile phones. Participants use web conferencing software to sign into the same webpage or application. To speak to each other, participants can either join a conference phone call or use their computer microphones and speakers. One user serves as the host and can share their desktop with the group.

During the online session, the host can display a document or other content from their own monitor that participants see at the same time. Most web conferencing software features a whiteboard where the presenter and participants can annotate. If the host edits a shared document, everyone sees the changes as they are made. Participants can use a **chat window** to send typed messages to each other during the web conference. Participants might also be able to share files.

Conferencing programs generally allow a meeting "wall," a background displaying the host company's logo and profile photo. They might also feature automatic language translation, instant captioning for the hearing impaired, and braille translation for those who are visually and hearing impaired. Popular business video conferencing programs with these types of features include Zoom, GoTo Meeting, Microsoft Teams, WebEx, and Google Meet.

Figure 11-12: A video conference

Ground Picture/Shutterstock.com

Webinars   Similar to a web conference, a **webinar** (short for web-based seminar) is a presentation an audience accesses over the web. It shows a shared view of the presenter's screen, might include audio and video of the presenter, and might even allow for audience participation. It's often used to present lectures, demonstrations, workshops, or other types of instructional activity.

Define Common Types of Digital Social Networking

Social media and social networks are now used by large segments of the population worldwide. As they have grown, they have become more specialized to suit the needs and interests of their users.

Social Media   Social media refers to many of the ways individuals and businesses share information and interact using the Internet. The information they share ranges from stories, photos, news, and opinions to complete diaries, daily life updates, professional networking, and job searches, as well as sophisticated games. Social media differs from other forms of communication because it is immediate, interactive, and widespread. The research company Statista estimates there are nearly 5 billion social media users worldwide as of 2023.

Social media helps people form online communities among users with similar interests around the world. **Table 11-1** lists the most common types of social media used today.

Social Networks   A social network, also called a social networking site, is a website that encourages members in its online community to share their interests, ideas, stories, photos, music, and videos with other registered users. Social networking was made

Table 11-1: Types of social media

Type	Lets you	Includes	Examples
Social networking	Share ideas, opinions, photos, videos, websites	Personal and business networking, chat, video chat and video conferencing, instant messaging, online dating, social memorials	Facebook, LinkedIn, Instagram, Snapchat, Discord, Google Chat
Blogging and microblogging	Create and update an online journal that you share with readers	Personal journals, expert advice, information on special areas of interest	Blogger, Substack, WordPress, Tumblr, Mastodon, Weibo
Media sharing and content sharing	View and distribute pictures, videos, audio files	Photo and video sharing, podcasting, news sites, online learning, distance learning	YouTube, Twitch, Teachable, Dailymotion, Flickr, Photobucket, Google Photos
Collaborative projects	Read, add, and discuss articles about topics of interest	Online encyclopedias, forums, wikis, message boards, news groups,	Wikipedia, Answers, Fandom, MediaWiki
Social curation, bookmarking, and social news	Tag (mark) and search websites; share websites, articles, news stories, media	Tagging; knowledge management	Reddit, Digg, Pinterest
File sharing	Send and receive files from others on an Internet location	Free or paid access to file storage locations on the Internet	Box, Google Drive, Microsoft OneDrive, Egnyte, ShareFile, Hightail, Dropbox
Virtual social worlds	Play games with others; create a simulated environment	Virtual reality games	World of Warcraft, Steam, Minecraft
Crowdfunding	Raise funds for a project, cause, or business	Websites that let anyone contribute; site takes a percentage of funds raised	GoFundMe, Indiegogo, Kickstarter, Startsomegood

possible by the growth of social media. Popular online social networks include Facebook, TikTok, Instagram, Snapchat, and LinkedIn. A news or activity **feed** on the site provides a listing of the most recent content posted to the network.

Businesses use social networking to learn more about their customers by collecting their feedback in the form of comments and experiences. A company's social networking site might advertise its products, services, and events. Nonprofit organizations use social networking to promote their activities, accept donations, and connect with volunteers.

Some online social networks have no specialized audience; others are more focused. You have probably viewed an online video, and chances are it was posted to YouTube. YouTube is the best-known example of a media sharing network.

A media sharing site, or media sharing network, lets users display and view various types of media. With photo sharing sites such as Instagram, Flickr, Photobucket, and Shutterfly, you can post photos and then organize them into albums, add **tags** (descriptive text) to categorize them, and invite comments (**Figure 11-13**). Photos and other posts on social network sites also include information that generally does not appear to site users, called **metadata**, which is data that describes other data. Metadata for a photograph includes the GPS location coordinates where it was taken, when it was posted, and who posted it.

Video sharing sites such as YouTube and Vimeo let users post short videos called **clips**. You can set up a post so that anyone, or only people you invite, can view or comment on your clip. On many of these sites, followers give feedback on shared media with a thumbs-up "like" or a thumbs-down "dislike."

Other social networks focus on the types of connections you can expect to make on the site. For example, with the professional networking website LinkedIn, you can keep in touch with colleagues, clients, employers, and other business contacts. LinkedIn is also a valuable social network for businesses, especially those that want to market a product or service. Businesses can create a company page and build connections to customers and clients. They also can join groups, post answers to user questions, advertise, and write articles. LinkedIn also offers online training courses for professional development.

Some social networks target more specific audiences around shared interests. For example, Behance is an online platform that allows those with creative talent to showcase their work. Like a more general-purpose social network, Behance supports profiles, media

Figure 11-13: YouTube and Flickr media-sharing networks

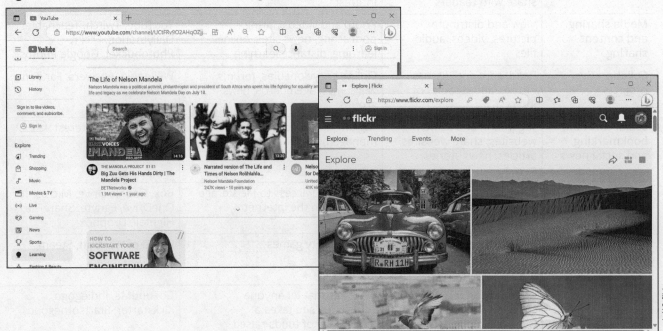

sharing, and activity feeds. Similarly, Discord is an online platform originally developed for gamers to share ideas, tips, and accomplishments. Due to its popularity, Discord is now used by many other types of communities as well.

With the growth of online shopping, users need a way to evaluate products before they buy. **Consumer review networks** let purchasers post online ratings and reviews of practically any product or service. For example, TripAdvisor helps travelers choose accommodations, flights, experiences, and restaurants by providing price and feature comparisons and customer ratings and reviews. Yelp helps consumers find professionals of all kinds, such as dentists, hair stylists, or mechanics, while Angi helps people search for service professionals, such as contractors or plumbers, in their area. Shopping sites such as Amazon also feature review capabilities to help users decide what products to buy.

A **message board**, also called **Internet forum**, is an online discussion site where people with a common interest participate in a conversation by posting messages. You can find forums dedicated to and have online conversations on any topic. For example, Quora features discussions built around questions and crowd-sourced answers. You can follow topics you select, and post questions, opinions, and links. You can also receive notifications when others post to a topic that interests you. The site lets you **upvote**, or promote, answers you find useful.

Social Curation Tools　　A business blog or website often provides links to relevant websites in their field, a practice known as aggregating content. However, this can be an enormous task, given the sheer volume of information on the Internet. From the early days of the Internet, **social bookmarking** sites allowed users to mark (or bookmark) websites to which they wanted to return. But to help find the most relevant, high-quality information, collect it, and share it with others, businesses now use social curation sites and tools.

Social curation sites let users share and save links to websites on selected news topics to target the most relevant, useful, and high-quality information. For example, a human resource manager might want to share media content about interviewing techniques with other department managers to ensure they can best match candidates with company needs and requirements. A social curation site lets users collect this information in one place and share it. In addition, automated social curation software tools can help filter, analyze, and rate content using keywords to make the job easier, faster, and more efficient.

For instance, Digg (**Figure 11-14**) and Slashdot collect news stories on science, politics, and technology. Personal social curation sites include Pinterest, where users can "pin" links to digital images and videos into collections called pinboards, similar to physical bulletin boards. Users can "like," "repin," and add comments to pins, and "follow" pinboards on topics that interest them.

Figure 11-14: Digg social curation site

Use Digital Communication Tools

While many college students are familiar with some forms of digital communication, today's job market requires that prospective employees can communicate using all forms. Multiple digital skills translate into increased salary, increased professional growth, and higher levels of career advancement.

Follow Netiquette Guidelines

Knowing how to use digital tools is critical, but learning how to use them effectively is equally important. This section begins with general netiquette guidelines for various types of digital communication, followed by basic information on how to use these digital tools in your personal life and professional career.

Internet Etiquette Guidelines   In any of your interactions on the Internet, follow these guidelines:

- Treat others as you want them to treat you. If you wouldn't say something to a person's face, don't write it in an electronic message.
- Be polite in your online communications. Avoid wording that might seem offensive, passive-aggressive, suggestive, or argumentative. Take care when using humor or sarcasm, which can be misinterpreted easily.
- Consider taking a neutral or moderated stance on controversial subjects, especially political ones.
- Read your messages before sending them, and correct errors in spelling, grammar, and tone. Consider using tools such as Grammarly or the built-in Word spell checker to help identify errors. You can also use generative AI (artificial intelligence) tools such as ChatGPT to check content before sending it.
- Consider email as public communication because people might forward your message to others without your knowledge.
- Remember that a human being is at the other end of your communication.

Personal Social Networking Guidelines   The fundamentals of netiquette apply to social networks just as they apply in other online communications:

- Respect other participants.
- Introduce yourself and get to know other members before adding them as friends. Don't overshare; show consideration for their time by keeping your messages short and focused.
- Before posting a comment, ask yourself how readers will react to it. If it is offensive, don't post it.
- Do not take an online discussion in a different, unrelated direction (called "hijacking a thread"). Stay on the current topic or start a new discussion on a different one.
- Do not post annoying or unwelcome messages or other information that might be considered harassment.
- Do not use social networks to monitor or keep track of a user's activities or whereabouts.
- Protect your **online reputation**, which is information about you that others can find on the Internet. Make sure your posts won't embarrass you someday.

Professional Social Networking Guidelines   When you create blogs posts, webpages, and social media posts in business, you should follow all netiquette guides. If you are using social media on the job, keep in mind the dos and don'ts in **Table 11-2**.

Table 11-2: Dos and don'ts for using social media in business

Do	Don't
Create a profile for your business connections apart from your personal ones.	Invite visitors to play games or join other activities that could waste their time.
In the professional profile, use your full name or a professional pseudonym, and a photo of yourself (not a photo of your pet, for example).	Use a pseudonym that is a reference to a joke or is offensive.
Offer information that visitors to your page will find valuable. Understand who visits your page (such as colleagues or clients) and adjust the content for these visitors.	Post anything that you don't want a future or current boss, colleague, client, or other professional contact to read.
Learn about the people who want to follow you or be your friends. Doing so is good business and helps you avoid an embarrassing connection.	Publish posts or comments when you are tired or angry because you might regret the post later when you have had time to consider it.
Post photos, messages, and videos that reflect a professional image and appropriate online reputation. When posting content that may be controversial, strive to be civil and respectful of everyone.	Publish posts or comments about controversial subjects that others might find offensive without thinking through the potential consequences and striving to be respectful of everyone.

Table 11-3: Don't include these in professional messaging

Message element	Examples	Guidelines
Abbreviations	TTFN BRB	Abbreviations such as TTFN ("ta-ta for now") or BRB ("be right back") are too informal for professional communications.
Emoticons/emojis	 Kristyna Henkeova /Shutterstock.com Sunflower /Shutterstock.com	An **emoticon** (short for emotion icon) is a symbol for an emotional gesture, such as a smile or frown, that you create using keyboard characters or insert as an image, such as a colon and a closing parenthesis for a smiley face. An **emoji** is an image that expresses an idea or concept, such as a picture of clapping hands to mean congratulations. Emoticons and emojis are very informal, so you should use them only in casual messages, and sparingly.
Personal information	"I've never told anyone this, but I really don't like our boss."	Avoid revealing personal information or any other information you wouldn't want known publicly.

Professional Messaging Guidelines   Originally, text messaging and chat were a new way to take advantage of emerging technology to exchange messages among friends. Because they're now valuable business tools as well, you need to follow the professional guidelines listed in **Table 11-3** when sending instant messages at work or participating in company chat rooms.

Blog Guidelines   If you participate in blogs as someone who posts entries or makes comments, you should be aware of blog guidelines for both roles:

- As a blogger, you're publishing information online that others might rely on to make decisions. Make sure the information you post is accurate and up to date.

- Acknowledge any connections you have with companies and people you endorse. If you review travel destinations, for example, and a hotel gives you a free vacation, disclose that information when you post a review of the hotel.

- As a commenter, read the commenting guidelines on the blog, which usually encourage you to use good judgment and basic courtesy.

- In particular, don't engage in **flaming**, which is posting hostile or insulting comments about another online participant.

Communicate with Digital Tools

Interactive conversations can be carried in many digital formats using any of the digital communication tools discussed so far. This section discusses how to use many of these tools for conversations online.

Email   In addition to learning the everyday features of your email program to send and receive messages, you should also learn appropriate email standards for your business or industry.

- Pay attention to the forms of address used for other employees, formality level, and signature conventions.

- Use CC and BCC fields judiciously.

- Learn how to transmit and respond to meeting requests that are tied to calendar programs. If a coworker wants to request a meeting with you, they may send an emailed meeting request. You can click Accept to automatically add the meeting time and details to your calendar program or respond to the sender if you are unable to attend at that time.

- Learn to use your email program's automatic reply features, also called autoreplies, when you are unavailable. Many of these tools will allow you to send different automatic replies to people inside your organization from those outside your organization. Consider carefully what information you include in these automatic replies. Informing coworkers you are on vacation until a certain date might be okay. However, replying to the general public with this information could result in attackers confiscating your email account to communicate as you, or could result in someone breaking into your home because you've given them the knowledge that you are out of town.

Digital Calendars   Another way to communicate briefly with others is through personal information apps such as calendars and address books. Calendar apps, including Google Calendar and iCal, let you keep track of appointments and events and communicate with others who need to know the schedule or events in the calendar. Most email apps such as Outlook also include a calendar feature (**Figure 11-15**). You can invite others to an event through the calendar. To schedule an appointment or event, you usually select the date on the calendar and then enter details, including the start and end times, location, invitees, notes, and time zone, if necessary.

To coordinate and communicate activities, you can share calendars with other people. Most calendar apps include a Share feature that lets you enter the email address of the person you want to share your calendar with. That person receives an email invitation to view your calendar but cannot make changes to it unless you allow them to do so.

Blogs   Blogs can be a source of valuable information in almost any area of interest. There are many millions of blogs on the web today and the number continues to grow. How can you find only the blogs you're interested in? You have several options:

- **Search engines:** One way is to use a search engine and search on text such as "blogs on careers," and you'll see many relevant blogs listed. Some search sites, such as Google, have specific blog searching capabilities.

Figure 11-15: Scheduling an appointment in the Outlook app

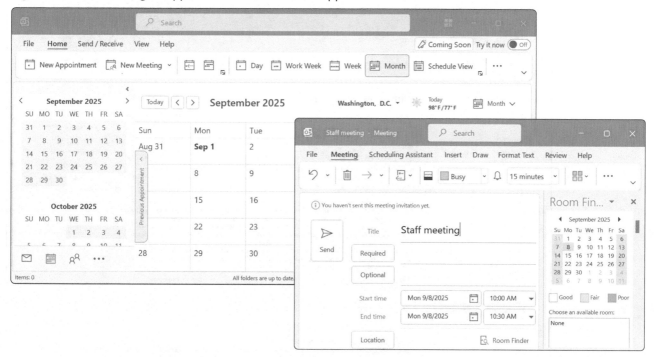

- **Blog search sites:** Sites like Blogroll (Blogroll.org) feature blog listings by topic.
- **Blog directories:** Numerous blog directories and catalogs let you browse for interesting blogs or search them using topics or keywords.
- **Search blog sites:** Go to a blogging site such as WordPress or Blogger and search for popular tags, such as business, technology, or culture.

Suppose you are developing a new business and want to publicize it. One way to spread the word is to create your own blog. As a blogger, you can use blogging software, available at sites such as Blogger.com, to create and publish your entries.

Microblogs   Tumblr and Instagram are examples of microblogging websites where you can post short text messages, links, photos, and videos from a smartphone or other computing device. Microblogs help you keep track of topics that interest you and let you repost content from other users. Most also notify you if another user reposts your content. All the content is posted for public consumption.

To receive posts from microbloggers, you follow them. New messages appear as soon as they are posted, which makes microblogs popular for people participating in the same activity, such as watching a sporting event. Like blogs, microblogs provide a way to categorize posts into topics or conversations so that other people can easily search for other posts about those topics. Instead of tags, microblogs use hashtags. A **hashtag** is a word(s) preceded by a hash (#) symbol that describes or categorizes a post, such as #cengageunlimited, and hashtags do not allow spaces. For example, #StudyAbroadSydney indicates the post is of interest to users who are studying or want to study in Sydney. Social networking sites such as TikTok, Facebook, and Instagram also use hashtags.

Wikis   You can view a public wiki the same way you would view any website; you can search on a keyword or click a link to a page. Before adding comments or content to a wiki, you usually need to register for the site by creating an account and then signing in. Typically, you select an Edit button or link and then make the desired changes. For example,

Figure 11-16: Editing a Wikipedia article

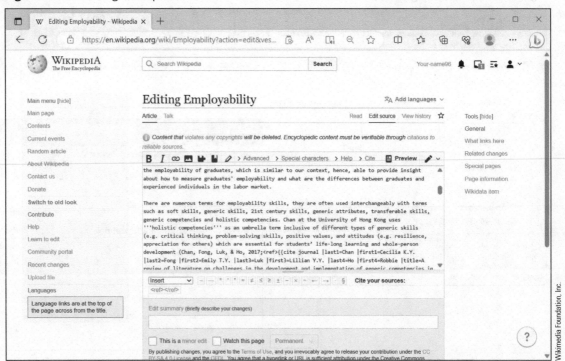

the Wikipedia entry for "employability" in **Figure 11-16** is being edited. In many wikis, edits are not posted immediately; instead, they are held until an editor or website manager can review them for accuracy. Unregistered users can review the content but cannot edit it or add comments.

As a form of business communication, some wikis have been replaced by other sites like Slack or Google Workspace, with better curation and search capabilities and more robust business collaboration features.

Message Boards   A message board, or Internet forum, temporarily saves messages and often uses a moderator to approve messages before they are posted for others to read. A **thread**, or threaded discussion, is a conversation that consists of text exchanges and includes the original message and all the replies. For example, technology companies host forums so users can get help from experts and other users. The Microsoft Support Community (answers.microsoft.com) is a free forum for asking and answering questions about Microsoft products. Groups such as sports teams, political organizations, and news websites also have dedicated message boards to exchange ideas and information.

Instant Messages   If your computer or mobile device does not already have a messaging app, you can download one from the Google Play Store or the Apple App Store. You can then exchange typed instant messages with people on your contact list, which consists of other IM (instant messaging) users you've selected or approved.

Instant messaging can also keep you informed about important events. You can sign up for a website or app to send alerts about breaking news, weather events, or sports scores to your mobile device, for example. Many workplaces now have messaging platforms.

In addition to text, you can include emoticons and emojis in a message. However, in many industries, emoticons and emojis are only appropriate for casual personal communications; even in industries or situations where emoticons and emojis are acceptable, they should be used sparingly. Avoid using text messages at work for bad news or important decisions, and always use professional language.

Anonymous Messaging Apps   When you visit websites or use social networking tools, the sites usually collect information from your profile and browsing history, so they can send targeted advertisements and gather usage data. In some situations, you might prefer that your information and browsing history remain private. **Anonymous messaging apps** let you send messages without including your identity. While some might use this capability for illicit purposes, others use it in a more positive way. The anonymous messaging app Sarahah lets businesses get honest, anonymous feedback from employees, without disclosing their identities. A drawback of anonymous messaging apps is that they can be used for cyberbullying.

Podcasts   You can download a podcast as a file and listen to it or watch it at any time, or you can stream the media file. With streaming media, you start playing the content right away without having to wait for the entire file or broadcast to download to your computer.

You can subscribe to podcasts using apps such as iTunes or Google Podcasts so podcasts are pushed to you when you refresh, update, or sync your mobile device. **Figure 11-17** displays the Google Podcasts app on a smartphone.

Figure 11-17: Various podcasts available in the Google Podcasts app

Create Digital Content

Digital communication tools are not used only for consuming content but also for creating it.

Microblogs   The brief messages that you can create using microblogs can be important in developing an online presence for yourself or a business, especially when combined with photos, audio clips, and video clips. Choose a microblogging platform such as Tumblr or Instagram, which will let you post updates from any of your devices, track activity, and interact with content posted by others. Download the app or plugin. You can set it up to notify you whenever someone mentions you or re-blogs your post.

In business, active microbloggers keep customers up to date on day-to-day happenings with a company's products or services. Microblog posts might educate readers or pique their curiosity, so they will want to visit a company's blog or website. To use microblogging most effectively, blog and re-blog frequently. The most successful microbloggers post content at least once a day, including personal updates or observations, brief opinion statements, links to online content, reactions to events, and other types of short information.

Blogs   To create, edit, and maintain a blog, you use blogging software, also known as **blogware**. This type of software is classified as a content management system (CMS), software that lets a group of users maintain and publish content of all kinds, but especially for websites. Blogware provides graphics, photos, standard text, and tools for web publication, comment posting, and moderation.

Popular blogware includes Blogger and WordPress. Google runs Blogger as a service that publishes blogs with time-stamped articles, or posts. A blog consists of separate pages, which are webpages displaying a single post. Your home page lists many posts with the most recent ones at the top of the list. To create a blog in Blogger:

1. Sign into Blogger using a Google account, and then select the New Blog button.
2. Enter a title and web address for the blog, and then select a template, which provides basic design elements such as colors, fonts, and graphics.
3. Use Blogger's tools to write and publish a post, add images and videos, customize the design, and view the activity on your blog, such as the number of **pageviews**, which indicates the number of times your blog has been viewed in a browser.

After creating a home page, you should create an **About page**, which is where you describe yourself, list any relevant experience or skills, and insert a photo and display name. If you assign your blog to one or more categories, which characterize your content in general, the category list appears on the About page. Anyone on the web can learn more about you and your blog by visiting your About page.

To attract an audience to your blog, you can include tags and links to other webpages. A tag (also called a **label**) is a key term associated with a post. For example, if you publish a post on how to find a job, one tag might be "findajob," so that people looking for jobs can find your blog post.

Network with Digital Tools

Although all communication is a form of networking, some digital communication tools are purpose-built to help people find and connect with others in various communities, industries, or interest areas.

Social Networks   Most social networks are open to the general public, and only require that you provide a name and password and complete an online form to create a **profile**, information about yourself that forms your online identity. You can provide as much or as little information as you like in your profile. You can expand your profile to describe your interests and activities and invite friends to visit your page. Friends can leave messages for you, and you can keep in touch with them by including links to your blog or by sharing media such as photos and videos.

Online social networks let you view profiles of other users and designate them as **friends**, or contacts. Some sites, such as Facebook and LinkedIn, require friends to confirm a friendship, while others, such as Instagram, allow users to follow any public accounts without confirmation.

You can expand your online social network by viewing your friends' friends and then, in turn, designating some of them as your friends. Friends of your friends, and their friends, form your **extended contacts**. Extended contacts on a personal social network, such as Facebook, can introduce you to others at your school or from your hometown, or enable you to stay in touch with those who have interests similar to yours.

Extended contacts on a professional network, such as LinkedIn, can introduce you to people who work at companies where you might seek employment. You can share employment history and skills in your profile, enabling potential employers who look at your profile to learn about your specific skills.

Personal uses of online social networks include sharing photos and videos as well as status updates to inform friends about what you are doing. You can **like**, or show appreciation for, the posts of your friends. When you do, people who see the content will know that you like it, and the person who posted it is notified. All your updates, likes, posts, and events appear in your account's **activity stream**. Activity updates from friends might appear on your news or activity feed. (Note that these streams are usually permanent unless you explicitly remove them or delete your account, meaning things that you posted or liked even years ago can still be found.)

Many social networks allow you to include hashtags to identify topics. Users can search for posts on a topic by searching for a hashtag. Some social networks list trending topics based on popular hashtags. Many television broadcasts, advertisements, and businesses post hashtags to encourage viewers and customers to share comments on TikTok, LinkedIn, or Facebook.

Social Shopping Networks   Social networking tools are useful not only for keeping in touch with customers, friends, and family; they can help you obtain needed items as well. **Social shopping networks** bring together people interested in buying similar kinds of products. Sites let shoppers share ideas and knowledge about products and prices.

Figure 11-18: Shopstyle, a social shopping network

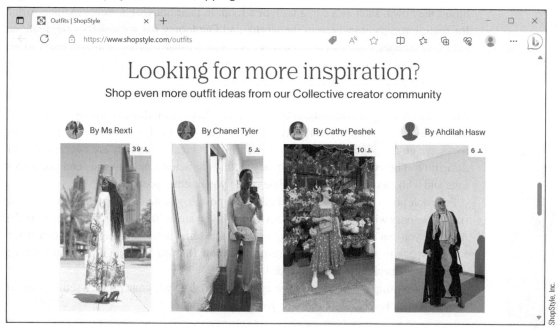

ShopStyle, Inc.

Shoppers might recommend products or hold product-related conversations. Some sites let users buy and sell merchandise, and buyers and sellers communicate directly with each other. For example, Etsy connects buyers and sellers of creative, unique handcrafts and vintage items; Etsy's community forums also provide a place for sellers to collaborate and share insights and solutions. Other sites encourage users to recommend collections of products. For example, in ShopStyle's Collective program, influencers present collections of products that match unique and individual fashion styles (**Figure 11-18**).

Groupon is an online marketplace where users and groups can share product information and purchase products at wholesale prices. Fab.com features unique accessories, accent pieces, and eye-catching technology products created by artists and designers.

Interest-Based Networks   Interest-based networks are similar to social networks but are targeted to a particular audience and subject. You can find interest-based networks on any topic, including those listed in **Table 11-4**.

Table 11-4: Examples of interest-based networks

Area	Examples	What it does
Home design	Houzz	Connects homeowners to professionals to help them with design and repair projects.
Idea sharing	Pinterest	Lets you post, search, and follow linked images you share with others, in interest areas such as food, technology, or decorating. You click pins, which are images representing links, to learn more. You can also save and share pins.
Sports	Fancred, Rooter	Connects sports fans; lets you check scores and chat live with other fans.
Fitness	Fitocracy	Lets you set and achieve workout goals while getting support from others.
Social causes	Care2	Joins users in a community that works toward social progress, kindness, and lasting impact. Interest areas include green living, animal rights, civil rights, and environment and wildlife.
Books	Goodreads	Connects readers who find and share books that interest them.

Figure 11-19: A post on Facebook, a social network

Meta Platforms, Inc.

Sharing Economy Networks   In **sharing economy networks**, people rent out things they own, such as a car, a tool, or a room in their house. Examples include Airbnb for renting rooms anywhere in the world, and Outdoorsy for renting RVs (recreational vehicles), camper vans, and travel trailers. Such sites usually have a search feature, so you can find what you need, as well as a review section, so you can tell others about your experience. Some allow owners to rate renters as well.

Messages on Social Networks   If you have something to say, you can find a quick way to say it on a social network. Most social networking sites let members post messages on the pages of other members, which is ideal when they are not online at the same time (**Figure 11-19**). Select privacy settings to determine who can send you a message and who can post on your timeline or tag you in other posts.

For each post, you can decide whether the post is visible to the public, to only your friends, or only within your friends' networks. If you are online at the same time as another member, you can use a chat feature to exchange text messages or engage in a video chat to see and speak to another member in a chat window (**Figure 11-20**). GPS-enabled devices allow you to check in to indicate your location.

If you are using a workplace messaging platform, check your privacy settings and be aware that employers might monitor your digital presence.

Attend Webinars and Video Conferences

Figure 11-20: Instant messaging on a social network

Bsd/Shutterstock.com

Video conferences have become essential for holding meetings with management, staff, vendors, and customers at remote locations. Training sessions can now use video conferencing tools (**Figure 11-21**). There's a good chance that some of your job interviews will take place via video conference, which increases productivity by reducing travel time and expense and allowing more people to participate.

Webinars   Webinars are ideal for education and training. They are an efficient and low-cost way to help you develop almost any skill, such as business writing, customer service, trade skills, or learning compliance requirements for payroll or human resources.

Figure 11-21: A video training session

Andrey_Popov/Shutterstock.com

Figure 11-22: Webinar on employability

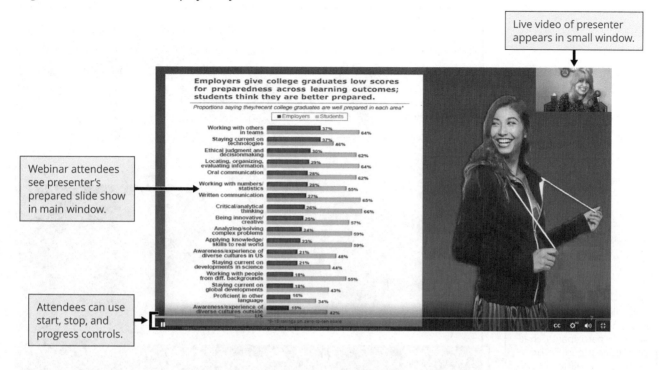

Live video of presenter appears in small window.

Webinar attendees see presenter's prepared slide show in main window.

Attendees can use start, stop, and progress controls.

Businesses also use webinars to promote their brands and establish their credibility to customers and potential customers. **Figure 11-22** gives an example of a webinar designed for college technology instructors.

Some webinars involve one-way communication, in which the presenter speaks and demonstrates, and the audience listens. Other webinars are more interactive and collaborative, especially if they allow polling to survey the audience on a topic or if they let participants ask and answer questions.

Webinars and web conferences often include slide show presentations and videos. Some include electronic whiteboards, where participants can record and save notes, and provide tools for activities such as brainstorming and problem solving.

Video Conferences   To participate in a video conference, you need to have a video camera, microphone, and speakers, earbuds, or headphones connected to your computer. Because video conferences let many people from different geographic locations meet electronically, they are different from some video calling programs, which usually connect only two people online. A video conference allows participants to see and hear each other, while a web conference does not.

Video conferencing might require that participants run compatible software on their device and might require that attendees set up an account. Downloading software may be as simple as clicking a link and waiting a few moments as you join a meeting, as with Zoom video conferencing (**Figure 11-23**), which does not require attendees to create an account.

Some software doubles as both video conferencing for groups and video chat software for just two people. With simpler tools like Google Chat, small businesses can set up free voice and video conversations for a few people. However, video chat software that allows group calling might not have the group participation tools, such as surveying or breakout rooms, that more complete video conferencing software has, or capabilities such as recording the conversation or providing live closed captioning.

Figure 11-23: Participating in a video conference using Zoom

Live video image of participants from their computer cameras.

Controls let participants start and stop video, invite and view participants, chat with other attendees, or record or leave the meeting.

iStock.com/Fizkes; LDprod /Shutterstock.com; iStock.com/m-imagephotography; LDprod /Shutterstock.com; Zoom Video Communications, Inc.

Figure 11-24: Video calling on FaceTime

Apple Inc.

Figure 11-25: Video job interview on HireVue

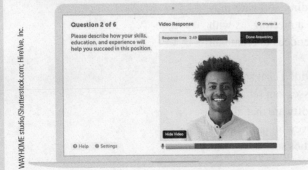

WAYHOME studio/Shutterstock.com; HireVue, Inc.

In any video conference, be sure that your background visible to others is neat and clean. Avoid having food or beverages in the area. Work associates and job recruiters will form opinions of you based on your surroundings, just as they would if they visited you in an office.

Video Chats   One of the best-known video calling apps is Skype. Skype is a Windows app for making video and voice calls. To use it, set up a Skype account. Add contacts by searching for them using their email address or Skype account name. Click the contact to call that person, and then click the camera icon to make a video call or the phone icon to make a phone call. You can leave a message if the person is offline.

You also can video chat with other Facebook users by opening a conversation in Facebook Messenger and clicking the video button. On Apple devices, FaceTime (**Figure 11-24**) allows video calling, while on Android devices, Google Chat and WhatsApp are popular video calling apps. Snapchat also features video chat.

Video Job Interviews   A video job interview might be conducted with one individual or with a group; it might be live in real time; or it might be one-way, where you record your answers to specified questions, or even respond to game-like tasks designed to assess cognitive and work style. Some programs allow you to do practice interviews online and submit your recorded interview when you are satisfied with the results. Your responses might be scored using digital and artificial intelligence tools. Popular video interviewing programs include VidCruiter, Breezy HR, and HireVue (**Figure 11-25**).

Evaluate the Impact of Digital Communication on Everyday Life

From email to social networks to online purchases, life today is filled with digital communications of all kinds, and nearly everyone feels their impact every day. While newer industries might thrive due to the spread of digital communication, some older industries suffer, affecting entire communities and countless lives. Some digital tools, like email and video conferencing, make it possible for people to work with others in remote locations, bringing people closer together. Yet others will say that digital communication, in fact, isolates people by decreasing face-to-face interaction. As you become familiar with digital tools, evaluate how you want to use them in your life to match your personal and professional goals.

Evaluate Pros and Cons of Social Media

As you have learned, social media refers to the many ways computer users receive and share information and interact using the Internet. It includes web and mobile technologies such as videos, blogs, online forums, news sites, file sharing, gaming, and crowdfunding. Social networking is an important part of social media. In the last 20 years, social media and social networking have changed how people communicate, shop, work, learn, relate with others, and spend their time, with both positive and negative effects.

Positive Effects of Social Media Social media has revolutionized how people learn and communicate, enabling personal growth and real-time interactive communication.

- **Expand learning opportunities:** Social media makes it easy to learn anything you want at any time. You can find a YouTube video for almost any purpose, whether you need to maintain your computer, practice yoga, play an instrument, or take better pictures. Consumer review sites such as Yelp can help you make informed buying decisions. TripAdvisor and Airbnb can help you plan personal and business travel with built-in ratings. Free online learning sites let you improve your math skills, learn a language, or learn economics; you can even watch free university lectures online (**Figure 11-26**). Using social media tools, you can learn at your own speed and check your progress with online evaluations.

Figure 11-26: Free online learning sites

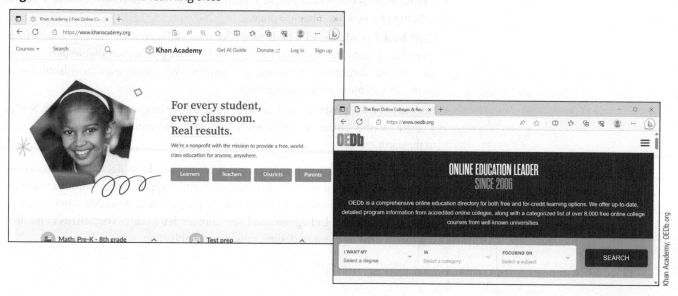

Khan Academy; OEDb.org

Figure 11-27: Social media used for public safety messages

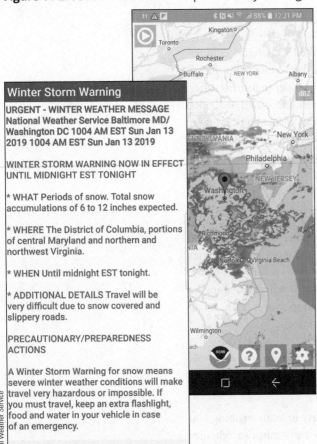

- **Distribute information:** You might already use social media tools to read or watch news and find information on your career, hobbies, and interests. You can learn about new products, social trends, weather, and emergency information. For example, you can choose to have your laptop, tablet, or smartphone alert you to imminent flooding danger or storm warnings in your area (**Figure 11-27**). Social media is gradually replacing traditional media such as newspapers, TV, and radio for broadcasting such events to help keep you informed and safe.

- **Enable interactive communication:** Social media can turn digital communication from the content creator into an interactive dialogue with the audience. You can post a video on YouTube that others can comment on and share. You can play online games with friends or strangers, anywhere in the world. Social media lets you collaborate and share ideas with others, whether it's sharing a proposal to develop a business strategy or discussing topics of mutual interest.

Gather Support with Social Media Social media has become a major way for individuals and organizations to gather knowledge, support, or contributions from a worldwide audience. Such support might include physical labor, data collection, research, or financing.

Crowdsourcing uses the Internet and the "intelligence of the crowd" to accomplish a task or solve a problem for the benefit of all. Project leaders put out a public request on the Internet, sometimes called an "open call," and motivated people respond. Examples of crowdsourcing include:

- **Community projects**, such as a beach cleanup or electronic petitions to accomplish community change. Nextdoor.com facilitates information sharing among neighbors.
- **Creative projects**, where people contribute ideas such as designing a new public building or a new state license plate.
- **Skill-based projects**, in which people donate skills such as editing, translation, scanning, or data transcription to create or improve publicly available data (census information, databases, or historic newspapers). Wikipedia uses crowdsourcing in its use of volunteer writers and editors.
- **Location-based projects**, such as wildlife counts or language use surveys; a NASA website recruits citizen astronomers to help locate asteroids that may pose a threat to the earth.

A particular type of crowdsourcing is **crowdfunding**, in which individuals come together on the Internet to provide funding that will support others in an endeavor. **Figure 11-28** gives an example of a crowdfunding project on GoFundMe. Other popular crowdfunding sites include Indiegogo and Crowdfunder. Kickstarter specializes in funding creative projects such as those in design, music, and publishing.

Figure 11-28: Crowdfunding on GoFundMe

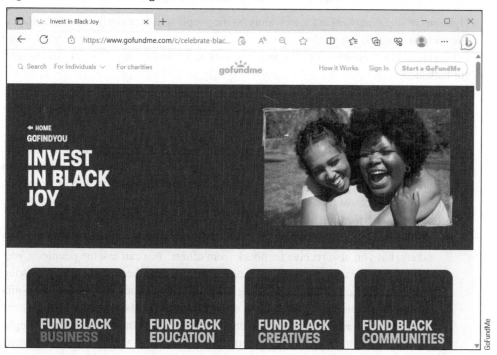

Negative Effects of Social Media
While social media has allowed people to communicate in unprecedented ways, it also entails risks.

- **Inaccurate information:** Not all the information on social media is current or correct. While traditional news outlets have standard procedures for verifying the news they publish, social media sites generally let anyone post ideas, information, points of view, and instructions, without anyone else verifying it. Some people intentionally release inaccurate information, called **disinformation**, to influence or harm the reputation of others, especially in a highly charged political environment, with potentially worldwide implications. The recent rise of "fake news" shows how inaccurate information can be used to influence and manipulate people.

- **Scams:** Unscrupulous people often use social media to try to take advantage of others for their own gain. They might seed websites with malware that will try to gather personal information on your computer, such as your passwords or bank account information. Predators with fake profiles on social networking sites might take advantage of legitimate users.

- **Technology addiction:** Some technology users become obsessed with computers, mobile devices, and the Internet, and might feel great anxiety if they are not connected using a device. They might choose interactive technology over interaction with people, even if friends or family are present. Technology might take over someone's entire social life. Addiction is a growing health problem, but it can be treated through therapy and support groups.

- **Technology overload:** People suffering from technology overload feel stressed and overwhelmed with the amount of technology they need to use. Both addiction and overload can have a negative impact on work and relationships.

Evaluate Pros and Cons of Social Networking

Opinions of social networking vary widely: some people use it regularly and can't imagine life without it; others are suspicious and avoid it completely. What are the effects of social networking? Is it a positive force in people's lives or a negative one? You can find support for both sides.

Positive Effects of Social Networking   Social networking offers many benefits to individuals, businesses, and other organizations.

- **Social connections:** Social networking is an efficient way to stay in touch with family, close friends, and acquaintances. You can share life details using status updates to keep others posted on what you're doing, including important events, opinions, pictures, and stories. You can share links to news sources. Many people use social networking to revive relationships with people from their past.

- **Interactivity:** Not only does social networking let you share your information with others, but you also receive feedback from others. You can ask the people in your network for ideas and information, and converse with them about proposed solutions to problems. Social networking tools let you flag topic categories and notify others when you post. You can join **online communities**, groups of people who share a particular background or interest and interact on the Internet. For example, you might join a Facebook group centered on wildlife in your state or area, where users contribute pictures of animals that other wildlife lovers in your area would appreciate. Whether you're in a remote location, or away from others due to illness or other circumstances, the interactive features of social networking can help you feel connected to, and less isolated from, the world.

- **Career growth:** In the same way that networking with others over the phone or in person can help you get a job, social networking on the Internet can help you grow professionally. Various surveys have found that nearly all recruiters use social media to find qualified candidates or to research candidates. You can use a LinkedIn or AngelList profile to post your resume, and then use its tools to develop extensive contacts in your field of expertise and be informed of new job opportunities. Sites like CareerBuilder and Monster can help you learn about careers and find jobs (**Figure 11-29**). You can like or follow any companies that interest you and learn about their products and available job openings. Participating in forums can establish you as an informed resource in your field. Following a company's social media posts will keep you informed on hiring trends.

- **Immediacy:** Social networking lets you share information instantaneously. With one mouse click, you can communicate with one or a thousand people and receive feedback just as quickly.

- **Information control:** Using social networking to stay in touch doesn't always mean your life is an open book. Smart users control what they share with others by using privacy settings in social networking programs. For example, on the Privacy Settings page on Facebook, you can choose who can see your posts, who can tag you, and who can send you friend requests (**Figure 11-30**).

- **Businesses networking:** Businesses use social networking to promote their products and services. They count on people to "check in" at the business's location to promote their museum, activity, restaurant, hotel, or other venue. Businesses can communicate easily with customers and receive their reactions. Newspapers and news programs use social networking to post breaking news and receive contributions of news items from their audience. Some businesses use live broadcasts on Facebook to display their expertise and educate their customers. For example, a research hospital might use a broadcast to explain the advantages of a new procedure or vaccine.

Figure 11-29: Building your career using social networking tools

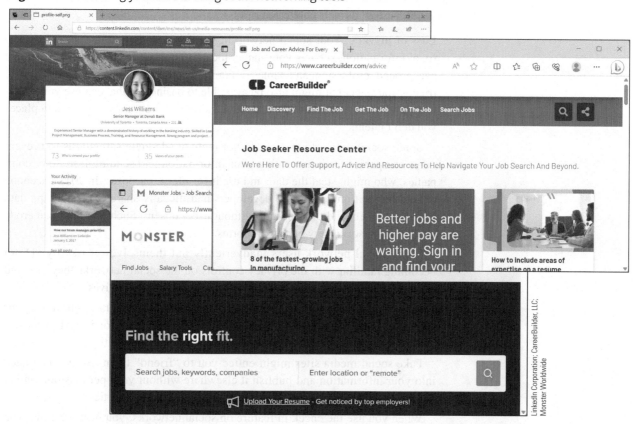

LinkedIn Corporation; CareerBuilder, LLC; Monster Worldwide

Figure 11-30: Facebook privacy settings

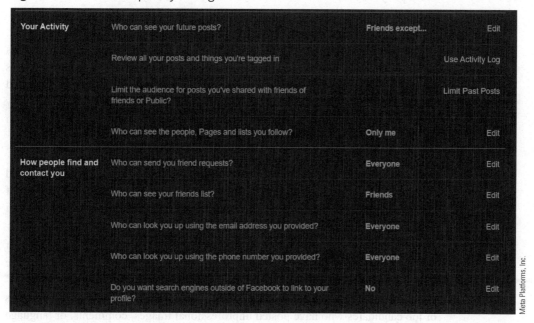

Meta Platforms, Inc.

If a business has a public relations issue, such as a product flaw or service outage, it can use social media to send immediate status updates and communicate the company's position. Social media gives the business an opportunity to inform its users directly and to help communicate its goals and control its image.

Negative Effects of Social Networking   Many people avoid social networking altogether because of its well-publicized risks.

- **Loss of privacy:** Your social networking profile might contain a wealth of personal information, such as your name, location, contact information, educational background, profession, and names of family members. These details are visible to friends you select but might also be available to businesses that can use your information to send you intrusive, targeted ads. Your photographs might reach places you don't intend.

  Some social networking sites do not include adequate safeguards to prevent other companies from harvesting your information and sending it to other companies, who might steal the data and use it for illegal purposes. In 2018 Facebook announced that one of its app developers had illegally shared personal app data with researchers and third parties without user consent. Such practices can erode confidence in social networking platforms.

  Some social network users inadvertently put themselves at risk by (1) not becoming familiar with the privacy controls on the social networks they use, and (2) **oversharing**, or sharing too much information about their lives.

- **Exposure to illegal and criminal activities:** Data harvesters might track your online activity and use the information for advertising or for illegal purposes. Hackers might use your personal information to steal your identity.

  Fake social media sites might entice you to "friend" them, so they can hack into your information and publish it elsewhere without your permission. Online acquaintances might misrepresent themselves using false identities.

  When you use the check in feature on social networks, you broadcast that you are not home at the same time you identify your whereabouts. And repeated use of such features might reveal patterns of your behavior without your intending it. This could put you, your loved ones, and your home at risk by anyone who wishes to do you harm.

- **Loss of information control:** Once your content is posted, you lose control of it. A photo or comment can make its way across the world and be replicated millions of times in a short period. Someone could send your personal details to audiences you might not have intended. For example, in 2009, several news agencies reported on an American couple who learned from friends traveling overseas that a family photo they had posted on social media was being used in a grocery store poster in Europe, without their knowledge or permission.

  Sharing inappropriate personal information can increase the risk that this information is misused in a public space and that it will impact your professional and personal relationships long into the future. Your **digital footprint**, the records of everything you do online, is nearly impossible to erase. Information about you can be forwarded, captured in a screenshot, or archived in a database.

- **Decreased employability:** Once an inappropriate photo or a thoughtless comment has been released on social networks, it can be difficult or impossible to undo the damage. Employers routinely search the web and social networks for job candidates' background information. Hiring managers might form unfavorable opinions of job candidates who have posted unprofessional images, comments, or language in the past. Recent industry surveys of human resource professionals reveal that two-thirds or more of employers use social networking sites to research job candidates, and over half of survey respondents report discovering content that caused them to eliminate a candidate from consideration for a job.

- **Downsides for businesses:** By having a robust social networking presence, many businesses inform everyone—including their competition—of their upcoming plans. Hiring notices on social networking sites can reveal potential, but unannounced, products to competitors. And, if a business has problems with products, services, or employees, social networking can magnify them by unleashing unflattering public responses.

Consider both the positive and negative effects of social networking, and determine what platforms and usage level are right for you, for your personal safety, privacy, and employability.

Module 11 Summary

Digital communication is the transmittal of data, instructions, and information from one computer or mobile device to another, often via the Internet. The principal types of digital communication include email, blogs, wikis, messaging, podcasts, video calls, online conferences, social media, social networks, and social curation tools. Following netiquette principles on the Internet, as well as guidelines for personal and professional social networking, professional messaging, and blogging, helps you to stay safe online, protect your reputation, and engage in meaningful, positive communication with others. Many types of digital communication, such as blogs, rely on written materials. Others, such as podcasts and online conferencing, are focused less on text and more on audio or visual media. Digital social networking connects people asynchronously, that is, participants can share information at different times instead of being online at the same time.

Developing competency in many digital communication tools is critical to many businesses and job roles, and plays an important role in creating many types of content. The skills required and the guidelines for how to use these tools can vary according to the industry. Some digital communication tools help people find and connect with others in various communities, industries, or interest areas. For instance, online social networks let you view profiles of other users and designate them as friends, or contacts. Social shopping networks can help you obtain needed items as well. Video conferences have become essential for holding meetings with management, staff, vendors, and customers at remote locations. Webinars are an efficient and low-cost way to help you develop almost any skill.

Nearly everyone feels the impact of digital communications in everyday life, with both positive and negative effects of social media and social networking. Positive effects include the ability to use social media to gather support for important causes. Negative effects include the quick spread of disinformation. There is support for both sides of the discussion about the effects of digital communications. Each person can determine what platforms and usage level is right for their situation, for their personal safety, privacy, and employability.

Review Questions

1. As you use digital communication, you can protect yourself, your family, and your career by following the rules of _____.

   a. netiquette
   b. social curation
   c. social media
   d. privacy

2. To remove older email messages from your mailbox without deleting them, you can _____ them.

   a. attach
   b. reply to
   c. courtesy copy
   d. archive

3. A town or municipality might inform its residents of an impending tornado using a(n) _____.

    a. podcast

    b. aggregator

    c. microblog

    d. media-sharing network

4. Which of the following statements is true for video conferences?

    a. They can only have two participants at one time.

    b. They may require you to download software and set up an account.

    c. They are the same as video chats.

    d. They do not allow participants to see or hear each other.

5. (True or False) Social curation sites restrict what sites and information users can access.

6. Which of the following groups might see an email you send directly to a coworker?

    a. Only the coworker

    b. Only your project team

    c. Your coworker and anyone specifically CC'd on the email

    d. The public

7. Typically, who edits wiki articles on public wiki sites?

    a. Anyone

    b. Registered users

    c. Wikipedia employees

    d. Government officials

8. To learn about a blogger's experience or skills related to the blog content, check their _____ page.

    a. About

    b. Home

    c. Settings

    d. Company

9. If you want a social media post to show up in user searches on that topic, you add a(n) _____ to the post.

    a. profile

    b. like

    c. hashtag

    d. comment

10. Which of the following apps is specific to Apple devices?

    a. FaceTime

    b. WhatsApp

    c. Skype

    d. Snapchat

11. (True or False) Social media can provide an effective option for accomplishing community change.

12. Which of the following is a positive effect of social networking?

    a. Communicating only with people you know

    b. Opportunities for career growth outside your local area

    c. Harvesting of personal information for marketing purposes

    d. One-way communication from businesses to customers

Discussion Questions

1. Identify one or two types of digital communication tools you have used in your schoolwork, your job, or your personal life, and explain how you have used these tools. How have these tools enabled communication that would have been difficult or impossible before these tools existed?

2. What are two or three differences you notice between the netiquette guidelines for personal social networking and professional social networking? Considering the career you would most like to pursue, discuss one or two ways social networking can help you promote yourself and achieve your professional goals.

3. Which digital communication tools can you use to find information when researching problems or tasks in your industry? How can you use digital communication tools to ensure you continue to learn about your profession and keep your knowledge up to date? How concerned are you about encountering inaccurate information through these digital communication tools?

4. Choose the three types of social media that you use the most. Approximately how many hours per day do you spend on them? What is the role they play in your life? What do you find are the advantages and disadvantages of using them? Do you believe they have an overall positive or an overall negative effect in your life?

Critical Thinking Activities

1. A group of your friends has recently started a small catering business. They know all about food, but not very much about digital communication. They have asked you what types of digital communications would best help them to build their brand and get customers. Discuss how they might use the following forms of digital communication for their catering business: Email, blogs, online conferences, and social networking.

2. You work as a hiring manager for your company, and you need to evaluate three qualified candidates for an accounting position. How can you use digital communication tools to further research each candidate? What kinds of information might you look for on each candidate that would differentiate one from the others as being the best fit for your company? What limitations do you think should be in place to prevent employers from digging into applicants' private lives?

3. You have applied for your dream job, and you just found out your first round of interviews will be conducted by video call. What differences should you anticipate for a video call interview compared to a traditional, face-to-face interview? What preparations should you make to give the best impression? What questions should you ask when scheduling the interview to understand the hiring manager's expectations for this interview? Do you think you are able to present yourself at your best in a virtual interview or in an in-person interview, and why do you think this format is optimal for you?

4. You volunteer for an organization that helps place rescued pets with homes. The organization has recently accepted more foster pets than usual, after a hurricane left several pets stranded and displaced when their families could not take them to shelters during the storm. You've decided to turn to social media for help. What tools will you use to garner community support and additional funding? How can you use social media and networking tools to help connect families with their rescued pets? What challenges do you anticipate in being able to meet your fundraising goals?

Apply Your Skills

Jordan Kinthe is a "digital nomad." Jordan works as a project coordinator for a nonprofit organization that partners with schools to help at-risk students and travels to various schools. When traveling, Jordan uses their laptop in shared office spaces, uses car- and bike-sharing when possible, participates in audio and video conferences with the nonprofit's home office, keeps up with the news using podcasts, and offers their condo as a short-term rental while they're on the road. Jordan contributes to a professional blog designed to help students and keeps in touch with family and friends using instant messaging. When communicating with digital tools, Jordan is careful to abide by the rules of netiquette to protect their professional and personal reputation.

Working in a small group or by yourself, complete the following:

1. Some of Jordan's video calls are conducted with coworkers, but in other calls, Jordan is interacting with customers and investors. Considering these high stakes, what are some considerations Jordan should keep in mind when needing to participate in video calls while traveling? How can Jordan ensure that each call provides a quality experience for the other party? Do you think a video call for work or school would be more stressful or less so than participating in an in-person meeting or class?

2. When Jordan rents out their condo, the renters must be able to contact Jordan easily and quickly when needed. What digital communication tools are best suited to ensuring Jordan is consistently available to respond to concerns from condo renters? Considering that some messages from renters are urgent while others are not so time sensitive, how many different avenues of communication should Jordan make available to their renters? In your chosen career, do you think it will be reasonable for you to be expected to respond to messages during off-times, or do you think this is an invasion into your personal time, and why do you think this way?

3. Jordan uses digital communication tools both personally and professionally when traveling. What precautions might Jordan take to ensure these different uses do not overlap in ways that could be problematic? Should Jordan use the same tools and accounts for all communications? Which types of tools might require different accounts? During one trip, one of Jordan's neighbors posts a comment to Jordan's work blog about problems with a renter at Jordan's condo. How should Jordan handle this conversation to address the problem with the renter while not allowing this personal issue to affect their professional reputation? Do you use the same tools and accounts for all communications, or do you separate them? Do you feel this arrangement is working for you or against you?

Digital Transformation

In This Module

- Explain the basic concepts of cloud computing
- Describe ways companies do business on the Internet
- Characterize new technologies
- Use AI technologies

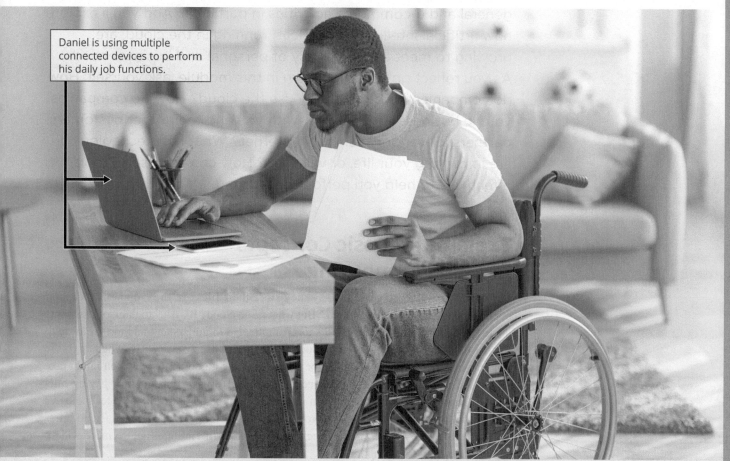

Daniel is using multiple connected devices to perform his daily job functions.

Prostock-studio/Shutterstock.com

Daniel Matheson has just been awarded an internship at the home office of a large floor covering manufacturer that embraces digital technology tools. The company sells its products nationwide to home improvement stores and also operates a local chain of direct-to-consumer stores. Both sales channels rely on e-commerce transactions through the company website. Daniel has learned the company uses several cloud-hosted applications, and a large part of his job will be helping with business-to-business (B2B) customer interactions through the website chat feature. As Daniel explores the company's website the night before his first day on the job, he finds that the website also includes a customer service chatbot.

Technology is changing the ways people live and the ways companies do business. The process of digital transformation encompasses all these changes. **Digital transformation** is the integration of digital technologies into business activities, organizational cultures, and customer experiences. Digital transformation is enabled by emerging technologies such as cloud computing, e-commerce, virtual reality, and artificial intelligence.

In this module, you will learn about several technologies that contribute to the process of digital transformation and how these technologies impact business in new and innovative ways. For example, understanding the basic characteristics of cloud computing will help you understand how the cloud is different from more traditional computing options. You'll see how cloud computing enables widespread advancements in e-business in general and e-commerce activities in particular. And you'll explore how artificial intelligence services, running in the cloud, are growing to meet a wide variety of personal and business needs. As you reflect on what you learn in this module, ask yourself: How do companies in your industry use the cloud? How do companies you do business with connect with you and their other customers, partners, or vendors using the Internet? What new technologies are impacting your life, or will soon? How can you use AI tools effectively to help you perform tasks more efficiently?

Explain the Basic Concepts of Cloud Computing

You've probably heard someone say they store their files "in the cloud" or that their application is running "on the cloud." But what is the cloud? It's easy to think of it as some abstract, undefined technology that's too complicated to understand and too far away to matter. In reality, you probably use cloud technologies nearly every day, whether you're doing homework for an online class or binge watching a good TV show. You might take advantage of cloud-based e-commerce by shopping for a birthday gift or paying bills online. Often, even the businesses you interact with in person rely on cloud technologies for security monitoring, transaction processing, and personnel management. Cloud infrastructure also makes other modern technologies like artificial intelligence more widely available for mass consumption.

The term cloud is often used to refer to services and resources accessed over a network. At a very basic level, cloud computing refers to providing and using technology tools, such as software or storage, via the Internet. While there are exceptions to this definition (for example, you could run cloud technologies on your own hardware in a **private cloud** that does not use the Internet), the most widespread use of cloud computing is the **public cloud**, where multiple customers use the same, Internet-connected cloud that is running on hardware owned by a cloud service provider. Additionally, each cloud provider runs their own cloud on their own hardware. In fact, it's common for businesses to use multiple clouds when they use cloud services from multiple cloud providers who each manage their own underlying cloud hardware. This section focuses on characteristics of the public cloud.

Identify Defining Characteristics of the Public Cloud

It's important to remember that the term "cloud computing" is not synonymous with "the Internet." They're two different things. The Internet is a tool that makes public cloud computing possible. In a public cloud, a person or business pays a fee to use someone else's hardware to:

- Perform computing tasks such as running an application
- Store files or databases
- Connect resources across geographical distances, even around the world

Think about how a website is built and managed. As illustrated in **Figure 12-1**, the files you create to build and run a website can be hosted on your own web server at your physical location where you live or work. This is called **on-premises** hosting when files, databases, or applications are hosted on your hardware in your office or data center. Alternatively, those files, databases, and relevant applications could be stored, managed, and run on cloud servers that are shared by many customers of a cloud provider who runs a large data center hosting many cloud services.

Figure 12-1: Web server on-premises vs. web server in the cloud

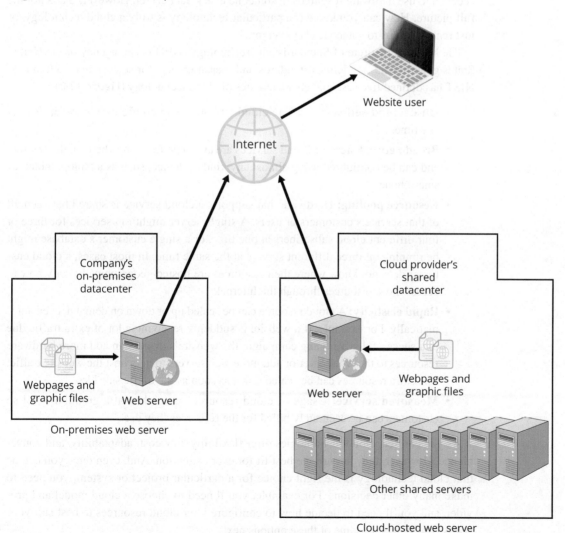

Figure 12-2: Five essential characteristics of cloud technology

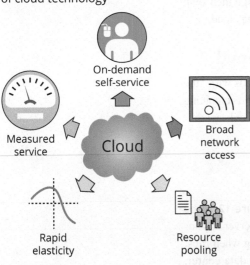

Both scenarios provide files that make a website work so users can access information from the company's website. However, the first scenario takes a more traditional approach in which the website owner must purchase, maintain, and run enough web servers to meet the demands of their website visitors even at the busiest of times. In the second scenario, the website owner can lease hardware resources from a cloud provider in a "pay-as-you-go" arrangement. The website owner, who in this situation is the cloud customer, pays the cloud provider a fee for the amount of hardware resources their website used that month. If the website had a lot of traffic, that cost is higher; in a slow month, the cost is lower. A business that hosts a website or other process in the cloud pays very low up-front cost, with monthly expenses varying according to each month's needs.

Why is this significant? In the past, only companies that could invest large amounts of money up front for expensive hardware could reasonably run popular websites to support their businesses. By using cloud resources, small startups with very little capital can create innovative websites that support a lot of traffic from customers as quickly as demand increases. Technology expenses for these startups will grow as the business grows. In many ways, cloud technology levels the playing field so that small, creative businesses can successfully compete with large corporations.

The Internet makes public cloud computing possible by allowing cloud customers to access and use hardware resources in someone else's data center. However, that's not the full picture. How can you know if a particular technology is truly a cloud technology, or just remote access to someone else's servers?

The National Institute of Standards and Technology (NIST) is an agency of the United States government that defines standards and measurements for science and technology. NIST has defined five essential characteristics of cloud technology (**Figure 12-2**):

- **On-demand self-service:** The cloud customer can configure cloud services at any time.
- **Broad network access:** Cloud services are available from anywhere on the Internet and can be configured using almost any kind of device, such as a laptop, tablet, or smartphone.
- **Resource pooling:** Hardware that supports a cloud service is shared between all of that service's customers or users. A single server might run services for three or four different cloud subscribers at one time, or a single customer's database might be running on three different servers at the same time. In most cases, a cloud customer does not know where their resources are hosted geographically, only how to access those resources through the Internet.
- **Rapid elasticity:** A cloud resource can be scaled up or down on demand, even automatically. For example, if a website is suddenly receiving a lot of extra traffic due to a successful advertising campaign, the website's owner can add more hardware resources to the web server or add more web servers to help host the website traffic. The extra resources can be scaled down as soon as the traffic subsides.
- **Measured service:** Usage of cloud resources is tracked at a granular level so customers can be accurately billed for the resources they use.

As you can see, cloud technologies offer flexibility, low cost, adaptability, and convenience. However, they are not the best fit for every situation. And, even once you decide that cloud technology is the right choice for a particular project or system, you need to make many other decisions. For example, you'll need to choose a cloud model and provider, and you'll need to decide how to configure your cloud resources to best suit your needs. You'll explore some of these options next.

Compare Common Cloud Models

In public cloud computing, functions and resources that are normally provided by servers on a local network are instead provided by one or more large data centers via the Internet (**Figure 12-3**). Companies can even spread their resources across many cloud hosting data centers around the world, which provides a better experience for their own customers. For example, a web site might be hosted on lots of web servers located in different countries, and each collection of web site files in each location might include different languages, cultures, or other variations appropriate to the surrounding region. Users within each country, then, don't have to wait as long for data to reach them from the closest web server, and that data might be customized to those customers' needs and interests, even though all customers from all regions enter the same web site address to reach the site. This design is called **distributed computing**, which is a way to design a system so various components run on multiple computers but work together as a single system. With the cloud, distributed computing can spread these components around any geographic area—even around the world—to place data and compute processes closer to the users who need them.

A function or resource provided through a cloud service is sometimes referred to with the phrase, "as a service." For example, if you run a cloud-hosted firewall application for your remote office locations or for your work-from-home employees, this cloud service might be called a Firewall as a Service (FWaaS). If you run a database using cloud-hosted technology, it might be referred to as a Database as a Service (DBaaS). Even some hackers have jumped on the -aaS bandwagon and offer Ransomware as a Service (RaaS)!

Cloud services generally can be categorized according to the service's role. Three common categories are:

- **Software as a Service (SaaS):** Cloud consumers most commonly interact with SaaS (pronounced *sass*), also called web apps, which is software that is distributed online and sometimes costs a monthly subscription or an annual fee to use. Google Docs is an excellent example. Dropbox, an online file storage app, and Zoom, an online conference call app, are also popular examples of SaaS.

Figure 12-3: The cloud runs on many large data centers throughout the world

Frame Stock Footage/Shutterstock.com

Figure 12-4: Cloud service categories and typical users for each category

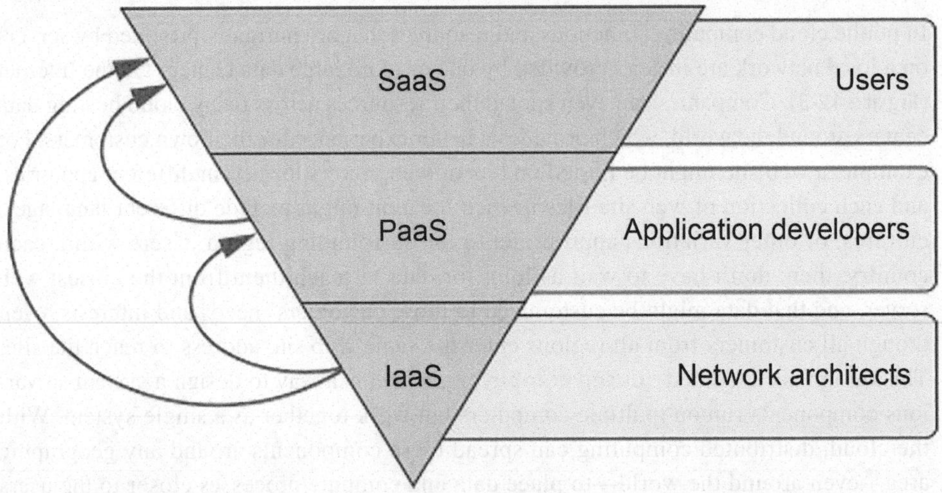

- **Platform as a Service (PaaS):** PaaS (pronounced *paz*) provides a platform from which cloud customers can run their own applications without having to manage underlying servers. For example, a company can run a website on a cloud service that does not require configuration of a web server. This is especially helpful with complex websites, such as those that allow for buying and selling online.
- **Infrastructure as a Service (IaaS):** IaaS (pronounced *i-az*) is a type of cloud service that allows cloud customers (usually businesses) to configure cloud-based networking infrastructure the way they want, such as routing, servers, operating systems, storage spaces, and security settings. While the customer can't configure the physical hardware that supports the cloud services, the customer does have much deeper control on how the cloud infrastructure is configured than with other cloud models. Working with IaaS services typically requires a lot more technical expertise than most other types of cloud services.

A major element distinguishing each of these cloud service models is the type of customer that typically uses these services. **Figure 12-4** compares the distribution of customers across all three categories, with users generally interacting with SaaS cloud services, application developers often needing PaaS services, and network architects incorporating IaaS services into their cloud-hosted networks.

Identify Major Cloud Providers and Cloud Risks

A handful of companies have emerged as leaders in the cloud provider market. Amazon Web Services (AWS) is a subsidiary of Amazon that is currently at the top of the pile. Other leading providers of PaaS and IaaS services include Microsoft Azure, Google Cloud Platform, IBM Cloud, and China's Alibaba Cloud. Leading SaaS providers include Salesforce, which provides companies with **customer relationship management (CRM)**, a set of services that help companies customize their interactions with customers through sales, marketing, communications, and customer loyalty programs (**Figure 12-5**), and Oracle, a market-leading provider of database management services.

You're likely to encounter cloud technology when you use free web-based services like email or cloud storage. For example, Google offers Gmail for free, and Microsoft offers free Microsoft accounts that use the outlook.com or live.com addresses. These email services are usually hosted in a cloud and are accessed over the Internet, meaning you can use nearly any Internet-connected computer to access your email.

Figure 12-5: Features of customer relationship management (CRM) systems

CUSTOMER LOYALTY   SERVICE   SALES   MARKETING   COMMUNICATION   DATABASE

Trueffelpix/Shutterstock.com

Many email accounts—even free ones—come with a certain amount of reserved cloud storage space. For example, at the time of this writing, creating a Google Account for your Gmail gives you a free 15 GB of storage space for your Drive, Gmail, and Photos storage. When you save files to your Drive folders over the Internet, you can access those files from any computer or mobile device with an Internet connection if you sign into your Google Account on that device. You can also share those files with other people, even allowing them to work on the files at the same time. Similar services include Microsoft's OneDrive and Apple's iCloud. Some cloud storage providers offer storage as a standalone service. Examples include Dropbox, Box, and Amazon Photos (which includes free photo storage for Amazon Prime members).

While free storage sounds great and has a lot of advantages, you should be aware of the risks. Storing your files on someone else's servers means you don't have to provide your own hardware for saving that data. However, it also means you don't have full control over where that data is located, who has access to it, and what happens if something goes wrong or if the storage service is canceled. The following list explores why these issues could be important to you:

- Especially in the workplace, you'll find that a lot of data is protected by law. For example, medical data is protected by the Health Insurance Portability and Accountability Act (HIPAA). Some of these laws require that data be physically stored within state borders or within the company's or customer's own country. When you store data in the cloud, you typically have no way of knowing where that data is saved geographically, which means you might not be in compliance with state or federal laws. With especially sensitive data (such as medical or financial data), cloud storage isn't always a reasonable option.

- When data is stored on your own computer, you have physical control over who can access your device and hence, your data. When you store data across the Internet, you're trusting that the cloud storage provider is protecting your data and the servers where that data is stored. Most reputable cloud companies do a good job of this, and in fact, many cloud storage services provide better security against ransomware or physical attacks than home or small business users can do for themselves. Still, you might want to encrypt sensitive data yourself before you upload it to cloud storage, or keep that data on-premises. While encryption adds a reassuring layer of protection, it also adds complexity and might prevent you from being able to use your data while it's still in the cloud.

- Although cloud storage providers generally offer reliable security for data on their servers, most cloud storage services do not include free backup. In other words, if something happens to their system where they lose data or their servers go down, you might lose files or access to your files in the process. Many users rely on cloud storage as their primary file storage solution without backing up that data anywhere else. Duplicating important files across at least two or three locations helps ensure you'll always be able to get to your data when you need it.

Describe Ways Companies Do Business on the Internet

Now that you understand what cloud computing is, you're ready to learn more about some of the ways businesses use cloud technologies and the Internet to conduct business on a day-to-day basis.

Explain How Cloud Services Are Used in the Workplace

IT professionals are rethinking how data centers are structured and how best to incorporate cloud technologies into their work processes. Cloud computing affects many non-technical job roles as well. For example, people in a variety of fields, from marketing to certain types of health care, can perform their work remotely rather than commuting to an office or facility. With communication software such as video conferencing applications, productivity software that can be run on any computer with an Internet connection (**Figure 12-6**), and data access provided by global cloud storage, many workers can telecommute occasionally or regularly. Companies can also hire qualified employees or consultants from anywhere in the world without requiring geographical proximity.

Many companies use SaaS products in their normal business processes. For example, sales representatives might track customer interactions in a web-based customer relationship management (CRM) application. A company's human resources department might track employee benefits, training, or hours worked in a SaaS system. An accountant might file taxes using an online portal, or a marketing team might use a web-based video conferencing app to collaborate with consultants across town or around the globe.

Figure 12-6: Web apps can run on many different kinds of devices

fizkes/Shutterstock.com

If you work for a company that uses cloud services (which is likely), you might use cloud-hosted resources to complete many tasks for your job:

- Track your work schedule and hours worked
- Make changes to your tax withholdings or benefits disbursements
- Share files with colleagues at your own or partner companies
- Collaborate with teammates on projects, deadlines, and events
- Complete on-the-job training customized for your job role
- Access your customized workstation from any computer
- Use robust applications on your own computer without having to install expensive software
- Work with expansive company data from across multiple departments
- Keep a more flexible work schedule that better fits your lifestyle

All these examples show how companies can use the Internet to conduct **e-business**, which is any kind of business activity conducted online. Some e-business processes might use cloud-hosted resources, such as a video conferencing web app. Other e-business activities rely on websites, Internet-based communications (such as email), or virtual private network (VPN) connections to remote resources. Note that, while e-business *can* use cloud-hosted resources such as a SaaS product running in a public cloud, it doesn't have to. So long as the activity relies on a computer network of some kind (especially the Internet), the activity is classified as e-business.

A specific type of e-business is e-commerce, where buy and sell transactions are conducted on an electronic network such as the Internet. Most companies these days have reached the conclusion that e-commerce is a necessary component to their overall business strategy. Modern consumers expect to be able to interact with a company and complete a transaction entirely over the Internet if they choose to do so. And major distributors have developed impressively efficient methods of delivering purchased goods to the consumer's doorstep. In **Figure 12-7**, conveyor belts in one of Amazon's massive fulfillment centers are used to ship products 22 hours a day (with two hours of daily downtime for maintenance).

Most physical stores are associated with an e-commerce website, and many retailers exist entirely online. Some of these companies were built with the intention of functioning entirely over the Internet while other companies have closed or are in the process of closing their physical stores in favor of their online presence. Interestingly, however, some Internet-native stores, such as Amazon, are migrating toward opening and maintaining

Figure 12-7: Conveyor belts sorting packages at an Amazon fulfillment center

Jill West

Figure 12-8: Omnichannel marketing methods of interacting with potential customers

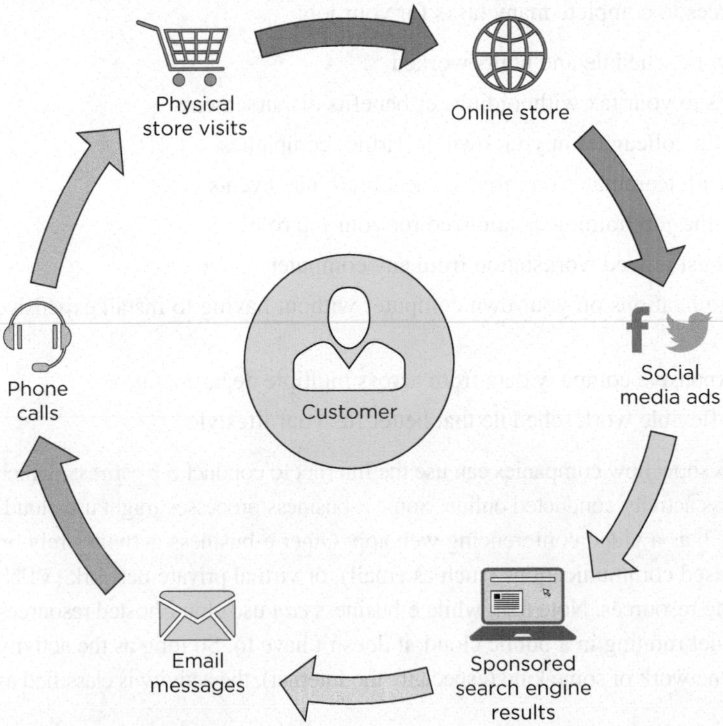

physical stores. While most of their customers will continue to prefer online shopping, many companies are finding that customers appreciate the option to visit a physical store and personally examine a product before buying it. These companies are shifting their strategy to use physical stores as acquisition- and marketing-opportunities for building customer relationships rather than primarily as distribution centers.

Retailers increasingly use multiple types of contact, such as an online store and a physical store, to reach a customer, which is considered an **omnichannel** strategy. This strategy typically includes targeted ads on social media, paid results on search engines, or contacts by email or phone (**Figure 12-8**). Have you ever googled a product on your laptop, and then, over the next few days, noticed several ads for that item appear on your favorite social media sites when you're browsing on your phone? This is omnichannel marketing at work.

A well-executed omnichannel strategy tracks a potential customer through several points of contact, such as a Google search, a "like" on Facebook, a product search on the retailer's app, or a visit to a physical store (possibly detected by the proximity of the customer's phone to the store's location). All these contacts track the progress of the customer's relationship with the company, detecting cues such as what size or color of item the customer likes or whether the customer might want to finance their purchase. At each point in the process, the company attempts to match the customer's specific interests and emphasize its **unique selling proposition (USP)**, which is a statement about how the company and its products are different and better than the competition's.

Compare Types of E-commerce Platforms

E-commerce generally revolves around three types of transactions:

- **Business-to-consumer (B2C):** Involves the sale of goods and services to the general public
- **Consumer-to-consumer (C2C):** Occurs when one consumer sells directly to another
- **Business-to-business (B2B):** Consists of businesses providing goods and services to other businesses

While typical consumers are probably most familiar with B2C transactions, both C2C and B2B e-commerce drive a major percentage of global commercial activity. C2C e-commerce transactions are represented by sites such as eBay or Facebook Marketplace, where users can post their own items for sale to other users. B2B transactions occur at several points along the supply chain, from the purchase of raw materials by a manufacturer to the sale of finished products to retailers. Shipping companies, vendor services, and warehousing processes all play significant roles in a complex supply chain, requiring transactions between businesses at every step. Many of these transactions today occur through an e-commerce service to maximize efficiency.

A variety of e-commerce platforms have emerged to meet rising demand:

- **Online storefront:** A retailer can create their own website or smartphone app for buying and selling products or services. The website or app includes a shopping cart and can receive payments of some kind. These online storefronts commonly incorporate existing e-commerce software (usually a PaaS offering, not SaaS) to provide the transaction processing components of the website instead of building these components from scratch. For example, Adobe Commerce is a free and very popular e-commerce solution incorporated into successful websites owned by companies such as Krispy Kreme, T-Mobile, and Coca-Cola.

- **Online marketplace:** Instead of building their own website, many retailers choose to join an online marketplace. In many cases, the online marketplace doesn't sell its own inventory, but provides a virtual meeting place for buyers and sellers. Etsy, eBay, and Amazon are all online marketplaces.

- **Social media:** In the past, social media sites such as Facebook and Instagram provided an opportunity for sellers to showcase their products or advertise their websites, with the actual sales transactions completed in some other way (through an e-commerce website or even in person). Today, many social media platforms include features that allow buyers and sellers to complete transactions directly within the social media site—for instance, Facebook Marketplace (**Figure 12-9**).

Figure 12-9: Buyers can pay for items directly on the Facebook Marketplace website

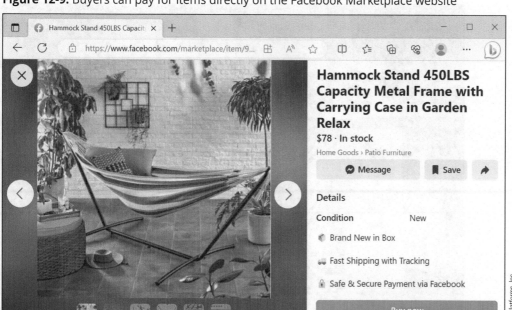

Meta Platforms, Inc.

Describe High-Growth Jobs in E-commerce Industries

As retailers grow into the expansive potential of the e-commerce economy, the workforce also benefits from expanded job opportunities. In the interest of responsibly managing costs, large online retailers and distributors often choose locations distant from large cities, thereby increasing employment opportunities for many disadvantaged populations and untapped job markets. Further, these positions generally pay well above minimum wage in addition to offering other worker benefits. The following is a list of high-growth occupations available within the e-commerce industry:

- **Customer service representatives:** Despite the self-service nature of e-commerce, customers still want an accessible point of contact with retailers to handle complaints, assist with orders, or provide additional information. Phone- and chat-based representatives provide personalized interactions with customers. These employees might specialize in particular services, such as order processing or technical support, or they might offer more generalized support to address whatever concern the customer raises. The retailer relies heavily on high-quality customer support to earn positive ratings and reviews from customers.

- **Shipping, receiving, and traffic clerks:** Distribution and fulfillment warehouses often require massive numbers of employees to process orders nearly 24 hours a day. Shipping, receiving, and traffic clerks help track shipments both into and out of the warehouse, checking for accuracy and ensuring timeliness.

- **Hand pickers and packagers:** Pickers often push carts throughout a warehouse, filling bins with items from the shelves to fill a few orders at a time. This process might be coordinated by a computer that intelligently determines which orders can be filled by a single picker while minimizing that person's travel time among the shelves. Amazon, for example, uses a random shelving system where items seem to be stored haphazardly throughout the warehouse instead of grouped by item or category (**Figure 12-10**). However, the computer knows where every item is located and will select specific items for the order that are in close proximity to each other. Packagers then take each order's items and prepare them for shipping. Amazon's computers tell packagers which size box to use and even cut the needed length of tape for that box.

Figure 12-10: Items on shelves at an Amazon fulfillment center

David Paul Morris/Bloomberg/Getty Images

Figure 12-11: Drone delivery territories will expand as laws adapt

Flystock/Shutterstock.com

- **Freight, stock, and material movers:** These workers help move large volumes of inventory as shipments arrive at or leave loading docks at the warehouse and as pallets of inventory need to be moved around within a distribution center. Forklift and other heavy machinery operators typically require special training and licensing.

- **Transport and delivery truck drivers:** As consumers increasingly rely on e-commerce, transport and delivery services must provide a more robust workforce to meet the rising demand. Some of the largest distributors or retailers are even developing their own delivery services, such as Amazon's last-mile delivery service and the emerging drone delivery technologies being explored by many retailers (**Figure 12-11**).

- **General and operations managers:** A warehouse manager and other management roles help in optimizing work schedules, overseeing operations processes, designing and enforcing policies, and generally supporting the on-site workforce.

- **Market research analysts and marketing specialists:** Not all e-commerce jobs are directly related to warehouse or distribution functions. Trained market analysts and specialists work to further evolve e-commerce marketing techniques. E-commerce opens expanded market opportunities that are no longer limited by geographical proximity.

- **Application and web developers:** Application and web developers are also seeing dramatic job growth in the e-commerce sector, developing both customer-facing and internal solutions that support e-commerce business processes.

Explain How to Build Trust through a Good E-commerce Website

As shoppers shift their buying habits to rely more heavily on e-commerce, retailers need to build relationships with their customers using channels that are unlike anything used in the past. Customers want a seamless experience, regardless of the device or other means of contact they use. They want convenient access at times that best suit their needs. They want easy access to the information required to determine whether a retailer is trustworthy and whether a product is what it seems to be. And they want the experience to be personalized to their interests and habits. The fact that shoppers are quick to abandon a website or items in their cart for a wide variety of reasons presents a challenge to retailers, forcing them to anticipate shopper needs at every step of the process.

Retailers use a variety of strategies and techniques to meet these shifting customer expectations:

- Post clear and well-lit product photos.
- List shipping and other add-on expenses on each product page.
- Add security seals and license badges.
- Extend customer service hours.
- Offer flexible return policies.
- Publish personalized information on the company's "About" page that shows the personality and passion of the company's team (**Figure 12-12**).

From this list, you can see a pattern emerging: A successful e-commerce website offers informative *content* that is relevant to site visitors, a sense of *community* to offer a personalized relationship with each customer, and effective *context* that adapts to each customer's preferences, location, and buying process. Collectively, this approach is sometimes called the 3 Cs of e-commerce.

E-commerce companies also build trust with customers by consistently complying with applicable laws, standards, and guidelines. For example, the major credit card companies Visa, MasterCard, Discover, and American Express developed a set of security standards, called the **Payment Card Industry Data Security Standard (PCI DSS)**, that applies to all merchants who use their services. These standards are enforced by the credit card companies themselves. Merchants are required to take specific measures to protect cardholder information, such as the credit card number and cardholder name. For example, cardholder data must be encrypted when it's being stored and also when it's being transmitted.

Figure 12-12: A personal statement appeals to a company's market

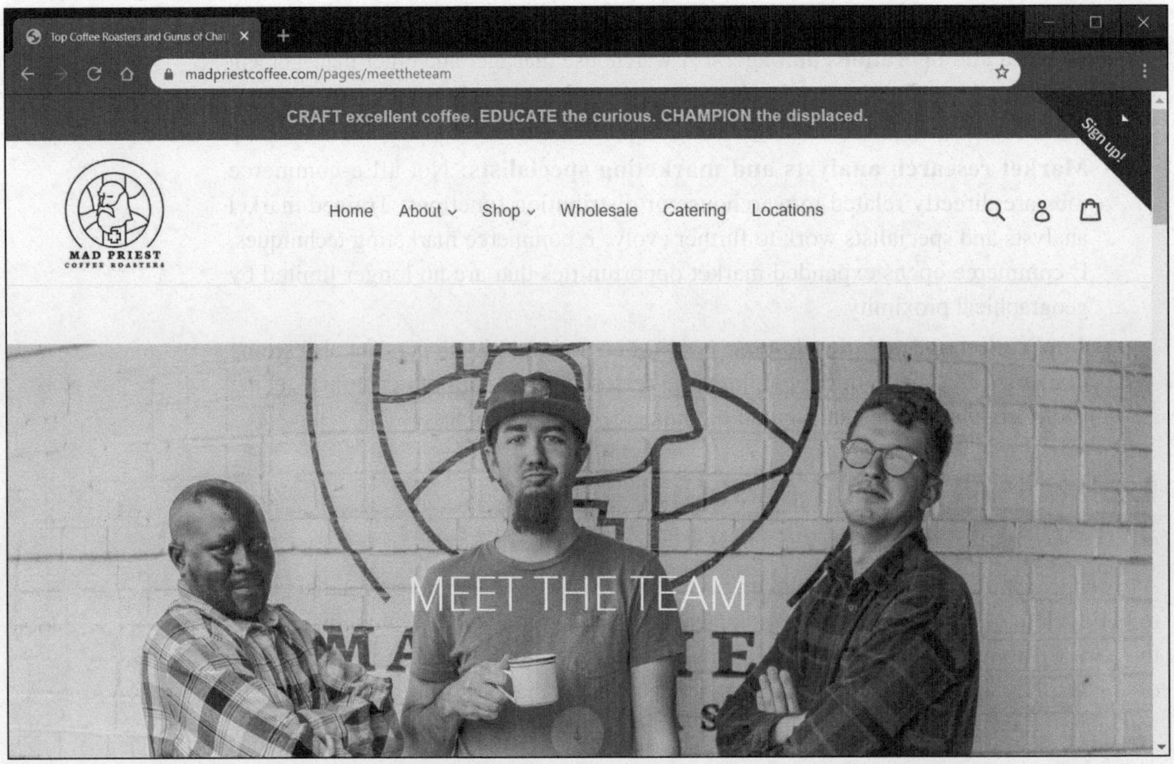

Mad Priest Coffee

Many other PCI DSS requirements are applied to participating merchants according to the number of transactions they process each year. While large companies must comply with extensive and very strict regulations, even the smallest business with only a handful of transactions a year must maintain compliance with the regulations that apply to them. Basically, if the business has any access to cardholder data, even if it's only for a few transactions, the business is subject to PCI compliance standards.

This is one area where relying on cloud technologies can be particularly beneficial to an e-commerce company. Businesses that use a SaaS e-commerce platform typically benefit from built-in PCI compliance configurations and capabilities.

Characterize New Technologies

The idea of virtual reality started with early science fiction stories, such as the holodecks on the sci-fi series Star Trek, where people could bring their imaginary worlds to virtual life. When you think of robots and artificial intelligence (AI), perhaps heroes in the Star Wars films asking droids for critical information during a hyper-space mission come to mind. While today's robots and AI-powered applications are not yet that advanced, these technologies can already perform some impressive tasks and processes.

Explain the Impact of Virtual Reality and Robotics

Virtual reality (VR) is the use of computers to simulate a real or imagined environment that appears as a three-dimensional (3-D) space. These simulations use 3-D images that enable users to explore and have a sensory experience through visual and sound effects. You can use VR in gaming to interact with a virtual environment and digital beings. **Augmented reality (AR)** is a type of VR that uses an image of an actual place or thing and adds digital information to it. A photo of a location overlaid with information about places of interest (**Figure 12-13**) or a football broadcast that shows a first-down marker are examples of AR.

Although VR developers work mostly with digital graphics and animation, they also use AI when creating virtual characters that make decisions and change their behavior based on interactions with others. A VR developer can create an entire 3-D environment that contains infinite space and depth.

Figure 12-13: Augmented reality combines real images with digital information

Figure 12-14: Robot used to detect weeds and spray chemicals

Zapp2Photo/Shutterstock.com

Robotics is the science that combines engineering and technology to create and program robots. Robots are useful in situations where it is impractical, dangerous, or inconvenient to use a human, such as cleanup of hazardous waste and materials, domestic uses such as vacuuming, and agricultural and manufacturing uses (**Figure 12-14**).

Robots can also assist surgeons. A robotic arm or instrument can be more precise, flexible, and controlled than a human hand. 3-D cameras enable the surgeon to see inside the body. Robotic surgeries often take less time to heal and can reduce risk of infection because they require a smaller incision site. However, robots still require a surgeon to control and direct the operation. Surgeons must be trained not only medically, but also in how to manipulate the robot.

Self-driving cars use cameras to change speed in response to traffic. They rely on GPS to navigate the best and fastest route. The proponents say that self-driving cars reduce dangers related to human error. One of the biggest concerns about self-driving cars, however, is that they might contribute to accidents caused by distracted driving when the human drivers rely too heavily on the car's technology instead of paying attention to quickly changing traffic conditions.

Similar to gaming uses, science and medicine use VR for training and research. For example, medical students can use VR to practice their emergency medicine skills. NASA uses VR to simulate space flight and the environments of other planets. Other commercial uses include enabling potential home buyers to move through a home's various rooms, or construction companies to show a preview of the completed building (**Figure 12-15**).

List Ways People Use Artificial Intelligence (AI) Technology

Artificial intelligence (AI) technology, which uses logic and prior experience to simulate human intelligence, has a variety of applications, such as speech recognition, virtual reality, logical reasoning, and creative responses. Computers with AI can collect information to make decisions, reach conclusions, and combine information in new ways, which is a form of learning.

Figure 12-15: 3-D modeling is used to build VR environments

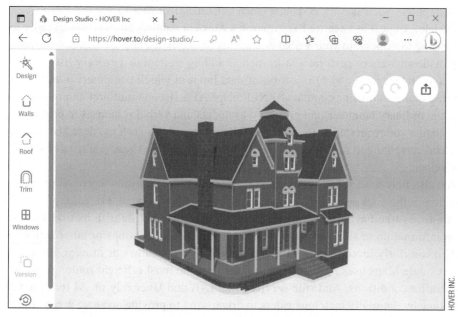

Computers with AI use machine intelligence rather than human intelligence to make decisions. The goal in creating AI devices is to minimize the gap between what a machine can do and what a human can do. Programmers train the computer to act when presented with certain scenarios by instructing the computer that "if *X* happens, then do *Y*."

You might have interacted with AI technology when contacting a website's customer service using a **chatbot** feature on a website or an app (**Figure 12-16**). While you can usually detect the robotic nature of AI's communications, today's AI-powered chatbots are learning to understand and use increasingly natural sounding language. This is accomplished through machine learning (ML), where the AI application uses statistics to learn from new data, identify patterns, and make decisions to progressively improve its performance. This learning process can be conducted by the software itself with little or no human intervention.

Figure 12-16: A chatbot app can provide AI-powered customer support

You might also have used AI technology when interacting with a digital assistant app on your phone (such as Siri), computer (such as Cortana), or smart speaker (such as Alexa or Google). **Digital assistants** like Amazon's Alexa or Apple's Siri use natural language processing to respond to your verbal commands or questions, and use search technology to provide answers or perform a task, such as adding an item to a grocery list. **Natural language processing (NLP)** is a form of data input in which computers interpret and digitize spoken words or commands. NLP helps AI assistants interpret commands you speak in ordinary language and give easy-to-understand verbal responses to provide the information you requested or to ask for additional input. Apps such as Alexa and Siri rely on cloud computing to function. Essentially, when you talk to Alexa, you're talking to the AWS cloud.

You also may have relied on AI technologies in many situations where AI processes function in the background of an application or website service. For example, social media feeds like Facebook's newsfeed run on AI-powered algorithms to determine what information to show you based on your previous interactions or other activities. Netflix similarly incorporates AI algorithms to suggest shows or movies you might like. Google Maps uses AI functions to determine the most efficient route, given current traffic conditions. And ride services like Lyft and Uber rely on AI to minimize wait time by optimally matching riders to drivers and to provide accurate arrival times. Many schools incorporate an AI-powered tool to detect plagiarism, and email providers use AI to continually improve their spam filters and adapt to shifting tactics used by spammers.

More recently, AI tools that generate text or images have risen in accessibility, popularity, and capabilities. Perhaps you have experimented with ChatGPT or Bing Chat, which are generative AI tools that respond to written prompts by generating text. For example, you could ask ChatGPT to write a cover letter for your resume. Although ChatGPT can write a professional-sounding letter, you would still need to edit the letter so it is more personal and more accurate. For example, you might need to incorporate your own personality, writing style, and relevant facts and context so the letter sounds like you and addresses specific details.

Figure 12-17: AI generated art sometimes gets details wrong

Bing Image Creator

Other generative AI tools, such as DALL-E or Bing Image Creator, can create images. Each image is unique; however, the AI tools do not yet fully understand concrete reality. And so AI-generated images often lack coherency or consistency. For example, it is not unusual for an AI generated image of a person to contain extra fingers or an extra arm, or an AI generated image of flowers to show blooms unattached to stems. **Figure 12-17** provides an example of AI-generated art resulting from the prompt, "border collie puppy with her paws up on a park bench, street art style, like dieselpunk." The details on the puppy aren't quite right, and the puppy has an extra front paw.

Practical Uses of AI   Some of the practical uses of AI include strategic gaming, military simulations, statistical predictions, and self-driving cars. For example, meteorologists use AI to analyze weather data patterns to create a list of possible outcomes for an upcoming weather event. The predictions made by the AI software then need to be interpreted, reviewed, and prioritized by people.

Some of the ways you might interact with AI on a daily basis include:

- **Virtual assistants:** Use voice recognition and search engines to answer, react, or reply to user requests.

- **Social media and online ads:** Track your data, such as websites visited, and provide ads targeted to your personal interests.

- **Video games:** Provide information to your virtual opponents based on your skill level and past actions.

- **Music and media streaming services:** Recommend options based on your past listening and viewing choices.

- **Smart cars:** Automate many driving tasks such as managing speed, steering to stay in a single lane of traffic, and avoiding collisions.

- **Navigation apps:** Provide you with information about traffic and the best routes, along with preferred stops along your way.

- **Security features:** Require your fingerprint to access your phone, or use facial recognition and motion-detection cameras that alert you to unusual or unauthorized visitors.

AI in the Workplace   Knowing what you might expect as you enter or advance in your chosen career can better prepare you to use AI technologies effectively at work. The following list explores some of the forms of AI you might need to interact with on the job:

- IoT and many other systems (such as customer management or inventory management systems) generate massive amounts of data. AI can help manage that data and detect patterns that improve business processes and answer questions related to strategic planning, a function called **data analytics**. For example, Coca-Cola collects sensor data from many of their vending machines around the world to monitor consumer interest, preferences, and flavor trends, such as the Freestyle machine (**Figure 12-18**) where consumers create their own flavor combinations. AI analyzes

Figure 12-18: Combining IoT and data analytics helps companies develop new offerings

Antonello Marangi/Shutterstock.com

the anonymous data gathered from these vending machine interactions to help the company develop new marketing strategies and track developing consumer interests. Similarly, credit card and insurance companies use AI to analyze vast data stores to detect signs of fraud. For example, many of these systems are looking for anomalies that show unexpected variations in a customer's spending habits. These anomalies might indicate someone other than the authorized card owner is using the credit account information. Many times, these automatic systems can flag suspicious activity within seconds of when the fraudulent transaction is attempted, prevent the transaction from being completed, and text the card owner to confirm whether the transaction is legitimate.

- **Robotic process automation (RPA)** refers to automatic processes running on servers that input or transfer data, such as transferring customer data from a call center system to a customer management system, updating records when a credit card is replaced, and synchronizing billing processes across multiple systems and document types.

- AI-powered chatbots can provide 24-hour support to customers, employees, and other decision makers. Intelligent chatbots serve a variety of purposes, such as FAQ (frequently asked questions) bots to answer common questions about typical business processes (like employee benefits or HR policies), conversational bots that can provide problem-solving support and assist in finding a product or service, and transactional bots that assist with making purchases and payments or returning items. A high percentage of chatbots are designed to support employees and management rather than customers. As an employee, you can become more productive in your job if you understand some basics about how AI systems work. As a customer, you can get the information you need more quickly if you know how to communicate with AI systems.

AI Training   AI relies on a variety of technologies that can be combined to create AI systems that meet specific needs (**Figure 12-19**).

One of the defining characteristics of AI is that it learns and improves over time. It somewhat simulates human intelligence to one degree or another in the way it absorbs new data and looks for patterns in the data that the system can use to generate insights, make decisions, or improve the system's own performance.

How does this learning happen? An AI system needs the input of a collection of data, called a **dataset**, to learn from. For example, if you're teaching an AI system how to identify the make and model of vehicles on a video stream (**Figure 12-20**), you'll need to give the system some videos to practice on.

In the past, programming relied on predictable inputs that resulted in predictable outputs. Today's developers are designing machines that seem to think for themselves, that produce output their users didn't necessarily expect. To do this, they use **artificial neural networks (ANNs)**, which are networks of processors that function similarly to the human brain by applying multiple layers of deep learning processes in a mesh network of signals (**Figure 12-21**). These kinds of processes require huge amounts of computing power and resources. The extensive hardware used to run cloud technologies are often required to develop and support AI services, and to transmit and host the massive amounts of data used by AI.

Figure 12-19: Many technologies contribute to a functioning AI system

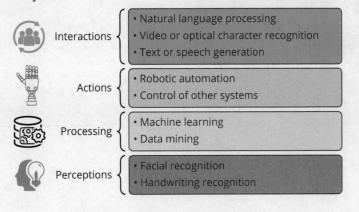

Interactions
- Natural language processing
- Video or optical character recognition
- Text or speech generation

Actions
- Robotic automation
- Control of other systems

Processing
- Machine learning
- Data mining

Perceptions
- Facial recognition
- Handwriting recognition

Figure 12-20: AI identifies and categorizes vehicles in a live video stream

Zapp2Photo/Shutterstock.com

Figure 12-21: Deep learning allows for pattern recognition

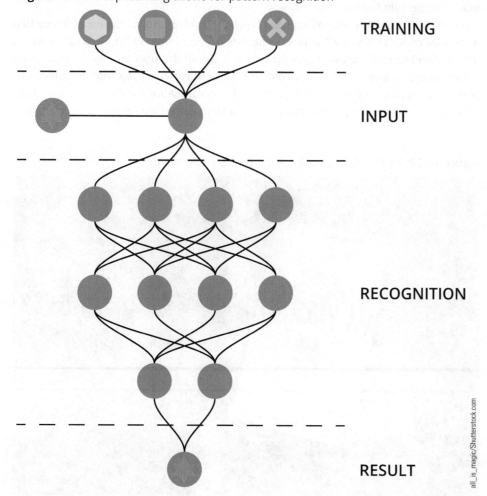

TRAINING

INPUT

RECOGNITION

RESULT

all_is_magic/Shutterstock.com

Use AI Technologies

AI is an integral part of most people's daily technological lives. Many of these processes happen in the background and don't require special knowledge on the part of the user. However, it's helpful to have a basic understanding of AI and its underlying technologies, particularly when you are using AI-controlled smart devices or using AI in the workplace.

Describe How AI Supports Smart Devices and the Internet of Things

When people think of AI today, they often think of smart home devices, such as smart locks, smart plugs, or smart security systems. These smart devices are considered "smart" because they can be programmed to make decisions without direct human intervention. For example, a smart lock on your front door (**Figure 12-22**) can be programmed to detect the presence of your phone as you walk up to your house and automatically unlock your door for you. A smart thermostat can detect when you're on your way home and turn on the heat. A smart coffee maker can be controlled by voice command. And a smart security system can alert you on your phone when it detects suspicious activity.

These items might be centrally controlled by a smart speaker that supports voice commands, such as Amazon's Echo device, a Google Home device, or Apple's HomePod speaker. In some cases, you can even adapt older devices to function as a smart device. For example, you might plug a standard coffee maker into a smart plug, or install a smart bulb in an existing light fixture.

AI's role in a smart home environment typically revolves around the user's interaction with voice commands as well as processing data collected from IoT devices (all of which rely on cloud services accessed over the Internet). Recall that natural language processing allows an application such as Alexa or Siri to understand your questions or commands, perform an appropriate action, and give a verbal confirmation or other response. Many smart devices also must process incoming data from embedded sensors. For example, a

Figure 12-22: A smart lock unlocks as the phone nears the door

Gabor Tinz/Shutterstock.com

Figure 12-23: Parking sensors provide data to a car to park itself

Chesky/Shutterstock.com

smart refrigerator can monitor its grocery contents and inform users when to add items to their grocery list. Another example is a smart doorbell that can tell the difference between the movement of a swaying branch versus a human approaching the house.

IoT isn't just for smart homes. Personal devices such as a smart watch or a medical sensor might incorporate AI capabilities for data processing or human interactions. Increasingly, automobiles are equipped with AI capabilities, such as monitoring maintenance needs, supporting human voice commands, and even providing self-parking capabilities (**Figure 12-23**).

Beyond the consumer market, IoT has also permeated the manufacturing, medical, and financial industries, as well as many others. For example, in a manufacturing environment, AI-powered IoT supports predictive maintenance to reduce equipment downtime. It monitors equipment for signs of needed maintenance before parts fail. IoT technologies track assets as small as shipped packages or as large as delivery trucks.

Figure 12-24: The Echo Dot is a smart speaker for Amazon's Alexa app

Effective AI Commands   If you use a virtual assistant app on your smartphone (such as Siri or Google Assistant), you might have been required to train the app to recognize your voice. This voice training process helps ensure the app can distinguish your voice from other people's voices. Typically, this process requires you to read aloud a few phrases when indicated on the screen.

These smartphone apps and the personal assistants on smart speakers (such as Alexa on an Echo device) listen for a **wake word**, a word or phrase that alerts the app to record and interpret whatever you say next. The Amazon Echo Dot in **Figure 12-24** is a smart speaker for

Anna Quelhas/Shutterstock.com

Alexa. If you want Alexa to give you the day's weather forecast, you might say, "Alexa, what's the weather for today?" Alexa detects the wake word "Alexa," and then records and interprets whatever comes next. Some of these assistants can be configured to use alternative wake words. For example, the Alexa app can respond to the wake words "Computer," "Echo," "Amazon," or "Ziggy." For the Google Assistant, you can use "Ok Google" or "Hey Google." (Currently, you cannot change the Siri wake word.)

It's also important to provide a clear break between your command to the AI system and any other comments irrelevant to the command afterward. The pause indicates the AI system should stop listening for additional commands. Similarly, if the radio or television is playing in the background when you try to talk to the AI system, it often won't be able to distinguish between your command and the background noise.

When programming Alexa, Siri, or Google Assistant to follow commands, developers use some standard approaches to designing interactions. First, consider the many possible variations in the ways different people might ask for a weather update:

- "Alexa, what's the weather for today?"
- "Alexa, what's today's weather forecast?"
- "Alexa, get me the weather forecast."
- "Alexa, what's the weather like?"
- "Alexa, how cold will it be today?"
- "Alexa, do I need an umbrella today?"

These are only a few variations for the same request for information on today's weather. Developers must program in the needed flexibility for Alexa to appropriately respond to all these variations. To do so, developers attempt to anticipate the many ways humans use language, including the use of contractions, informal words not found in the dictionary, and incorrect grammar.

Another layer of programming AI interactions involves designing commands in a way that is sufficiently structured for the AI system to interpret what the user wants. For example, consider the request for the weather forecast. Does the user want the forecast for today, for the upcoming weekend, or for a different day? Does the user want the local forecast or weather information for a different location? All these details provide important information for the AI system to respond appropriately. However, many users expect the AI system to make certain assumptions if the information is not specified. For example, if the user says, "Alexa, what's the weather," the user probably expects Alexa to provide information on the local weather at the current time, not next week's forecast for another city.

As a user, you can anticipate what the AI system needs from you in order to do as you ask. Provide sufficient detail in your request and phrase your requests in a way that clearly communicates what you want. If you're not getting the needed response, consider how to rephrase your question more efficiently or with needed detail.

You can also configure the AI system with personal details that help the system better understand you and anticipate your preferences. For example, if you program your Alexa app with your work address, you can ask, "Alexa, what's my commute like?" and it will know to check traffic between your home and work rather than give a general traffic report for your entire city.

Generate Content with AI

Recent developments in AI technology have resulted in several new tools for generating images and text. Tools such as DALL-E and Midjourney can be used to create images from text prompts. Tools such as ChatGPT and Bing Chat can help users write essays, compose emails, or develop checklists.

Tips for Using AI Text Generators   When ChatGPT was asked for tips on how new college students might use it, it generated the following response:

> ChatGPT can be a useful tool to increase productivity as a college student. Here are some tips on how to use it effectively:
>
> 1. **Quick Info:** Get fast answers on study topics.
> 2. **Brainstorming:** Generate ideas for papers and projects.
> 3. **Outlining:** Plan essay structures effectively.
> 4. **Writing help:** Improve grammar and phrasing.
> 5. **Time management:** Limit usage to stay focused.
> 6. **Task organization:** Seek scheduling tips.
> 7. **Complex concepts:** Simplify hard-to-understand topics.
> 8. **Language practice:** Practice languages with conversations.
> 9. **Review:** Reinforce learning by explaining concepts.
> 10. **Collaboration:** Use ChatGPT for group brainstorming.
>
> Remember that while ChatGPT can be a valuable tool, it's essential to combine it with traditional learning methods, engage with professors, and participate actively in your studies. Stay focused, use ChatGPT responsibly, and make the most of your college experience!

Notice the list is surprisingly thorough with a lot of variety and excellent grammar. ChatGPT even provided helpful context around using the tool in balance with other learning methods.

Limitations of AI Text Generators   Text and image generation tools can provide helpful assistance in the creative process. However, there are significant limitations to keep in mind when using these tools (**Figure 12-25**). AI text generators, for example, work by predicting the next most likely word based on the text samples it was

Figure 12-25: ChatGPT warns of inaccurate, offensive, or biased content in text output

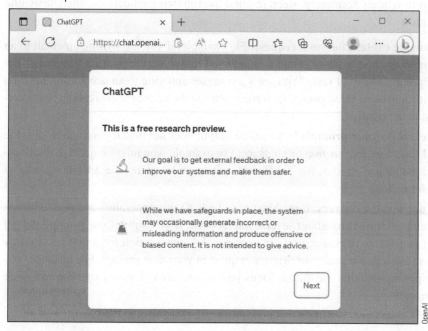

trained on. The text generation process is entirely mathematical in nature. The AI tool has no understanding of the context—it merely uses logical algorithms to predict the text the user has asked for.

Unfortunately, this process does not guarantee much accountability to reality. AI text generators are known to "hallucinate" facts. In other words, the AI tool generates text that seems to match the user's request, but any information in the text is not necessarily true.

For example, some researchers have noticed that ChatGPT's accuracy with even basic math tasks declined over the first several months of its availability to the public. Some AI text generators do not have access to the Internet and cannot fact-check information. Extreme caution should be used when working with any information provided by a text generator. These tools should primarily be used to generate text, and the user must provide their own expertise or other resources to verify any facts within that text.

Further, the increasing concerns surrounding copyright and ownership of content generated by these tools require serious consideration. Although there are many scenarios where AI content generators can serve as a useful tool in your toolkit to help brainstorm ideas and organize your thoughts, many situations preclude the use of AI for generating text or images. For example, your school might have published a statement or Acceptable Use Policy (AUP) regarding if or when AI tools may be used for schoolwork. Similarly, many companies are developing guidelines and rules around AI usage, because these AI tools present certain risks related to copyright, cybersecurity, and protection of proprietary information. These developments put a responsibility on you, the user, to consider the legal and ethical implications of using these tools. Always check any relevant policies, restrictions, or guidelines before using AI tools in your school or work activities.

Prompt Engineering   A request to an AI-powered content generator (such as ChatGPT) is called a **prompt**. The process of designing a prompt and editing it to get the desired result is called **prompt engineering**. You might need to add details, context, or other guidance so the AI tool will generate the text you want. You might also need to tackle smaller components of your overall project to ensure the AI tool can process your request accurately. Keep in mind the following guidelines when designing your prompts:

- **Provide context for your request:** For example, if you are writing an email to an employer about a job offering, assign the AI tool your role in order to generate the appropriate type of text: "You are a job seeker applying to an accounting position with a medium-sized company. Write a letter to the employer expressing your interest in the position."

- **Iterate on your prompt:** If the initial output does not match your needs, give the AI tool more information or guidance. For example, you might request that the output be longer, shorter, use a different writing style, or include different pieces of information.

- **Continue the conversation:** Most of today's AI text generators are able to follow a conversation throughout several interactions. If you submit one prompt and get an inadequate response, you can continue the conversation from that point rather than having to repeat your original request in your next prompt. For instance, you might request that the output focus less on one area of your expertise and more on another.

- **Simplify the request:** Break down larger projects into smaller components. You can even use the AI tool to help you list the steps of a larger project, and then prompt the AI tool for portions of the text along those steps. For example, work with AI to develop a job hunt plan. Then use the AI tool for each separate step: suggest job search terms, list most-requested skills and talents, develop and then format the resume.

- **Ask for alternatives:** You can request multiple alternatives in a single prompt. For example, you might ask for five metaphors to explain an abstract concept, and then select the one or two you find most helpful.

- **Perform your own editing:** Do not rely on any information presented by an AI-powered text generator. These tools are intended to generate text, not facts. In some cases, you can legally use the AI tool to help you draft text. However, you must do your own fact-checking to ensure all the information is accurate and relevant. One of the most obvious indicators an AI tool was used to generate text is when it confidently presents fiction as fact. Additionally, generously edit the text to incorporate your own writing style and personal information.

Communicate Proficiently with AI Systems

AI chatbots and other interactive AI technologies are designed to communicate with users as much as possible in ways that feel natural to humans. A significant goal of AI developers is to advance AI technology sufficiently so that human users can't tell the difference between a machine or a human on the other end of a conversation. For example, suppose you call into a customer service line. A sufficiently advanced AI system could sound just as natural and be just as responsive as a human technician, and is never distracted, tired, or annoyed (**Figure 12-26**). This challenge, which AI has not yet fully met, was first posed by computing pioneer Alan Turing in 1950, who theorized a test scenario with a human asking the AI system questions in an attempt to determine if the system is human or machine. To pass what was soon known as the **Turing Test**, the AI system must trick the human evaluator into

Figure 12-26: AI systems are designed to emulate human patterns of interaction

Phonlamai Photo/Shutterstock.com

thinking the system is a real person for at least five minutes. Surprisingly, this requires the AI system to be able to answer questions incorrectly, such as when the human interrogator asks a math question or asks the machine if it's a computer or a human. For example, if the machine always answered math questions correctly, that would indicate it's a machine and not a human who makes occasional mistakes.

Some systems have managed to trick users in specific situations. For example, in May of 2018 during a conference demonstration, Google Assistant powered by Google Duplex AI technology called a hair stylist to make an appointment for a client. The Google voice had been programmed with typical human idiosyncrasies, such as saying "um" or pausing before answering a question, as if it was thinking. The hair stylist was not informed the caller was an AI system. The system was able to schedule the appointment, despite some issues with a schedule conflict, without alerting the human to its true nature. Therefore, some experts believe that in this case, Google Assistant passed the Turing test, although other experts disagree because the human was not informed of the test and had no reason to question whether the caller was an AI.

However, these specific situations tend to be very limited in scope, such as a conversation for making an appointment. Additionally, the human, especially in the case of the hair appointment, is often not aware that their conversation partner's true nature is in question. Still, AI continually shows impressive progress in this area.

Some developers and ethicists question whether this goal is appropriate. Many users might feel betrayed if they discover they're talking to a machine when they thought they were talking to a human. For this reason, many companies incorporate disclosure notices of some kind to ensure their users know when they're interacting with a machine.

Despite the ability of some AI systems to sound increasingly natural, users can still benefit from having a basic understanding of how to most efficiently communicate with AI. Avoiding cultural slurs, speaking clearly, and understanding what AI can or can't do makes communicating with an AI system more productive. To understand better what an AI system needs from users, it helps to look at how AI is programmed to understand human language.

Module 12 Summary

Cloud, e-commerce, and artificial intelligence technologies are making technology more accessible, supporting a global economy, and helping to streamline repetitive or predictable tasks. Collectively, the impact of these advancements on the way business is conducted is known as digital transformation. Cloud computing often provides the infrastructure that enables these technologies and brings them to wider, global markets. Cloud computing is the process of providing or using computer tools over the Internet. In the public cloud context, customers use a cloud provider's hardware to do computing tasks. When hosting a website or other process in the cloud, there's very little up-front cost, and expenses vary each month according to the amount of cloud services used. Because the cloud offers flexibility, low cost, adaptability, and convenience, cloud technology levels the playing field so that small, creative businesses can successfully compete with large corporations.

Many companies use the Internet to conduct business, which is called e-business. A specific type of e-business is e-commerce, which is the process of conducting buy and sell transactions on an electronic network such as the Internet. Most companies have reached the conclusion that e-commerce is a necessary component to their overall business strategy. Retailers increasingly use multiple types of contact, such as an online store and a physical store, to reach a customer. High-growth occupations in the e-commerce industry include positions such as customer service representatives, hand pickers and packagers, and delivery truck drivers. A successful e-commerce website offers informative *content* that is relevant to site visitors, a sense of *community* to offer a personalized relationship with each customer, and effective *context* that adapts to each customer's preferences, location, and buying process.

Several emerging technologies impact daily and work lives for many people. Virtual reality (VR) is the use of computers to simulate a real or imagined environment that appears as a three-dimensional (3-D) space. Augmented reality (AR) is a type of VR that uses an image of an actual place or thing and adds digital information to it. Robotics is the science that combines engineering and technology to create and program robots. Robots are useful in situations where it is impractical, dangerous, or inconvenient for a human to perform a particular task.

Artificial intelligence (AI) is the technological use of logic and prior experience to simulate human intelligence. AI devices often rely on natural language processing (NLP) to help interpret voiced commands and give verbal responses to provide the information requested or to ask for additional input. People commonly encounter AI in a variety of scenarios: interacting with a chatbot, using a digital assistant app, AI-powered algorithms in the background of applications or websites, or generative AI tools such as ChatGPT, Bing Chat, or DALL-E. Text and image generation tools can provide helpful assistance in the creative process. However, there are significant limitations to keep in mind when using these tools. Extreme caution should be used when working with any information provided by a text generator.

Users can benefit from having a basic understanding of how to most efficiently communicate with AI. Avoiding cultural slurs, speaking clearly, and understanding what AI can or can't do makes communicating with an AI system more productive. A voice training process helps ensure an AI app can distinguish the user's voice from other people's voices. Understanding how AI systems process commands and providing sufficient detail and structure to your requests can help you get the desired response from AI-powered systems. Most importantly, AI technology users need to understand the legal and ethical implications of AI-generated output so they can use these tools responsibly. Simultaneously, developers continue to advance AI technology in ways that are intended to better serve human progress.

Review Questions

1. What characteristic of cloud technology helps minimize storage costs by allowing customers to pay only for what resources they use?

   a. Broad network access
   b. Measured service
   c. Resource pooling
   d. On-demand self-service

2. Your website development team is setting up a new website for your company, and you've decided to host this website in the cloud. However, in the interest of improving the website's performance, you don't want to have to manage underlying servers. What kind of cloud service will best meet your needs?

   a. SaaS
   b. FWaaS
   c. IaaS
   d. PaaS

3. (True or False) Automatic data backup is typically guaranteed when storing sensitive files in cloud storage.

4. What marketing strategy can help streamline contacts with customers and target customer interests?

   a. E-business
   b. Unique selling proposition
   c. Omnichannel
   d. Online storefront

5. (True or False) Online storefronts typically are built on SaaS products hosted in the cloud.

6. The e-commerce job role with the most direct influence on customer satisfaction ratings is a _____.

   a. shipping clerk
   b. customer service representative
   c. marketing specialist
   d. transport truck driver

7. What set of standards requires retailers to encrypt customers' payment information?

   a. PCI DSS
   b. HIPAA
   c. RaaS
   d. CRM

8. What technology is most directly used to increase production of high-demand products, such as cars?

   a. Augmented reality
   b. Artificial intelligence
   c. Virtual reality
   d. Robotics

9. To find information about a product a customer is interested in purchasing, a call center technician most likely would refer to _____.

   a. robotic process automation
   b. data analytics
   c. artificial neural networks
   d. a chatbot

10. How can your smartphone's virtual assistant determine if you're giving it a command or if your comments are directed at someone else?

   a. You pause before asking your question.
   b. You say the correct wake word.
   c. You include details in your request.
   d. You complete the voice training process.

11. When an AI text generation tool presents false information in its output, the tool is said to be _____.

   a. hallucinating
   b. lying
   c. engineering
   d. editing

12. When interacting with an AI system, which of the following methods would result in worse outcomes for the user instead of getting the desired response?

   a. Avoid cultural slurs.
   b. Speak clearly.
   c. Provide proprietary information.
   d. Develop realistic expectations.

Discussion Questions

1. You and your business partner have developed an innovative new product that will appeal to a wide range of potential customers. However, you don't have much money to help you get your company off the ground. What budgeting methods would be available with a cloud service versus purchasing all the computer hardware you might need?

2. Think of a website you've used recently to make or consider an online purchase. What features of that website helped build your trust in that company sufficiently that you would buy from them? When selling your own items online, what measures could you take to earn trust from your buyers?

3. Some people prefer to interact with a chatbot while others would rather talk to a human. Which do you prefer and why? Have you used an AI assistant like Siri, Alexa, or Google Assistant? What kinds of tasks do you think these assistants are most helpful with?

4. IoT technology has come a long way in just a few years. However, many people still have extensive concerns about using smart technology due to perceived security threats. Would you be comfortable having a smart lock on your front door, and what is your reasoning for your response? What other smart devices would you like to have in your home? What security concerns do you have with these devices?

Critical Thinking Activities

1. Your company is looking at options for migrating some of their web servers to a cloud service. However, no one on the team currently knows much about cloud providers and what kinds of services they offer. Research the top three public cloud service providers. Each of these providers offers a variety of cloud services that could be used for hosting a web server. Create a list of one service from each provider that your company might use to run a virtual machine in the cloud for their web servers.

2. You own a small shop that sells sports gear with a special focus on outdoor sports like bicycling, hiking, and kayaking. You have a small website, but it doesn't yet support online purchases. You've decided to expand your business by targeting a larger geographical region, and that means your website needs extensive upgrades. You're concerned, though, about what kinds of regulations you will have to meet in order to handle online transactions and customer payment information. Research basic PCI requirements for small businesses. Who do these standards apply to? What are the cutoff points for each level of compliance requirements according to number of transactions per year? Include your information source(s).

3. You are designing a new AI-powered application that will automatically match resumes with available job openings based on a wide variety of job applicant and job role characteristics. You plan to train the system using resumes of current employees in similar job positions who have received favorable reviews from their employers. However, you recognize there could be some bias represented in the current employment pool regarding employees' race, gender, marital status, and other characteristics. You want to ensure the AI system does not incorporate existing bias and make sure it evaluates potential employee matches based on their qualifications. At the same time, you hope to give the AI system enough information so it can detect currently unknown patterns of what characteristics contribute to employee success in their job roles. Do some research online about what factors make for high quality training datasets. List three factors that will help you choose the best training data for your AI application. What strategies can you use to help eliminate bias in your AI application?

4. Your company is developing a therapy chatbot that will provide short-term support for people experiencing a mental health crisis, until a human therapist can arrive on the line. The company expects the chatbot to provide faster response times for incoming calls and texts at suicide and crisis help clinics during times of high call volumes. You need to develop some guidelines on what kind of information is given to a caller up front so each person is aware they're talking to a chatbot until a live operator is available. Do some research online about people's preferences when using a chatbot and what current expectations are for these interactions. What insights should you keep in mind as you're designing these guidelines? If you were using a chatbot on a retail site to get customer support, what design characteristics would you want the chatbot to have that would make it more user friendly for you?

Apply Your Skills

Daniel Matheson has just been awarded an internship at the home office of a large floor covering manufacturer that embraces digital technology tools. The company sells its products nationwide to home improvement stores and also operates a local chain of direct-to-consumer stores. Both sales channels rely on e-commerce transactions through the company website. Daniel has learned the company uses several cloud-hosted applications, and a large part of his job will be helping with business-to-business (B2B) customer interactions through the website chat feature. As Daniel explores the company's website the night before his first day on the job, he finds that the website also includes a customer service chatbot.

Working in a small group or by yourself, complete the following:

1. As an intern supporting customer interactions, which category of cloud services is Daniel most likely to interact with: SaaS, PaaS, or IaaS? What are some tasks Daniel might be expected to do that likely will use the company's cloud resources? For what kind of data stored in the cloud might Daniel need to be especially careful to do his part in protecting that data?

2. Although Daniel's company offers a chatbot on their website, Daniel will still engage in many interactions with customers. At times, customers will begin their conversation with the chatbot, and then the conversation will be handed over to Daniel to continue the conversation and provide customized support. What skills might Daniel need so he can perform well with these online chats? What questions should Daniel ask his supervisor before taking his first customer chat assignment? If you were working in this type of internship, how would this kind of experience benefit you in your chosen career?

3. Daniel wants to develop some standard responses to common customer questions that he can copy-and-paste into the chat to provide faster response times. He's decided to use ChatGPT to help him develop some of his standard responses. Suppose a common question from customers is, "How will new flooring affect the noise level in my office space?" Design a prompt for ChatGPT that gives a list of different types of flooring and their effects on noise levels. What is your prompt? Refine the prompt so it presents this information in a more succinct way and with a more conversational tone that is appropriate for a chat conversation online. What is this refined prompt? What information provided in the output by ChatGPT might need to be fact-checked? What is another common customer question for which ChatGPT could generate a reasonable and helpful response?

Databases

In This Module

- Discuss the importance of databases
- Use a database management system
- Explain how data informs business decisions

Safia monitors statistics for recent property sales.

She uses queries to identify properties most interesting to prospective buyers.

BongkarnGraphic/Shutterstock.com

Safia Karimi works for a real estate broker's office. One of her responsibilities is to pull lists of properties that meet a range of requirements for clients looking to buy a home. Buyers might want a property in a certain part of town or with a certain number of bedrooms and bathrooms. And of course, there's always a budget to consider. As Safia is fine-tuning a list of properties for one client, she's also advising property owners on what prices to list their properties according to current market demands for different kinds and locations of comparable homes. Safia tracks all this information through a variety of databases that constantly monitor property sales throughout her region.

What databases have you used today? Chances are, you've interacted with several databases and didn't know it. Did you check your email today? Sign into a social media account? Buy something online or check your bank account balance? You don't even have to be on the Internet to interact with a database. Did you fill your car with gas or buy a bus ticket? Take the drive-through for coffee or lunch? Use your credit card at a store? All these activities require interactions with a database, either to pull information from the database (such as when signing into an account) or to add information to a database (such as when making a purchase). Businesses use databases to track information over time.

In this module, you learn how and why databases are used, and you gain familiarity with basic concepts related to working with a database management system. You'll also explore how businesses analyze massive amounts of data to make strategic decisions. As you reflect on what you learn in this module, ask yourself: What makes databases so important? How could you use a database management system to help with your own projects? How can data inform the decisions you need to make?

Discuss the Importance of Databases

Because a database allows you to efficiently collect, access, retrieve, and create reports of data, they are crucial to running many types of organizations. A retail business might use a database to store customer information, details on sales transactions, or an accounting of inventory in stock. A medical office might use a database to track patients' medical histories, appointments, test results, and doctor's notes. A school might use a database to record student contact information, grades, and attendance. Data is the lifeblood of most organizations, and databases are entrusted with the critical job of organizing this data, making it easily accessible when needed, and ensuring the data is kept safe and secure.

Compare Spreadsheets and Databases

Since organizations have to store so many different kinds of information, you might wonder why they don't just create files in a word processing program or a spreadsheet application. Those apps can be used to store information, right? Why complicate things by using a database?

While documents and spreadsheets do store information, generally that information is isolated from the information held in other documents or spreadsheets. Document and spreadsheet files are stored as unrelated objects in a file system; you can open one file and use it, but the data inside it is not connected in any way to data in a different file. Databases offer the advantage of showing connections between different sets of data. The following side-by-side comparison of spreadsheets and databases will help clarify the critical differences between these two types of data storage.

You might have used a spreadsheet to track some basic information, such as a directory of contact information or expenses in a budget. However, a spreadsheet can't keep up with the complexity of data that a database can. While spreadsheets fill an important role, they can't do the work required of a database.

Spreadsheet software was originally intended as an electronic alternative to paper ledgers. A spreadsheet app such as Excel or Google Sheets is designed to store numbers, charts, and other data in a gridlike format where it can perform automatic recalculations as data changes. And while you can have multiple worksheets within a spreadsheet, these worksheets are not designed to fluidly interact with each other. In other words, the spreadsheet software is not aware of any significant relationships between each worksheet except in the form of performing calculations.

In many cases, a database will also store data in a grid format. These storage objects are called tables (**Figure 13-1**), and they appear very similar to a worksheet. Each column in the table is a field, with its field name at the top. In Figure 13-1, the fields are named StudentID, LastName, FirstName, City, State, and Major. Each row in the table is a record containing information for each member of the table, such as enrollment information for each student, contact information for each club member, each order placed by a customer, or each employee at an office location. Each table is a collection of records for a single subject, such as all students, all club members, all customer orders, or all employees.

However, unlike a spreadsheet, the database can show relationships between tables. A **relationship** is an association between entities that shows how data in one table relates to data in another table. For example, one table might show a list of Customers while another table might show a list of Orders. A relationship between these tables can show all the orders for each customer.

This relationship can streamline data entry. For example, the customer's shipping address can be stored in the Customers table. Each order in the Orders table can pull that information from the Customers table when it's needed without having to store that information over and over for every order. This method reduces the quantity of data stored in a

Figure 13-1: A database table is organized by fields and records

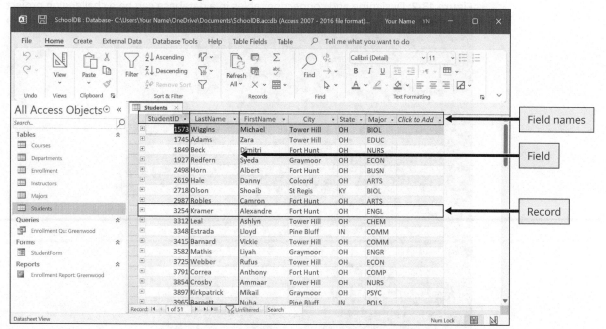

database by cutting down on data duplication across multiple tables. This, in turn, reduces the chances for errors and inconsistencies. It also makes data updates, such as updating a customer's address, much faster and easier to do. Spreadsheet software cannot track this kind of connection between different types of data.

There are many other fundamental differences between what a spreadsheet can do well and what a database can do well. Consider the following advantages of using a database:

- **Data relationships:** As already mentioned, databases can show relationships between tables, which streamlines data entry and reduces the chances for errors or inconsistencies.
- **Data updates:** Updates to data in a database are more efficient than when using spreadsheets.
- **Data validation:** Databases can validate new data as it's added to each table, such as making sure that a phone number with the expected number of digits is entered into a CellPhoneNumber field. This helps ensure that the right data is being added.
- **Data quantity:** Databases can easily handle a lot more data than a spreadsheet can. Where a spreadsheet might be limited to about a million rows, a database table can hold tens of millions of records. Some types of databases don't rely on tables at all and can store even higher volumes of data.
- **Data sharing:** Databases are optimized to allow many users to see new or changed data as soon as it's entered and, unlike spreadsheets, can track who made what changes and when.

Despite these many advantages of using a database, a major challenge of databases is that they're complicated to design and set up, requiring intricate knowledge of the data to structure it appropriately (**Figure 13-2**). The people who create and maintain databases must have special training. These databases also require high performance hardware with high-capacity memory and processor resources. Further, databases typically contain sensitive or mission-critical data that requires special protection. The database must be adequately secured to protect against intruders, and it must be sufficiently backed up in case of data loss or hardware failure.

Figure 13-2: Designing and connecting tables in a database can be a challenging project

Semisatch/Shutterstock.com

Define Relational Databases

The discussion so far has focused on relational databases, so called because of the relationships between various types of data in the database. Other kinds of databases exist as well, many of which have emerged in recent years to meet the needs of e-business and other Internet-enabled activities. You'll learn more about other types of databases later in this module. For now, developing a deeper understanding of relational databases will help you to better understand some basic database concepts and skills.

Because relational databases rely on relationships between types of data to show how some data is related to other data, they are best suited to data that can be organized into tables where each record in a table stores the same pieces of information. For example, each customer record in the Customers table will contain the same information for every customer: CustomerID, FirstName, LastName, Address, PhoneNumber, etc. And each order record in the Orders table will contain the same information for every order: OrderID, PurchaseDate, OrderStatus, etc.

Most relational databases are managed using SQL (Structured Query Language), which is pronounced *S-Q-L* or just *sequel*. Database managers and experienced users use the SQL programming language to configure and interact with the database's objects and data. Some examples of SQL commands are provided later in this module. But you don't have to learn programming to work with databases. Database software can make these tasks much easier.

The structure and design of relational databases focus on the consistency of the data held within these databases. Each time a change is made to a database, the database must be locked to ensure that conflicting changes aren't made at the same time. Each of these changes is called a transaction. Relational databases are often measured against the principles of a database transaction model called the **ACID (Atomic, Consistent, Isolated, Durable) model**, which is used to ensure each transaction is reliably processed. If something goes wrong when processing a transaction, an ACID-compliant database will handle the error gracefully and avoid problems that could invalidate data in the database. These four principles define the elements needed for this level of reliability:

- **Atomic:** Once a transaction is started, it is either completed or the database is reverted back to its previous state. For example, if you are transferring money from your account to a friend's account, and an error is encountered during the transfer, the money cannot be lost. The money either stays in your account, or it is transferred to your friend's account. The database will not allow only one part of that transaction to persist if there is an error during the transaction.

- **Consistent:** No processed transaction can change the database's design in ways that might compromise the integrity of the database. For example, when transferring money from your account to your friend's account, the amount deducted from your account must match exactly the amount added to your friend's account.

- **Isolated:** Each transaction is handled independently of all other transactions. For example, you cannot transfer money into your friend's account and transfer that same money to a different person's account at the same time. Although multiple transactions might happen quickly, they are still being handled one at a time within the database.

- **Durable:** Even if the system fails, all completed transactions will survive the failure. For example, if the bank experiences a power outage immediately after you transfer money to your friend's account, the transaction will still persist even once power is restored and the database again becomes available.

Define Nonrelational Databases

In many situations, the enforced consistency of a relational database (with the same kinds of information in every record in a table) is an advantage. However, this consistency comes with the limitation that data must generally be represented by text or numbers rather than images, videos, or other file types. As web applications became more popular, this restriction led to the emergence of more powerful database technologies better suited to managing massive amounts of data. For example, **NoSQL databases**, or **nonrelational databases**, resolve many of the weaknesses of relational databases. "NoSQL" originally stood for "non-SQL," but more recently has been called "not-only SQL" because some of these systems do support SQL-based languages. Popular nonrelational database applications include MongoDB, CouchDB, Oracle NoSQL Database, and Apache Cassandra.

These unstructured or differently structured databases use a variety of approaches to store many kinds of data. One simple example is a key-value database. **Key-value databases** (also called key-value stores) create any number of key-value pairs for each record. For example, for a student database, you might store each piece of a student's contact information in a separate key-value pair in a list:

Key	Value
Street Address	123 Artist Way
City	Martin
State	OH

However, you could also create unique key-value pairs for any student in the database. Suppose a student placed first in a road derby competition. You could store a key-value pair for that unique piece of information, even though no other student in the database might have participated in that kind of event:

Key	Value
Road Derby Competition	1st place

Nonrelational databases don't offer the same kind of data consistency or validation as relational databases. However, the hardware and software resources available to the database, as well as the database structure, can be more easily increased to handle the massive volume of Big Data, which continues to increase indefinitely. This is possible because a nonrelational database can be distributed across multiple servers, which makes it easy to add more servers without compromising the database's design. Also, even during some types of system or hardware failure, users can still access a nonrelational database, which is to say the database offers **high availability**.

Whereas the design of relational databases emphasizes consistency, the design of nonrelational databases emphasizes availability. In contrast to the ACID model for relational databases, nonrelational databases are measured by the **BASE (Basically Available, Soft State, Eventually Consistent) model**, which is used to ensure data in the database is highly available even during a failure of some sort. These three principles define the elements needed for this level of availability:

- **Basically Available:** Copies of new data are spread across multiple hosts so that, even if one host fails, other hosts still have the correct data.
- **Soft State:** It takes time to copy the data to other hosts, and during this time, the hosts temporarily have different information. If a request is made to one host that has not yet received the updated data, the host will present outdated data during that time.

- **Eventually Consistent:** The data will eventually be consistent across hosts, given sufficient time to make all the copies. This is very different from relational databases where the data must be immediately consistent. One common way to choose between nonrelational DBMSs is to compare the average time needed to reach consistency. Especially for cloud-hosted nonrelational database services, this time to consistency might be measured in seconds rather than minutes or hours.

Nonrelational databases serve different purposes with different priorities than relational databases. For something like bank transactions where data must be immediately consistent, nonrelational databases typically aren't a good fit. But for something like social media posts, a nonrelational database is an excellent tool to handle massive volumes of data that should be highly available to optimize the user experience.

Describe the Effects of Cloud Computing on Database Technology and Methods

Traditionally, the structure and size of a database were limited by the hardware available to host that database. With the emergence of cloud computing, businesses now have many more options for designing, hosting, and managing a database.

Cloud providers, such as AWS (Amazon Web Services) and Microsoft Azure, have developed cloud-based database services that are not restricted by the size or capabilities of a company's own, on-premises hardware. For example, AWS offers a service called Amazon RDS (Relational Database Service) that lets customers host their databases on AWS hardware using virtual machines from the EC2 (Elastic Compute Cloud) service (**Figure 13-3**).

RDS, as its name implies, uses a relational database structure, and it works very similarly to more traditional database systems. However, other cloud database services are more cloud-native in design, meaning they were designed from the beginning to intentionally take advantage of the benefits of cloud computing. For example, AWS offers a key-value database service called DynamoDB, which is a serverless database service. With a **serverless** service, a customer does not have to manage the underlying host, and the customer only pays for the resources they use, such as storage space, and the time spent interacting with their data (**Figure 13-4**). With this service, a customer can expand the size of their database almost indefinitely.

Figure 13-3: A virtual server in the AWS cloud runs on a physical server in the AWS data center and hosts an RDS database

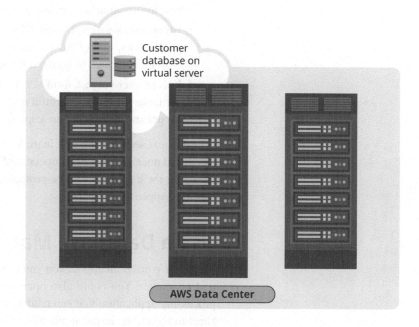

Customer database on virtual server

AWS Data Center

Figure 13-4: AWS manages the physical hardware and the virtual server; the customer manages the database and its interactions with users

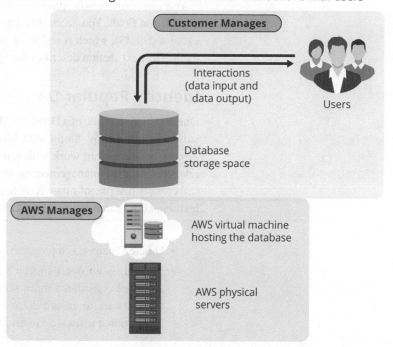

Customer Manages

Interactions (data input and data output)

Users

Database storage space

AWS Manages

AWS virtual machine hosting the database

AWS physical servers

Cloud-based database services offer the potential for significant cost savings along with many other benefits:

- **Increased scalability:** Scalability is the ability of a resource to increase in size as demand increases. Scalable, cloud-based databases provide small or new companies with access to sophisticated database technology that can quickly expand to meet the business's growing needs over time.

- **Reduced latency:** Latency is the brief delay between when a request is made and the response is received. In some cases, multiple copies of a database can decrease response times and improve user experience, and many cloud database services include the ability to create many database copies and place those copies globally where needed. Copies of a database used only to retrieve information (not to write new information) are called read replicas.

- **Increased security:** Cloud databases typically have industry-leading security protections, and cloud-hosted databases can offer faster data access speeds to customers located throughout the world.

- **Faster recovery:** Cloud services in general—and cloud database services in particular—include insightful monitoring options so customers can identify problems sooner and even automate responses to those problems for faster recovery times.

In the next section, you will learn how a database management system is set up, organized, and managed. A key component of this process is the organization of the data itself. However, the data must also be protected from threats and backed up in case something harmful happens to the data.

Use a Database Management System

Microsoft Word is an application you use to open and work with a document that contains text or images. You could also open that document in Google Docs or a similar word processing application that can read a document file. Similarly, when you open a spreadsheet in Excel, the Excel application allows you to access the numbers and calculations contained within the spreadsheet. You could instead open the spreadsheet in Google Sheets or a similar spreadsheet application.

You can see a similar pattern with databases. The database itself contains the data records and fields. You access the data in the database through a database management system (DBMS), which is software used to create databases and then manipulate data in them. The next section describes the options available when choosing a DBMS.

Identify Popular Database Management Systems

One common example of a DBMS is Microsoft Access, which is a part of the Microsoft 365 suite of applications, along with Word, Excel, PowerPoint, and others (**Figure 13-5**). Access is designed to work with relational databases, so it's more specifically called a relational database management system (RDBMS).

Access is just one of many RDBMSs, but it's the one many users begin with as they're learning about database concepts. Other examples of RDBMSs that also use SQL include the following:

- Oracle Database is a proprietary RDBMS offered by Oracle.

- MySQL is an open-source RDBMS. Open-source programs such as MySQL are often considered more secure because users can evaluate the source code of the software to ensure there are no loopholes left open for attackers to exploit. Open-source software can also be customized by technically skilled users.

Figure 13-5: Access is one application in the Microsoft Office suite of applications

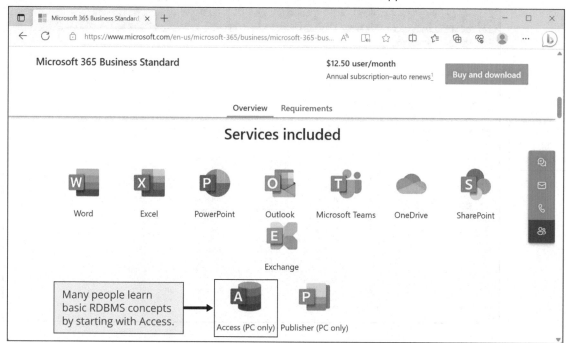

- Microsoft SQL Server, like Access, is produced by Microsoft. However, it's designed to handle much greater volumes of data.
- MariaDB is a free RDBMS developed by the same people who built MySQL.
- PostgreSQL is another free and open-source RDBMS.
- Amazon's Aurora is a **Database as a Service (DBaaS)**. This means the DBMS runs on servers owned by a cloud provider, and users access the database remotely through a web browser. Because the service relies on robust cloud provider hardware, it can provide sophisticated features and expand almost indefinitely to meet the needs of high-demand customers.

You can also use other kinds of database management systems that rely on different kinds of technologies, so it's sometimes helpful to specify that a particular DBMS is designed to work with relational databases by using the more specific term relational database management system (RDBMS). All the DBMS options in the preceding list are also considered RDBMSs.

Organize Data in a Database

Access, like most other DBMSs, includes both front-end and back-end elements. Unlike most other DBMSs, it's only suitable for use by one person at a time or by a few users accessing the database in the same location (like a small office) on a single network. Larger databases accessed across large corporate networks or the Internet (like through a website), or accessed concurrently by many users, require more robust back-end database software, such as Microsoft SQL Server.

Data in a database is organized to allow for quick searches and to support connections between data in relationships. While this organization can expand into a highly complex and intricate structure, there are basic concepts used throughout the structure that help make sense of the data and that help ensure the data makes sense.

Figure 13-6: You can toggle between Datasheet View and Design View in Access

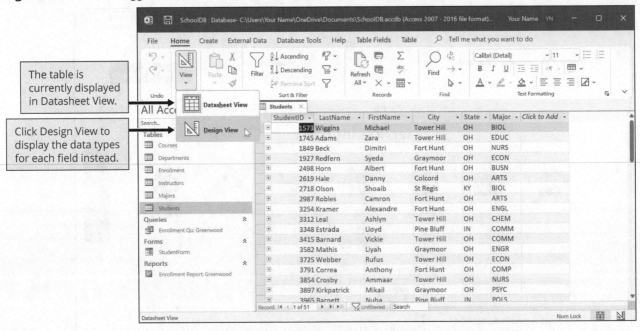

Recall that data in a relational database is stored in tables, and that tables are made up of fields and records. Each field has a unique name based on the information it holds—no two fields in a table can have the same name. The design of these field names is important because database users often pull information from certain fields when working with the data. Fields are further defined by their data type and length—that is, the type of data they are designed to hold, and the amount of data they are designed to hold.

To create a useful database table, you start by figuring out exactly what information you want the table to hold, and then create all the necessary fields with the right data types and lengths before entering data. Choosing appropriate data types ensures that your database will work as efficiently as possible. And choosing appropriate field lengths helps protect the database from certain kinds of security risks.

So far, the examples in this module have only used Datasheet View in Access, which displays the table in a grid view with all its fields and records. Alternatively, you can use Design View instead to display the data types and other properties for all fields in a table. The View button toggles between Datasheet View and Design View (**Figure 13-6**).

Figure 13-7 lists the data type for each field in a Students table using Design View. Some data types not shown in the Students table include Currency, AutoNumber (a number automatically assigned by the DBMS), Yes/No (allows only two values, such as True/False or On/Off), and Hyperlink (such as an email address or web address). You set the data type to control the kind of data stored in each field. For example, setting a field to the Date/Time data type can ensure that users enter date information in the field and not text or other kinds of numbers. Note, however, that fields containing numbers not used for calculations (such as phone numbers) are usually set with a text data type.

Data Validation   Controlling a field's data type is an important part of **data validation**, which is a process that sets cells so the values they accept are restricted in terms of type and range of data. This helps ensure the data entered into a database makes

Figure 13-7: Use the data type to control the kind of data stored in each field

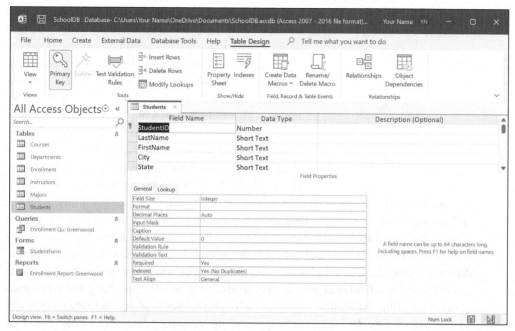

sense and meets certain criteria. Data validation can enforce other criteria with various types of validity checks. The following list explains some of the more common kinds of validity checks:

- **Data type check:** Field data types ensure that the right kind of data is entered into a field. For example, a number data type won't allow alphabetic characters.

- **Presence check:** This check, when turned on, requires the user to add information to a particular field and won't allow the user to leave a field blank.

- **Field property check:** Some field properties can be used to validate data entry. For example, a maximum field length of 5 can be used on a zip code field to prevent the entry of longer numbers.

- **Uniqueness check:** This check, when turned on, requires the user to enter information unique to that record. For example, if someone has already created an account with a certain username, no one else can create another account with that same username.

- **Range check:** A range limitation might require a number to be positive or a date to fall within a certain range, such as only in the past.

- **Format check:** Access allows the use of an input mask to control how data is formatted in a field; an **input mask** is a field property that provides a visual guide for users as they enter data. For example, an input mask might require that a date be entered using a four-digit year.

- **Multiple choice check:** This check can be enforced by using a data type that allows users to choose from a pre-existing list, such as a list of days of the week.

While these validity checks can't guarantee that the data matches reality, they can serve as a guide to help database users notice if they're entering incorrect data. For example, if you start to type your street address into a phone number field, the database will alert you to the problem and ask for more appropriate information.

Now you're ready to learn about how data stored in a database is organized.

Figure 13-8: The key icon indicates which field is the table's primary key

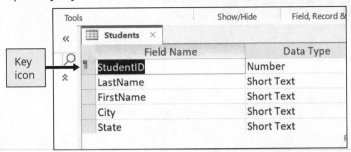

Primary Keys and Indexes

Each record in a table must be unique in some way, different from all other records in the table. You might initially think that each student's name in the table would be unique. However, it's possible for two students to have the same name. For this reason, most tables include a numeric field that contains a unique number of some kind, such as a student ID number. This field is called the **primary key** and must contain unique information for each record; it is also called a unique identifier. In Design View, a small key symbol indicates a table's primary key. In **Figure 13-8**, the StudentID field is the Students table's primary key.

Typically, every table in a relational database has a primary key. If the information in a table doesn't naturally include a field with unique information, such as a part number in a list of products, the database can assign an automatically generated number to each record that is unique, and then use that number field as the primary key. The primary key helps improve database performance by creating an **index** for the table, which is a database object that is created based on a field or combination of fields. It can be a field property that keeps track of the order of the values in the field, and a list that relates field values to the records that contain those values. An index speeds up searching and sorting records in a table. The index on the primary key field keeps a constantly updated list of all records in that table sorted in numerical order by those unique numbers. Even if users re-sort the records according to last name in alphabetical order or in chronological order by birthdate, the DBMS can always very quickly reorganize the records by the primary key because of the index on that field.

Other fields can be indexed as well. Think about the index in the back of a book. It lists topics that are commonly searched in that book and gives one or more page numbers for each of those topics. A database index works in a similar fashion. It provides a pre-sorted list of values in a particular field so the database can quickly home in on the information it needs. Imagine you are working with a table containing a million customer records, and you want the DBMS to find only the hundred or so records for customers who live in Chicago. If the DBMS already has an index of customers sorted by city, it will quickly be able to reduce that list to only the records you want. This is how an index speeds up data processes in a database.

You can create an index for any field you search often. For example, **Figure 13-9** displays two indexes for the Students table: one for the StudentID field (which is the primary key of the Students table) and one for the Major field, which will keep an updated list of students that is always sorted by their declared major.

Figure 13-9: The PrimaryKey index was created automatically, while the Major index will speed up searches for records matching each listed major

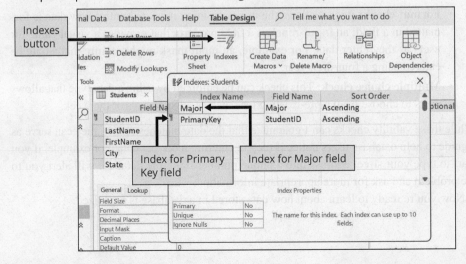

Relationships The primary key in each table also enables relationships between tables. As you've already learned, a relationship connects data in one table with data in another table. For example, Figure 13-6 earlier displayed the fields in the Students table. Notice the Major field on the far right. This field requires the database user to select one of the majors listed on the Majors table. **Figure 13-10a** shows the Majors table in Datasheet View, and **Figure 13-10b** shows the Majors table in Design View. Note that the primary key in the Majors table is the MajorID field.

Figure 13-10a: The Majors table provides a list of available majors

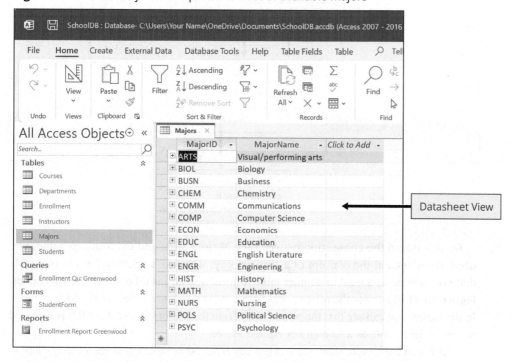

Figure 13-10b: The Majors table uses the MajorID field as its primary key

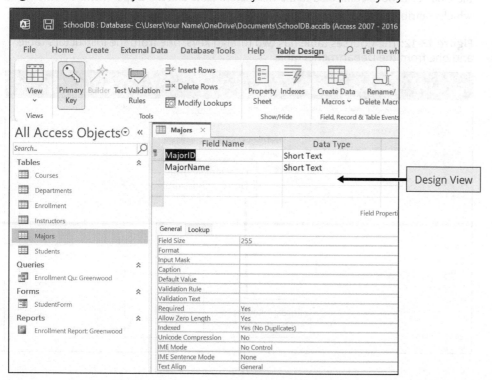

Figure 13-11: In a relationship, one table's primary key becomes a foreign key in the other table

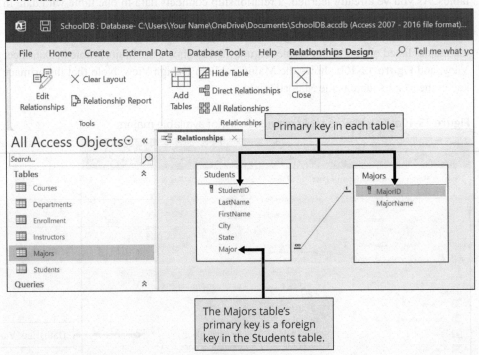

To understand the connection between the Majors table and the Students table, you need to understand the concept of a **foreign key**, which is a primary field in one table that you include as a field in another table to form a relationship between the two tables. **Figure 13-11** illustrates the relationship between the Students table and the Majors table. In the figure, you can see that the primary key from the Majors table (MajorID) is included in the Students table as a foreign key named Major.

A table can have more than one foreign key from other tables, and each foreign key in a table must be a primary key in the field's linked table. For example, in **Figure 13-12**, the Courses table is connected to the Instructors table and the Departments table, both of which contribute a foreign key to the Courses table.

Figure 13-12: The Courses table has two foreign keys: one from the Instructors table, and one from the Departments table

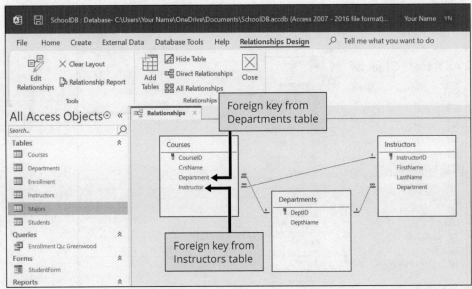

Notice the small "1" and "∞" symbols at each end of each relationship. There are different kinds of relationships depending on how many items on one end of the relationship can relate to each item on the other end of the relationship. For example, each order in a sales database will be connected to only one customer, but each customer can have many orders. Together, these two constrictions create a one-to-many relationship (one customer to many orders). The following list explains the three most common types of table relationships:

Figure 13-13: A one-to-many relationship

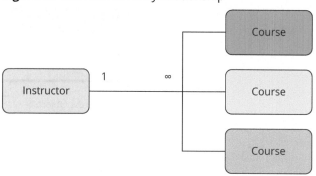

- A **one-to-many relationship** is a relationship between two tables in a database in which a common field links the tables together; the linking field is called the primary key field in the "one" table of the relationship and the foreign key field in the "many" table of the relationship. For example, most schools assign exactly one instructor to each course, and each instructor can teach many courses. This creates a one-to-many relationship (**Figure 13-13**).

- A **one-to-one relationship** is a relationship between two tables in which each record in the first table matches, at most, one record in the second table, and each record in the second table matches, at most, one record in the first table. For example, a school's student council likely has only one president's position, and only one elected student can fill that position. This creates a one-to-one relationship between the position and the student who can fill it (**Figure 13-14**).

- A **many-to-many relationship** is a relationship between two tables in a database in which one record of one table relates to many records in the other table and vice versa. To create such a relationship, you must establish a third table called a junction table that creates separate one-to-many relationships with the two original tables. For example, each student at a school can take more than one course at a time, and each course will typically have more than one student in it. The junction table might be an Enrollments table to show each student-course match. This creates a many-to-many relationship (**Figure 13-15**).

Figure 13-14: A one-to-one relationship

Figure 13-15: A many-to-many relationship with a junction table

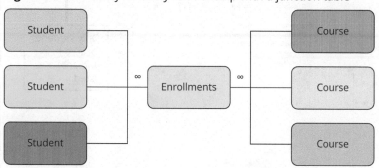

Figure 13-16: The Students table is sorted alphabetically by Major

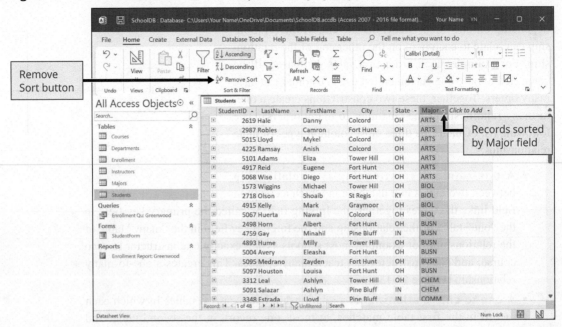

Sorts and Filters You can sort the records in a table according to the contents of one or more fields. For example, you could sort the records in a table alphabetically by last name, or numerically by zip code. You can choose to sort records in ascending order (A to Z, or lowest number to highest number) or in descending order (Z to A, or highest number to lowest number). Typically, however, a table is sorted by its primary key. In **Figure 13-16**, the Students table is sorted alphabetically by major. In Access, click the Remove Sort button to return the records to the default order according to the primary key values.

You might also want to temporarily hide some of the records in a table while you work with a few, specific records. To do this, you can apply a filter. For example, you might want to see a list of all students who live in Indiana (IN). To do this, filter the State field for all records where State equals "IN" so all other records are hidden (**Figure 13-17**). The other records aren't gone, they're just temporarily not visible. Click the Toggle Filter button to remove the filter.

Figure 13-17: The Students table is filtered to show only students who live in Indiana

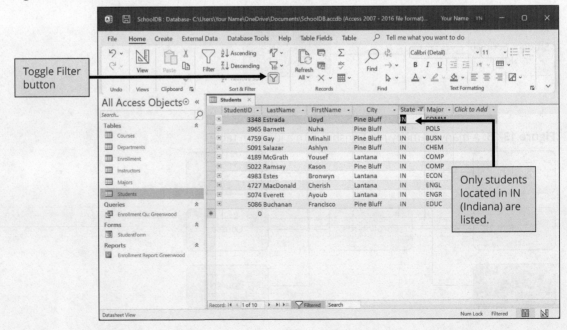

Queries   Sorts and filters are helpful when working with a single table. However, most of the work you'll do in a relational database requires working across multiple tables. In fact, this is essentially the point of having the relationships between tables: you want to find patterns and insights based on data held in various tables. To do this, you use queries. A query extracts data from a database based on specified criteria, or conditions, for one or more fields. For example, in the sample school database, you could run a query that shows all the students taking any class taught by a particular instructor, even though there is no field in any existing table that currently links the data in that way. **Figure 13-18** displays the results of this query. **Figure 13-19** illustrates how the tables and fields are related in the query.

Figure 13-18: A query showing all students enrolled in one instructor's courses

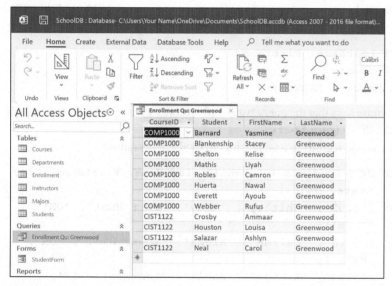

Figure 13-19: Four tables contribute data to this query

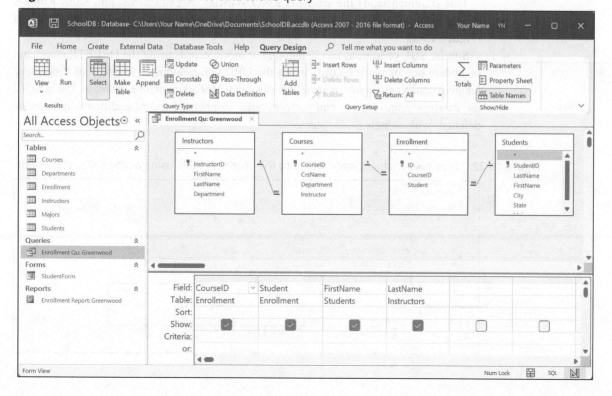

Figure 13-20: This query shows the names of all students from the Students table

Examine Structured Query Language (SQL)

You can use queries for more than just pulling data from tables to see it. You can also edit records, add records, and delete records using query functions. This is commonly performed using a query language such as Structured Query Language (SQL)

Common SQL operations include: SELECT, DELETE, INSERT, and UPDATE. The SELECT operation is used to pull information from a database, similar to the query provided earlier in this module. Consider this simple example:

```
SELECT LastName, FirstName
FROM Students;
```

This SQL statement would output a list of every student's last name and first name from the Students table (**Figure 13-20**).

To limit this list only to those students with an Arts major, you would need this SQL statement:

```
SELECT LastName, FirstName
FROM Students
WHERE Major = "ARTS";
```

The WHERE phrase says that the query wants only records where the Major field equals the Arts MajorID value (**Figure 13-21**).

Similarly, you can add records to a table with the INSERT operation:

```
INSERT INTO Students (StudentID, LastName, FirstName, City,
        State, Major)
VALUES ('5102', 'Whitley', 'Kody', 'Fort Hunt', 'OH',
        'CHEM'),
        ('5103', 'Cairns', 'Alexa', 'Tower Hill', 'OH',
        'MATH'),
        ('5104', 'Robson', 'Sahil', 'Lantana', 'IN',
        'POLS');
```

This statement adds the students Kody Whitley, Alexa Cairns, and Sahil Robson to the Students table along with their relevant information for each field listed (**Figure 13-22**).

Similar SQL operations can delete one or more records using the DELETE command or update one or more records using the UPDATE command. Mastery of this query language can significantly increase the efficiency of working with a database. Using SQL, the database administrator can perform large numbers of record additions, updates, or deletions with a single SQL statement.

Figure 13-21: This query shows the names of all students with an Arts major

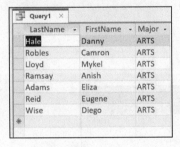

Figure 13-22: Three new students were added to the Students table using a single SQL statement

Compare Front-end and Back-end Database Components

A DBMS is used to manage data in the database; however, most non-technical users don't interact directly with the DBMS. For example, if you have a social media account like Facebook or Instagram, your account information is stored in a database. You can make changes to that information whenever you want even though you don't have direct access to the DBMS that manages the data. Instead, you sign into your account through your web browser and make changes on a user interface webpage.

When you interact with your social media account on a website, you're using the **database front-end** user interface, which is designed to be user friendly while also limiting and streamlining the kinds of tasks a user can complete within the database. This type of user interface is commonly built using web languages such as HTML, CSS, and JavaScript (**Figure 13-23**). A database front-end helps preserve the database's integrity and security. For example, it would not be a good idea to give non-technical users the ability to delete an entire table in the database! Interacting with the front-end interface also requires little to no understanding of the database's underlying structure, relationships, and format.

In contrast, database designers and administrators interact with the database's back end. This **database back-end** includes the database server hosting the data, some aspects of the DBMS, and the database itself. For example, most websites rely on database back-ends to hold information about users, blog posts, videos, inventory posted for sale, transactions, or even the webpages themselves.

Database back-ends are typically created when the project files, such as files for a website project, are first created. The developer chooses a database type they think will be the best fit for the data, based on their experience and expertise. The developer chooses a relational or nonrelational database product, such as MySQL, MariaDB, or MongoDB, that will support the data to be stored and that will function within the required environment, such as the web server's operating system, any programming languages being used, and any access permissions the server must provide.

Figure 13-23: Users interact with the database front-end; data is stored in the database back-end

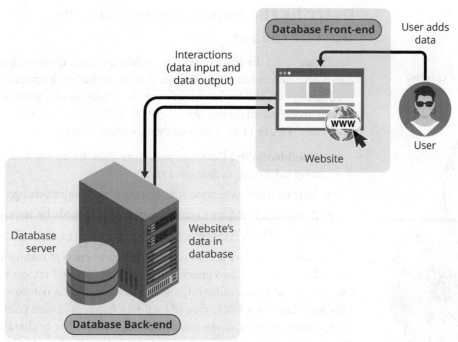

Specially trained **database administrators (DBAs)** work with the back-end components to ensure a company's business data is safe, secure, and well-managed. Web developers also distinguish between the front-end and back-end portions of application development. With large, complex applications, some developers will specialize in back-end development while others focus more on front-end development.

Explain How to Secure a Database

As you might imagine, database security is a critical issue for companies who store highly sensitive and valuable data in their databases. Whether the database contains financial information, medical data, purchase transactions, or user passwords, the business has a responsibility to protect that information and ensure it does not fall into the wrong hands. A data breach can be costly in terms of negative media exposure, loss of trust with customers or business partners, and government fines or even jailtime. What techniques can companies use to secure their databases?

The following lists several best practices in database security:

- Users given access to the database should be required to create long, secure passwords for their accounts. Each user should only be given the minimum access privileges required to do their job, such as the ability to view data but not change it or delete it, which is a common cybersecurity strategy called the **principle of least privilege**.
- Web servers are designed to be accessible to the open Internet, but database servers should reside in more secure segments of the network behind one or more firewalls and other types of network security.
- Sensitive data in a database should be encrypted. If a hacker manages to access a password database, for example, encryption can provide a last layer of defense that might prevent the attacker from actually using the stolen information. Not all data in the database must be encrypted, as this could severely slow the database's overall performance. However, data that indicates a person's identity (such as a name or social security number), contact information, or other personal information (such as medical records) should be encrypted, as required by law or industry standards. Any backup files should also be encrypted.

Describe the Importance of Backing Up a Database

Not all threats to a database come from potential attackers. Ensuring that data is accessible when it's needed and that no one has made unauthorized changes are also key aspects of database security. In fact, a classic security model called the **Confidentiality, Integrity, and Availability (CIA) triad** (**Figure 13-24**) addresses these concerns directly:

- **Confidentiality:** Refers to protecting a database from unauthorized access, as discussed earlier.
- **Integrity:** Refers to protecting data from unauthorized changes.
- **Availability:** Refers to ensuring data is accessible by authorized users when needed.

Techniques to secure access to a database and encrypt sensitive data address the first two concerns, confidentiality and integrity. One way to address availability of data is to back up a database. This way, data is not lost in case of hardware failure, software problems, human error, or environmental threat (such as fire or flood). The database can be recovered, sometimes automatically, and data access can be restored with (hopefully) minimal disruption.

Figure 13-24: The CIA triad is a classic security model for protecting data

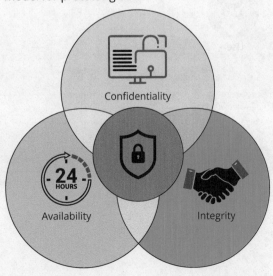

The backup process for a sizable database is not as simple as creating a second copy of a database file. The data in a database changes frequently, so backups must be created or updated on a regular basis. For this reason, many DBMSs include built-in backup tools, and some of these tools can perform automatic backups. These backups might include information about the state of the database at a particular point in time and a log of any changes to data since the previous backup, along with information about who made the changes and when. In some cases, the database is backed up continuously.

When needed, a database can be restored using the backup files. This recovery process might be applied only to a single object or record, or to the entire database, depending on the situation. This process is usually performed using a recovery utility of some kind. The backup copies might also be used as read replicas. These extra read replicas can help speed up the performance of a database whose data must be retrieved frequently.

Explain How Data Informs Business Decisions

You've learned a lot about data stored in databases and how to access that data. However, data by itself doesn't mean much. Raw and unorganized facts are not immediately valuable to organizations. But when data has been processed in a way that reveals patterns, relationships, and other insights, it becomes information. And information is extremely valuable.

To get meaningful insights, you need a large volume of relevant data. Database technologies have evolved over the years to handle massive amounts of data.

Describe the Significance of Big Data

Have you recently posted information to a social media site, such as Facebook or Instagram? Have you purchased an item online based on a recommendation from the website (**Figure 13-25**)? Did you read customer reviews about that item, look at customer photos, or even watch a customer-posted video?

All these activities generate and interact with data that is stored, analyzed, and referenced when making business decisions. However, the massive volume of data kept by a typical organization complicates storage and analysis processes, especially when you consider that data is often not structured in a way that allows it to be stored in traditional relational database tables.

Figure 13-25: The Amazon website tracks views of each product to recommend similar products

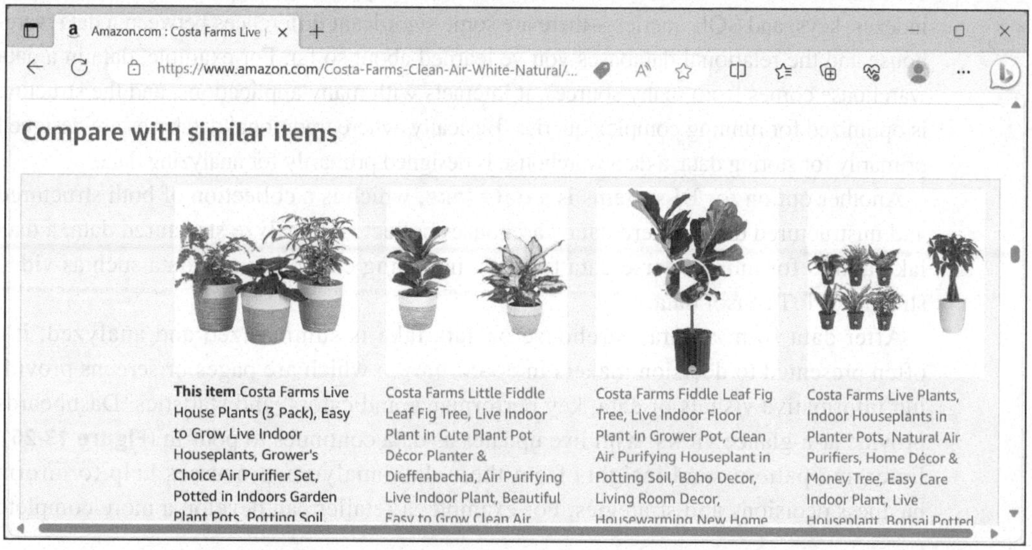

Examples of large and complex data sources, called Big Data, include the following:

- Data streams from Internet of Things (IoT) devices that monitor a passenger plane's engine performance
- Constantly changing ownership and valuations of stocks on the New York Stock Exchange
- Transactions recording items purchased, coupon usage, type of checkout used, and payment types at every register of a grocery store chain
- Student responses and scores, attendance, time on task, and discussion board messages in a learning management system
- Biological data collected by wearable fitness trackers
- Posts, reactions, blocks, and account settings on a social media website or app
- Video footage from traffic cameras at intersections and along highways
- Historical, current, and forecasted weather and environmental data

This list describes only a few examples of the terabytes of Big Data (a terabyte is about a billion kilobytes) generated every millisecond on Earth. In fact, Big Data is often identified according to three Vs:

- **Volume:** The massive amount of data that must be stored and analyzed
- **Variety:** The different formats in which this data can exist, such as music or video files, photos, social media texts, financial transactions, IoT sensor data, and more
- **Velocity:** The fact that this data is often generated and received at high speeds

Two additional Vs often used to describe Big Data include the following:

- **Value:** The helpfulness of the data in making strategic decisions
- **Veracity:** How accurately data reflects reality

Summarize the Impact of Business Intelligence

The analysis of Big Data benefits businesses by providing a bird's eye view of how well the business is functioning and giving insights into how to improve business processes and increase productivity. This analysis is performed by **business intelligence (BI) tools**, which are software features that analyze data to answer sophisticated business questions.

BI systems might collect data from existing databases (such as a product database) and from live data streams (such as an online transaction processing system) into a central repository called a **data warehouse**. While a data warehouse is a type of database—and most use tables, indexes, keys, and SQL queries—there are some significant differences between a data warehouse and the relational databases you've learned about so far. For example, data in a data warehouse comes from many sources, it interacts with many applications, and the structure is optimized for running complex queries. Basically, where traditional databases are designed primarily for storing data, a data warehouse is designed primarily for analyzing data.

Another option for BI systems is a **data lake**, which is a collection of both structured and unstructured data. Where data warehouses collect and analyze structured data, a data lake allows for more diverse data formats, including collecting raw data such as video streams or IoT sensor data.

After data from a data warehouse or data lake is summarized and analyzed, it's often presented to decision makers in **dashboards**, which are pages or screens providing informative visuals of data, key performance indicators, and statistics. Dashboards provide at-a-glance views, with live updates as data continues to pour in (**Figure 13-26**). Emerging patterns and insights from these data analytics processes help to inform business decisions and strategies. For example, a retailer can develop a more complete

Figure 13-26: Dashboards often update automatically as data continues to stream in

understanding of customer interests and preferences. The retailer might discontinue a product, reposition a product, or create new products based on this information. It might also adjust its marketing strategies, offer new financing options, fine-tune product or service pricing, or shift its customer service priorities.

Module 13 Summary

Data is the lifeblood of most organizations, and databases are entrusted with the critical job of organizing this data, making it easily accessible when needed, and ensuring the data is kept safe and secure. However, the many advantages of databases come at a cost; databases are complicated to design and set up, requiring intricate knowledge of the data in order to structure it appropriately. Relational databases rely on relationships between types of data to show how some data is related to other data. Most relational databases are managed using Structured Query Language (SQL). For additional flexibility, a database can be hosted in the cloud.

The data in a database is accessed through a database management system (DBMS), which is software used to create databases and then manipulate the data in them. One common example of a DBMS is Microsoft Access. Others include Oracle Database and MySQL. Data in a database is organized to allow for quick searches and to support connections

between data in relationships. Controlling the data type of a field is an important part of the data validation process, which ensures that the data entered into a database makes sense and meets certain criteria. Each record in a table must be unique in some way from all other records in the table. Most tables include a numeric field used to assign each record a unique number of some kind, which is called the primary key. DBMSs offer several tools to help streamline data entry and analysis processes and get the most benefit from data stored in a database. You can edit records, add records, and delete records using a query language such as Structured Query Language (SQL). Mastery of this query language can significantly increase the efficiency of working with a database.

A data breach can be costly in terms of negative media exposure, loss of trust with customers or business partners, and government fines or even jailtime. Each user should be required to use long, secure passwords and should only be given the minimum access privileges required to do their job, which is called the principle of least privilege. Database servers should reside in more secure segments of the network behind a firewall. Sensitive data in a database should be encrypted. One way to address availability of data is to back up a database. Backups must be created or updated on a regular basis.

Large and complex data sources that defy easy handling with traditional data processing methods are called Big Data. Being able to analyze Big Data provides a bird's eye view of how well a business is functioning and gives insights into how to improve business processes and increase productivity,

which collectively is called business intelligence (BI). BI systems might collect data from existing databases and from live data streams into a central repository called a data warehouse. Where data warehouses collect and analyze structured data, a data lake allows for more diverse data formats, including collecting raw data such as video streams or IoT sensor data. Data from a data warehouse or data lake is summarized and analyzed, and then it's often presented to decision makers in dashboards with live updates. Emerging patterns and insights from these data analytics processes help to inform business decisions and strategies.

Review Questions

1. In a veterinarian's database, data about an individual pet would be stored as a separate _____.

    a. table
    b. column
    c. field
    d. record

2. Aimee works for a martial arts studio. Which of the following tables will give her contact information for a student who requested more information about a new class being offered?

    a. Classes
    b. Locations
    c. Instructors
    d. Students

3. (True or False) Nonrelational databases offer the same kind of data consistency and data validation as relational databases do.

4. To handle a quickly increasing number of files, a cloud-based database for a website where thousands of users will post their own photos needs to be highly _____.

    a. available
    b. scalable
    c. consistent
    d. distributed

5. Carlos's small start-up company can't afford their own servers, but they need a robust database for their new web app. Which of the following is the best fit for Carlos's needs?

    a. Microsoft Access
    b. Google Docs
    c. Amazon Aurora
    d. Microsoft Excel

6. (True or False) One table's primary key can be another table's foreign key.

7. Which SQL statement would show the type of pet most preferred by people over the age of 64?

    a. INSERT INTO TblPets (Owner, Species)
       VALUES ('Retired', 'Pet')
    b. SELECT OwnerAge
       FROM TblOwner
       WHERE OwnerAge >64
    c. SELECT Species
       FROM TblPets
       WHERE OwnerAge >64
    d. SELECT Species
       FROM TblOwners
       WHERE Pet='Yes'

8. Chantelle wants to change the color scheme for her company's web app, and she needs to get the logos updated. What kind of developer would be best for Chantelle to talk to?

    a. Back-end
    b. Front-end
    c. DBA
    d. Mobile

9. Which of the following techniques most likely would be detrimental to the security of an insurance company's database?

    a. Require long account passwords.
    b. Encrypt customer contact information.
    c. Install the database server behind a firewall.
    d. Allow any user to add new tables.

10. Which aspect of the CIA triad requires that databases be backed up often?

    a. Availability
    b. Integrity
    c. Scalability
    d. Confidentiality

11. What's the most important reason that Big Data is often managed in a cloud environment?

    a. Volume
    b. Veracity
    c. Value
    d. Variety

12. For updated, at-a-glance information on current stock prices, a financial planner can check their _____.

    a. data warehouse
    b. relational database
    c. dashboard
    d. data lake

Discussion Questions

1. What do you think is the biggest advantage a customer database can offer a small business over keeping lists of customer information in a spreadsheet? If you were a small business owner, what are two ways you could use a customer database to better serve your customers? Identify one or two databases you believe you have interacted with as a consumer.

2. The module described key-value stores as a type of nonrelational database. Do some online research and make a list of three more types of nonrelational databases. In comparing relational and nonrelational databases, which do you think you would prefer to work with and learn more about, and why?

3. You are designing a database for a non-profit that will serve economically disadvantaged children by connecting them with mentors in the local business community. What are three tables you will need to include in your database? If you were creating a new database to use in your own life, what kind of data might the database track?

4. Many companies use Big Data to develop deeper insights into existing markets and potential new markets. However, data analysis of smaller portions of a data warehouse or data lake is often more informative than an attempt to analyze the entire thing. Do some online research to find out what a data mart is. Explain how a data mart differs from a data warehouse. Give two examples of a data mart.

Critical Thinking Activities

1. You work as a database administrator, and you've been asked by your employer to serve on a project team developing a new vendor database. You believe a relational database would be the best fit, given the project parameters and the requirements for immediate consistency. However, you need to supply your team members with some explanation as to why this is your recommendation. How would you explain the differences between the ACID model and the BASE model? Why is ACID compliance so important for relational databases?

2. You are creating a database to support an e-commerce website that sells gaming merchandise. Because you need to balance security with performance, you must choose only some parts of the data to be encrypted. Thinking about the data that might be stored in this database, which parts of that data would you say most need to be encrypted? How did you decide which parts of the data require that level of protection?

3. In your work as a database administrator for a manufacturing plant, you must decide how often your inventory database should be backed up. Inventory levels change throughout the day, and the company would be temporarily at a standstill and unable to function if the database was unavailable. However, every time you create a backup copy of the database, network speeds across the company slow down and negatively impact other workflows. How often do you think this database should be backed up? Where could you store the backup so it would not be affected by a destructive event, such as a fire or flood, at the manufacturing plant? Do you back up your own, personal files and photographs? What kinds of backup methods could you use for your own data?

4. The use of Big Data offers both benefits and risks. Benefits include better understanding of issues and interests as well as more effective technology to meet current needs. Risks might include less privacy for the people whose data is collected, inflated expectations, and greater dependence on technology. Research the pros and cons of collecting and using Big Data to make business decisions. Do you think the use of Big Data is worth the risks, and why do think this way? What concerns should be considered in determining which data can be collected and how?

Apply Your Skills

Safia Karimi works for a real estate broker's office. One of her responsibilities is to pull lists of properties that meet a range of requirements for clients looking to buy a home. Buyers might want a property in a certain part of town or with a certain number of bedrooms and bathrooms. And of course, there's always a budget to consider. As Safia is fine-tuning a list of properties for one client, she's also advising property owners on what prices to list their properties according to current market demands for different kinds and locations of comparable homes. Safia tracks all this information through a variety of databases that constantly monitor property sales throughout her region.

Working in a small group or by yourself, complete the following:

1. Some databases are intended for internal use only, while other databases are built for customer access. What is an example of each—an internal database and a customer-facing database—that a real estate office might use? Which of these databases do you think would most benefit from being stored in the cloud instead of on the real estate office's own servers? If you were shopping for a new home, what kind of information would you want to be able to find about properties in a real estate database?

2. Safia needs to find a list of low-cost homes for a small family of two adults and one child. Which SQL command will help her find this information, and how could she use it to query the database? Thinking of the different tables a real estate database might contain, on what table would she likely run this query, and why do you think this table would be helpful? What factors might she need to include in the query to restrict the results only to relevant properties?

3. Safia's boss has asked her to help research some ideas for how they might adjust their advertising strategies to expand their customer market. What are some Big Data topics or sources that might help Safia uncover and develop ideas for new markets? How could Safia's company use Big Data to improve their marketing efforts? Thinking about your chosen career path or your dream job, in what ways might using Big Data help with your work? What skills might you need to work effectively with Big Data in the future?

Digital Ethics and Lifestyle

In This Module

- Define the legal and ethical responsibilities of a digital citizen
- Explain the importance of information accuracy
- List ways to ensure content is accessible
- Explain how to promote a healthy digital lifestyle

Ilana knows that being a digital citizen includes being able to identify inaccurate information and ensuring digital inclusion.

Ilana's posture helps her avoid text neck.

Tomorrow Ilana will put away her devices and have a digital detox.

Tatiana Buzmakova/Shutterstock.com

Ilana Goldberg is studying to be a paralegal. While doing an internship with a local law firm, she became aware of many of the legal and ethical issues related to technology use. She wrote guidelines to distribute to members of the law firm on information accuracy and accessibility of technology and content. Since returning to school, Ilana has looked up her school's policies regarding appropriate technology use and is planning a monthly digital detox.

Users of modern technology must navigate a challenging and ever-changing landscape in which the difference between right and wrong is not always clear. Being a good digital citizen encompasses many concepts with which you should be familiar, including green computing, getting permission to use others' content, and protecting your devices from hacking. Your goal, as a responsible digital citizen, is to strive to always behave ethically. This means staying aware of your legal and ethical obligations to avoid breaking the law or causing harm to others or yourself. It also means using available technologies in a way that respects others' privacy, does not provide or endorse misleading information, promotes accessibility, protects your identity, and safeguards your behavioral and physical health.

In this module, you will explore and recall issues and practicalities surrounding digital ethics. You will investigate the importance of information accuracy, accessibility, and impacts on your health and privacy. As you reflect on what you learn in this module, ask yourself: What do I need to do to be a responsible digital citizen? How can I identify inaccurate information? What is my responsibility to provide accessible content to others? How can I protect my personal information?

Define the Legal and Ethical Responsibilities of a Digital Citizen

Digital ethics is the set of legal and moral guidelines that govern the use of technology, including computers, mobile devices, information systems, databases, and more. Ethical questions arise in every aspect of technology. Every digital citizen is responsible for educating themselves about their obligations, as well as their own rights. Not knowing or understanding the laws and rules that apply to you often is not recognized as a reason or excuse for not following them.

Simply following existing laws may not cover all aspects of being a digital citizen, as the laws that govern technology are not always as specific as others, such as traffic laws and building codes. Technology changes so quickly that it often raises issues not covered by current law. Because the average person doesn't follow technology developments closely, society as a whole often lags in its ability to develop a consensus about the ethics of technology-related situations. That means responsible digital citizens must sometimes make their own decisions about what's right and what's wrong, always keeping in mind that violating digital ethics has negative consequences for themselves and others beyond violating laws. You have learned about various technologies, and some ethical issues have been addressed (**Figure 14-1**), but others also exist.

Figure 14-1: Common digital ethics issues

Internet of Things
Green Computing **Net Neutrality**
Closed vs. Open Source code
Copyrights Hoaxes **Robotics**
Piracy **Big Data**
Zombies Responsive Design
Netiquette Spyware Cybersecurity
Artificial Intelligence

Figure 14-2: Technology raises many ethical and legal questions

> ✓ Is it ever acceptable to use a fake name online?
> ✓ What laws exist to monitor cyberbullying?
> ✓ How can I prevent distracted driving?
> ✓ Can I use my company-issued device for personal communication?
> ✓ Why is digital inclusion an important ethical issue?
> ✓ How can I recognize a deep fake?
> ✓ Should I do a digital detox?
> ✓ Why is keyword stuffing unethical?

Like many ethical questions, digital ethical questions don't always have easy answers. They can involve complex issues related to privacy and protecting the identity, rights, and behavioral health of individuals (**Figure 14-2**).

Differentiate between Digital Literacy and Digital Citizenship

Digital literacy is having a current knowledge and understanding of technology and an ability to use it, combined with an awareness of commonly used technologies. Digital citizenship refers to the ethical, legal, and productive use of technology. Keep in mind that you can be digitally literate without being a responsible digital citizen. For example, digitally literate people know how to copy and paste information from one source into another. Digital citizens know when it is appropriate to copy and paste information, how to properly credit the source, and the ramifications of violating copyright restrictions.

Other facets of digital citizenship include adhering to the relevant laws, abiding by commonly accepted etiquette guidelines, staying aware of your rights and the rights of others, keeping your information secure, and taking care not to adopt unhealthy technology habits. These aspects guide how you access, communicate, shop, and more with technology.

Because lawmakers are struggling to adapt existing laws to cover technology, it can be difficult to know how to address the legal, ethical, and moral consequences. Making things more complicated, actions can be legal but not ethical, or legal and ethical, but not moral (**Figure 14-3**). An action is legal if it breaks no laws. An action is ethical if it adheres to certain defined standards, often spelled out in a code of ethics or generally agreed on by society. Whether an action is moral often is a relative question, depending on the standards of individual people. Your code of what is right and just influences whether you consider your actions or

Figure 14-3: Technology use can have legal, ethical, and moral consequences

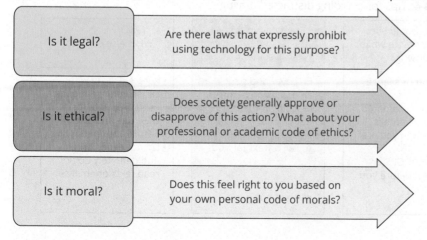

Is it legal? — Are there laws that expressly prohibit using technology for this purpose?

Is it ethical? — Does society generally approve or disapprove of this action? What about your professional or academic code of ethics?

Is it moral? — Does this feel right to you based on your own personal code of morals?

those of others to be moral. However, others' moral codes may differ from yours based on their experiences and situations. For example, it is legal for a lawyer to help prevent a client from going to jail, even if the client admits to a serious crime. Not only is it legal, the ethical code of conduct for lawyers makes it mandatory for a lawyer to do so. However, individual people might consider it immoral to help keep an admitted criminal from going to prison.

The first step in evaluating a situation involving digital ethics is to consider whether an action is acceptable if it were done without using technology. For example, speaking negatively about another person can be harmful when done face to face. If done through messaging or social media, it can cause even more damage as the message or post can be shared, reposted, and distributed to many.

While questions related to the use of technology do not always have clear answers, a digital citizen always tries to behave in a socially responsible manner, remaining aware at all times of the potential impact of their behavior on others. It can be helpful to think of the dangers and unintended consequences of your behavior on yourself, others, and society as a whole.

Describe Restrictions Regarding Technology Use

Many laws are being debated, revised, and passed to deal with how technology complicates problems like harassment or bullying, abuse of or attacks on free speech, invasions of privacy, and copyright infringement. Online activity allows for some level of anonymity, making it challenging to identify the perpetrators. Laws, which vary widely, are being adapted to address these problems. Companies and schools struggle to monitor and regulate use of technology while also respecting employees' and students' privacy and rights.

Technology Laws   Missouri is one state that has attempted to define and enact punishment for cyberbullying. A Missouri statute defines cyberbullying as bullying "through the transmission of a communication including, but not limited to, a message, text, sound, or image by means of an electronic device." The law states that schools are required to report any instances of cyberbullying, and that perpetrators can be convicted of a felony.

Other states, such as Massachusetts, have enacted "hands-free" laws to prevent distracted drivers from causing accidents. **Distracted driving** means driving a vehicle while focusing on other activities, typically involving an electronic device such as a cell phone. The law prohibits texting and all other activities while driving. Other recommendations exist that help drivers understand their role in keeping themselves and others safe (**Figure 14-4**).

Connecticut is one of many U.S. states that is attempting to regulate use of artificial intelligence (AI). The state legislature recently passed a law requiring the state's Department of Administrative Services to provide a list and complete an inventory of all systems used by state agencies that use AI. The law also included a provision requiring that lawmakers create policies and guidelines regarding use and development of AI systems.

Figure 14-4: Tips for avoiding distracted driving

What should I do with my device while driving?	What if I remember that I need to text or call someone?	What else can I do?
• Turn it off or silence it. • Set up an automated response that tells people when you are driving. • Set up your GPS or maps app before you start driving.	• Pull over and park in a safe location before reaching for your device. • Ask your passengers to call or text for you.	• Keep kids safe with car seats or seat belts, as appropriate for their age and size. • Secure your pets. • Do not eat or drink, and definitely do not read texts or emails.

Figure 14-5: Applications of the right to be forgotten

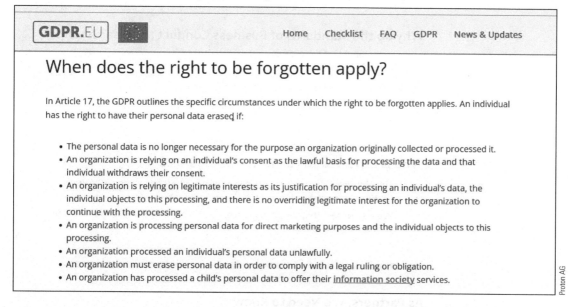

The European Union's General Data Protection Regulation (GDPR) also is called the "Right to be Forgotten" (**Figure 14-5**). Under these provisions, individuals have the right to request that their personal data be erased in certain circumstances. For example, if the data no longer is necessary for the original purpose under which it was collected, if the individual withdraws their consent after first agreeing to it, if the data was illegally collected, or if the data only was collected for marketing purposes.

Acceptable Use Policies   Schools, businesses, and organizations often lay out their expectations and rules for digital citizenship in acceptable use policies. An **acceptable use policy (AUP)** is a document that lists guidelines and repercussions of use of the Internet and other digital company resources, including network storage and email servers.

An AUP is distributed in part to reduce an organization's liability and to clarify what is and isn't a fireable offense (**Figure 14-6**). For example, if an employee uses their company's email server to send harassing email or uses the company's network resources to hack into

Figure 14-6: Portion of an AUP from the University of Texas at Austin

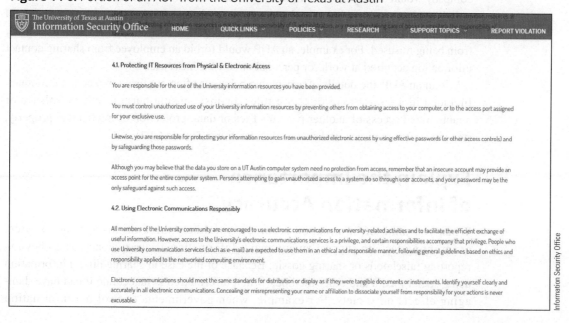

Figure 14-7: Portion of Code of Conducts for Starbucks

Why do the Standards of Business Conduct (Standards) Exist?
- As a global company, we are subject to the highest standards of ethical conduct and behavior
- The Standards help us make decisions in our daily work
- The Standards demonstrate that we take our legal and ethical responsibilities seriously

Who is Expected to Follow the Standards?
- The Standards apply to all partners, officers, and board of directors, as well as temporary service workers and independent contractors
- We also expect that third parties working on our behalf will follow similarly high ethical standards

As Partners, We Need to Know:
- Know and follow the Standards and company policies that apply to our jobs
- Ask questions when we are unsure of the right course of action
- Speak up when we see or suspect misconduct

Leaders and Managers Set the Tone
- Set high expectations for partners and lead by example
- Foster an open-door culture where partners feel comfortable asking questions and reporting concerns
- Be alert to possible misconduct in the workplace
- Promote ethics and compliance through continued learning opportunities

Starbucks Coffee Company

another website, and that employee has signed an AUP forbidding such behavior, then the company would clearly have the right to terminate the employee. AUPs typically cover not only illegal or unethical behavior but also actions that waste company resources or time. Companies also use AUPs to protect company data, such as customer contact information, from being misused. For example, an AUP would forbid an employee from sharing contact information acquired at work for personal or non-business use.

Within an AUP, the details of acceptable behavior often are listed in a code of conduct. Included in a **code of conduct** are rules against causing harm to others, misuse or unauthorized access of another person's files or data, protection of intellectual property, stealing, software piracy, and social considerations (**Figure 14-7**).

Explain the Importance of Information Accuracy

When you think of information accuracy, you likely think of misquoting a source, or inventing facts to support an argument. Information accuracy concerns go beyond reporting falsehoods or sharing gossip. Because of the ease in sharing digital information using social media and other methods, when information is inaccurate it can have damaging effects on society. For example, when governments control the information their citizens can access, and only permit sponsored or approved content to be available, their citizens are at a global disadvantage. As a digital citizen you should recognize the impact of inaccurate or incomplete information.

Citizen journalism is the involvement of non-journalists to write, edit, create, and distribute news content. Citizen journalists often collaborate with others to source and analyze information in order to report on it. While there is nothing illegal or unethical about citizen journalism, there are guidelines professional reporters use to create accurate, unbiased, and responsible content that will be published by reliable news sources. These guidelines cover including sources and giving the opportunity to show both sides of a story. Because citizen journalists can self-publish information using social media and blogs, they are not held to the same standards required of reporters submitting content to established news sources. Proponents of citizen journalism argue that not being held to these guidelines enables their reporting to uncover and share information that may not be available to professionals. In addition, for local coverage, citizen journalists often can approach and elicit information from sources whom they know, but who may not feel able or be authorized to speak with members of the press.

List Examples of Deception

The use of digital technologies to misrepresent or mislead is difficult to monitor or recognize. The practices you have already learned about, including evaluating the source of information, is just the start. Identifying additional ways technology is being used to create false information will help you evaluate and promote accuracy.

- One issue that has legal, ethical, and moral implications is the use of fake names or IDs online. It may seem harmless, or even safer, to use a fake name, but bad actors do this regularly to harm other people. The term **catfishing** refers to a deliberate attempt to mislead people about your identity by creating a fake online profile. People might do this to lure someone into a relationship on false pretenses on an online dating site in order to humiliate or extract money from the victim, or to leave malicious comments on a website. Using a fake name to hide or obscure your identity can sometimes be a security measure and is not always immoral or bad. For example, using a nickname to protect your identity is acceptable; attempting to impersonate a celebrity or other person is not. Some social media sites require you to use your real name. Others allow you to create a profile using any name you like but have a verification process to identify the official account of a celebrity or public figure to protect them from impersonation.

Figure 14-8: Deep fakes alter images such as faces

- A **deep fake** is a video or other digital content that has been altered or created to digitally replace a person with a different person (**Figure 14-8**). Typically this type of content is meant to embarrass, slander, or cause legal issues to the person being targeted. An example is creating a video that alters the appearance of someone doing an illegal act with the face and body of someone well known, such as a politician.

- AI can be misused to create seemingly real text or visual content, including deep fakes. AI-generated content, even when well-intentioned, needs to be fact-checked for accuracy. In one example, an attorney was punished for submitting a legal brief generated using AI that cited several cases that did not exist.

- **Deceptive design**, also called **dark patterns**, are techniques used in app and web design to get the user to unintentionally sign up for or buy something. Examples include making it difficult to find or access options to unsubscribe or to change privacy or notification settings, automatically subscribing a user to a paid version of an app after a "free" trial, or requiring users to enable features that allow the app or website to monitor user's activities.

Describe Ethical SEO Practices

Search engines rely on several factors to prioritize the links to results, including SEO. Recall that search engine optimization (SEO) is the use of tools to allow search engines to better find or index a website. Search engines use **algorithms**, processes or sets of rules, to create and then determine the order and scope of the search results.

As a user of the web, you rely on web developers' ethical uses of SEO practices to ensure that the search results you get truly match and are relevant to your search keywords. You may be searching for a specific website or webpage, for more information about a topic, or for a product to buy. Your search terms will differ depending on your purpose; the SEO used to promote the website should do the same.

Common SEO practices include:

- Identifying a target keyword. A **target keyword** is the search term users are most likely to use to find the webpage. The target keyword should appear in the webpage's title, URL, and in the content.
- Using **meta tags**, which are HTML specification tags that tell search engines what data to use (**Figure 14-9**). Meta tags can exist for every page in a website and should be descriptive but concise.

Figure 14-9: Sample meta tags

iinspiration/Shutterstock.com

Figure 14-10: Sample clickbait headline phrases

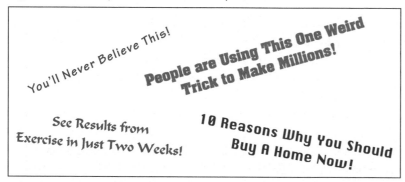

- Keeping the website organized with folders and subfolders for categories of webpages. As the folders and filenames appear in the webpage's direct URL, this will further help users find specific content within your website.

Being aware of unethical SEO practices is one way to evaluate web content for accuracy and reliability. Practices that are not recommended, and which may get your website penalized by being removed from a search engine, include:

- **Keyword stuffing**, which is the practice of using irrelevant keywords in meta tags and other website content.

- Front-loading ads at the top of the webpage, making it difficult for users to find content. This is not illegal but may violate some search engines' evaluation and ranking standards.

- **Clickbaiting**, which is using sensationalized words or phrases in your webpage titles, descriptions, and other content in order to draw users in (**Figure 14-10**). Examples include using claims to save or make money, lose weight, or learn secrets about celebrities.

List Ways to Ensure Content Is Accessible

Digital inclusion is the movement to ensure that all users, regardless of economic or geographic constraints, have access to the devices, data, and infrastructure required to receive high-speed, accurate, reliable information. The goal of digital inclusion is to ensure that everyone has access to all the resources offered online, including education, participation in local and national government, employment listings and interviews, and healthcare access. The following are some barriers to digital inclusion:

- Geographic areas that lack the infrastructure necessary to provide reliable Internet access
- Government restrictions or censorship
- Lack of affordable devices or connections
- Lack of education
- Lack of understanding of the value of technology

Define Accessible Web Development

The Americans with Disabilities Act requires online content, including websites, to be accessible to people with disabilities. Screen readers describe visual screen elements and read content aloud to users with visual impairments, and screen magnifiers let them adjust the size of screen content. Assistive listening devices interpret audio content for users with hearing impairments. Alternative keyboards and pointing devices assist those with physical impairments to navigate screen content. When working to make a website digitally

Figure 14-11: Content accessibility checklist

✓ Consider all users, including those with visual and hearing impairments, color blindness, and more.
✓ Make sure your content will work as recommended for all assistive devices, including screen readers, assistive listening devices, and adaptive input and output devices.
✓ Include captioning for all video and audio content.
✓ Add alt text for all non-text objects.
✓ Ensure the content follows a logical order as many screen readers will read from the top of a page down.
✓ Use recommended fonts, font sizes, and colors to make your page easier to read for users with learning disabilities or color blindness.
✓ Use headings to distinguish content sections.
✓ Include inline hyperlinks to external webpages or websites.
✓ Write to a ninth-grade reading or lower reading level by using shorter sentences and considering word choice.
✓ Avoid using idioms or phrases that may not be able to be translated using Google Translate or other services used to present content in a user's primary language.

accessible, it's also important to consider that some users may be color blind, or may be prone to seizures triggered by flashing animations. Being aware of methods to make your content accessible is critical to publishing content (**Figure 14-11**).

Apps used to publish online content, including content management systems and apps that save files in web-friendly formats, often include tools to check content for accessibility. One of the most important considerations when creating accessible content is to include alternative text, or alt text, which provides descriptions for all visual elements or non-text objects. Alt text should be written so that a user can understand the visual information, context, and purpose of an object. Before publishing online content, take advantage of these tools to ensure your content meets the latest accessibility standards (**Figure 14-12**).

Figure 14-12: Accessibility Toolbar plug-in options for WordPress

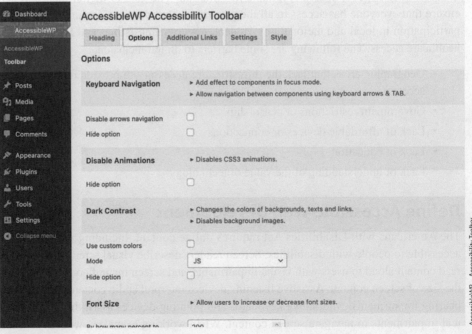

Describe Accessible App Development Practices

In addition to the same principles used in accessible web development, such as color contrast, use of alt-text, and clear and consistent navigation, there are other ways developers take accessibility into consideration.

- Keep text and font choices simple and remember that users with dyslexia and visual impairments find some fonts and text styles easier to read than others.
- Offer personalization options that allow users to change the screen orientation, font and font size, and screen resolution so that users can customize their experience to meet their needs and preferences.
- Test your app with a wide audience, and include options for users to review and submit feedback about their experiences.
- Allow for a variety of input methods, including choice of gestures and voice input.

List Examples of Content Bias

You may assume that, since technology at its roots deals with numbers and code, technology is unbiased. However, many technological developments have resulted in apps and systems that carry unintended content biases. Bias refers to any prejudice or favoritism towards a group, such as an ethnicity, gender, or identity. A **content bias** is when information being presented or interpreted excludes or shows preference to a group. Bias is not always obvious, especially in technology, where it can be an unintentional part of the app code or available data. Recognizing and working to correct these biases will help you understand how to ensure equality in access to and representation in technology.

Speech Recognition Apps   Speech recognition apps often have trouble recognizing certain accents, including those associated with certain ethnic and geographical groups. This is due in part to the way these apps are trained. Developers start with a set of voice samples, which may not fully reflect the voices of the population. American English often is used as the default for recognizing accents and speech patterns, making the technology more difficult, if not impossible, especially for non-native English speakers.

To overcome these biases, some users may resort to using speech patterns that are more commonly recognized by speech recognition apps, essentially hiding their true accent. Having to adjust in this way prevents these from benefitting equally from the technology. It also harms society at large, because it perpetuates a reduced set of voices contributing to what is average or perceived as standard. And because the technology may be more difficult to train for some, they may give up using it, further restricting their voices and contributions.

Automated Screening Processes   Content bias also affects automated screening processes, such as resume screening or facial recognition. For example, a technology company realized its resume filter prioritized verbs that were associated with male-identifying applicants. Facial recognition apps can also have trouble making distinctions between people of certain racial backgrounds, such as people who are Black or Asian, because the identifying features used by the technology may not take into account physical traits associated with those ethnicities.

Data Pools   In a data pool used to train AI systems or used in other technologies, if one group is under- or over-represented, it can skew not only the data but the resulting output. A **data pool** is the source, often a database, of values used by a technology. Because of this, not only are certain ethnic or societal groups ignored, such as minorities, those with non-binary genders, or people with certain religious beliefs, but the results can include a confirmation bias that makes assumptions about certain groups' influence or participation. Some AI content-generating apps have been accused of having a liberal political bias. AI-generated content makes assumptions based on the data to which it has access. Ensuring better representation of data pools can help remove these biases.

To reduce content bias, developers of speech and screening technologies increasingly are adapting the apps and increasing the scope of their data pools so that they recognize a wider, more diverse array of individuals. Recognizing the limitations of these apps and technologies and actively working to improve and avoid content biases is essential to providing equal access and opportunities.

Explain How to Promote a Healthy Digital Lifestyle

Technology makes many things in your life more convenient. You should consider how it affects your ability to manage your time, and whether ultimately technology makes you more or less efficient. Responsible digital citizens regularly evaluate their use of technology to make sure it really is making their lives better.

Technology use can have positive and negative impacts on an individual socially, legally, physically, and mentally. Knowing the risks can help you protect your health, identity, and position in society.

Create a Digital Wellness Plan

While you likely are familiar with some of the physical and behavioral concerns with technology use, you also should learn how to prevent them or minimize their impact. Physical risks include repetitive strain injuries (RSI) that impact your muscles, nerves, tendons, and ligaments in joints such as elbows, wrists, and shoulders, as well as your neck, hands, and forearms. Poor postures can lead to **text neck**, which is tightness or discomfort in the neck due to looking down at your phone or device for long periods. Spending too much time looking at devices can cause eyes to be itchy, sore, or dry, or cause headaches due to **eye strain**.

To prevent or reduce the physical effects of long-term technology use, follow these practices:

- Take hourly breaks. Consider setting an alarm on your device as a reminder. During a break, move your body and don't look at your screens.
- Correct your posture. Keep your shoulders relaxed, and, if looking at your phone for long periods, put it in front of your face to avoid looking down.
- Don't text and walk. Distracted digital users are more prone to falls or getting hit by a moving vehicle.
- Stand up while you work at your desk. Use props to place your computer at a comfortable height or a desk that converts from sitting to standing height (**Figure 14-13**).
- Resist succumbing to a sedentary lifestyle. Do not substitute technology use for regular exercise.

Experiencing anxiety when you cannot check your phone for a prolonged period is a sign of technology addiction. This type of addiction, in which a person is obsessed with using technology and feels anxiety when away from devices, can actually result in lower productivity and lower quality of life. Using devices before bed can make it difficult to sleep. Psychological issues that can be increased with overuse of technology include social anxiety, depression, feelings of isolation, and lower life satisfaction. Use of technology can hinder or impair social skill development.

Figure 14-13: Convertible stand up desk

Michael O'Keene/Shutterstock.com

To prevent or reduce the behavioral health effects of long-term technology use, follow these practices:

- Take frequent breaks, and consider a digital detox if you see signs of technology addiction.

- Turn off devices at least an hour before bedtime to make it easier to fall asleep.

- Use social media moderately. Consider your motivations and expected response before posting or commenting to avoid creating conflicts. Remember that much of what people post is only a small part of their life, and that people tend to post more positive than negative aspects of their lives.

- Restrict use of devices during social interactions, such as dinners with friends or family, to maintain your social connections.

- Safeguard your identity and privacy to avoid identity theft or invasions of privacy, which are stressful situations.

One concern is that for smartphone users technology access is always at your fingertips. It can be hard to create separation from the physical devices as well as the information, entertainment, and communication opportunities.

Experts recommend taking occasional breaks from digital devices. A **digital detox** is a period of time during which an individual refrains from using technology. Participation in a digital detox has behavioral health benefits, including better sleep, less anxiety, and more productive thoughts. A break from devices also can help alleviate physical problems such as eye strain and repetitive stress injuries.

Understanding the effects of technology on time management is another way to protect your behavioral and social health. Keep a log for several days about how much time you spend using devices in ways that are productive or unproductive. Analyze how your technology use affects your productivity. Be accountable for managing your time using apps that prohibit specific technology uses, such as gaming or social media, during work or school hours.

List Steps to Safeguard Your Information

Personally identifiable information (PII) is anything that can be used to uncover an individual's unique identity, such as fingerprints. Since many people have the same name as others, a person's full name typically isn't considered PII. Handwriting and facial recognition sometimes are considered PII, but aren't as exclusive as numerical data. Examples of numerical PII include:

- Social security number (SSN)
- Email address
- Phone number
- Driver's license number
- License plate number
- Credit card number

Hackers attempt to collect PII from a variety of sources, including:

- Personnel or student databases, which often include SSN, email, and phone numbers
- Motor vehicle registration or car insurance databases, which would include a license plate and driver's license number
- Retail businesses, which would include a person's credit card information

Collecting PII can be lucrative for hackers, as it can enable them to take out bank loans, incur charges on a new credit card, or make purchases or borrow funds that can ruin the financial credit of the person whose PII was used.

In addition to hackers, smart technology such as electric meters, smart TVs, wearable technology, and GPS devices submit data about your usage to companies that then use it for their own purposes—often to sell you more products or track your whereabouts. To protect yourself and limit your exposure to data collection, be sure to enable privacy settings on your IoT devices. Watch the news for companies or products that experience a **data breach**, which is any unauthorized collection or distribution of data. If you discover that a company with which you do business has been hacked, contact them to see if your data was accessed, change your passwords, and keep an eye on any suspicious activity.

Module 14 Summary

Digital ethics refers to the legal and moral guidelines for all uses of technology. Digital citizens should understand their responsibilities to be digitally ethical, as well as their rights. Laws and society often lag behind in developing legislation and opinions on ethical technology use. Ethical questions arise around privacy, and protection of identity and rights of others.

Digital citizens know not only how to use technology, but what uses are ethical and unethical. Digital citizens also should know the laws, accepted etiquette, rights, and how to develop healthy technology habits. They also should

understand how to identify if something is ethical, moral, and/or legal.

States and governments are attempting to keep up with laws that cover use of new and developing technologies, especially in areas such as cyberbullying, distracted driving, artificial intelligence (AI), and digital privacy. Acceptable use policies (AUPs) define accepted uses and restrictions on the use of technology at a school, business, or organization. Often a code of conduct is included in an AUP, which outlines acceptable behavior.

Concerns regarding information accuracy include not only reporting false information, but other practices that may result in inaccurate or misleading information. Citizen journalism has its positive and negative aspects and is not illegal or unethical. The lack of restrictions placed on professional journalists enables amateur writers to publish and quote information that may not meet all journalistic standards for ethics.

Examples of deceptive technology practices include catfishing, deep fakes, misuse of AI, and deceptive design. Catfishing occurs when a person misleads another about their online identity. Deep fakes are the use of AI and other technologies to create content that shows a person doing or saying something that they did not do. Deceptive design is a technique used by website and app developers to trick users.

Search engines use algorithms to determine search results. To promote their content in search engines' result lists, ethical web developers use target keywords, meta tags, and web folders to identify their content clearly and accurately. Unethical development practices used to attempt to get higher in SEO results include keyword stuffing (using irrelevant keywords), front loading ads, or using clickbait headlines to lure people in.

Digital inclusion is the effort to ensure all users have access to devices, data, and infrastructure needed to quickly access reliable information. Barriers to digital inclusion include: geographic lack of infrastructure, government restrictions, lack of affordable devices, or connections, and lack of education or understanding of the value of technology.

Accessible web content is regulated by the Americans with Disabilities Act. Factors include: optimizing content for screen readers and assistive listening devices, allowing adjustment in screen content size, and allowing flexibility in navigation. Website publishing apps often offer tools to check content for accessibility.

It is important to acknowledge and identify technological biases. Speech recognition apps often default to certain accents and are not easy to use for people from certain ethnic or geographic groups. Resume screening algorithms have been found to focus on certain phrases or words that are associated with different genders. Another bias exists in the data pools used to train AI and other systems. If the data pool is not diverse enough, it can instruct the technology to make assumptions and distinctions that do not represent all users.

Text neck and eye strain are two well-known physical risks to prolonged technology use. A digital wellness plan may include recommendations such as: taking breaks, using correct posture, not texting and walking, and using a stand-up desk. Behavioral health risks can be prevented by turning off devices before sleep and using social media moderately. A digital detox is a time when a user refrains from using technology to improve sleep and decrease anxiety, for example.

Hackers use personally identifiable information (PII) to create fake profiles or take out loans or credit cards in another person's name. Examples of PII include fingerprints, email, social security numbers, and vehicle license plate numbers. Smart devices that track and sell your PII are another risk. Look out for data breaches, which are known examples of successful hacking that resulted in unauthorized distribution of PII.

Review Questions

1. (True or False). An action is ethical if it breaks no laws. An action is legal if it adheres to certain defined standards, often spelled out in a code or generally agreed on by society.

2. The EU's GDPR regulates _____.
   a. information privacy
   b. AI usage
   c. distracted driving
   d. cyberbullying

3. AUP stands for _____ use policy.
   a. activity
   b. acceptable
   c. app
   d. administrative

4. The involvement of non-journalists to write, edit, create, and distribute news content is known as _____ journalism.
   a. citizen
   b. populist
   c. amateur
   d. social

5. The deliberate posting of content intended to cause harm or mislead people by tricking them into believing something that is false is known as _____.
   a. deep fakes
   b. deceptive design
   c. dark patterns
   d. catfishing

6. An HTML specification tag that tells search engines what data to use is a(n) _____ tag.

   a. beta
   b. SEO
   c. meta
   d. accessible

7. The movement to ensure that all users have access to devices, data, and infrastructure to receive high-speed, accurate, reliable information is referred to as digital _____.

   a. ethics
   b. inclusion
   c. citizenship
   d. literacy

8. So that a user can understand the visual information, context, and purpose of an object, you should include _____ in your website content.

   a. HTML tags
   b. SEO techniques
   c. alt text
   d. content management systems

9. Including options for gestures and voice for _____ is an important part of accessible app development.

   a. input
   b. output
   c. screen size
   d. alt text

10. (True or False) Since technology at its roots deals with numbers and code, technology is unbiased.

11. A period of time during which an individual refrains from using technology is known as a digital _____.

   a. divide
   b. quarantine
   c. vacation
   d. detox

12. SSNs and driver's license numbers are examples of _____.

   a. SEO
   b. PII
   c. AI
   d. HTML

Discussion Questions

1. Describe a situation that has legal, ethical, and moral implications—for instance, seeing someone cheating on a test, or noticing that a colleague is falling for a catfishing scheme. How can you determine which elements of the situation are legal or illegal, which are ethical or unethical, and which you would consider moral or immoral? What is your responsibility to step in to help address the situation? Explain your answer.

2. Define citizen journalism. Give one pro and one con to citizen journalism. Have you ever been tempted to write a blog or article about a local event or issue? Describe a situation in which you wrote about a local event or issue as a citizen journalist. If you have not, describe what your situation would be as a citizen journalist writing a blog or article—for instance, what event or issue might you write about and what considerations would be important to you?

3. List two examples of content bias. What are the repercussions to the biases? Have you ever been affected by content bias? Name a situation in which you did or might encounter bias and what you can do to identify and fix the situation.

4. Define PII and list three examples of it. Explain how PII might get into the wrong hands. What PII have you recently submitted, and under what circumstances? Do you have concerns about your privacy? Why or why not?

Critical Thinking Activities

1. What are the characteristics of digital ethics? List two examples of technology laws. What is covered in an AUP? Have you ever had to follow an AUP and/or a code of conduct? What guidelines did or could they cover?

2. Give two examples of ethical SEO practices. Give two examples of unethical SEO practices. Why is it important to understand SEO as a digital citizen?

3. List three examples of accessibility guidelines that apply to both app and web development. In what ways have or would you personalize an app or website to meet your individual needs?

4. Define the term, digital detox. Have you ever participated in a digital detox? For what reason? If you haven't, why would it be helpful? List three activities you personally did or would miss during a digital detox. Describe how a digital detox could help someone struggling with technology addiction.

Apply Your Skills

Ilana Goldberg is studying to be a paralegal. While doing an internship with a local law firm, she became aware of many of the legal and ethical issues related to technology use. She wrote guidelines to distribute to members of the law firm on information accuracy and accessibility of technology and content. Since returning to school, Ilana has looked up her school's policies regarding appropriate technology use and is planning a monthly digital detox.

Working in a small group or by yourself, complete the following:

1. Before Ilana left her internship, she wrote a draft of an AUP for the law firm. List three areas she should cover in the AUP. Which is most important in your opinion? Why?

2. The law firm represented someone who was a victim of a deep fake video that was created about them. What technology might have been used? Why is a deep fake so harmful? What would you do in this situation?

3. Ilana was raised abroad. She has a speech recognition app she uses to dictate notes to herself while working. Often the app will incorrectly translate her speech because it does not recognize her accent. What are the negative repercussions of this type of bias? What are developers doing to avoid this situation?

4. While at the law firm, employees were asked to fill out a survey about their workspaces and how to make them more comfortable and physically healthy. List two physical problems Ilana might have written as concerns. Explain what accommodations she might ask for. Have you ever used a standing height desk? Why did or would you use one?

Index

Note: **Boldfaced** page numbers indicate key term introduced.

deception
examples of, CC 14-7–14-8
deceptive design: A technique used in app and web design to get the user to unintentionally sign up for or buy something. **CC 14-8**
deep fake: A video or other digital content that has been altered or created to digitally replace a person with a different person. **CC 14-7**
deep learning, CC 12-21
default setting: Standard setting that controls how the screen is set up and how a document looks when you first start typing. **CC 4-12**
deliverable: Any tangible item, such as a chart, diagram, report, or program file, created during development. **CC 8-5**
denial of service (DoS) attack: A type of attack, usually on a server, that is meant to overload the server with network traffic so that it cannot provide necessary services. **CC 10-15**
deprecated tag: In HTML, describes an older tag whose continued use is discouraged because newer techniques have been created to accomplish the same result. **CC 9-32**
designer, CC 8-3
design phase (SDLC): A phase of the software development lifecycle when the project team acquires the necessary hardware and programming languages/tools, as well as develops the details of the finished product. **CC 8-8**–8-9
desktop: The main workspace of an operating system. **CC 4-3**
desktop computer: Computer that typically consists of the system unit, monitor, keyboard, and mouse. **CC 3-5**
desktop operating system: An operating system installed on a single computer. **CC 4-7–4-8**
desktop publishing, CC 5-11
development: The process of creating programs and apps from the idea stage to distribution to users. **CC 8-2**
methodologies, CC 8-10–8-11
process components, CC 8-4–8-5
reasons for, CC 8-4–8-5
team role and responsibilities, CC 8-2, CC 8-3
tools and strategies, CC 8-11–8-18
device
input, CC 3-2
output, CC 3-3
device driver: A program that controls a device attached to your computer, such as a printer, monitor, or video card. **CC 3-19**
device management app: An app that provides tools for maintaining your computer or mobile device. **CC 5-7**
DevOps: A software development approach that encourages collaboration between the development and operations, produces programs quickly, and then offers continuous updates to increase the functionality of the program. **CC 8-10–8-11**

dialog box: A window with controls that lets you tell Windows how you want to complete an application program's command. **CC 4-4**
Digg social curation site, CC 11-15
digital assistant: An app like Amazon's Alexa or Apple's Siri that uses natural language processing to respond to your verbal commands or questions, using search technology to provide answers or perform a task, such as adding an item to a grocery list. CC 7-23, **CC 12-18**
digital audio: A type of sound that is recorded and stored as a series of 1s and 0s. **CC 7-4**
live audio feed, CC 7-16
streaming, CC 7-16
digital calendar, CC 11-18, CC 11-19
digital camera: A camera that creates a digital image of an object, person, or scene. **CC 3-15**, CC 7-18
digital certificate: A technology used to verify a user's identity by using a digital key and that has been "signed" by a trusted third party. This third party verifies the owner and that the key belongs to that owner. **CC 2-12**
digital citizen: Person familiar with how to use technology to become an educated and productive member of the digital world. **CC 1-7**
legal and ethical responsibilities, CC 14-2–14-6
digital communication: The transmittal of data, instructions, and information from one computer or mobile device to another, often via the Internet. **CC 11-2**
audio and visual, CC 11-11–11-13
impact on everyday life, CC 11-27–11-33
and netiquette principles, CC 11-2–11-3
types of written, CC 11-6–11-11
digital coupons, CC 2-15
digital detox: A period of time during which an individual refrains from using technology. **CC 14-13**
digital device: A machine that reads and produces digital, or binary, data. **CC 7-6**
digital divide: The gap between those who have access to technology and its resources and information, especially on the Internet, and those who do not. **CC 1-7**
digital ethics: The legal and moral guideline that governs the use of technology, including computers, mobile devices, information systems, databases, and more. **CC 14-2**
digital footprint: The records of everything you do online; can be nearly impossible to completely erase. **CC 11-32**
digital forensics examiners, CC 1-15
digital graphic, CC 7-3
2D and 3D, CC 7-3–7-4
digital inclusion: The movement to ensure that all users, regardless of economic or geographic constraints, have access to the devices, data and infrastructure required to receive high-speed, accurate and reliable information. **CC 14-9**
digital lifestyle, healthy, CC 14-12–14-14

G

interest-based network: A social network that is targeted to a particular audience and subject, such as cat lovers or book lovers. **CC 11-23**

Internet: A global collection of millions of computers linked together to share information worldwide. **CC 2-2**, CC 2-6

companies doing business on, CC 12-8–12-15

e-business, CC 12-9

e-commerce, CC 12-9, CC 12-10–12-15

etiquette guidelines, CC 11-16

omnichannel marketing, CC 12-10

standards, CC 2-7

Internet Engineering Task Force (IETF): A nonprofit group that sets standards to allow devices, services, and applications to work together across the Internet. **CC 2-7**

Internet forum: On a forum, an online discussion site where people with a common interest participate in a conversation by posting messages; also called a message board. **CC 11-15**

Internet of Things (IoT): An environment where processors are embedded in every product imaginable (things), and these things communicate with one another via the Internet or wireless networks. **CC 1-3**, CC 8-18

AI-powered, CC 12-22–12-24

in business, CC 1-6

at home, CC 1-5–1-6

network, CC 10-10–10-12

Internet peer-to-peer (Internet P2P) network: A type of P2P network where users share files with each other over the Internet. **CC 10-6**

Internet Protocol (IP) address, CC 2-5

Internet protocols, CC 10-8–10-9

Internet Service Provider (ISP): A company that sells Internet access. **CC 2-6**, CC 10-3, CC 10-12, C 11-5, CC 11-11

Internet telephony: Voice communications over the Internet; sometimes called Voice over Internet Telephony. **CC 11-11**

interpreter: Translates and executes one statement in a program at a time. Interpreters do not produce or store object code. Each time the source program runs, the interpreter translates instructions statement by statement. **CC 8-16**

intranet: A private network for use by authorized individuals; organizations use intranets to communicate internally and can allow users to use a web browser to access data posted on webpages. **CC 10-8**

invoice scam, CC 6-8

iOS, CC 4-9

IoT. *see* Internet of Things (IoT)

IPv4 (Internet Protocol version 4), CC 10-9

IPv6 (Internet Protocol version 6), CC 10-9

IrDA, CC 10-9

IT consultant: A professional who is hired based on technical expertise, including service and advice. CC 1-15, **CC 8-6**

IT department, CC 8-3

J

JavaScript: A popular language for writing scripts that run in your browser to control a webpage's behavior and often make it interactive. **CC 9-2**

use in website development, CC 9-3

and webpages, CC 9-40–9-42

Jobs, Steve, CC 1-3

joint-application design (JAD) session: Consists of a series of lengthy, structured group meetings in which users and IT professionals work together to design or develop an application. **CC 8-13**

joystick: Game controller with a handheld vertical lever, mounted on a base, that you move in different directions to control the actions of the simulated vehicle or player. **CC 3-16**

JPEG (Joint Photographic Experts Group), CC 5-26, CC 7-8

K

kernel: The core of an operating system; memory, runs programs, and assigns resources. **CC 4-12**

keyboard: Input device that contains not only characters such as letters, numbers, and punctuation, but also keys that can issue commands. **CC 3-14**, CC 4-13–4-14

keyframe: A location on a timeline that marks the beginning or end of a movement, effect, or transition. **CC 7-20**

keylogger: Malware that silently captures user's keystrokes, screen images, and other information without the user's knowledge. **CC 6-6**

key-value database: A database that creates any number of key-value pairs for each record. Also called a key-value store. **CC 13-6**

keyword: In a search engine, a descriptive word or phrase you enter to obtain a list of results that include that word or phrase. **CC 2-18**

keyword stuffing: The unethical SEO practice of using irrelevant keywords in meta tags and other website content. **CC 14-9**

kilobyte (KB): Thousands of bytes of data. **CC 4-18**

kiosk: A freestanding booth usually placed in a public area that can contain a display device used to show information to the public or event attendees. **CC 1-5**

L

label: In a blog, a key term associated with a post; also called a tag. **CC 11-22**

landscape orientation: The position of a page, slide, or worksheet so that the page, slide, or worksheet is wider than it is tall. **CC 5-11**

laptop: A portable computer that is smaller than the average briefcase and light enough to carry comfortably; often called a notebook. **CC 3-4**

power-on self test (POST): At startup, a sequence that tests all computer components for proper operation. **CC 3-9**

power settings, CC 4-16–4-17

predictive development: Software development that uses a linear, structured development cycle. **CC 8-10**

predictive technologies, CC 8-18

presentation: A document that lets you create and deliver a dynamic, professional-looking message to an audience in the form of a slide show. **CC 5-16**

animations in, CC 5-19

design and delivery, CC 5-19–5-21

formatting, CC 5-18

sharing and displaying, CC 5-19

template and slide master, CC 5-19

transitions in, CC 5-18

presentation app: An app that lets you create visual aids for presentations to communicate ideas, messages, and other information to a group. **CC 5-16**

primary key: The field in a database that contains unique information for each record; also called a unique identifier. **CC 13-12**

principle of least privilege: A cybersecurity strategy in which each user is given the minimum access privileges to a database required to do their job. **CC 13-20**

printer: Creates hard copy output on paper, film, and other media. **CC 3-17**

3D printer, CC 3-18

types of, CC 3-17

privacy

loss of, CC 11-32

securing, CC 6-18

private cloud: A cloud technology run on your own hardware that does not use the Internet. **CC 12-2**

procedural language: A third-generation programming language that uses a series of English-like words to write instructions. **CC 8-15**

process manager, CC 8-20

processor, CC 3-8

cache, CC 3-8

multi-core, CC 3-8

processor cache: Stores frequently used data next to the processor so that it can easily and quickly be retrieved. **CC 3-8**

multi-core, CC 3-8

productivity app: An app for personal use that you may use to create documents, develop presentations, track appointments, or to stay organized. **CC 5-8**

features of, CC 5-8–5-24

productivity suite: A collection of productivity apps such as Microsoft Office 365, Apple iWork, G Suite, or Apache OpenOffice. **CC 5-8**

professional messaging guidelines, CC 11-17

professional social networking guidelines, CC 11-16

profile: On a social networking site, information about yourself that forms your virtual identity. **CC 11-22**

programmer: The person who creates app code. **CC 8-2**, CC 8-3

language and tools selection, CC 8-14

programming language: A set of words, abbreviations, and symbols. A programmer or developer uses a programming language to create instructions for a program or app. **CC 8-8**

differentiating among, CC 8-14–8-16

programming tools

differentiating among, CC 8-16

program window: On a desktop or laptop computer, displays a running program., **CC 4-15**

project: In an IDE, the files and folders relating to a website being developed. **CC 9-9**

project leadership, CC 8-3

project management: The process of planning, scheduling, and then controlling the activities during system development. **CC 8-11**

apps, CC 8-12–8-13

data and information gathering techniques, CC 8-13–8-14

techniques, CC 8-11–8-14

project management app: An app used to assist developers in planning, scheduling, and controlling development projects. **CC 8-11**

project manager, CC 8-3

projector: Displays visual output from a computer on a large surface such as a wall or screen. **CC 3-17**

project team: Consists of users, the system analyst, and other IT professionals. **CC 8-2**, CC 8-3

prompt: A command to an AI (artificial intelligence) tool that generates a particular response, such as text generation, from the tool. **CC 12-26**

prompt engineering: The process of designing a prompt and editing it to get the desired result. **CC 12-26**–12-27

protocol: A standardized procedure computers and devices use to exchange information. **CC 2-5, CC 10-8**

prototype: A working model that demonstrates the functionality of the program or app. **CC 8-8**

public cloud: A cloud service where multiple customers use the same, Internet-connected cloud that is running on hardware owned by a cloud service provider. **CC 12-2**

characteristics of, CC 12-3–12-4

public domain: The item, such as a photo, is available and accessible to the public without requiring permission to use, and therefore is not subject to copyright. **CC 2-22**

apps, CC 8-19

programs, CC 8-19

Public Technical Identifiers (PTI), CC 2-7

publish: To post a website to a web server online, or if using a content management system, to upload content to a content management systems, so it is visible on a website on the Internet. **CC 9-14**

makes it easy to transport folders and files to other computers; also called a pen drive, flash drive, jump drive, keychain. **CC 3-8**

USB hub: An external device that contains many USB ports. **CC 3-6**

user account: Identifies the resources, such as apps and storage locations, a user can access when working with the computer. **CC 4-18**

User Experience (UX): The focus on the user's reaction to and interaction with a product, including its efficiency, effectiveness, and ease of use. **CC 8-4**

users with disabilities, and technology, CC 1-9–1-11

U.S. Federal Communication Commission (FCC), CC 2-20

utility: An app or program that enables you to perform maintenance-type tasks related to managing the computer or device. **CC 4-7**

V

vacuum tube: Cylindrical glass tube that controlled the flow of electrons, used in the first generation of computers. **CC 1-2**

value-added reseller (VAR): An organization that purchases products from manufacturers and then resells these products to the public, offering additional services with the product. **CC 8-6**

vector graphic: A format for storing digital images that tend to be simple images composed of shapes, lines, and diagrams. **CC 5-25**, CC 7-3

vendor proposal
  decisions, CC 8-6
  requests, CC 8-6
  technical specifications, CC 8-5
  testing, CC 8-6

video
  capturing, CC 7-23–7-24
  developing original, CC 7-23–7-24
  hardware and apps, CC 7-16
  streaming, CC 7-15–7-16
  on the web, CC 7-16

video calling: A face-to-face conversation held over a network such as the Internet using a webcam, microphone, speakers, display device, and special software; also called video chat. **CC 11-11**

video card: A circuit board that processes image signals. **CC 3-20**, CC 7-16

video chat, CC 11-26

video conference: A meeting among several geographically separated people who use a network or the Internet to transmit audio and video data; also called a web conference. **CC 7-16**, CC 11-25–11-26

video console: A hardware device with special controllers that let you play video games. **CC 7-11**

video editing app: An app that allows you to modify a segment of a video, called a clip. **CC 5-28**, CC 7-24

video file format, CC 7-9–7-10

video file resolution, CC 7-7–7-8

video game, CC 12-19

video job interview, CC 11-26

video messaging: Leaving a video message for a recipient to pick up later. **CC 11-12**

video podcast: A file that contains video and audio, and is usually offered as part of a subscription to a podcasting service. **CC 11-11**

view-only link: A link to a workbook on a OneDrive that can be viewed by users. **CC 5-12**

viral: A video that has been shared millions of times over social media in a short period of time. **CC 7-16**

virtual assistant, CC 12-19

virtualization: The practice of sharing computing resources, such as servers or storage devices, among computers and devices on a network. **CC 4-9**

virtual machine (VM): Enables a computer or device to run another operating system in addition to the one installed. **CC 4-17**

virtual memory: The capability of an operating system to temporarily store data on a storage medium until it can be "swapped" into RAM. **CC 3-10**, CC 4-11

virtual private network (VPN): A private, secure path across a public network that allows authorized users secure access to a company or other network. **CC 10-8**

virtual reality (VR): The use of computers to simulate a real or imagined environment that appears as a three-dimensional (3-D) space, **CC 7-4**, CC 7-5, **CC 12-15**, CC 12-16

virtual social world, CC 11-13

virtual world: An environment simulated by virtual reality software to appear as a real or imagined 3-D space. **CC 7-12–7-13**

virus: A computer program designed to copy itself into other programs with the intention of causing mischief or harm, usually without the user's knowledge or permission. **CC 6-7**

Visa, CC 12-14

VisiCalc, CC 1-3

vlog: A video blog consisting of video clips. **CC 11-8**

VLOOKUP function, CC 5-15

voice mail: A voice message, a short audio recording made using digital technology and sent to or from a smartphone or other mobile device when the recipient did not answer a phone call. **CC 11-10–11-11**

voice memo: A short audio recording created in a messaging app instead of sending a text message. Also called a voice note. **CC 11-11**

voice messaging: The recording and posting of digital messages for another person. **CC 11-10–11-11**